the
Modern British Party System

PAUL WEBB

SAGE Publications
London • Thousand Oaks • New Delhi

To Laura, Michael and Alice

First published 2000

Apart from any fair dealing for the purposes of research or private
study, or criticism or review, as permitted under the Copyright,
Designs and Patents Act, 1988, this publication may be reproduced,
stored or transmitted in any form, or by any means, only with the
prior permission in writing of the publishers, or in the case of
reprographic reproduction, in accordance with the terms of licences
issued by the Copyright Licensing Agency. Inquiries concerning
reproduction outside those terms should be sent to the publishers.

SAGE Publications Ltd
6 Bonhill Street
London EC2A 4PU

SAGE Publications Inc
2455 Teller Road
Thousand Oaks, California 91320

SAGE Publications India Pvt Ltd
32, M-Block Market
Greater Kailash – 1
New Delhi 110 048

British Library Cataloguing in Publication data

A catalogue record for this book is available from the British Library

ISBN 0 8039 7943 6
ISBN 0 8039 7944 4 (pbk)

Library of Congress catalog card number **132724**

Typeset by M Rules
Printed in Great Britain by The Cromwell Press Ltd, Trowbridge,
Wiltshire

CONTENTS

PREFACE

Between 1945 and 1970, it was orthodox to regard Britain as having a very stable, centralized and party-oriented political system. Parties were vital to a number of interconnected and critical aspects of politics in the country: they structured and organized elections and the work of the national legislature; shaped the political agenda and informed citizens about public policy issues; fostered political representation and participation; recruited and socialized the political elites who occupied elective and appointive office; and provided accountable governance. So central were they, that it was quite impossible to conceive of political life in the country without thinking first and foremost of *party* political life. While there is no doubt that parties remain at the heart of political life in Britain today, it is equally plain that they have come under considerable pressure to adapt in the last third of twentieth century. This book seeks both to show how parties remain of central importance, and the ways in which they and the party system have changed.

Change in British party politics is not hard to discern. It can be observed in a host of interconnected developments, including: the erosion of two-party electoral domination; partisan and class dealignment within the electorate; the emergence of new lines of political conflict which cut across traditional linkages between parties and voters; the emergence and growing relevance of various minor parties; the growth of backbench dissent within parliamentary parties; an increasingly audible chorus of complaint about the supposed iniquities of the electoral system; a more diverse electoral geography; and greater variety of regional party system dynamics. In the light of these changes, a number of questions arise. What is the exact nature and scope of change? What are the sources of change? What are the effects of change? And how have parties responded to the pressures imposed by their changing environments? Broadly speaking, this book is driven by an underlying concern with these questions.

The opening chapter seeks to provide a broad overview of party system change. In doing so, it argues that British society as a whole has become more heterogeneous, and that this is reflected in the greater pluralism and diversity of the various party systems found in the UK. Overall, these changes now make the country's traditional 'two-party' designation seem inadequate. In

Chapter 2, the nature, scope and consequences of electoral change are considered in greater detail; in particular, the gradual opening up of the electoral market since 1970 is traced through a detailed examination of the sources of dealignment and realignment. Such change implies greater scope for competition over voter support, but begs the question of how modern British parties compete: the answer is elaborated over the course of the ensuing three chapters. In Chapters 3 and 4, the importance of party ideologies and election programmes, on which formal models of party competition routinely and justifiably lay emphasis, is discussed. But this only provides a partial insight into the competition for votes, and Chapter 5 therefore investigates the increasingly important realm of political marketing, imagery and media effects. The phenomenon of political marketing, it should be noted, provides an especially powerful example of how parties respond and adapt to their changing environments. This is important, for it serves to make the point that parties are not simply the passive victims of a changing external environment over which they have no control; by adapting, they survive and retain a degree of autonomy to shape public life.

The next three chapters switch focus to the internal life of political parties. Chapter 6 examines the increasingly important issue of conflict and cohesion within parliamentary parties, while Chapter 7 moves beyond the legislature to consider the changing balance of power between party elites and grass-roots memberships. Here again we shall see parties adapting to changing circumstances, something which is no less true of the way in which they obtain and deploy the resources they need to operate effectively, the subject of Chapter 8. Finally, in Chapter 9 we shift focus from the internal life of modern political parties to their consequences for the wider political system. How well does the party system as a whole function on behalf of the political system and how might it do better? This is a vitally important question which bears heavily on the quality of democracy in modern Britain, and turns on the often-alleged 'failure' or 'decline' of parties in advanced industrial democracies. Though it is possible, and in some ways justifiable, to argue that their systemic performance is flawed, it will be contended here that the 'decline of party' thesis is greatly exaggerated in respect of Britain.

A feature of this book is the use of general comparative models. It is almost intuitively obvious that it can be instructive to view British politics through the lens of comparative theory, yet it is striking how seldom general books about party politics in the country have embraced such an approach. (See Maor [1997] for a rare counter-example.) This insularity is surprising, for it seems to imply that Britain is so exceptional as to lie beyond the reach of comparative models, something which is plainly not the case. Though any party system comprises a unique blend of institutions, behaviours and practices, this does not usually mean that the tools of comparative empirical analysis are fundamentally inappropriate or valueless. Consequently, the perspectives of comparative politics often surface in the pages that follow, most obviously in respect of subjects such as the classification of party systems, the

measurement and explanation of electoral change, processes of party competition and political marketing, the distribution and organization of intra-party
power, and the systemic performance of parties. In this sense, then, the book
may be regarded as an extended case-study of party system change in the
world of contemporary industrial democracies.

ACKNOWLEDGEMENTS

In the course of writing this book, I have incurred a number of debts which I should very much like to acknowledge. Though it seems an unconscionably long time ago now, I must thank Peter Mair for first suggesting the idea of a book on the British party system. In addition, he and a number of others have performed an invaluable service in reading and commenting on various chapter drafts; these include Roger Scully, Ian Holliday, Shaun Bowler, Thomas Poguntke, David Farrell, Susan Scarrow, Jim Tomlinson, Justin Fisher, Ben Seyd, Phil Cowley and Tim Bale. Furthermore, the feedback I have received from conferences and seminar presentations over the years has proved very helpful in respect of some of the ideas and material included in this book, notably the 'Party Politics in the Year 2000' conference staged in Manchester (1995) and the British Politics Group panels at APSA Annual Meetings in San Francisco (1996) and Boston (1998). Notwithstanding the intellectual debts I owe to these groups and individuals, the usual disclaimer of responsibility applies, of course.

I am grateful to the Data Archive at the University of Essex for providing British Election Survey data, Conservative and Labour Party Membership Survey data, and British Candidate Survey data; to Ian Budge for providing me with Comparative Manifesto data, and to Pippa Norris for supplying British Representation Survey data. Frank Cass Publishing kindly permitted me to draw extensively (in Chapter 6) on my article, 'Attitudinal clustering within British parliamentary elites: patterns of intra-party and cross-party alignment', which was first published in *West European Politics*, 20: 89–110; Cambridge University Press permitted me to reproduce Figure 2 of Herbert Kitschelt's article, 'Class structure and social democratic party strategy' from the *British Journal of Political Science* (23/3: 309); and Sage Publications have permitted me to reproduce Table 2.7 from Geoff Evans and Pippa Norris (eds) *Critical Elections: British Parties and Voters in Long-Term Perspective* (1999: 97). I am much obliged to the British Academy for funding my research on party employees (grant number APN8695), which proved valuable in writing Chapter 8; Jacqueline Stevenson proved a willing and able research assistant in respect of this component of the book, moreover. I should also like to thank a number of individuals working for the political parties who have accommodated my not inconsiderable intrusions on their time: these include Jonathan Seller, Jonathan Upton, Carol Linforth, Neil Bendle, Jackie Stacey, John Braggins, Linda Kelly, Nick Smith and Lesley Quinn (Labour Party); and Lisa Gregory, Stephen Phillips and Philip Smith (Conservative Party).

It goes without saying, however, that the biggest debts of gratitude are owed to my family, of whose support there is never any doubt. This goes for my wife Susan and my parents, and in a special way for my children, Laura, Michael and Alice, whose births span with uncanny precision the period in which this book was written. There may be some deeper significance to this fact, though if so, I confess it is beyond me; in any case, they remain quite my favourite party animals, so I gladly dedicate this book to them.

PDW
London

1

PARTY SYSTEMS IN THE UK:
AN OVERVIEW

CONTENTS

The aim of this chapter is to provide an overview of contemporary party systems in the UK. This serves as an important contextual preface to the detailed account of party politics which follows in subsequent chapters. But what is a party system? In general, a 'system' consists of a recurring pattern of interaction between a set of component elements; thus, the term 'party system' refers to a recurrent pattern of interaction between a set of political parties. Furthermore, it is useful to think of parties as competing and/or cooperating with one another. From this, we may infer that a party system is *a particular pattern of competitive and cooperative interactions displayed by a given set of political parties*. This definition is particularly significant since the central argument of this chapter will be that, since 1970, the UK has moved some way from its traditional status as a classic exemplar of *majoritarian democracy* towards its polar antithesis as a model, that of *consensus democracy*. Fundamental to these alternative models of democracy are the twin phenomena of competition and cooperation between party elites; although it would be quite wrong to suggest that cooperation between parties never occurs in majoritarian systems, there can be no doubt that it is far more prevalent in consensus democracies. Accordingly, this chapter can be understood as arguing, *inter alia*, that inter-party cooperation has become somewhat more typical than hitherto in the UK.

The majoritarian and consensus models of democracy were developed as ideal-types by Arend Lijphart in order to illuminate a basic dichotomy which characterizes the world's democracies. As he says, these models provide fundamentally different solutions to the problem of how to ensure democratic rule:

> Who will do the governing and to whose interests should the government be responsive when the people are in disagreement and have divergent interests? One answer is: the majority of the people . . . The alternative answer to the dilemma is: as many people as possible. (Lijphart 1984: 4)

The essence of the former approach lies in the idea that the majority (which may in fact be a simple plurality rather than an absolute majority) takes full and undiluted control of the reins of power. This 'winner-takes-all' principle generates a set of features which Lijphart identifies as innate to a majoritarian democracy. These include: the concentration of executive power in the hands of one-party governments; the 'fusion' of executive and legislative power so that the cabinet (sustained by the disciplined support of a cohesive majority in parliament) dominates the legislature; a two-party system based on a single dimension of competition and a first-past-the-post electoral system; pluralist competition between interest groups; a centralized system of unitary government; the sovereignty of parliament; 'asymmetric bicameralism' in which the lower house of parliament (wherein resides the government's majority) takes clear precedence over the upper house; a flexible, uncodified constitution which cannot restrict the sovereignty of the parliamentary majority; the absence of mechanisms of direct democracy (such as referenda) which might interfere with the sovereignty of parliament; and a central bank which is subject to control by the political executive.

By contrast, the consensus model of democracy entails all that is contrary to majoritarianism, including: the sharing of power in coalition governments; a clear separation of legislative and executive power so that it is impossible for the latter to dominate the former; a multi-party system based on multiple dimensions of political conflict and a proportional electoral system; a coordinated or corporatist system of interest group behaviour in which compromise is the aim; decentralized or federal government; a system of judicial review under which the constitutionality of parliamentary law can be determined by courts; 'balanced bicameralism' in which minority representation is the special preserve of an upper house with powers that are genuinely countervailing to those of the lower house; a codified constitution which guarantees minority rights; recourse to direct democracy; and an independent central bank which cannot be controlled by the political executive (Lijphart 1984: chs 1, 2; Lijphart 1999: 3–4).[1] Although neither of these models has existed anywhere in its pure form, there are cases which have come close to exemplifying them. Thus, while Switzerland and Belgium are cited by

Lijphart as the nearest empirical referents of the consensus model, the UK and New Zealand (until 1996) can be regarded as their majoritarian equivalents. Consensus systems are best suited to the needs of 'plural' (which is to say divided) societies in which rival linguistic, ethnic or religious groups can all share power, whereas the majoritarian principle is most functional in relatively homogeneous countries like Britain, in which there are held to be no great cultural divisions.

Even from this very brief account, it is apparent that the party system can best be understood as part of a wider political and institutional settlement. Two points about the place of the party system in this settlement require particular emphasis. First, the classification of the party system according to the numerical criterion (two-party or multi-party?) is important. Second, as we have already seen, the extent of inter-party cooperation varies between these different types of system: for instance, in a two-party majoritarian system parties do not expect to share office, whereas they do in multi-party consensus democracies. Therefore, the analysis of party system development which follows focuses particularly on the number of parties in the system (or to put it differently, on the extent to which the system is fractionalized), and on changing patterns of inter-party competition and cooperation.

In addition, it should be noted that parties interact in more than one *political arena* and at more than one level of *political jurisdiction*. Specifically, party systems operate in electoral, legislative and executive arenas, and at local, regional, national and European levels of jurisdiction. Within England, elective regional political authorities do not currently exist, but within the UK as a whole a broader conception of 'regional' jurisdiction is emerging. As a result of referenda held in 1997 and 1998, a separate Scottish parliament, and assemblies for Northern Ireland and Wales have been established.[2] Moreover, these directly elected representative bodies are accompanied by political executives,[3] which means that it is appropriate to conceive of party systems operating within the electoral, legislative and executive arenas of each region.[4] The European level is somewhat different, however, for thus far British parties' interaction in the European Union is restricted mainly to the electoral arena (that is, through contesting European parliamentary elections). In the legislative arena (the European Parliament), they generally operate as members of transnational party groups (such as the Party of European Socialists to which the Labour Party federates itself), rather than as discrete national entities (Hix and Lord 1997). Moreover, there is no 'European government' based on political parties, which means that national parties do not really interact in the EU's executive arena at all. Thus, the one EU arena in which UK parties clearly operate as distinct entities is the electoral one – and in fact it is even questionable just how far there really is an authentically 'European' electoral arena in a British context given the 'second-order' nature of elections to the EP (Reif and Schmitt 1980). That is, the major British parties and most voters appear to regard EP elections largely as mid-term referenda on the national government's record in office, which seriously undermines these contests' status as 'European' elections

(Heath et al. 1999). For these reasons, the analysis which follows excludes any attempt to account for the manner in which UK parties interact at the level of the EU.

In view of the foregoing discussion, it is apparent that statements to the effect that 'Britain has a two-party system' are in reality gross simplifications which beg questions about which level of political jurisdiction and which arena of party interaction one is talking about. To put it another way, it implies that the country actually has more than one party system, and that quite different patterns of party interaction may be found within these different systems; thus, we would doubtless discover, should we care to look, a variety of systems across the 440 principal local authorities which currently exist in Britain, many of which contrast quite starkly with that which we associate with Westminster. It is equally plain that the Scottish party system is significantly different to the Westminster party system, whichever political arena one refers to.

That said, it remains common practice to speak of 'the party system' and to mean by this the pattern of party interaction we find in the various national level political arenas. This has not been entirely unreasonable in view of the fact that since 1945 the UK has broadly been a majoritarian democracy with a centralized and unitary state, subject to the formal sovereignty of the parliamentary majority in Westminster. However, given that (a) this tradition of majoritarianism has generally come under some pressure since 1970, and (b) the specific advent of devolution has formalized the political significance of (some) regional jurisdictions in the UK, it has become more appropriate to take account of party system change at central, regional and local levels. We shall start, therefore, by considering the national party system, before evaluating regional and local systems.

The Westminster party system

1945–70: the era of classic two-party majoritarianism

Explicit in much of the literature on electoral behaviour and party competition in the UK is the notion that something started to change after the general election of June 1970. From 1945 to 1970 it is perfectly appropriate to speak of party interactions in Britain in terms of the classic two-party system which is inherent to majoritarian democracy; thereafter, matters are not so clear-cut. Of course, it has never been literally true that only the two major parties have contested or won voter support in Westminster elections, nor even that only they have won representation in the House of Commons. So why should we insist on speaking of 'two-partism'? Because, of course, in some sense it seems to us that only the two major parties are really important to an understanding of the essential dynamics of the system. This, in turn, reflects the fact that the major parties in 'two-party' systems (a) absorb most of the votes cast in elections and (b) are consequently able to dominate the business of government.

Thus, only two parties in the system really 'count'. While Giovanni Sartori has suggested widely acknowledged 'rules for counting' parties (based on what he calls their 'coalition' and 'blackmail' potential [1976: 122–3]), Lijphart has pointed to anomalies generated by these rules (1984: 117–18) and directs us instead towards a well-known measure developed by Markku Laakso and Rein Taagepera (1979). Their formula for counting the 'effective number of parties' takes account of both the number of parties in the system and their relative strength. This is a very intuitive and useful technique of measurement since it tells us, for instance, that in any system comprised of just two equally strong parties, the effective number will indeed be 2.0, while a system consisting of three equally strong parties will generate an effective number of 3.0, and so on. This measure can be calculated either on the basis of party shares of the popular vote (the effective number of electoral parties [ENEP]), or on the basis of shares of seats won in parliament (the effective number of parliamentary parties [ENPP]).[5]

Table 1.1 reports general election results since 1945 and clearly shows a growth in the effective number of parties after 1970. Given the distorting effect of the 'first-past-the-post' single-member plurality (SMP) electoral system (see Chapter 9), this is less pronounced in respect of parliamentary parties than electoral parties, though it is still apparent. Thus, while the average ENPP for 1945–70 was 2.05, it increased to 2.18 for the period from 1974 to 1997; the ENEP average shows a more marked increase, from 2.36 (up to 1970) to 3.17 (post-1970). In effect, there is now a two-party system in the national legislative arena, but a multi-party system in the national electoral arena.

It is possible to elaborate considerably on the essential nature of the classic two-party system in the period up to the mid-1970s. In doing so, it is especially helpful to utilize criteria devised by Jean Blondel (1968) and Giovanni Sartori (1976). These suggest that two-partism consists of a number of key features. From Blondel, we understand it to be defined by (a) the high proportion of votes absorbed by Labour and the Conservatives up to and including the election of June 1970 (90.3% on average after 1945) and (b) the high degree of electoral balance between these parties (the mean difference between them in terms of the percentage of the national vote won being 3.9%). Together, these two conditions ensure that competition in the electoral arena was almost entirely about direct confrontation between the two major parties – third parties rarely intruded. In 1964, for instance, the major parties finished in the first two places in some 93% of constituency contests in mainland Britain (574 out of 617).

From Sartori, we see that two-partism consists of three further conditions which particularly relate to the legislative and executive arenas. First, there should be a predominantly 'centripetal' pattern of competition between the major parties as they seek the support of the median voter; that is, major parties on both the left and the right can be expected to adopt ideologically moderate programmes in an attempt to maximize their electoral support. (Implicit in this, you will note, is Lijphart's view that majoritarian two-party

TABLE 1.1   *UK general election results since 1945*

| | Conservative | | Labour | | Liberal Dem. | | Others | | | | |
	Vote	Seats	Vote	Seats	Vote	Seats	Vote	Seats	ENEP	ENPP	Turnout
1945	39.8	213	48.3	393	9.1	12	2.7	22	2.52	2.07	72.8
1950	43.5	299	46.1	315	9.1	9	1.3	2	2.40	2.07	83.9
1951	48.0	321	48.8	295	2.5	6	0.7	3	2.13	2.05	82.6
1955	49.7	345	46.4	277	2.7	6	1.1	2	2.16	2.03	76.8
1959	49.4	365	43.8	258	5.9	6	0.9	1	2.28	1.99	78.7
1964	43.4	304	44.1	317	11.2	9	1.3	0	2.53	2.06	77.1
1966	41.9	253	47.9	363	8.5	12	1.7	2	2.42	2.03	75.8
1970	46.4	330	43.0	287	7.5	6	3.1	7	2.46	2.08	72.0
1974F	37.8	297	37.1	301	19.3	14	5.8	23	3.13	2.25	78.8
1974O	35.8	277	39.2	319	18.3	13	6.7	26	3.16	2.25	72.8
1979	43.9	339	37.0	269	13.8	11	5.3	16	2.87	2.14	76.0
1983	42.4	397	27.6	209	25.4	23	4.6	21	3.45	2.09	72.7
1987	42.3	376	30.8	229	22.6	22	4.4	23	3.33	2.17	75.3
1992	41.9	336	34.4	271	17.8	20	5.8	24	3.03	2.26	77.7
1997	30.7	165	43.3	419	16.8	46	9.3	29	3.21	2.11	71.5

Notes:
'Liberal Dem.' refers to the Liberal Party for the period 1974—79, and the SDP-Liberal alliance in 1983 and 1987. 'ENEP' refers to Laakso and Taagepera's index of the effective number of electoral parties in a system; 'ENPP' refers to the effective number of parliamentary parties (Laakso and Taagepera 1979). See also note 1.5.

Sources:
Nuffield election studies; British Governments and elections website (http://www.psr.keele.ac.uk/area/uk/uktable.htm).

systems are characterized by competition along a single predominant ideological dimension.) As we see in Chapter 4, the logic of centripetal competition has been broadly appropriate to Britain in the post-war era. This is not to suggest that the major parties lack distinctive ideological identities, and neither is it to deny that there have been periods of ideological polarization when one or other (or even both) of the major parties have moved away from the ideological centre-ground; this happened, for instance, during the mid-1980s. However, those parties departing from the logic of centripetal competition have generally met with electoral disappointment and have eventually sought a return to the centre (New Labour being a notable example). Thus, centripetal competition may reasonably be regarded as a model of long-run equilibrium in the post-war British context.

This in itself is interesting since it implies a surprisingly high degree of shared ground between the parties. Indeed, it may well be that without this, majoritarian democracy could not be as stable as has generally proven the case in the UK; were governmental programmes to oscillate wildly from one extreme to another, the essential homogeneity of interest which underpins majoritarianism would be undermined, as would system performance and legitimacy. Perhaps it is not surprising, therefore, to discover that research conducted by Hans-Dieter Klingemann and his colleagues reveals that, in much of the period between 1945 and 1985, British governments were prone to taking over 'obviously popular ideas' from opposition party agendas (1994: 262). This suggests that at least some of the apparent adversarialism of British party politics is surface rhetoric; indeed, during periods of relatively close proximity to each other, confrontational language is a virtual necessity in order for the major parties to distinguish themselves in the eyes of ordinary voters. (By contrast, consensus democracies require parties to tone down their very real differences of identity and interest in order that divided societies do not disintegrate politically.) The danger, however, comes if one party wins power so emphatically or consistently that it feels tempted to ignore completely the agendas of other parties or social minorities; in such circumstances, it might be suggested that two-partism gives way to dominance by a particular party, something which some commentators alleged happened in respect of the Conservative Party in the Thatcher-Major years (King 1993; Heywood 1994).

The second feature of two-partism to which Sartori draws attention is the ability of one of the major parties to govern alone. The refusal of majority parties to share the spoils of executive office with rivals is one of the main aspects of competitive behaviour found in a two-party system. Indeed, genuine two-party systems are almost bound to result in competitive behaviour in the executive arena, for they are zero-sum games in which one contender's losses are the other's gains (Ware 1996: 154). Parties follow competitive strategies since there is no incentive to share power and no one else to form a coalition with, except in the historically rare circumstances which induce 'grand coalitions' – that is, broad coalitions of all major parties. In a two-party system this usually occurs only during a time of national crisis; for instance, during the Second World War the normal processes of competitive party politics were suspended as Labour and Liberal frontbenchers joined Winston Churchill's coalition government. At all other times, however, two-party systems adopt the 'winner-takes-all' rule – a highly competitive relationship between major parties in the executive arena. Even on the rare occasions since 1945 when the largest single party has not been able to command an overall majority in the Commons, it has been the norm to continue in office as a minority administration rather than to seek to form a coalition (see Table 1.2).

Finally, Sartori explains that two-partism is defined by a regular alternation in power of the major parties. This is essential if the 'winner-takes-all' principle is not to result in permanently excluded minorities. Such a scenario could ultimately undermine the legitimacy of the entire regime, a point attested to by the experience of Northern Ireland, where the 51-year rule of the Unionist majority between 1921 and 1972 engendered an upsurge of civil rights protest and militant republicanism in the Catholic community from the late 1960s. Thus, the exercise of the majority principle in the executive arena is only acceptable when the current opposition (and its supporters in the electorate)

TABLE 1.2   *Party composition of national government since 1945*

Dates	Party of government	Status	Prime minister
07/45–10/51	Labour	Majority	Attlee
10/51–04/55	Conservative	Majority	Churchill
04/55–01/57	Conservative	Majority	Eden
01/57–10/63	Conservative	Majority	Macmillan
10/63–10/64	Conservative	Majority	Douglas-Home
10/64–06/70	Labour	Majority	Wilson
06/70–02/74	Conservative	Majority	Heath
03/74–03/76	Labour	Minority/Majority[1]	Wilson
03/76–05/79	Labour	Majority/Minority[2]	Callaghan
05/79–11/90	Conservative	Majority	Thatcher
11/90–05/97	Conservative	Majority/Minority[3]	Major
05/97–	Labour	Majority	Blair

Notes:
1   From March to October 1974 Harold Wilson led a minority government, but achieved a
    small overall majority in parliament at the general election held in the latter month.
2   Labour lost its parliamentary majority in November 1976. Between March 1977 and August
    1978, the Labour government's majority was effectively restored thanks to the negotiated
    support of Liberal MPs (the so-called 'Lib-Lab pact'). This was only an agreement on
    parliamentary support; the Liberals did not participate directly in government.
3   John Major's government technically lost its parliamentary majority between November
    1994 and April 1995 when 8 Eurosceptic Conservative backbenchers had the party whip
    removed from them, and a further individual resigned the whip.

recognize that its turn in office will come around again before long. One
might say that whereas power is shared between the main protagonists *con-
secutively* (that is, one party at a time) in a stable majoritarian democracy, it is
shared *concurrently* in a consensus democracy.

Post-1974: the emergence of latent moderate pluralism

Thus, the Westminster party system prior to 1974 was a classic case of two-
partism and was absolutely integral to the majoritarian model of adversarial,
'winner-takes-all' politics which the country exemplified. By the middle of the
1970s, however, changes were under way which began to affect a number of
the core features of British majoritarianism; the cumulative effect of these
changes has been such that, while it would be quite wrong to suggest the
country has been transformed into a consensus democracy in Lijphart's sense,
there is little reasonable doubt that it is less purely majoritarian than formerly. Indeed, almost all of Lijphart's defining features of majoritarian
democracy have been affected by this process, including the party system. Of
particular note are the following points about party system change.

   First, the numerical criterion. As already noted, the effective number of
parties increased after 1970 with the result that it is no longer possible to
regard Britain as a clear-cut case of two-partism in the electoral arena, and this

status has become less certain in the legislative and even executive arenas. This is further illustrated if we return to Blondel's criteria for classifying party systems, which suggest three important developments. First, the average share of the vote absorbed by the major parties, which stood at 90.3% for the period 1945–70, has fallen to 74.8% for subsequent elections (1974–97). Second, the degree of electoral imbalance between the major parties has grown perceptibly, from a mean difference of 3.9% in their levels of national support up to and including 1970, to 8.2% in the period since. Third, and as a corollary of major-party decline, we have witnessed the emergence of significant 'minor' parties since 1970; most notably, of course, the Liberal Democrats (and their predecessors) have achieved an average vote of 19.1% in the elections since this date (compared to just 7.1% previously), while the Scottish and Welsh nationalists have emerged as significant electoral forces in their respective regions. As a consequence, the pattern of constituency contests in Westminster elections is no longer dominated by the major parties to the extent it once was: whereas 93% of such contests in Britain were direct confrontations between Labour and the Conservatives in 1964 (remaining high at 92% in 1970), just 67% (432 of 641 constituencies) were in 1992; this shift in the pattern of competition at constituency level dates very clearly from February 1974 (Johnston et al. 1994: 260–1). Taken together these developments imply that, in the electoral arena at least, Britain now has what Blondel calls a 'two-and-a-half party system' rather than a pure two-party system; that is, the major protagonists in the competition for seats at Westminster are two large parties and one smaller, but significant, party.

A second aspect of UK majoritarianism which has come under some pressure since 1970 is the 'unidimensional' nature of party conflict. Between 1945 and 1970, party conflict was overwhelmingly structured by the class cleavage and the attendant ideological conflict between socialism and capitalism; the most convenient and widely used form of shorthand to describe this state of affairs was the 'two-class, two-party' model of politics. However, since 1970 parties have increasingly been drawn into conflict over issues which do not neatly fit this classic British agenda of class-related politics. The extent of such change should not be exaggerated; indeed, in Chapter 4 we see that issues relating to the conflict between socialism and capitalism still predominate in the competition for seats at Westminster. Nevertheless, two refinements of this basic position need to be stated. First, examination of party manifestos reveals some increase since the 1960s in emphasis on the 'second dimension' of competition (which deals with issues of social morality rather than class ideology – see Table 4.1). The centre parties have proved especially likely to focus on such issues, which is important given their growing significance as an electoral force since 1970.

Second, the analysis in Chapter 4 does not in any case take full account of a broader growth in the complexity of issue agendas since 1970. This is largely because it is possible to achieve parsimonious explanations of party competition at the national level by reference to the two main issue dimensions which have been salient throughout the period as a whole (the *socialism* and *liberty* dimensions, as they are generally referred to in this book). But this is not to pretend that issues which lack a clear relationship to these dimensions have not also been important. In particular, the examination of intra-party politics in Chapter 6 reveals something of the growing importance of the question of European integration – potentially or actually a 'third dimension' of party conflict in the UK. Just as critical, however, has been the recrudescence of nationalist politics in Britain's 'celtic fringes'. This has not only contributed directly to a growth in the effective number of parties, with the Scottish Nationalist Party (SNP) and Plaid Cymru (PC) both gaining representation at Westminster, but it has obliged the major parties to adapt their agendas. This they have just about managed to do, with the Conservatives generally adopting a unionist and anti-devolutionist stance, and Labour a pro-devolutionist position, but this has not been achieved without a degree of internal conflict in either case. In addition, a number of other issues which do not fit neatly into 'the old boxes' of two-party politics, as Anthony King has put it, have emerged to suggest a multiplicity of potential or actual issue dimensions with which parties must now contend (1993: 229). These include issues of environmental protection, educational reform, women's rights, ethnic and sexual minority rights, animal rights, urban–rural tensions, and so on. In short, new dimensions of political conflict have been generated which often cut across established patterns of class alignment.

In effect, this increasing complexity of issue agendas reflects the growing pluralism of British society over the period since the 1960s. This is not to suggest that Britain has been transformed from a homogeneous society, lacking significant distinctions in all but socio-economic class, into the sort of culturally plural society on which the classic examples of consensus democracy have been built. Such societies are clearly divided between distinct subcultures based on ethnicity or religion (as in Switzerland or the Netherlands) and subcultures of this nature do not really exist outside of Northern Ireland in a UK context. Indeed, such societies are probably better described as *segmented* rather than merely 'plural'. Contemporary British society is plural in a somewhat different sense however; rather, it has become more varied and diffuse as class has lost its overwhelming predominance as a source of social identity. Instead, many citizens are now likely to take their primary sense of identity or interest from the region in which they live, the sector in which they work or consume services, their attitudes towards industrial society and the environment, their racial origins, their sexual orientation or their gender.

What are the consequences for the party system of this growing complexity of issue agendas? First, it creates problems of demand-aggregation for parties; that is, it is difficult for them to find ways of bundling together the various demands made by competing and cross-cutting social groups (see Chapter 9). Moreover, it further tends to undermine their internal attitudinal cohesion. Or as King says, 'the domain within which the traditional Conservative-Labour party debate still holds sway has shrunk considerably; outside that domain the parties have ceased to put down anything like unambiguous markers' (1993: 229). This in turn suggests that the traditional domination of the legislature by the executive may be less assured than the pure majoritarian model suggests; though governments with large majorities may continue to feel secure, the growth of backbench dissent since 1970 (see Chapter 6) means that a number of administrations have found their situations precarious (most notably the minority governments of James Callaghan in the 1970s and John Major in the 1990s).

One effect of this can be to place pressure on the capacity of parties in the executive arena to govern alone. In part, governing parties have adapted to this by modifying constitutional practice: Lijphart himself noted that the significant increase in parliamentary defeats for major government proposals had brought about a lapse in the old convention that governments should resign on such occasions; instead, since 1970 'the new unwritten rule is that only an explicit vote of no confidence necessitates resignations or new elections' (1984: 11). Beyond this, there have been a number of occasions since 1970 when governing parties have had possible or actual recourse to seek the support of non-governing parties in order to continue governing 'alone'. Thus, on failing to be returned with an overall majority (indeed, without even achieving a plurality of seats) in February 1974, Conservative premier Edward Heath unsuccessfully sought the support of Jeremy Thorpe's Liberals in an attempt to remain in office. From March 1977 to August 1978, Jim Callaghan's minority Labour administration sustained itself with the parliamentary support of David Steele's Liberals – regular 'consultation' rather than ministerial portfolios being the price paid for this 'Lib-Lab Pact'. When the pact broke, moreover, the same government relied on the Scottish and Welsh nationalists in the final tortuous months of its existence, though the outcome of the 1979 devolution referenda effectively scuppered this relationship (Thorpe 1997: 199). Finally, though never formally acknowledged, it was widely suspected that John Major's Conservative government relied on an unofficial deal with the Ulster Unionists from 1993 to 1997 (Norton 1998: 87). None of these were formal coalitions in which government portfolios were shared between the parties involved, but they clearly involved inter-party cooperation in the legislative and executive arenas. Interestingly, despite its huge parliamentary majority after May 1997, the Blair government chose to maintain the unusually cooperative relationship which had been established with the Liberal Democrats in opposition. This relationship has been expressed in a number of ways, including the latter's decision to abandon a stance of 'equidistance' between the major parties in 1995 in favour of an explicitly left-of-centre stance, coalition agreements in local government, joint policy-making on constitutional reform and the establishment of a joint cabinet committee after the 1997 general election. Although not universally welcomed among either party's backbenchers or members, Lib-Lab 'consultation' was, as in the 1970s, once again the practice.

None of this is to ignore the fact that national government is still single-party government, but it does point to a certain evolution of party behaviour in the legislative and executive arenas. More precisely, it suggests that what

Gordon Smith has defined as the 'party system core' has altered since 1970. For Smith, a 'core party' must have potential or actual relevance for inter-party dynamics and alignments (1989: 161). This criterion is similar to Sartori's notion that a party is only 'relevant' if it has either 'coalition' or 'blackmail' potential (1976). From this perspective, it is apparent that minor parties such as the Liberal Democrats, the Scottish and Welsh nationalists, and the Ulster Unionists have all gained in coalition potential since 1970; there are times when one or more of these parties may become critically important junior partners to the major parties, if only in the legislative rather than the executive arena. Hence, they have shifted from the periphery towards the core of the Westminster party system.

Moreover, it should be noted that, were it not for the mediating impact of the SMP electoral system, the growing multi-dimensionality of political conflict in Britain since 1970 may well have fragmented the Westminster party system further than it actually has. In general, there is a clear correlation between the number of issue dimensions and the number of parties in a system (Lijphart 1984: 148), but it is certain that institutional contexts strongly affect this relationship. Thus the SMP electoral system, by imposing a very high threshold for small parties to surmount before they can gain parliamentary representation, keeps the ENPP artificially low. However, it cannot prevent the emergence of parties with geographic concentrations of support – which explains the relative success of the nationalists in Scotland and Wales since 1970.

So the growing heterogeneity of British society since 1970 has produced a more complex issue agenda, which in turn has generated a number of problems for the main parties, including a reduced capacity to aggregate interests, lower internal cohesion, and less certain control over the legislative and executive arenas. This is not to suggest that *every* aspect of party system change can be traced back to wider societal changes: for instance, we see in Chapter 2 that the important electoral arena development of partisan dealignment owes something to voter perceptions of policy failure by governing parties, and such problems of party government do not necessarily derive from the growing pluralism of society. Nevertheless, the striking changes to the Westminster party system, outlined above, all fundamentally reflect the greater pluralism of British society. In the light of this, it is hardly surprising that pressure has grown for a variety of institutional reforms which, if fully enacted, would touch every remaining component of the classic majoritarian stereotype. Most notably, resentment against the unitary state has generated a measure of devolution for Scotland and Wales. In Northern Ireland, moreover, the peace process has brought legislation reintroducing self-rule for the six counties, and a power-sharing executive based explicitly on the prescriptions of consensus rather than majoritarian democracy. Thus, the UK has become an idiosyncratically and asymmetrically decentralized state (that is, with different models of devolved power for different regions).

Equally significant has been the growing pressure for reform of the electoral system. Criticism of the adversarial and unrepresentative nature of the

British party system has become harder for SMP apologists to ignore since 1970, and for obvious reason; the disproportional effects of this system mattered relatively little when the major parties absorbed over 90% of the national vote and alternated with some regularity in office, as was the case during the heyday of majoritarian democracy. Since then, as we have seen, minor parties have come to account for a quarter of the vote on a regular basis, and, given their lack of particular regional strength, the Liberal Democrats and their predecessors have suffered particularly from the workings of the electoral system (see Chapter 9). Not surprisingly, therefore, the influential critiques of academics such as the late Samuel Finer (1975, 1980) and David Marquand (1988) have been wholeheartedly expounded by the centre parties, and have found a certain resonance at the popular level. For instance, British Election Survey data in 1992 revealed that one-third or more of the electorate wanted the system reformed and two-fifths felt that the country would be better served by the introduction of coalition government to replace the single-party model that has been so characteristic of post-1945 Britain. By 1997, fully 55% of ICM poll respondents agreed with the statement 'this country should adopt a new voting system that would give parties seats in parliament in proportion to their votes', while only 35% agreed that 'we should retain the current voting system as it is more likely to produce a single party government' (Dunleavy and Margetts 1997: 240). Finally, in 1998 the Blair government established an independent Commission (chaired by Lord Jenkins) to investigate and make recommendations on electoral reform for elections to Westminster (of which more in Chapter 9). It should also be noted that the UK has in any case become an increasingly heterogeneous laboratory for those investigating the impact of different electoral systems: since 1999, a regional list-PR system has been employed for elections to the European Parliament; the Scottish Parliament, Welsh Assembly and Greater London Assembly use (slightly different versions of) the Additional Member System; London's directly elected mayor is chosen by the Supplementary Vote, while elections to the Northern Ireland assembly at Stormont Castle utilize the Single Transferable Vote (STV). Thus the principle of single-member plurality elections has already been well and truly breached, and this institutional cornerstone of majoritarian democracy is under some pressure at the national level, although its passing should not yet be considered a certainty.

In short, most components of Britain's majoritarian model of democracy have been modified since 1970,[6] and the simple two-party system which is integral to it neither seems a convincing description nor a rational prescription any longer. Were it not for the retention – for the time-being – of the SMP electoral system for Westminster elections, one could speculate that a more appropriate label than two-partism would probably be Sartori's category of 'moderate pluralism'. Such a categorization is helpful since it allows for a system which gravitates around three to five relevant parties, and thereby allows for the increased effective number of (electoral) parties since 1970. However, it also entails alternation in power between competing parties or blocs of parties, and (like two-partism) an essentially centripetal model of party competition. Furthermore, moderate pluralism has the advantage of describing systems in which there is scope for inter-party cooperation in the legislative and executive arenas, something which, as we have seen, seems to have become a more significant part of party behaviour since 1970. Overall, then, moderate pluralism may well be a preferable label for today's party system – or rather it would be, were it not for the impact of SMP voting. That this key institutional constraint has limited the growth of the effective number of parliamentary parties, and therefore permitted single-party governments to endure, implies that we should regard moderate pluralism as 'latent' rather than actual for the present.

It is important, however, to note that the transition from two-partism to even a latent version of moderate pluralism has not occurred in a smoothly linear fashion. For notwithstanding the sustained increase in EPEN after 1970, the lack of alternation in government between 1979 and 1997 suggests an intervening period of dominance by the Conservatives. Certainly, following their fourth consecutive national victory in April 1992, a number of observers suggested that the UK had developed a 'dominant party system' (King 1993; Heywood 1994). Indeed, Sartori's own criteria for classifying party systems seem to lend support to this view since 'predominance' (as he prefers to call it) exists when a major party repeatedly wins an overall majority of seats. He suggests that: 'three consecutive absolute majorities can be a sufficient indication, provided that the electorate seems stabilized, that the absolute majority threshold is clearly surpassed, and/or that the interval is wide' (1976: 196). Add to this the Conservatives' unprecedented exploitation of the quangocracy, their centralization of Britain's unitary state (Jenkins 1995), and the lack of freedom of information or other countervailing provisions in the constitution, and it is obvious that the growth of predominance seemed a persuasive rationalization of the contemporary party system at the time. However, it is now possible to look back on this lengthy interlude with the benefit of hindsight. Plainly, the outcome of the general election of May 1997 rendered the dominance thesis untenable; more than this, however, if we refer again to Sartori's definition, it can be argued that dominance was never quite an appropriate classification since Conservative electoral success was not built on 'stable' structural factors. The Conservatives' apparent dominance was more transient than that of other parties which have been identified as dominant (such as the Italian Christian Democrats from 1948–94, the Swedish Social Democrats from 1932–76, or the post-war Japanese Liberal Democrats) because it was always contingent on their maintaining a reputation for competent economic management (which they failed to do after 1992) and the disarray in which their opponents found themselves for much of the period. Furthermore, in so far as 'dominance' did develop, it was restricted to the legislative and executive arenas (and then only for the period 1979–92, given the precarious nature of the Major government's parliamentary position). In the electoral arena, the relative strength of the Conservative Party was never really such that it merited the adjective 'dominant'.

More than anything, the 1979–97 period is fascinating for the manner in which it serves to highlight the dangers of a majoritarian institutional frame-work and ethos in an increasingly heterogeneous society. Overall, this framework allied with more contingent factors (such as Labour's disarray in the 1980s) to ensure the continued exclusion of partisan minorities (who cumulatively amounted to a majority, of course) from government, while at regional level partisan minorities often went heavily under-represented in parliament (Dunleavy et al. 1993). Neither did they even have recourse to a compensating degree of devolved executive power given the highly central-ized nature of the state during the period. In this context, the 'winner-takes-all' principle and the adversarial nature of the British political system began to show considerable weaknesses to some observers. Most sig-nificantly, one of the two traditional beneficiaries of the majoritarian system – the Labour Party – came to question it. The party's long exclusion from national office and the undermining of its power bases in local government gradually induced it to embrace a programme of reform that would strike at much of the majoritarian institutional infrastructure, via devolution, reform of metropolitan government, the ceding of further powers to Europe, the intro-duction of an entrenched Bill of Rights, and even electoral reform. Therefore, while there is an obvious case for describing the 18-year rule of the Tories as an era of dominance, it was in fact a surprisingly shallow kind of dominance and proved transient. Underlying it all was the latent outline of a system of moderate pluralism in the electoral arena, whose expression in the legislative and (especially) executive arenas was suppressed by the workings of the elec-toral system.

Regional party systems

As we see in Chapter 2, the Scottish party system is somewhat distinct from that of the rest of the UK and has been so for some time. This is all the more true of the system in Northern Ireland. Moreover, the Blair government's programme of constitutional reform has generated an ambitious, if asym-metrical, set of devolutionary reforms which serve further to enhance the significance of these distinctive regional party systems. Each is worthy of particular attention.

Scotland

The protagonist unique to Scotland which most lends it a distinctive party system is the Scottish National Party (SNP). Founded in 1934 out of the merger of the Scottish and National parties, it was soon distinguished by the demand for a separate parliament which would have 'final authority on Scottish affairs' (Garner and Kelly 1998: 186). Though it first returned an elected member to Westminster in 1945, it was not until the late 1960s that its political fortunes began to surf on a developing wave of popular nationalist sentiment. A famous by-election victory at Hamilton in 1967 is often cited as the symptomatic turning point in the party's history, and in 1974 it enjoyed an unparalleled surge in electoral support, first to 21.9% of the vote in Scotland and 7 seats at Westminster (February), and then to 30.4% of the Scottish vote and 11 seats (October). While it endured a slump in support and a period of factionalism in the 1980s, it has nevertheless remained a critical actor in the system, winning 22% of the Scottish vote and returning 6 MPs in 1997.

Pressure for devolution in Scotland came gradually from the 'bottom-up' (Keating 1997), and Scottish public opinion swung heavily in favour of it during the long period of Conservative government from 1979–97. While Scots have always been able to draw upon their own strongly developed national and cultural traditions, institutions and laws, the experience of 'English' Thatcherite government during the 1980s only served to increase the sense of a need for greater national autonomy. The change in public opinion is easily demonstrated by the results of the two referenda on the question of Scottish devolution held in 1979 and 1997 respectively; while the former (on a 64% turnout) produced a bare (and insufficient) majority in favour (51.6%), the latter (on a 60% turnout) generated overwhelming support for devolution (74.3%). The Scotland Bill, which was published following the September 1997 referendum, established a new Scottish parliament in Edinburgh empowered to take responsibility for domestic policy in Scotland over areas such as education, health, housing, the legal system, the environment and transport. While a number of matters remain the preserve of Westminster (including foreign and defence affairs, constitutional issues, economic policy, energy and social security), this gives the new Scottish authority considerable power. Note too that while economic and fiscal policy is largely reserved for Westminster, the parliament in Edinburgh has the right to adjust public expenditure by varying the income tax imposed on Scots by plus or minus 3% with respect to the level set by the national government in London. The new parliament at Holyrood has 129 members who are elected under a variant of the Additional Members System (AMS). Thus, while 73 (57%) are elected by the SMP method using the existing Westminster constituencies, a further 56 'additional members' are elected by a closed list system using Scotland's eight European Parliamentary constituencies. The additional members are allocated in such a way as to ameliorate the disproportional effects of the results in the SMP seats. Scottish representation in London is altered in a number of ways as a result of these devolutionary measures: Westminster MPs – including those representing Scottish constituencies – lose all responsibility for those issues now devolved on Holyrood; there is no further need for a Select Committee on Scottish Affairs; moreover, the number of MPs sitting for Scottish constituencies is likely to be reduced.[7]

What are the implications of all this for the Scottish party system? The first thing to note is that the advent of devolution may yet serve to alter the relative electoral strength of the various protagonists in ways largely unforeseen by its progenitors. When Labour came into power nationally in 1997 it promised devolution as a means of sustaining the Union; that is, in recognizing the strength and extent of the demand for a degree of autonomy north of the border, Labour argued that the overall legitimacy of the UK would be enhanced by devolution. The SNP, however, while supporting the Scotland Bill, made it quite plain that devolution was to be regarded as but a step along the road to eventual national independence for Scotland. Whether or not they were inspired by nationalist sentiment, it soon appeared that the reality of devolution might engender a dramatic change in the projected partisan preferences of many Scottish voters. In little more than half a year following the publication of the Scotland Bill there was something of a reversal in the relative opinion poll strengths of these two parties. However, this did not endure (perhaps because of internal tensions between the SNP's 'gradualist' and 'fundamentalist' wings), and by the time of the inaugural elections in May 1999, the SNP had lost some of its projected support to the apparent advantage of both the Liberal Democrats and the Conservatives (Lynch 1998). Nevertheless, the SNP still performed better than it had generally done in previous Westminster elections, which may in part reflect the boost that devolution has given to nationalist sentiment north of the border.

Note that the AMS electoral system itself might be a source of changing electoral behaviour. Table 1.3 records how Labour remains overwhelmingly the largest party in Scotland in terms of the constituency races (winning 53 of its 56 seats by this means in 1999); however, the SNP and the Tories particularly profited by the additional member component of the system, which

TABLE 1.3   *Electoral support and representation in Scotland, 1974-99*

Date	Labour		SNP		Conservative		Liberal Democrat		ENPP
	%	Seats	%	Seats	%	Seats	%	Seats	
Feb.1974	36	40	22	7	33	21	17	3	2.40
Oct.1974	36	41	30	11	25	16	8	3	2.44
1979	42	44	18	2	31	22	9	3	2.07
1983	35	41	12	2	28	21	25	8	2.37
1987	42	50	14	3	24	10	19	9	1.93
1992	39	49	22	3	26	11	13	9	1.99
1997	46	56	22	6	17	0	13	10	1.59
May 1999	33	56 (53 + 3)	28	35 (7 + 28)	16	18 (0 + 18)	16	17 (12 + 5)	3.24

Notes:
Results are for Westminster parliamentary elections, except for 1999, which reports the result of the first election to the Scottish Parliament. The figures in parentheses are respectively for the number of constituency MSPs and regional ('additional') MSPs. In addition to the 4 main parties listed above, 3 other MSPs were returned to Holyrood in 1999: Dennis Canavan as an Independent for Falkirk West; Tommy Sheridan as a Scottish Socialist for the Glasgow region; and Robin Harper as a Green for the Lothian region. 'Liberal Democrat' refers to the Liberal Party for the period 1974–79, and the SDP-Liberal alliance in 1983 and 1987. 'ENPP' refers to the effective number of parliamentary parties.

Sources:
Nuffield election studies; Scottish Parliament website
(http://www.scottish.parliament.uk/msps/results).

may in part have reflected the fact that voters did not feel a vote for these parties was 'wasted', even in what might have been hitherto safe Labour
constituencies. This could be one reason why many Scottish voters may come
to behave differently in the context of different elections, perhaps being more
likely to favour the SNP in Scottish politics, while retaining a preference for
Labour in so far as UK politics is concerned (Brown 1997: 162).

The second unquestionable implication of Scottish devolution is that it
fosters a more consensual brand of party politics than has been the norm for
Westminster. For one thing, most of the politicians are able to draw on more
than a decade of cross-party campaigning for devolution, and in particular on
the experience of working in the Scottish Constitutional Convention which
met to prepare detailed devolution plans between 1989 and 1995. More to the
point, however, the nature of the AMS electoral system and the typical distribution of partisan support is almost certainly going to generate a consistent
need for coalition governments in Edinburgh. Table 1.3 illustrates this plainly
enough. The effective number of parliamentary parties at Holyrood is around
3, which is clearly somewhat greater than it is at Westminster, and it is not
surprising that no single party achieved an overall majority in 1999. Indeed,
the opinion polls indicated that coalition government was clearly in prospect
well before the election, though the precise complexion and legislative programme of a coalition was uncertain. For instance, had the party elites
applied 'minimum-winning coalition' logic after the election, an
SNP/Conservative/Liberal Democrat government should have been formed.
To clarify, this would have been the smallest coalition that would have guaranteed an overall majority in the Holyrood parliament; these parties could
have combined to garner 70 seats, thus surpassing the necessary majority
threshold of 65. No other multi-party combination surpasses the threshold by
so few. The strictly utilitarian logic of William Riker's famous minimum-winning model dictates that self-interested parties will not wish to dilute their
share of governmental spoils any more than is strictly necessary, and will thus
ally themselves with the smallest rival party or group of parties that permits
them parliamentary control (1962). Why form a coalition with legislators who
are not strictly necessary to the majority?

The answer to this question is, of course, that policy considerations may
well render minimum-winning coalitions unfeasible – and Figure 1.1 illustrates why. Assuming that the most salient policy dimensions in Scottish
politics have come to be the classic left–right distributional dimension and the
conflict between Scottish nationalism and UK unionism, then it is apparent
that the SNP and the Tories are virtually ideological antipodes. While the
SNP are widely held to be to the left of both Labour and the Liberal
Democrats now (Laver 1998: 343), the Tories are plainly the most right-wing
party in the system; and it is equally obvious that while the SNP represents
the most nationalist point of the party system in Scotland, the Tories remain
the party most wedded to the notion of a unitary state in the UK. In short, any
coalition involving these two parties is simply not feasible since one could not
begin to envisage the governmental programme on which they might agree.

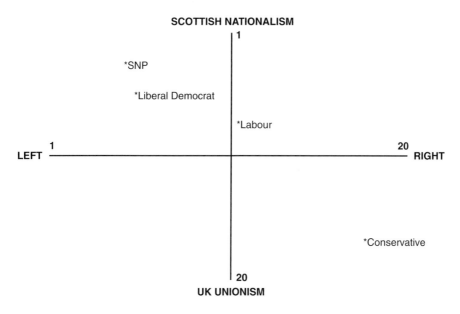

SCOTTISH NATIONALISM

*SNP

*Liberal Democrat

*Labour

LEFT 1 ——————————————————————— 20 RIGHT

*Conservative

20

UK UNIONISM

Note: Party locations on each dimension are derived from the 'expert scales' devised by Michael Laver. Thus, '1' represents the most left-wing (that is, pro-tax and public services) position on his economic scale, while '20' represents the most right-wing position. The Scottish nationalism/UK unionism' dimension is derived from Laver's 'decentralization' scale, on which '1' represents the most pro-devolutionist position and '20' the most anti-devolutionist (see Laver 1998)

FIGURE 1.1   *A two-dimensional representation of the Scottish party system, 1997*

Logic dictates that coalition-building should take account of policy considerations as well as the office-seeking ambitions of politicians. Hence, our perspective shifts to that of Robert Axelrod's' minimum connected winning coalition' model (1970). This is a coalition which is 'minimum-winning', but subject to the vital proviso that the parties involved are ideologically 'connected' (or proximate) to each other. For the sake of realism, we might accept a relaxed interpretation of Figure 1.1 according to which Labour and the Liberal Democrats are understood to occupy sufficiently similar ideological space for any combination of Labour, Liberal Democrat and Scottish Nationalist politicians to be feasible. The only one which would be both ideologically connected and minimum-winning, however, is the alliance of Labour and the Liberal Democrats; while an SNP-Liberal Democrat coalition could not have controlled a parliamentary majority (with only 52 seats), a Labour-SNP coalition would have achieved an unnecessary 'surplus' (with 91 seats) compared to the Labour-Liberal Democrat option. The actual coalition which did emerge in May 1999 coincided neatly with the formal logic of political science, therefore (though reality is not always so perfect, it should be said [Laver and Schofield 1998: 100]). *Partnership for Scotland* was signed by the new First Minister (Labour's Donald Dewar) and his Liberal Democrat counterpart and Deputy First Minister (Jim Wallace) a week after the elections and committed the parties to a governing alliance that was intended to last for the four-year parliamentary term. Its general thrust confirmed what had long been apparent, that Scottish politics was set to be dominated by parties which operate in broadly centre-left and devolutionary ideological space, and which will be prepared to share power and cooperate in a more consensual manner than has typified post-war behaviour in the majoritarian and adversarial context of Westminster.[8]

Northern Ireland

The dimensions and dynamics of party interaction in the province of Northern Ireland are quite unlike those found in any other part of the United Kingdom (as we see in Chapter 2). The less salient of the two main dimensions of competition is the classic left–right axis of distributional politics, while the most important dimension is the nationalist one (pitting Irish national identity against loyalty to Britain). In Ulster, identification is at least as important as competition when it comes to understanding the nature of party/voter linkages; traditionally, most voters have identified with either British or Irish nationality, and there has consequently been very little scope for electoral competition between unionists (British) and nationalists (Irish), although competition for electoral support has undoubtedly intensified within each bloc since 1970.

Between 1922 and 1972 Northern Ireland maintained a considerable degree of devolved power with the focal point being the parliament at Stormont Castle. The Unionist Party, supported by Ulster's Protestant majority, enjoyed permanent legislative control throughout this period before the outbreak of inter-communal strife in 1969 led to the suspension of devolved government for the province and the imposition of direct rule from London. From this point Unionism began to fragment, with the birth of Ian Paisley's Democratic Unionist Party (DUP) in 1971 being particularly significant. The DUP came to represent a more militant and populist unionist voice than the Ulster Unionist Party (UUP). Furthermore, the distinction between the two main Unionist parties can be drawn in terms of both constitutional and class ideology. The DUP has been able to appeal to the economic insecurities of the Protestant working class (a far from insignificant factor in, for instance, a declining industrial city like Belfast), while the UUP has traditionally been the party of the dominant Protestant middle class. Thus, the former is clearly the more left-wing of the two Unionist parties, and research suggests that social class has a significant impact on which of these parties loyalists vote for; indeed, left–right ideology 'not only cross-cuts the effects of constitutional ideology, it is a more powerful predictor of intra-communal political division than is the constitutional issue' (Evans and Duffy 1997: 70). This is not to deny that the DUP's stance on the Union has also generally been more radical, however. Thus, while both parties broadly favoured the maintenance of the link with mainland Britain (despite a shared suspicion about the intentions of British governments), the more conciliatory UUP (led by David Trimble) became the key Protestant interlocutor in the Peace Settlement of 1998. The DUP, by contrast, refused to compromise its stance by taking part in the multi-party talks and embraced a position highly critical of the eventual settlement. For instance, it would not countenance any form of cross-border or all-Ireland structures, though these were eventually guaranteed in the form of a new North/South Ministerial Council which emerged from 'strand two' of the talks. Moreover, it has always rejected any form of consensus democracy for the government of Ulster. This was why Paisley and the DUP actively supported the loyalist Ulster Workers' Council strikes in 1974 which were designed to undermine the introduction of a consociational power-sharing executive; equally, this was why the DUP opposed the highly consensual power-sharing arrangements (see below) introduced by the new settlement in 1998. Instead, it has always seen itself as a staunch upholder of the principle of simple majoritarian democracy, given that Protestant loyalists have always outnumbered Catholic Irish nationalists in the province.

The nationalist parties in Northern Ireland are motivated both by the goal of a reunited Ireland, and by the desire to enhance the lot of the Catholic population in the province, which they believe to have suffered undue discrimination at the hands of the Protestant and unionist majority. The major nationalist party is the Social and Democratic Labour Party (SDLP), founded in 1970 out of the union of the old Nationalist Party, the National Democratic Party and the Republican Labour Party. The SDLP quickly came to represent the legitimate face of nationalism for most observers, and certainly became the party of the majority of Catholics in the North, broadly winning from one-fifth to one-quarter of all votes cast in the province at general elections after 1974 (see Table 1.4). The other major nationalist force is Sinn Fein. The origins of this party lie in the organization founded in 1905 to fight for an independent Ireland (the name is Gaelic for 'we ourselves'), though the organization in Northern Ireland really dates, once again, from the enormously volatile period of the early 1970s. Following a split among republicans in 1970, the provisional IRA's 'political wing', provisional Sinn Fein, emerged as the voice of militant republicanism. Since both the SDLP and Sinn Fein occupy left-of-centre positions on class ideology, the dimension of constitutional ideology is all-important in explaining intra-bloc differences in the nationalist community.

The SDLP has always supported the reunification of Ireland by peaceful constitutional means, and the devolution of government in Northern Ireland based on consensual and power-sharing structures. The leader of the party since 1979, John Hume has become one of the major protagonists in the politics of the province and a joint recipient (along with the UUP's David Trimble) of the Nobel Peace Prize in 1998. While always intent on obtaining the consent and cooperation of the unionist population, Hume has sometimes sought prior agreement with the British and Irish governments as a way of exerting external pressure on unionist politicians (Fisher 1996a: 135); this was particularly evident in the 1985 Anglo-Irish Agreement and, more

TABLE 1.4   *Electoral performance and representation in Northern Ireland*

Date	UUP		DUP		Other Union		APNI		SDLP		SF		Other		ENPP
	%	Seats	%	Seats	%	Seats	%	Seats	%	Seats	%	Seats	%	Seats	
1974F	32	7	8	1	24	3	3	0	22	1	–	–	10	0	2.40
1974O	36	6	8	1	17	3	6	0	22	1	–	–	10	1	3.00
1979	36	5	10	3	11	2	12	0	18	1	–	–	12	1	3.60
1983	34	11	20	3	3	1	8	0	18	1	13	1	4	0	2.17
1987	38	9	12	3	5	1	10	0	21	3	11	1	3	0	2.86
1992	35	9	13	3	8	1	9	0	24	4	10	0	2	0	2.70
1997	33	10	14	2	4	1	8	0	24	3	16	2	1	0	2.75
1998	21	28	18	20	11	10	6	6	22	24	18	18	3	2	5.24

Note:
All results are Westminster elections, except for 1998, which relate to the Northern Ireland Assembly at Stormont. UUP – Ulster Unionist Party; DUP – Democratic Unionist Party; 'Other Unionists' includes Vanguard Party, pre-1974 Faulknerites, PUP, UDP, UKU and various Loyalist groups; APNI – Alliance Party of Northern Ireland; SDLP – Social Democratic and Labour Party; SF – Sinn Fein; 'Other' includes Northern Ireland Labour Party, and various independent candidates. 'ENPP' refers to the effective number of parliamentary parties.

Sources:
Nuffield election studies; http::/ /explorers.whyte.com/allsum.htm.

generally, at various points throughout the peace process leading to the negotiated settlement of 1998. The SDLP tabled proposals to the 'Peace Forum' of parties involved in talks on the settlement which included classic consociational devices such as a power-sharing executive for the province, weighted majority voting and 'sufficient consensus' criteria to ensure cross-communal support for important decisions, and a framework of human, political and cultural rights.

Sinn Fein distinguished its position from the SDLP in a number of ways during the two decades or more following the outbreak of the Troubles in Northern Ireland. For one thing, it steadfastly refused to condemn the IRA's strategy of violent confrontation; for another, it sought to undermine the legitimacy of Northern Ireland by canvassing support from the nationalist community while rejecting participation in electoral politics. It was only in 1982, after the relative success of the republican prisoners' hunger-strike campaign in the Maze prison, that Sinn Fein modified this non-electoralist stance. Seeing the capacity of the campaign to rekindle militant opinion in the nationalist community – especially in the context of hunger-striker Bobby Sands's successful campaign in a Westminster by-election in 1981 – Sinn Fein decided upon a strategy of contesting seats in European, general and local elections, while refusing to take its places in the latter two of these assemblies: to do so would have been, from Sinn Fein's perspective, to legitimize British rule in Northern Ireland and to recognize the partition of Ireland. In recent years

Sinn Fein has effectively modified its position; it was brought into the peace process thanks in no small part to the efforts of the SDLP's John Hume, though its right to participate directly in peace talks was constantly derided by Unionists and undermined by the IRA's decision (early in 1996) to reverse the ceasefire it had announced in 1994. However, when the ceasefire was restored in July 1997, and Sinn Fein accepted the 'Mitchell principles' of democracy and non-violence, Northern Ireland Secretary Mo Mowlam declared that Sinn Fein had met the conditions permitting it to participate in multi-party talks. Not that Sinn Fein's proposals to the Peace Forum were likely to be accepted, however, given that they included provision for a national parliament for a united Irish state. Nevertheless, Sinn Fein has come a long way towards the legitimate political mainstream since the 1970s, something from which it has almost certainly derived electoral benefit during the 1990s; thus, during the three sets of elections which took place in 1996–97 (for the Peace Forum, local government and Westminster), Sinn Fein averaged 16.5% of the vote in the province, compared to 11.2% between 1982 and 1994 (O'Leary and Evans 1997: 166).

Clearly, the Peace Agreement of 1998 establishes an important new institutional context within which party politics in Northern Ireland will develop, so it is essential to say something about this. The Agreement signed on Good Friday established a 108-member Assembly elected by Single Transferable Vote (STV) from party lists within the 18 Westminster constituencies. In taking responsibility for matters hitherto the preserve of the Northern Ireland Office, the Assembly gained jurisdiction over issues such as agriculture, education, transport, health and tourism, while Westminster retains reserved powers over economic policy, foreign and defence affairs, and the highly sensitive issue of policing remains in the hands of the Secretary of State for Northern Ireland. The Assembly's procedures are highly consensual and sensitive to the need to protect minority rights; thus, the 'parallel consent' of a majority of unionist and nationalist representatives or a weighted majority of 60%, including at least 40% of each bloc of representatives, is required. Cross-community support is similarly required for the election of the First Minister and his or her Deputy, while the Executive's various ministerial portfolios (and Committee positions) are shared out on a proportional basis (Cm.3883: Strand 1). This Agreement was put to a referendum of all citizens living in Northern Ireland and drew the support of 71.1% of them (on a turnout of 80.1%).

At the time of writing, successful implementation of the Peace Agreement hangs in the balance. While Assembly elections took place in June 1998, it met initially only in 'shadow' mode, which is to say without full legislative or executive powers, in order to select an Executive, resolve its standing orders and working practices, and make preparations for the effective functioning of the Assembly and other bodies established by the overall Agreement, such as the North/South Council and the British-Irish Council (op. cit.: Strand 1, para. 35). Final implementation of the Agreement was subsequently prevented by a protracted dispute over the vexed issue of the decommissioning of paramilitary groups' weapons, with the result that the Assembly and Executive at Stormont were stripped of their powers by the British government in February 2000, just a few weeks after acquiring them.

In essence, the current party system of Northern Ireland can be portrayed in the terms described in Figure 1.2. It should be said, however, that this figure does not include all party organizations contesting elections in Ulster, but only the major protagonists. This is not to suggest that the minor parties in the province lack all significance. Two particular points may be made about them. First, unionism has been further fragmented in recent years as a direct result of the peace process, with the Progressive Unionist Party (PUP) and the Ulster Democratic Party (UDP) emerging as the legitimate electoralist front organizations of loyalist paramilitary organizations which declared cease-fires during or after 1994. Though small, these parties appear to have drawn working class support away from both the UUP and the DUP. While this serves to intensify yet further the process of electoral competition within the unionist bloc, it should be noted that there are signs that the unionist parties have responded by recognizing the 'ethno-national imperative'; that is, in certain seats they forged ad hoc electoral arrangements in the general election

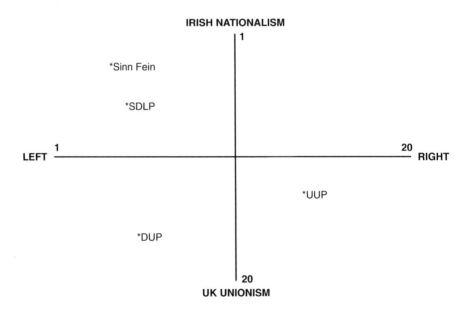

Note: The spatial locations of parties on this diagram are not, as in the case of Figures 1.1 and 1.3, derived from Michael Laver's expert scales, since his research does not incorporate estimates of the ideological positions of parties in Northern Ireland. Neither is it possible to compile a full map of ideological locations from the comparative manifesto data set (see Chapter 4) given that some important parties are excluded from this. Consequently, this figure simply draws on personal qualitative judgements about party ideologies in the province.

FIGURE 1.2   *A two-dimensional representation of Northern Ireland's party system*

of 1997 so as not to split their support and thereby allow the 'ethnic competitor' (that is, the nationalist bloc) to triumph (O'Leary and Evans 1997: 168). Second, it is conceivable that the Alliance Party (APNI), another small party in Northern Ireland, will come to play an increasingly significant role as a coalition-building pivot in the system. Alliance, though an offshoot of the unionist bloc, has always sought to build an explicitly cross-communal identity and basis of support in arguing for consensual and bridge-building structures, not only within the province but also between the North and the South. While unable to surmount the high representational obstacles of Westminster's electoral system, it has maintained a significant level of cross-communal support in local elections. Brendan O'Leary and Geoff Evans argue that, with the Catholic community outbreeding the Protestants and set to become the majority bloc by the year 2020, 'APNI will have a social base for its self-professed role at the beginning of the next century because it will hold a pivotal electoral share of the votes' (op. cit.: 164). The results of the first elections to the new Assembly at Stormont point to the potential significance of APNI and, indeed, the other small parties of the province (see Table 1.4). Furthermore, Table 1.4 demonstrates how the use of STV rather than the SMP electoral system employed in Westminster elections permits a dramatic increase in the effective number of parliamentary parties in Northern Ireland (see column headed 'ENPP').

To summarize, the nature of the party system in Northern Ireland has long been distinct, and the dramatic political developments of the past few years have induced changes which are already altering patterns of inter-party competition and cooperation, and are likely to do so further. Until the Good Friday Agreement, little genuine competition for votes took place between the two main party blocs, although there was plenty of competition within them. A combination of demographic change and the Peace Agreement has generated: (a) the continuing, if gradual, electoral decline of the unionist bloc; (b) the further fragmentation of the unionist bloc; and (c) the need for enhanced cooperation within the unionist bloc in order to fend off the common threat it faces from the nationalists. Meanwhile in the electoral arena, competition has tended to continue unabated between the main two nationalist parties; it is conceivable, however, that electoral pacts between Sinn Fein and the SDLP may emerge in respect of Westminster elections. Just such an agreement was proposed by Sinn Fein during the run-up to the 1997 election, but rejected by the SDLP because of the IRA's resumption of violence in 1996. In any case, overshadowing all developments in the electoral arena is the possibility of greater cooperation in the province's legislative and executive arenas; if the politicians and paramilitary organizations can overcome the various obstacles to implementation of the Peace Agreement, the consensual and power-sharing institutional context of devolved government in Northern Ireland will guarantee as much.

Wales

Having lost its independence as long ago as 1536, Wales has not retained the degree of institutional and legal distinctiveness from England that Scotland has enjoyed; almost paradoxically, however, a relatively high proportion of its people (approximately 20%) remain Welsh speakers and these are central to Welsh cultural identity and nationalism. Living largely in northern and western Wales, they provide the basis of a political cleavage which has left its mark on the principality's party system in the shape of the Welsh Nationalist party, Plaid Cymru (PC). Founded in 1925, PC has articulated the grievances of those Welsh voters who have sought to protect the Welsh language and identity, and who have aspired to a degree of home rule for their country.

During the 1950s and 1960s the party began to develop a broad programme of economic and social policy, something which it had hitherto lacked, partly in an effort to spread its appeal to the largely English-speaking communities of south Wales. As with Scottish nationalism, the electoral growth of Welsh nationalism became evident in the decade following the middle of the 1960s: by-election success at Carmarthen in 1966 helped spawn the Welsh Language Act 1967 (giving greater prominence to the use of Welsh in the public services); and an electoral breakthrough occurred in February 1974, with PC securing over 10% of the vote in the principality and returning two MPs to Westminster. This level of electoral support has been broadly maintained for elections to Westminster, though the number of representatives elected to the Commons increased to four in 1992 and 1997. That said, 'unlike the SNP, Plaid Cymru's support is strongly concentrated, with 37% of the vote in Gwynedd and 22% in Dyfed, but little outside their linguistic base' (Norris 1997: 17). Thus, all four PC parliamentarians represent constituencies in North Wales (Ynys Mon, Caernarvon, Merionnydd Nant Conwy and Ceredigion), while the party lost deposits in 25 of the 38 Welsh seats it contested in 1997 (Garner and Kelly 1998: 192).

Ideologically, PC has taken some time to develop a broad programme and it has not been achieved without considerable tension between the party's various internal tendencies. Quite obviously, PC's primary dimension of appeal relates to the question of Welsh independence. Here it pursues a general strategy of decentralization, supporting the Labour government's devolution legislation in 1997–98. These provisions were quite different to those put forward in respect of Scotland, and have been characterized as 'devolution without autonomy' (Lynch 1998: 7). Labour has long been aware of the challenge posed to its traditional electoral hegemony in Wales by the rise of Welsh nationalism, and sought to provide a satisfactory response in the 1970s through the establishment of the Welsh Development Agency (1974) and proposals for devolution – though the plans were emphatically rejected by the Welsh people in the referendum of 1979. Its criticisms of the way in which the Conservatives governed Wales via the quangocracy during the 1980s and 1990s, plus the belief that regional economic development might be enhanced through some measure of devolution, led to the Blair government's new plan for an elected Welsh Assembly in 1997 (Eurig 1999: 89). This Assembly (the *Senedd*) only has 'secondary' legislative powers, it should be noted; its main prerogative is to implement and scrutinize laws made at Westminster, and it has no independent tax-raising powers. It does, however, have the right to determine different spending priorities within the overall block grant (initially set at £7 billion) made by Westminster in respect of policy areas such as agriculture, education, economic development, health, local government and the environment. Moreover, the Secretary of State for Wales is obliged to consult the Assembly about any legislation outlined in the Queen's Speech. In the 1997 general election PC articulated a policy of support for devolution, followed by a five-year period of transition to full autonomy within the European Union; indeed, PC has (like the SNP) become a devotee of the 'Europe of regions' concept which would guarantee Wales's existence as part of a non-English-dominated geo-political region. In the event, Labour's Welsh devolution proposals were popularly ratified by the narrowest imaginable margin of 50.3% to 49.7% in September 1997, on a turnout of just 50.1%. Though clearly representing an advance on 1979 in the degree of public support for devolution in Wales, these figures illustrate the constraints on PC's project.

Beyond devolution and decentralization, PC has officially been socialist since 1981; at the 1997 general election, for instance, it proposed a public sector job-creation programme funded by tax increases. That said, there has been a long-standing tension between the socialist wing of the party and the rural landowning and petit bourgeois conservative wing. This tension is not necessarily eased by the party's environmentalism (as demonstrated, for instance, by its proposal for a polluter-pays tax), though electoral pacts with the Green Party have occasionally been fruitful (for instance, in local and European elections). Given that it finds itself occupying devolutionist and left-of-centre territory in common with Labour, it is not surprising that it seeks to distinguish its own brand of 'community socialism' from Labour's 'state socialism', though such distinctions may be purely rhetorical (Fisher 1996a: 129).

What does all this mean for the nature of the party system in Wales? The electoral system used for the Senedd is very similar, though not identical, to that employed for Scottish Parliamentary elections. The Assembly consists of 40 members elected by SMP voting, plus 20 additional members elected by party list votes in the principality's five European parliamentary constituencies. Despite this, the typical patterns of voter preferences and party representation found in Wales up to the first Assembly elections of May 1999 meant that few observers foresaw much likelihood of coalitional arrangements. Labour had long enjoyed a degree of electoral dominance in the country such that it could generally expect to form a single-party executive; indeed, in 1997 the effective number of parliamentary parties in the principality was just 1.36 (see Table 1.5). Reflecting this, Welsh devolutionary arrangements did not so much emerge from the practice of consensual negotiation between parties (as in Scotland) as from Labour's own internal system of politics. In short, Wales has long had a dominant party system, in which the primary opposition to Labour has often been on the centre-left (that is, Plaid Cymru in parts of the North and the Liberal Democrats elsewhere) rather than the right. Thus, in 1997, the Conservatives were runners-up to Labour in 23 Welsh seats, whereas candidates from Labour, the Liberal Democrats or Plaid Cymru filled the leading two positions in 15 constituency contests.

In view of this, it came as a considerable surprise when Labour was denied an overall majority in the Assembly elections of May 1999. Table 1.5 shows how a strong performance by Plaid Cymru did much to leave Labour three seats short of the majority threshold. Nevertheless, Labour's leader in Wales and the new First Secretary of the Assembly, Alun Michael, rejected the idea of a coalition with the nationalists or Liberal Democrats, and chose instead to form a minority administration. Figure 1.3 illustrates the principal protagonists' locations in two-dimensional competitive space; it is apparent from this that the Welsh party system bears a striking resemblance to the Scottish system, with Plaid Cymru substituting for the SNP.

TABLE 1.5 *Electoral performance and representation in Wales*

Date	Labour		Conservative		Lib. Democrat		Plaid Cymru		ENPP
	%	Seats	%	Seats	%	Seats	%	Seats	
Feb.1974	47	24	26	8	19	2	11	2	2.00
Oct.1974	50	32	24	8	16	2	11	3	2.14
1979	49	22	32	11	11	1	9	2	2.13
1983	38	20	31	14	23	2	8	2	2.39
1987	45	24	30	8	18	3	7	3	2.20
1992	50	27	29	6	12	1	9	4	1.85
1997	55	34	20	0	12	2	11	4	1.36
1999	39	28 (27+1)	15	9 (1+8)	13	6 (3+3)	28	17 (9+8)	3.23

Notes:
Results are for Westminster general elections, except for 1999, which is the Welsh Assembly election result. The percentage for 1999 is the 'regional' (party) vote rather than the constituency (candidate) vote. The figures in parentheses are respectively for the number of constituency seats and regional ('additional') seats. 'Liberal Democrat' refers to the Liberal Party for the period 1974–79, and the SDP-Liberal alliance in 1983 and 1987. 'ENPP' refers to the effective number of parliamentary parties in Welsh constituencies represented at Westminster or in the Welsh Assembly.

Sources:
Nuffield election studies; The *Guardian*, 8 May 1999.

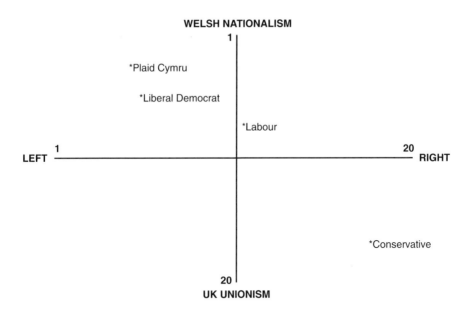

Note: Party locations on each dimension are once again derived from the Laver's 'expert scales' (1998), using the same method as for Figure 1.1.

FIGURE 1.3   *A two-dimensional representation of the Welsh party system, 1997*

Party systems in local government

The final political jurisdiction within which British political parties have operated is that of local government. There have been many changes to the institutional structure of local government since the nineteenth century, but of most significance for any understanding of contemporary party politics are those introduced in the early 1970s and the mid-1990s. The former reorganization saw the introduction of a system whereby major urban areas were governed by a single-tier district or borough authority, while remaining areas were subject to two tiers of local government (counties and districts). This greatly reduced the number of units of local authority (from 1800 to 500) and councillors (from 42,000 to 24,000) in the country (Mellors 1989: 71). During the 1990s, this basic pattern was disrupted to a significant extent in so far as two-tier government was replaced by single 'unitary' authorities in Scotland, Wales and many, but not all, parts of England. Consequently, the structures of local government in Britain are now as follows.

London   From the year 2000 the capital is to be governed by an executive Mayor, directly elected by Supplementary Vote, and a 25-member Greater London Assembly elected by AMS. In addition, there are 32 boroughs, elected quadrennially by Multiple-Member Plurality (MMP) voting: that is, voters express as many candidate-preferences as there are councillors to be returned; for instance, in a three-member ward, voters could make up to three choices, with the three candidates gaining the highest number of votes being elected.

English metropolitan boroughs   There are 36 of these all-purpose authorities operating in the major conurbations previously served by the metropolitan counties of Greater Manchester, Merseyside, South Yorkshire, West Yorkshire, Tyne and Wear, and West Midlands. Elections are by MMP voting three years out of every four, with one-third of the council elected each time.

English unitary authorities   There are now 46 of these all-purpose authorities which have taken on the functions of both county and district councils in their areas since the Local Government Review of the mid-1990s. Some elect their entire councils by MMP voting every four years, while others elect one-third in each of three years out of four.

English county councils   There are now just 34 counties whose major functions include education and social services. All elect their entire councils every four years by SMP voting.

English district councils   There are 238 districts, each constituting a second tier of local government within a county. Districts are responsible for functions such as local housing, refuse collection and council tax collection. Some elect their entire councils by MMP voting every four years, while others elect one-third in each of three years out of four.

Scottish and Welsh unitary authorities   Since 1995, there have been 32 all-purpose unitary authorities in Scotland, and 22 similar bodies in Wales. All are elected every fourth year by MMP voting (Rallings and Thrasher 1999: 195–6).

In this context of institutional change since 1970, the penetration of local government by parties has deepened appreciably. Notwithstanding the fundamental lack of constitutional autonomy which renders local government susceptible to the encroachments of central government, the scope of local jurisdiction remains important, accounting for 25% of public expenditure in the UK (Kingdom 1999: 592–3), and many of the major urban centres represent particularly attractive political prizes for the parties.

The (party) politicization of British local government probably started with the efforts of the old Liberal Party in the late nineteenth century (the best known example being provided by Joseph Chamberlain's famous party 'caucus' in Birmingham), while the pursuit of 'municipal socialism' by Labour in certain inner-city areas after 1900 did much to promote 'the emergence of the modern local party' (Kingdom 1991: 110). Throughout the twentieth century local government has gradually become party politicized, but the major reorganization of the sector under the Heath government of the early 1970s produced a dramatic surge in party penetration: thus, although 80% of councillors were already affiliated to the main national parties in 1975, over 94% were a decade later, and while 47% of authorities in England and Wales still retained independent (non-partisan) majorities in 1973, less than 10% did by 1987 (Mellors 1989: 77). Moreover, the party politicization of local government is revealed in further ways: for one thing, while the degree of cohesive party behaviour may still vary considerably from authority to authority (Gyford et al. 1989: 175; Mellors 1989: 80), it does generally appear to have increased (Chandler 1996: 151). For another, some party groups are not beyond attempting to 'politicize the bureaucracy' through 'judicious appointments and promotions' (Kingdom 1991: 114). Finally, and contrary to earlier claims on the subject, research demonstrates that it really does 'matter' which party or parties control a local authority in terms of policy and expenditure outcomes (Sharpe and Newton 1984: ch. 9). Indeed, this is strongly implicit in the lengths to which the Conservative central governments of the 1980s and 1990s went in order to constrain the financial and political autonomy of local government (Jenkins 1995).

It has frequently been argued that local elections are merely 'second-order' judgements on the performance of parties in central government. Though many voters probably do regard local elections in this light, there is a growing body of literature which suggests there must be more to local electoral behaviour than this. A number of studies in the 1980s and 1990s pointed to discrepancies between electoral choices in national and local elections (Miller et al. 1990: 28; Heath et al. 1999), and to the importance of local issues and considerations in determining choice in the latter (McLean et al. 1995). Moreover, evidence of 'split-ticket' voting was confirmed by a study of electoral behaviour in the parliamentary and local elections held simultaneously on 1 May 1997; for instance, support for the Liberal Democrats generally tended to be greater in the local government contests than in Westminster constituency races held that day, as illustrated by the case of Cambridge, where their candidates garnered 18,000 votes in the local elections, but only half this amount in the national contest (Rallings and Thrasher 1997b: 180–1). Overall, it even seems likely that the influence of national factors over local electoral behaviour may have declined somewhat since the 1970s (Rallings and Thrasher 1997a: 168).

That said, the most striking shift in local electoral behaviour since 1990 must largely have reflected the broader national political fortunes of the major parties; this is the precipitous decline of the Conservatives in local government, which started during the 1980s, but reached a nadir in 1995, when the first ever elections to the new unitary Scottish local authorities were held in April and the Tories returned just 11.3% of the overall vote cast, securing 7.1% of the council seats they contested. The Labour Party was the great victor of these elections, taking 43.7% of the vote and 53% of the seats, while the SNP won over a quarter of the vote and 15.7% of the councillors (McIver 1995: 73). Things did not go a great deal better for the Conservatives south of the border, moreover. In 1995, local elections in England and Wales were held for a mixture of metropolitan boroughs, districts councils and new unitary authorities, and the party's share of the overall vote fell (from what had hitherto been an historically low level on the previous occasion these councils had been contested in 1991) to 25%, as it lost a total of 2027 seats. By contrast, Labour's share of the national vote rose from 44% to 48% and it gained some 1799 seats; the Liberal Democrats surpassed the Conservatives by gaining 495 extra council seats to hold more than 5000 across England and Wales as a whole (Game and Leach 1995: 66–8). While the Conservatives lost control of 66 local councils, Labour gained control of 44 and the Liberal Democrats of 17. The Conservatives were left without control of a single unitary authority in Scotland and Wales, or of a single metropolitan district in England. While it is tempting to explain these results largely in terms of the intense mid-term unpopularity of what was then still the incumbent party of national government, Conservative decline in local government had in fact already been gathering pace for a decade or more, and owed much to the emergence of the Alliance parties/Liberal Democrats as a force in local politics (Rallings and Thrasher 1997a: ch. 8). By the time of the elections of May 1997 the contrast with the overall position of the parties in 1979 (when Thatcher's first government assumed office, of course) was stark indeed; as Table 1.6 reveals, the party's subsequent recovery has been very limited.

From our point of view, however, the most interesting feature of Table 1.6 is the penultimate row; this offers incontrovertible evidence of the growing number of 'hung councils' in which no single party manages to win an overall majority of the seats available. In 1979, at the peak of major party domination of local government, almost three-quarters of councils were either Tory- or Labour-controlled, but now less than half are (op. cit.: 120). The emergence of minor parties in local government has generated far more councils which are either Liberal Democrat-controlled or hung; moreover, with a third of all local authorities falling into the latter category, the possibility of coalition-building between parties is obvious. All this points to the considerable variety of local party systems which now exist. Indeed, it is possible to distinguish the following variants.

Dominant-party systems   These occur (taking our cue from Sartori's central criterion of 'predominance') when one party is repeatedly able to win overall control of a council in its own right. There are many examples, but a particularly clear illustration is provided by Wigan metropolitan borough, where Labour has won overall control at every election since 1973, and following the local elections of May 1999 held 70 out of the 72 seats on the council.

Two-party systems   There are many examples in local government of systems in which two parties tend to absorb most of the votes and seats, and in which they enjoy regular alternation of majority status in their own right. However, it is important to note that a range of two-party systems exists; while many councils continue to be characterized by the dominance of the contest between Labour and the Conservatives (for example, Bromsgrove district

TABLE 1.6   *Party representation in local government, 1979 and 1999*

Party	April 1979		May 1999	
	Seats	Councils	Seats	Councils
Conservative	12,140 (47.8%)	257 (49.2%)	6,148 (27.6%)	74 (16.8%)
Labour	7,350 (28.9%)	78 (14.9%)	9,140 (41.1%)	167 (38.0%)
Liberal Democrat	1,030 (4.1%)	1 (0.2%)	4,488 (20.2%)	27 (6.1%)
Nationalists	280 (1.1%)	5 (1.0%)	447 (2.0%)	4 (0.9%)
Independent/other	4,620 (18.2%)	102 (19.5%)	2,031 (9.1%)	18 (4.1%)
No overall control	–	79 (15.1%)	–	150 (34.1%)
Total	25,420 (100.1%)	522 (99.9%)	22,254 (100.0%)	440 (100.0%)

Note:
'Liberal Democrat' refers to the Liberal Party in 1979.

Source:
BBC 1999: 19; LGC Local Elections Centre website
(http://lgcnet.com/pages/products/elections/elec99.htm).

council), others revolve around the confrontation between Labour and the Liberal Democrats (Liverpool metropolitan borough council), the Conservatives and the Liberal Democrats (Chelmsford district council), and in Scotland between Labour and the SNP (East Ayrshire), or even the Liberal Democrats and the SNP (Aberdeenshire).

Moderate pluralism (two-and-a-half partism)   There exist local systems in which no single party is able to achieve an overall majority of the seats in a council, but where a third party holds the balance of power and may forge an alliance with one or other of the leading contenders. Solihull metropolitan district in the west Midlands is a good example: for seven consecutive elections during the 1990s, this council remained hung, with the Liberal Democrats always holding the balance of power; in May 1999, the Conservatives won 24 seats, Labour 15 and the Liberal Democrats 11, placing the latter in a position to form a coalition with either of the major parties in order to establish control of the borough.[1]

Diffusion   This term is borrowed from Gordon Smith (1979) to describe a situation in which no single party enjoys an overall majority, and coalition-building is fluid and irregular, with majority alliances shifting and subject to renegotiation from one issue to another. This diffuse pattern of party interaction will often be conducted in the formal context of a 'minority administration', and although it has sometimes been associated with unstable and immobilist political systems abroad – the post-war Italian republic being a classic example – Smith argued that it can also produce relatively stable and cohesive forms of politics. In fact, this model of politics is surprisingly common in British local government, as Colin Mellors has shown. Although his empirical analysis is now somewhat dated, it remains relevant: he discovered that 7 out of 20 hung county councils which he surveyed in the mid-1980s displayed no evidence of 'stable voting coalitions' between parties across a broad range of local issues. Rather:

> Formal pacts are unusual and agreements where they do exist tend to be informal, covert and avoid too close a commitment between parties . . . Policy alliances, therefore, tend to be loose, temporary and issue-specific. Tactical considerations are reinforced by the perceptions of many actors who regard multi-party politics and power-balances as essentially aberrations from the traditional two-party contest. (1989: 103)

Non-party systems Though increasingly rare, we should not overlook the continued existence of local party systems in which a relatively high proportion of councillors are formally non-partisan independents. This may well facilitate a 'non-politicized' model of 'community politics' in which the protagonists generally refuse to see purely local issues from any broader ideological or political perspective, and is now most likely to be found at the level of the parish council. However, an excellent example of a more significant non-party system can be found in Epsom and Ewell district council, which has been controlled by the representatives of various non-partisan ratepayers' groups since 1973. After the May 1999 elections, Epsom had 27 independent councillors, 9 Liberal Democrats and 3 Labour members.

Overall, even the brief survey offered here reveals the great diversity which exists in patterns of party interaction in British local government. Party systems vary from authority to authority and over time, and reflect a variety of factors including the local social profile, the particular issue agenda of a locality, the nature of interpersonal relations between local party elites, calculations by local politicians about how long a hung situation is likely to persist, and the local political culture. Such cooperation as exists between parties tends to occur mainly in the legislative arenas of local councils (over policies and committee positions). In the future, the promise of institutional changes such as the introduction of elected mayors for big cities and the possible use of proportional representation for local elections, may affect local party system development. For example, London's mayoral government is likely to encourage coalitional behaviour in the electoral and legislative arenas; the mayoral contest itself is to be decided using the Supplementary Vote electoral system, according to which voters will indicate a second preference to be counted in the event of no single candidate returning an absolute majority of first preferences. In such circumstances, it is not inconceivable that some candidates may be prepared to advise their supporters as to the supplementary choices they should make on their ballot papers. Even more to the point, however, the new Greater London Assembly will be based on an AMS electoral system which will almost certainly deny any single party overall control; so whoever is elected mayor is, rather like the US President, bound to become involved in building support coalitions in the Assembly – perhaps on an issue-by-issue basis. This system of elected mayors, moreover, may be adopted by other local authorities in the foreseeable future, thanks to further reforms of local government (Kingdom 1999: 592). In short, if the Blair government's new model of urban governance is to work, it will probably require local parties to eschew Westminster traditions of adversarialism in favour of the politics of consensus democracy. In view of this, it is interesting to note research suggesting that, where hung councils have persisted in certain localities, 'both councillors and officers have been willing to adapt to such a situation over time and to put in place more co-operative methods for policy review and decision' (Rallings and Thrasher 1997a: 205).

Conclusion

This chapter has surveyed the variety of party systems which presently exist in the UK to reveal two major findings. First, politics at most levels of political jurisdiction is heavily suffused with party activity; overall, indeed, party penetration of politics has increased given developments in local government since the 1970s. Second, the classic label of two-partism which has so often been applied to the UK as a whole, as if it were a monolithic system, obscures as much as it reveals. If it applies, then it is mainly at the national level and in the executive arena; the minor parties have become more relevant in both the electoral and (to a lesser extent) legislative arenas, which suggests that the 'core' of the Westminster party system extends beyond the major parties now. Moreover, there can be little doubt that systemic change would be considerably greater were it not for the constraining influence of an electoral system the future of which is uncertain (see Chapter 9). Two-party systems are also found in many local authorities, of course, but in general, majoritarian two-partism no longer seems a particularly convincing designation for the UK as a whole. In Scotland and Northern Ireland, and in many local councils across the country, multi-party politics and complex blends of competition and consensus-building characterize the interactions of political parties. In a way, this has long been the case: however, it has become more important to recognize the growing diversity of party system dynamics in the UK since 1970. Patterns of electoral support have become more regionally varied during this period (as we see in Chapter 2), and the advent of devolution has provided a newly institutionalized significance for this diversity.

In general, the changes we have reviewed in this chapter have often occurred first, or at least been most readily observed, within the electoral arena. Recall, for instance, that the increase in the effective number of electoral parties has been significantly greater than the increase in the effective number of parliamentary parties (Table 1.1). Similarly, it is implicit in some of the arguments made in this chapter that change in the electoral arena has catalysed change in the other arenas; for instance, the electoral growth of minor parties has compelled the major parties to cooperate with them in legislative and sometimes executive arenas at national, regional and local levels. Somewhat paradoxically, then, it seems that the tendency towards greater levels of inter-party cooperation within the legislative and executive arenas has occurred because of growing competition within the electoral arena. Given that this is so, it makes sense to move into a more detailed examination of party system change by focusing first on the electorate. Specifically, the underlying questions on which we need to focus are: 'How far do parties compete for electoral support?' and 'How do they compete?'

Notes

1   Note that Lijphart includes direct democracy in his original account of the distinction between majoritarian and consensus democracies (1984), but excludes it from his later formulation (1999). This is because of a certain ambivalence about which model it should properly be ascribed to. It is included as a component of the consensus model here on the grounds that (a) it clearly serves as a constraint on the classic majoritarian principle of the sovereignty of parliament, and (b) as Lijphart himself points out, the popularly initiated referendum can (paradoxically) be a powerful instrument of minority rights protection (1999: 230–1).

2   Some readers may prefer the adjective 'national' to 'regional' in this context. However, this usage would be confusing since the UK as a whole (or at least Great Britain) is so often referred to as a 'nation-state'. For the sake of clarity, therefore, Scotland, Wales and Northern Ireland are referred to as 'regions' of the UK in this chapter; in this sense, the region is intended simply to be understood as a level of jurisdiction falling between that of national government based in London, and purely local government.

3   While there is no Welsh 'government' as such, there is an Executive Committee comprising the various subject committee chairs of the Assembly; this is presided over by a First Secretary who is elected by the Senedd (Kingdom 1999: 147). It is therefore appropriate to speak in terms of an 'executive arena' operating in Wales.

4   Note that, at the time of writing, difficulties in the continuing peace process mean that the Northern Ireland executive at Stormont is still not operative; it cannot yet be safely assumed that it will ever be, although this remains the official intention of the British and Irish governments.

5   The effective number of parties is calculated by the formula:

$$\frac{1}{\Sigma p_i^2}$$

where pi is either the share of the vote won by the $_i$th party (for ENEP) or the share of seats won in parliament by the $_i$th party (for ENPP). For example, in 1945 the Conservatives won 33% of the seats in the Commons, Labour 61%, the Liberals 2% and the remaining parties and candidates 3% between them. (To simplify calculations I have counted the latter group as a single 'party', which means that the ENEP/ENPP figures cited in Table 1.1 are marginal underestimates.) Therefore, ENPP is:

$$\frac{1}{(.33^2 + .61^2 + .02^2 + 02^2)} = 2.07$$

6   Note that there are several remaining features of the majoritarian model which have not been discussed at length here since they do not bear directly upon the party system. This does not mean, however, that they are intrinsically insignificant. Indeed, most carry implications for the sovereignty of parliament and have been subject to change themselves. They include: (a) the accession of the UK to the European Community, which implies that the British state accepts the sovereignty of European law in certain areas; (b) the decision of the Blair government to incorporate the European Convention on Human Rights into British law, which challenges the sanctity of Britain's traditionally flexible and 'unwritten' constitution; (c) the decision of the Blair government to grant the Bank of England independence in establishing monetary policy; (d) the decision of the Blair government to establish the Wakeham Commission on reform of the House of Lords, which could weaken asymmetric bicameralism if it results in an elected upper house with increased powers; (e) the growing willingness of party elites since the referendum on EEC membership in 1975 to countenance the use of direct democracy.

7   This is a partial – and not wholly logical – response to the notorious 'West Lothian' question first raised in the 1970s by the Labour backbencher Tam Dalyell, when he asked how it could be justified that he, as member for West Lothian, could deliberate on 'English' matters, whereas MPs for English constituencies would no longer have a reciprocal right in respect of those Scottish issues which had been devolved on Edinburgh. The most logical answer to this problem is also the most radical; if the UK were transformed into a completely federalized state then it would be possible to devolve 'England-only' issues onto a new English parliament (or a set of regional English assemblies) which would be the functional equivalent(s) of Holyrood. Westminster would then be left with responsibility only for 'all-UK' issues which affected England, Scotland, Wales and Northern Ireland. Such a solution shows little sign of appealing to any of the major parties, and the main response of the Labour government has simply been to reduce Scotland's numerical 'over-representation' at Westminster as a rather unsatisfactory attempt to alleviate the so-called West Lothian anomaly.

8   Not that the coalition agreement did not provoke criticism on the part of some Liberal Democrat MSPs who resented elements of the deal, notably over controversial issues such as university tuition fees (Seenan and McAskill 1999); nevertheless, the deal was struck and supported at Holyrood by the overwhelming majority of Liberal Democrats.

2

THE ELECTORAL MARKET AND THE
COMPETITION FOR VOTES IN BRITAIN

CONTENTS

The underlying purpose of this chapter is to demonstrate that the country's electoral market place is more open than hitherto and that, consequently, the competition for votes in which parties engage is more extensive. The electoral market refers to all citizens who are enfranchised to vote in elections for public office, and it can be divided into 'open' and 'closed' sectors. The open part of the market comprises those voters whose support might plausibly be won by more than one party in any given election. By contrast, other sections of the electorate identify so closely with one particular party as to be effectively closed off to any of its rivals. In the short-to-medium term at least, it makes little sense to speak of parties 'competing' for the support of these strong 'identifiers' – their electoral choice is a foregone conclusion. In the face of these open and closed sectors of the electoral market, each party is confronted with a key decision about its basic electoral strategy, as Peter Mair says:

In the first place, they (the parties) can attempt to restrict or narrow that market and thus engage in primarily defensive electoral strategies, mobilizing existing adherents rather than attempting to win new supporters. Second, they may choose simply to compete on the market and so engage in primarily expansive electoral strategies, constantly searching for new voters and placing relatively little emphasis on the mobilization of existing loyalties. (Mair 1997: 158)

Whereas the former approach is limited to the inculcation and mobilization of enduring loyalties among certain groups of voters, only the latter truly involves two or more parties competing for the support of the same citizens. Hence, there is a basic strategic difference between a party which seeks to 'mobilize' the support of loyalists and one which genuinely 'competes' for uncommitted voters.

In the course of this chapter, it is argued that widely recognized processes of partisan dealignment and social change have helped to open up the market for votes in Britain and, therefore, obliged the major parties to embrace increasingly competitive strategies; more precisely, while parties have usually operated a mixture of 'mobilizational' and 'competitive' strategies, the balance has shifted towards the latter. There are a number of steps in the ensuing analysis, starting with a consideration of how the electoral market place came to be relatively 'closed' in the first place, which entails an account of the historically derived linkages between parties and social groups in Britain, and the social psychology of fixed political identities. Following this, we examine how the electoral market began to open up after 1970, and investigate the blend of realigning and dealigning forces which have been central to this process.

The social bases of party support and the closing of the electoral market in Britain

In seeking to understand the patterns of electoral linkage which anchored British political parties to society throughout much of the twentieth century, it is helpful to start with the seminal insights of Seymour Martin Lipset and Stein Rokkan (1967). The chief virtue of their influential account of the way in which historical factors have shaped European party systems lies in the sense of structure it brings to our perception of European party systems; that is, it shows how party political conflict is often structured by tensions between key social groups. These social conflicts are often rooted deep in a country's history, but can continue to shape social and electoral identities among today's citizens. Rokkan and Lipset's work is also valuable in so far as it establishes the contrast which exists between the British party system prior to 1970 and thereafter. This is because they concluded their argument with a statement of what has now become widely known as the 'freezing hypothesis': that is, across Europe as a whole 'the party systems of the 1960s reflect, with few but

significant exceptions, the cleavage structures of the 1920s' (Lipset and
Rokkan 1967: 50). The reasons for the apparent freezing of party systems
were complex but essentially connected with the narrowing of electoral markets as party organizations mobilized the bulk of 'available' voters during the
era when electoral franchises were democratized; hence, the notion that electoral markets had become relatively 'closed' (Bartolini and Mair 1990: 57).
This view may have been warranted at the time Lipset and Rokkan wrote but,
within a few years observers started to question its continuing validity as evidence mounted of what appeared to be new levels of voter instability across
Europe. One of the leading examples of such instability was provided by
Britain.

The first of these phenomena which swept across Europe (albeit much
Lipset and Rokkan emphasized the enduring impact of history and argued
persuasively that what happened in Europe as long ago as the sixteenth century has continued to shape twentieth-century party systems. In particular,
they drew attention to two great macro-historical processes (national revolution and industrial revolution), each of which generated socio-political
divisions (or 'cleavages') in modern societies.

The first of these phenomena which swept across Europe (albeit much
earlier in certain parts of the continent than in others), the national revolution,
refers to the process by which national consciousness developed and nation-
states came to be formed. Often the process was complex and slow-moving,
but Lipset and Rokkan argued that it fostered two enduring socio-political
cleavages which remain with us in contemporary Europe. The first of these is
the centre–periphery cleavage. The process of national revolution typically
entailed central nation-building elites seeking to subjugate local cultures and
jurisdictions. Their goal was to replace these sub-national identities and loyalties with new national equivalents, but the struggle to build the nation-state
sometimes left an enduring legacy of bitterness between centre and periphery.
This is particularly true where there are what Rokkan and Lipset refer to as
'ethnically, linguistically or religiously distinct subject populations in the
provinces and the peripheries'. In fact, there appeared to be few indications of
lasting centre–periphery tensions in Britain until the late 1960s. The most
obvious centre–periphery cleavage which had found expression in the British
party system until 1920 was the Anglo-Irish one. Those parties in Ireland
which steadfastly refused to embrace a British identity, such as the Irish Home
Rule Party and the Irish Nationalists, were both important to patterns of
party competition and realignment in the late nineteenth and early twentieth
centuries. By 1922, however, the systemic impact of this centre–periphery
cleavage based on conflicting ethnic identities seemed to have resolved itself
with the establishment of the Irish Free State, as the Nationalists and the Sinn
Feiners no longer sat in the House of Commons. But matters were not quite so
straightforward in reality. In the first place, it was this centre–periphery conflict between Britain and what had hitherto been 'the most religiously and
culturally distinct part of the British Isles' (Ware 1996: 206) that spawned the
various Ulster Unionist parties, which retained their representation at
Westminster; their continuing presence there has sometimes been of great

consequence for the task of maintaining governmental majorities. This was demonstrated in recent years, as the second Conservative government of John Major (1992–97) found itself confronting the tortuously difficult task of enacting a legislative programme in the face of an evaporating parliamentary majority; the support of Unionist parliamentarians sometimes proved critical in this context (Norton 1998: 87). Secondly, and of even greater significance for our analysis, since the 1960s there have been obvious signs of the re-emergence of centre–periphery conflicts within the country's party system. This has come partly in the form of Irish Republican parties and candidates winning representation in Northern Ireland's Westminster constituencies, but more obviously (as we saw in Chapter 1) in the shape of Scottish and Welsh Nationalism.

The second type of cleavage which Rokkan and Lipset claimed to have derived from the process of national revolution in Europe was religious in nature. In fact, they saw different types of religious cleavage emerging in various ways from the nation-building process; some countries were left with lines of socio-political tension between Catholic and Protestant communities, whereas other nations have been left with conflict between the (Catholic) church and a secular state. The potential for Catholic–Protestant tensions developed in the sixteenth and seventeenth centuries as nation-building leaders sought to establish national churches that would be independent of the universal authority claimed by Rome. Where societies were largely Protestantized (as in Scandinavia, for instance), there was little potential for lasting Catholic–Protestant conflict; neither was there any basis for such a cleavage in countries which remained largely untouched by Protestantism, or where the counter-reformation successfully obliterated it (most obviously true in the case of latin southern Europe). However, countries which were only partially Protestantized were left in a rather different situation. The classic example of this is the Netherlands, which maintained a highly segmented system of internal subcultures (or 'pillars') based on different religious denominations until the late twentieth century. Broadly speaking, Britain also falls into this indeterminate category of partial Protestantization. Henry VIII was a classic example of a nation-building ruler who established an independent national (Protestant) church, but neither he nor any of his successors ever succeeded in eradicating a sizeable Roman Catholic minority. Indeed, Catholic–Protestant tensions have provoked some of the bloodiest episodes in the country's history. During the nineteenth century, religion intruded into party politics, with Tories generally hostile to Catholic emancipation and radical Whigs (the party of freedom of conscience and religious toleration) in favour. That said, party politics in mainland Britain has never been based principally on a Catholic-versus-Protestant pattern of alignment. This may owe something to the fact that the Catholic Emancipation Act of 1829 (piloted through parliament, ironically, by the Tory prime minister Sir Robert Peel) eliminated much of the bitterness between the two denominations prior to the democratization of politics.

Catholic–Protestant conflict, however, has actively structured party politics in one part of the UK in the twentieth century – Northern Ireland. If anything, subcultural segmentation between Catholic and Protestant communities increased there after the onset of the 'Troubles' in the late 1960s, and religious identity serves as a badge of distinction between the two groups, each with its differing sense of national identity and loyalty. Indeed, it is not easy to distinguish the religious from the centre–periphery cleavage here since they overlap almost perfectly; Catholicism is overwhelmingly associated with Irish ethnicity while Protestantism is mainly correlated with British identity. Centre-periphery and religious cleavages are not always mutually reinforcing in this way (cf. countries like Belgium, Spain or France), but in Northern Ireland both cleavages derive directly from the creation of the British nation-state.[1]

To argue that Catholic–Protestant conflict has mattered little for patterns of mainland party political alignment in the democratic era is not necessarily to suggest that religion has been altogether without relevance. In fact, significant lines of party political distinction have been evident *within* Protestantism. Indeed, tensions between adherents of the established Anglican church and followers of Nonconformist varieties of Protestantism (such as Methodism or Baptism) may well have constituted one of the most important structural cleavages of the nineteenth-century party system. Until well into the 1800s Nonconformists, like Roman Catholics, were subject to various disability laws which excluded them from voting or holding public office. Again, it was the radical Whigs who demanded toleration and an end to such discrimination, and evidence suggests that Nonconformist support for their successors, the Liberals, endured long into the twentieth century (Wald 1983). Nevertheless, it is widely recognized that even this kind of religious cleavage (not dealt with specifically at any length by Lipset and Rokkan) was dwindling in importance by the 1920s, with the emergent industrial class conflict seeming to supersede it.[2]

Processes of national revolution have, then, in a variety of ways, generated both centre–periphery and religious conflicts which left their mark on the British party system as it emerged in the eighteenth and nineteenth centuries. However, it is the second kind of macro-historical process referred to by Lipset and Rokkan – industrial revolution – which has had the greater impact on the development of British party politics since then. They suggest that this has generated two kinds of socio-political cleavage: one between landed and industrial interests, another between owners and workers within the industrial sector.

Rather like religion, the land–industry cleavage largely played itself out in Britain prior to the democratization of politics. Industrialization produced conflicts between agricultural and industrial interests, and this was brought to a head in the continuing debate about whether the country should maintain tariffs to protect agriculture from cheap foreign imports or dismantle them in order to enhance the export opportunities of the burgeoning manufacturing sector. By the early nineteenth century, the Whigs had (despite their aristocratic traditions) come to articulate the aspirations of the emerging commercial and industrial elites, while the Tories remained primarily a party of the shires and the landed gentry. The issue of repealing the Corn Law tariff provoked a crisis within the Tory party in the 1840s as Peel introduced the reform which the industrial interests sought. In the longer run, however, the party managed to survive this and to adapt to the reality of Britain's growing economic dependence on industrial trade; by 1914, it had largely brokered a marriage of urban and rural interests (though the periodic re-emergence of the tariff reform issue could always be relied upon to generate a bout of intra-party dissensus). In the twentieth century, the modern Conservative Party has undoubtedly been the party of capitalism, and its ability to contain the tensions between industrial and agricultural sectors has meant that the land–industry cleavage has found little or no expression in patterns of voter alignment. Thus, it is implicit in this discussion that this cleavage has only occasionally surfaced within the Conservative Party, and almost never between it and other parties.

The second cleavage emanating from the process of industrialization has without doubt been the most significant for British party politics in the twentieth century. This is the industrial class conflict based on tensions between owners (and senior controllers) of capital and their employees. While the Liberal Party maintained its major-party status it was possible for the religious cleavage to share pride of place with the emerging class cleavage as a structural determinant of voter alignment, for both major parties won support from large numbers of recently enfranchised employee groups; in other words, occupational class locations were cross-cut by religious identities. However, once the Liberals were eclipsed by Labour during the 1920s, class interests became increasingly influential in determining both the agenda of party politics and patterns of electoral alignment. By the 1960s, Peter Pulzer was able to contend that 'class is the basis of British politics – all else is embellishment and detail' (Pulzer 1967: 98).

Care should be taken not to regard the British party system as determined by the structures of social group conflict alone; for instance, Lipset and Rokkan took pains to emphasize the ways in which institutional factors such as a country's electoral system can mediate and channel the impact of social structure. Nevertheless, the 'closing of the electoral market' was driven by the political mobilization of social groups by the main parties. At the time they wrote, a few years before the first signs that the electoral certainties of the post-war era might be starting to unravel, the structural basis of the British party system seemed relatively straightforward: land–industry and religious cleavages were a thing of the past (at least on mainland Britain), and, if only because 'nothing else' mattered (to paraphrase Samuel Finer), class was of obvious and overwhelming importance. What is more, it seemed perfectly appropriate to regard Lipset and Rokkan's freezing of party systems hypothesis as apposite in the case of the British party system.

Partisan identification and the frozen party system

The impression of a 'frozen' party system based on stable patterns of electoral alignment was reinforced in the 1960s by the influential electoral research of David Butler and Donald Stokes. At the heart of their account of the British voter lay the partisan identification model first developed by a team of researchers (of whom Stokes was one) based at the University of Michigan. In *Political Change in Britain*, first published in 1969, Butler and Stokes applied this model to the British electorate, successfully marrying an explanation based on social location with a psychological mechanism of how the voting decision is made.

The partisan *identification* model draws upon two key concepts. Identification itself refers to any long-term affective attachment to a 'group-object' in the social environment – such as a political party. The group-object acts as a reference point by which other objects in the social and political environment may be evaluated, becoming a source of cues for interpreting the political world. As one of the most striking and enduring objects in the political environment, political parties offer a comparatively stable guide to the evaluation of other political 'objects' (such as policy issues or candidates). Partisan identification leads to selective perception of the voter's political environment and so tends to be self-reinforcing. Put starkly, strong partisan identifiers are likely to believe what the party says about individual policies, whether or not they know anything about the issues in question.

The second concept fundamental to the partisan identification model is that of *socialization*. Mark Franklin suggests that this derives from the 'deep-seated human desire for conformity' (Franklin 1985: 50). Face to face contact tends to produce a mimicry of attitudes, values, speech and dress, and this is often enough to induce people to adopt a partisan identification during childhood, before they have any well-developed cognitive understanding of politics. This initial family socialization may later be reinforced by other primary and secondary group links so that partisan identification actually tends to harden with age. When the partisan identification model was adapted to the British case by Butler and Stokes in the 1960s, social class location played an important role as an additional agent of socialization; in effect, the partisan identification model subsumed cleavage theory, as each generation was deemed simultaneously to learn both political and class identities (see Figure 2.1). In short, *Political Change in Britain* provided the intellectual basis for understanding the 'two-class, two-party model' of British politics; the major parties absorbed an overwhelming proportion of the popular vote, apparently on the basis of enduring patterns of social group alignment. Although it was argued by some critics that the concept of partisan identification was not always relevant outside the American context for which it was originally designed (Budge et al. 1976), it quickly became central to the orthodox account of British voting behaviour in the 1960s. As subsequent commentators observed, this was effectively a highly 'closed' model of political behaviour in the country, implying that parties only competed over a rela-

FIGURE 2.1   *The partisan identification model of voting in Britain*

tively limited number of 'available' voters at elections. Most voters' preferences were seemingly determined well in advance of the election. As Richard
Rose and Ian McAllister put it:

> The most familiar model of electoral competition, class equals party, is a closed
> model. It is simple in the extreme, admitting the minimum number of classes and
> the minimum of parties. It also implies the minimum of change: little or no short-
> term movement of voters between two parties, and long-term changes following
> the gradual alteration in the relative size of the two classes. (1986: 1)

This image of socially structured simplicity was undoubtedly exaggerated by
an important institutional factor – the electoral system. As noted in Chapter
1, the SMP system clearly sets very high representational thresholds which
smaller parties have generally found extremely difficult to surpass; it has
almost certainly, therefore, served to reduce the 'realistic' choices facing
voters. This has entrenched the electoral superiority of the major parties and
the apparent impact of the main socio-political cleavage which distinguishes
them.

Nevertheless, there is little doubt that the stable electoral alignments that
persisted until the 1960s reflected high rates of class and partisan identification, and implied that comparatively few votes were available for the major
parties to compete over. This is not to say that there was nothing competitive
about British elections prior to the 1970s, but direct competition was effectively limited to a few key constituencies and limited numbers of unaligned
voters, though the battle over these key votes was always intense. Yet by the
early 1970s, evidence of emerging electoral instability in the country was
beginning to accumulate, and gave pause for thought about the old certainties
and simplicities of the closed-class model. Was the party system beginning to
'thaw'? And if so, did this imply that the electoral market place was opening
up to more extensive electoral competition?

Indications of electoral instability after 1970

The February 1974 general election represents the most obvious point of
departure from a pattern of stable alignment in post-war Britain (though

some commentators have argued that the roots of instability may predate this [see, for instance, Franklin 1985: ch. 7; Miller et al. 1986]). The election was characterized by the return of a minority Labour government and a surge in third-party support. The Liberals in particular made progress, achieving a post-war high of 19.3% of the vote (up from 7.5% in 1970). By contrast, the combined Conservative and Labour vote of 75% represented a notable fall from the levels achieved at previous elections. Labour called a further general election in October of that year, winning a slim (and precarious) overall majority. Nevertheless, the combined major-party vote barely advanced and, while the Liberals slipped back a little, gains were made by the nationalist parties in Scotland and Wales (Scottish National Party and Plaid Cymru). As a result of these developments, the party system started to take on more of a multi-party appearance. This fragmentation of the party system is most straightforwardly illustrated by the increase in the actual number of parties represented in parliament (from three in 1964 to eight a decade later, and ten by 1983). However, the additional parties represented at Westminster were all small, and did not necessarily do much to undermine the continuing dominance of the major parties; a more telling measure of party system fragmentation is the 'effective number' of parties, which takes into account both the number of parties and their relative sizes. Referring back to Table 1.1, it will be recalled that the effective number of electoral parties (ENEP) did indeed change after 1970, and even the effective number of parliamentary parties grew somewhat, despite the restrictive effects of the SMP electoral system. Given the growing coalitional relevance of minor parties at Westminster, it seems that the party system has shifted in the direction of moderate pluralism even within the legislative arena – and this is certainly true of the electoral arena.

The literature on voting behaviour has produced a variety of measures of electoral change, the bulk of which (even if derived from surveys of individual voters) are aggregated at the level of the national electorate as a whole. One of the earliest of these measures was utilized in an influential study conducted by Richard Rose and Derek Urwin (1970). Though replicated and updated by at least one subsequent author (see Maguire 1983), it is nevertheless hard to see any intrinsic logic in their suggestion that a 'significant' trend in a party's share of the vote is constituted by a minimum net change of plus or minus 0.25% per year.[3] A simpler but more effective way of demonstrating long-term instability in electoral support is to refer to standard deviations around the mean share of the vote won by each party. If we split the post-war era into two distinct time periods (1945–70 and 1974–97), these measures provide clear confirmation of the growth of electoral instability after 1970. The mean level of Conservative support dropped from 45.3% (1945–70) to 39.3% (1974–97), while Labour fell from 46.1% to 35.6% and the Liberals/Liberal Democrats rose from 7.1% to 19.1%. More to the point, however, standard deviations around these means were higher after 1970 in all three cases, indicating greater variation in levels of party support. For the Conservatives the standard deviation rose from 3.9 to 4.9, and for the Liberal Democrats from

TABLE 2.1   *Indications of electoral instability, 1964-97*

Year	Two-party swing	Mean annual range in monthly opinion polls	Pedersen volatility index	Block volatility 'A'	Block volatility 'B'	Switched vote from previous election	Decided in election campaign
1964	−3.2	11.0	6.0	5.6	0.3	18	12
1966	−2.7	na	4.2	1.1	3.8	na	11
1970	+4.7	18.9	5.9	5.9	4.9	16	12
1974F	−1.4	15.3	14.5	5.9	5.9	24	23
1974O	−2.1	na	3.0	1.1	2.1	na	22
1979	+5.2	25.7	8.1	6.7	2.2	22	28
1983	+5.5	26.8	11.6	2.2	2.2	23	22
1987	−1.7	21.5	3.2	0.4	0.4	19	21
1992	−2.0	23.3	5.2	1.2	1.2	19	24
1997	−10.1	na	12.3	7.9	7.9	25	27

Note:
Block volatility 'A' counts Labour and the various centre parties as 'class-left' parties throughout the time-series. Block volatility 'B' only regards the Liberals as 'class-left' once they joined the SDP in the Alliance of 1983 and 1987; hitherto in the series only Labour counts as class-left, therefore. Opinion poll range is measured by the difference between the highest and lowest support for the Conservatives in any one month plus the difference between the highest and lowest support for Labour in any one month.

Sources:
Heath et al. 1991: 15, 20; Crewe 1993: 101. Swing and volatility measures are author's own calculations based on election results reported in Table 1.1. 1992 and 1997 entries for last two columns of table are based on author's own analysis of British Election Survey data.

3.1 to 3.8; most dramatically, however, Labour's increased from 2.2 to 5.2. Thus, from having enjoyed the most stable level of support up to 1970, Labour came to have the least stable thereafter, suggesting that it might be central to the story of contemporary electoral change.

A number of other indicators seem to confirm the picture of rising electoral instability in the 1970s. It is apparent, for instance, in the two-party swing[4] and the parties' monthly opinion poll ratings reported in Table 2.1. Moreover, we have some evidence of growth in 'electoral hesitancy' in so far as the number of voters who did not decide how to vote until the election campaign itself doubled in February 1974 and has remained high ever since.[5] A similar pattern is evident in the number of voters prepared to switch from one party to another. One measure which has been widely employed in comparative studies of electoral change is Mogens Pedersen's index of net volatility (Pedersen 1979), and this too is reported in Table 2.1. This index aggregates for the party system as a whole the quantity of change in the various parties' levels of support across a pair of elections. As Pippa Norris explains, the index is calculated by 'summing the percentage point changes in each party's share of the vote compared with the previous election, and dividing by two'

(Norris 1990: 122–3). This is equal to the sum of the cumulative gains of all winning parties (or obversely, the sum of cumulative losses of all losing parties) at an election. For example, in a three-party system where party A lost 10% of the popular vote between elections t and t+1, party B gained 7% and party C gained 3%, total net volatility (TNV) would be:

$$\frac{(10 + 7 + 3)}{2} = 10.$$

Theoretically, TNV (or the Pedersen Index, as it is widely known) has a range running from 0–100, though a score above 10 usually signifies a high volatility election in a west European context (see Bartolini and Mair 1990: appendix 2). Compared to the rest of western Europe, the UK is generally characterized by relatively low levels of net volatility; since 1950, only Switzerland has experienced a lower average net volatility (Lane and Ersson 1999: 128). The moment of greatest volatility in the UK's electoral history was the dramatic election of 1931 (TNV = 19.1), which convulsed the Labour Party. Since 1945, the UK has not followed a neat secular trend, but fluctuated between low and high volatility elections (see Table 2.1). Nevertheless, if we employ the usual periodization of post-war elections, it becomes clear that average TNV is higher after 1970 (8.3 compared to 4.7).

In recent years, a major corrective to the way in which net volatility data are interpreted has been proposed by Stefano Bartolini and Peter Mair (1990). They argue that, on its own, the Pedersen index gives an exaggerated impression of meaningful electoral change. Rather, they contend, it is far more valuable to concentrate on block volatility (BV). That is: 'block volatility is actually *a part* of total volatility, and represents that part of the total net electoral interchange which occurs between the two groups of parties which have been aggregated into blocks' (Bartolini and Mair 1990: 23). The concept of block volatility has considerable significance for any assessment of the freezing hypothesis. This is because it enables parties to be grouped together according to which side of a cleavage they fall on; Bartolini and Mair were especially interested in the stability of the class cleavage in Europe, and discovered that there was relatively little evidence of electoral volatility across the line dividing 'class-left' parties (such as Labour) from their non-socialist rivals. For instance, across Europe as a whole, average TNV was 7.99 between 1966 and 1985, whereas average BV was only 2.41 (op. cit.: 100–2). Thus, only 30% of total volatility was accounted for by voters shifting between left-wing and right-wing parties; the remaining 70% was down to voters switching from one left-wing party to another, or from one right-wing party to another. This implies that most voters, even if they cannot be relied upon to be loyal to a single party over time, are still constrained by a clear sense of class politics. To this extent, the class cleavage (and perhaps other cleavages) may not yet be crumbling.

This is an issue we shall reconsider in a rather different way (through analysis of individual-level behaviour rather than through aggregate-level measures like volatility indices) when we turn to the debate over class dealignment in Britain, but it is interesting to examine the developments in block volatility in the country. For Europe as a whole, Bartolini and Mair acknowledged that block volatility data for the twenty years following 1965 did 'offer some slight evidence of class dealignment, with average volatility increasing to 2.39 as against 2.15 in the period 1945 to 1965' (op. cit.: 102). For Britain, however, their analysis suggests the opposite pattern; whereas TNV rose, on average, from 4.6 in 1945–65 to 6.7 in 1966–85, BV actually fell slightly from 2.4 to 1.6 (op. cit.: 111). If correct, this means that volatility across the left-right cleavage within the party system constituted more than half of all electoral volatility during the earlier period, but less than a quarter after the mid-1960s. As such, this places the frequently cited evidence of growing electoral instability since 1970 in an interesting light, in so far as it tends to undermine the widely held view that electoral change stems largely from the decomposition of the class cleavage (see below).[6]

However, the evidence on block volatility needs treating with some care. In particular, difficulties arise in distinguishing 'class-left' from 'bourgeois' parties. In Britain's case, this is especially problematic in respect of the centre parties; which ones should we count as 'class-left'? Bartolini and Mair's approach was to regard Labour and, after 1981, the breakaway SDP as class-left parties (that is, parties defined by a left-of-centre class ideology) while other competitors counted as part of the 'bourgeois' block (Bartolini and Mair 1990: 314). Yet it is hard to avoid the feeling that there is something anomalous about regarding the SDP as 'class-left' while not so regarding its Alliance partner (and future political spouse), the Liberal Party. How does one resolve this? One possibility is to count Labour and the Liberals/SDP/ Alliance/Liberal Democrats as 'class-left' throughout the entire period under analysis; this is not necessarily an indefensible position given the British Liberal Party's close identity with a left-liberal (or 'social-liberal') position after 1945 (see Chapter 3). An alternative way is to regard the Liberals as bourgeois until their alliance with the SDP; this would recognize that, while they did not historically derive from a class-left ideological background, their identity and strategy became so closely bound-up with that of the SDP that it was virtually indistinguishable after the early 1980s. After all, the block volatility argument is implicitly predicated on the notion that voters switching from, say, Labour to the SDP would not perceive themselves as crossing the party political class cleavage; if this is true, then it is difficult to assert that voters in 1983 and 1987 who chose to vote Alliance but only had Liberal candidates rather than SDP candidates running in their constituencies saw things any differently. In short, if a shift from Labour to the SDP did not constitute an erosion of the class cleavage, then neither did a shift from Labour to the Liberals.

These different approaches do occasionally produce contradictory results, most notably with respect to the elections of 1964 and 1979 (see Table 2.1). Block volatility 'B' (BVB) in Table 2.1 only counts the Liberals as part of the 'class-left' block once they forged the Alliance with the SDP in 1983 (and therefore comes closer to Bartolini and Mair's original conception), whereas block volatility 'A' (BVA) simply regards all centre parties as 'class-left' throughout. Two things stand out in the evidence about block volatility. First, both measures suggest that block volatility was elevated in 1970 and February 1974, while BVA also indicates a comparatively high amount of net switching of votes 'across the class cleavage' in 1979. Note particularly how, once again, the elections of 1970 and 1974 figure as some kind of turning point. Second, notwithstanding the irruption of the SDP on to the British political scene after the 1979 general election, inter-block alignments appeared to stabilize in the 1980s (which broadly confirms Bartolini and Mair's claims); it was only with New Labour's extraordinary landslide of May 1997 that a new post-war block volatility record was created, prompting speculation that enduring realignments across the old cleavage structure had been generated (Evans and Norris 1999).

However, it should be said that, while the concept of block volatility offers a persuasive counterpoint to the usual perceptions of growing instability, it only justifies tentative conclusions about the strength of the class cleavage. This is because it is impossible to be sure of the factors that influence electoral choices until one moves to individual-level analysis. For instance, while Bartolini and Mair are undoubtedly correct in alerting us to the fact that relatively little electoral change involves switching from left to right or vice versa, aggregate-level evidence such as this cannot tell us if people who vote consistently for either the left or the right are motivated by *class* considerations. Thus, left-wing voters in Britain might consistently choose Labour because they consider it to have better plans than the Tories for the National Health Service, or for generating and sustaining economic growth, or for protecting public services – but *not* because they are in any sense class ideologues. Therefore, Bartolini and Mair's evidence does not necessarily undermine the various individual-level analyses which have suggested a process of class dealignment in Britain (see below). In any case, their comparative work focuses almost exclusively on the class cleavage but tells us little about the decay or emergence of other cleavages. Hence, even if the aggregate levels of electoral support for left and right in Britain have been remarkably stable over time, we cannot infer anything from this about the extent to which it is based on the traditional cleavage structure, or whether the aggregate picture masks a pattern of underlying turbulence in which new sectoral, regional or ideological cleavages are coming to matter more.

In fact, much individual-level analysis does indicate the erosion of social structural factors in Britain. This evidence emanates largely from the debate about class dealignment, which we shall examine at greater length below, but it is useful at this point to highlight one or two broader findings. Mark Franklin, for example, has claimed that social structure accounted for about 80% of what it was possible to explain statistically in Labour's support in 1964, but for only 60% in 1983. Most social background factors (including occupational class) have lost impact over this period (although regional association has become a little more important); moreover, this declining structuration of the vote reflected (among other things) a pattern of generational change in so far as new voters entering the electorate after 1970 were generally 'less responsive to group loyalties' (Franklin 1992: 121). This line of argument supports the position adopted by Richard Rose and Ian McAllister in *Voters Begin to Choose* (1986), in which they argue that the bulk of the electorate is no longer anchored to a stable partisan loyalty determined by class and family socialization. By the 1980s social structure was of primary importance for a declining proportion of the electorate, and was chiefly related to Conservative 'core' supporters among non-unionized owner-occupiers and Labour's core of manual council house tenants. Party competition had effectively been rendered more 'open' and fluid than hitherto, and this placed a serious question mark over the continuing usefulness of the frozen party system scenario.

A further way in which electoral analysts have attempted to trace patterns of change is by focusing on trends in *partisan identification*. This is regarded by many as a valid measure of the size of the parties' blocks of core supporters within the electorate. Such an approach makes it possible to gauge the underlying trend in the number of citizens claiming to maintain affective party attachments undistorted by the effects of short-term factors which may be relevant only to specific election campaigns (such as candidate images, marketing approaches and special issues). Moreover, as we have seen, partisan identification is central to the orthodox account of British voting behaviour during the era of stable alignment.

Since the 1970s, there have been widespread claims that a cross-national phenomenon of *partisan dealignment* has afflicted western electorates, and the key indicator of this is the erosion of partisan identification (Dalton 1996: 208–13). Russell Dalton, for instance, has reported evidence that some 13 OECD countries (including Britain) display a significant reduction in the percentage of electors claiming a strong partisan identity (Dalton forthcoming). In Britain, as Table 2.2 reveals, the percentage of voters claiming some sort of a partisan identity has barely dropped since the 1960s (top row), but the percentage claiming to be very strong partisans has fallen appreciably (from 44% to 16%). Even if we follow the advice of authorities like Anthony Heath in refusing to read too much into the vague distinction between 'very' and 'fairly' strong partisan identities (Heath et al. 1991: 13), it is hard to avoid the conclusion that partisan sentiments have eroded across the period spanned by the data: in 1964 very and fairly strong partisans taken together constituted 82% of the electoral sample surveyed, but by 1997 they accounted for just 58%. Furthermore, it is interesting to observe that this is not a phenomenon which has been limited to a particular party. Unsurprisingly, in view of the Labour Party's general political tribulations between 1979 and 1992, we find that its partisan base in the electorate weakened over the period; in 1964, 88% of Labour's partisans claimed either a very or fairly strong identity, but by 1992 only 59% did. Naturally enough, however, this improved substantially to 69% in the landslide triumph of 1997; even so, this still left the party with significantly fewer strong partisans

TABLE 2.2   *Partisan identification in Britain, 1964–97*

	1964	1966	1970	1974	1979	1983	1987	1992	1997
% with partisan identification	93	91	90	90	90	86	86	86	91
% identifying with Conservatives	38	35	40	35	38	38	37	35	30
% identifying with Labour	43	46	42	40	38	32	30	33	46
Total Cons + Labour identifiers	81	81	82	75	76	70	67	68	76
% Very strong identifiers	44	44	42	26	22	26	19	17	16
% Fairly strong identifiers	38	38	37	40	46	38	40	40	42
% Not very strong identifiers	11	9	11	14	23	22	27	29	33
% No or other party identification	7	9	10	10	10	14	14	14	9

Note: 1974 figure is for February election only.

Source: Crewe, Fox & Day 1995: 47; British Election Study 1997.

than in the 1960s. The story is similar for the Conservatives; while 89% of their declared partisans were very or fairly strong in 1964, just 75% were in 1992 and only 62% were five years later. These figures reveal the extent of partisan dealignment, and provide a clear sense of the opening of the electoral market, in so far as weak partisans and non-partisans are known to be more likely to switch allegiance than strong partisans. For example, analysis shows that in 1997 some 74% of very/fairly strong partisans voted for the same party as in 1992, whereas only 48% of weak/non-partisans did.[7]

In summary, then, we obtain an undeniably conclusive impression from the evidence so far reviewed. Two-party swings, opinion poll ratings, the aggregate strength of partisan identification, some indicators of electoral hesitancy, the average Pedersen Index score, the stability of party shares of the vote and the growing effective number of parties all point to greater electoral instability after 1970. This much already implies an opening up of the electoral market to more extensive party competition. However, the story does not end here. Given the overwhelming importance of class politics in Britain throughout most of the twentieth century, it would be remiss to overlook the question of *class dealignment*. This is a concept which refers to the weakening propensity of British electors to vote according to their social class location, and it is a close correlate of general partisan dealignment. It is a theme which has been especially prominent in the literature about electoral change in Britain since the 1970s and it bears directly upon the opening up of the electoral market place.

The debate about class dealignment in Britain

Central to the debate over class dealignment are two questions: has it really occurred or not; and if so, why? We consider the latter question below during the discussion about the causes of electoral change; here we concentrate on the former issue. The dispute about whether or not there has been class dealignment in Britain peaked during the late 1980s, after the publication of Heath, Jowell and Curtice's *How Britain Votes* (1985). In this and subsequent publications (see especially Heath et al. 1991), they offered a carefully researched and strongly argued corrective to the class dealignment thesis which had been expressed in influential volumes such as Sarlvik and Crewe's *Decade of Dealignment* (1983) and Mark Franklin's *The Decline of Class Voting in Britain* (1985). The debate revolved both around theoretical questions (such as how best to define class[8]) and methodological issues (such as how best to measure class voting[9]). Heath et al.'s interventions succeeded in elevating the debate to a detailed and sometimes highly technical level, and stimulated notable exchanges between the main protagonists (see Crewe 1986; Heath et al. 1987; Dunleavy 1987).

More than a decade later, those who incline to the view that class dealignment has occurred can point to some striking evidence. For instance, the overall proportion of electors who vote according to their occupational class fell from 63% in 1964 to just 47% in 1983, recovering slightly over the next two general elections before slumping to a new low in 1997 (see 'absolute' class voting levels in Table 2.3). Similarly, Robert Alford's classic index of class voting (widely employed in comparative studies since he introduced it in the early 1960s) shows an equally definite drop in value. The Alford index is a simple measure normally calculated by subtracting the percentage of middle class voters supporting parties of the left from the percentage of working class voters doing so (Alford 1963). It is a measure of 'relative' class voting in so far as it captures the relative strength of a given party in two different classes; in Britain's case, it is generally used to contrast the levels of support for Labour among manual workers and non-manual employees (though as David Denver has pointed out, the index could justifiably be modified so as to gauge levels of relative support for the Conservatives [1989: 54][10]). Table 2.3 reveals three main steps down in the standard Alford index since the 1960s; first in 1970, then again in 1979, and finally in 1997. On the first two occasions, these sudden drops in class voting almost certainly reflected working class disenchantment with Labour governments (Heath et al. 1991: 77; Webb 1992a: 126; Norris 1996: 126), whereas 1997 seems to have had more to do with the increasingly heterogeneous social appeal of New Labour across a range of social categories (see 'Explaining electoral change' below).

An alternative way of capturing relative class voting is through the odds ratio, the preferred instrument of Heath et al. (1985: 31, 40–1). The simplest version of this compares the odds on a non-manual elector voting Conservative rather than Labour with the odds on a manual employee doing so (Heath 'A' in Table 2.3). A ratio of 1.0 would indicate that the relative

TABLE 2.3 *Measures of class voting in Britain, 1964–97*

Measure	1964	1966	1970	1974F	1974O	1979	1983	1987	1992	1997
Absolute	63	66	60	55	54	55	47	49	51	45
Alford	42	43	33	35	32	27	25	25	27	22
Heath 'A'	6.4	6.4	4.5	5.7	4.8	3.7	3.9	3.9	3.9	3.2
Heath 'B'	9.3	7.3	4.9	6.1	5.5	4.9	6.3	5.0	4.9	3.6
Scarbrough	3.7	3.5	2.2	1.5	1.5	1.7	1.2	1.2	1.0	0.3

Notes:
Absolute class voting is calculated by adding the number of non-manual workers voting Conservative to the number of manual workers voting Labour and calculating this total as a percentage of all voters.

The Alford index is calculated by subtracting the percentage of non-manual workers that voted Labour from the percentage of manual workers voting Labour. The index runs from 0 to 100, with 100 implying that all vote according to their social class and 0 implying that none do so.

Heath 'A' is the odds ratio calculated by the formula:
(Conservative vote/Labour vote within the non-manual sector)/(Conservative vote/Labour vote within the manual sector)

Heath 'B' is the odds ratio calculated by the formula:
(Conservative vote/Labour vote within the salariat)/(Conservative vote/Labour vote within the working class)

Scarbrough's odds ratio is calculated by the formula:
(Conservative vote/other party vote within the salariat)/(Labour vote/other party vote within the working class)

Sources: Denver (1989); Scarbrough (1986); British Election Survey data.

strengths of the two parties were identical in each class; the higher the value of the odds ratio, however, the more distinct the classes would be from each other in terms of party support (that is, the greater the level of class voting). The odds ratio proved to be a highly controversial element of the class dealignment debate and was subject to a variety of criticisms; some suggested that it was oversensitive to small changes in aggregate voting behaviour and was therefore unreliable (Crewe 1986; Dunleavy 1987), while others felt it could be of use if its construction was refined to take account of support for third-parties (Scarbrough 1986).[11] Whatever the arcane merits of these arguments, three different versions of the odds ratio are reported in Table 2.3 and it is plain that each mirrors the Alford index in displaying a general decline in class voting since the 1960s; moreover, like the Alford index, Heath's own preferred variant (Heath 'B') suggests that the elections of 1970, 1979 and 1997 saw notable downward steps in relative class voting.

It seems undeniable that a degree of class dealignment has occurred in British voting behaviour since the 1960s, albeit according to a somewhat irregular and non-linear pattern.[12] This would seem to constitute further evidence of the opening up the electoral market since the 1970s in so far as class dealignment erodes the 'closed-class' model of voting behaviour. This model, implicit in the two-class, two-party orthodoxy of the 1960s has been described in the following terms by Richard Rose and Ian McAllister:

> To say that parties compete is an exaggeration, for each party is not so much seeking to win votes from those committed to its opponent as it is seeking to mobilize the maximum vote from electors already predisposed in its favour by their social position. (1986: 11)

While it should be stressed that the electoral market was never completely 'closed', nor alignments totally 'frozen', the range of evidence reviewed on electoral change, and class and partisan dealignment seems to point to a scenario according to which British parties can now 'compete' for a greater proportion of the market than hitherto. However, we will not be in a position to assert this with complete confidence until the causes of electoral change have been examined. This is because the openness of the electoral market is determined by the relative degrees of *realignment* and *dealignment* which have taken place. If change has been generated mainly by a process of realignment, then the British electorate may simply have been undergoing a transition from one 'closed' model of voting behaviour to another; should electoral change have generally been prompted by the enduring dealignment of voters, however, then the scope for party competition over uncommitted votes will have increased. This is an issue which merits considerable attention.

Explaining electoral change: realignment or dealignment?

It has been suggested that while dealignment implies an opening up of the electoral market to new levels of competition, realignment does not. What do these terms mean? They were coined by the American political scientist VO Key (1955), who regarded electorates such as the USA's as inclined to prolonged periods of stable alignment in which certain social groups offered sustained support to their preferred party. Realignment refers to the process of transition which party systems periodically undergo when new ties between social and political structures are forged. Thus in the wake of a realignment there will exist a clear social group basis of party support, but this will not be the same as that which preceded the transition. Rather, new cleavages will come to structure the party system and patterns of electoral support in a new phase of stable alignment. By contrast, the process of dealignment is one whereby established connections between party and society break down, but are not replaced by new structural associations. Instead, the party system floats increasingly free of its social moorings, with only a relatively small proportion of the electorate maintaining any general partisan loyalty; consequently, factors which are only salient in the short-term context of specific election campaigns (such as candidate and issue assessments) are likely to have a permanently enhanced bearing on the voting decisions that people make. Fewer voters will maintain long-term predispositions to vote for a particular party, and consequently dealignment implies that a greater proportion of the electorate will be susceptible to the effects of party election campaigns.

Has Britain's electorate been realigning or dealigning? Almost certainly, a mixture of both processes has been taking place, but it is not easy to be more precise since the initial symptoms of both phenomena are similar – for instance, weakening partisan identification, declining electoral turnout and increasing volatility. However, in assessing the problem we are helped by the fact that a quarter of a century has now passed since signs of electoral change first became evident. A detailed review of the evidence about the causes of electoral change over this period will guide interpretation. In general, explanations which emphasize the emergence of new cleavages imply realignment, while those which stress the changing social psychology of voters or the behaviour of parties themselves imply dealignment.

Realignment and the emergence of new cleavages

The idea that new cleavages are emergent in Britain represents a direct challenge to Lipset and Rokkan's notion of a frozen party system, of course. Nothing in their macro-historical scheme of cleavage development takes account of the impact of post-war social, economic and political changes on the cleavage structure of the country. Yet prima facie one might assume that the latter half of the twentieth century, with its distinctive record of ever more rapid social and technological change, must have generated new lines of political conflict which could have found their way into the party systems of countries like the UK. There are a number of claimants to the status of potential 'new cleavages' that exert pressure upon established patterns of alignment in the country. The most likely cases for consideration include: sectoral cleavages; geographical cleavages; and the newly salient issue cleavages concerning the environment and European integration. Each of these deserves attention.[13]

Sectoral cleavages

In searching for the sources of new cleavages, one of the most obvious developments to consider in post-war Britain is the growth of the state. The burgeoning activities and responsibilities of the state have generated a number of interconnected lines of differentiation between public and private sectors. This has captured the attention of a number of political scientists and has produced some interest in the idea of sectoral cleavages. The most notable proponent of this theory has been Patrick Dunleavy (1979; 1980). He has suggested that public–private tensions express themselves in the form of at least two distinctive types of sectoral cleavage, relating to spheres of consumption and production.

The consumption sectors model offers an account of how the expansion of a variety of public and welfare services (especially in housing, health and transport) can differentiate citizens as consumers. If it can be plausibly demonstrated that (a) a conflict of interest exists between those who rely heavily on public sector services and those who purchase their housing, health care and so on privately, and (b) that this conflict has been translated into patterns of electoral alignment, then we may conclude that a cleavage based on consumption sectors does indeed structure modern party politics to some extent. The production sectors model is essentially similar except that it is based on the notion of differentiation between those who work rather than consume in the public and private sectors.

Why should people who depend on the state for jobs, services or benefits come into any sort of conflict with their counterparts in the private sector? There are at least three possible answers, listed below.

Ideological predisposition   Those who believe in the need for the state to intervene in providing services for all (including the underprivileged) may be predisposed to work as social workers or teachers, whereas those committed to ideals of individual achievement based on competition may well prefer to seek their goals in private industry. Strictly speaking, in such circumstances the appearance of a sectoral cleavage would amount to an effect rather than a cause (that is, alignment would be a corollary of self-selection by group members, quite possibly reflecting their underlying location on a left–right ideological dimension).

Interest   This is the line of explanation preferred by Dunleavy. In essence, he contends that tensions arise between those associated with the public and private sectors since it is generally in the interest of the former to seek the greatest possible expenditure on state services and/or job opportunities from which they benefit, while the latter will seek to minimize their tax bills by preferring parties and politicians who promise reductions in state programmes. Seen in this light, the 'tax/welfare backlash' which some observed in the mid-1970s appears to be some kind of a sectoral effect (Kuhnle 1997: 349; Walker 1986).

Socialization effects   Proponents of socialization theory might argue that certain groups whose members are frequently in close contact (for instance, council estate residents, or colleagues in schools or public sector agencies) will increasingly come to imitate each other in terms of values or political preferences. It should be said that this type of argument is *not* proposed by Dunleavy, though it does offer a plausible mechanism of public/private sector differentiation.

What evidence do we have for the existence of sectoral cleavages in UK party politics? With respect to consumption sectors, Dunleavy has argued that transport and housing are especially important, since the costs of these absorb over half the average household income and are of obvious importance to people. Moreover, the major parties have tended to prefer opposite sides in the conflict of sectoral interests. For instance, throughout the post-war period the Conservatives have been committed to the goal of a 'property-owning democracy', and have therefore encouraged private house building, defended mortgage interest tax relief, and tended to oppose subsidies to council house tenants. By contrast, Labour has favoured council house building pro- grammes and low rents for public housing. With regard to transport, it has generally been the case that since the late 1960s Labour has favoured subsi- dies to public transport, while the Conservatives have preferred to encourage private transport wherever possible, and the use of market criteria to guide public transport operations where not (Dunleavy and Husbands 1985: 23–4).

Thus, the consumption sector approach is inherently plausible. Housing in particular has attracted much attention as a line of potential electoral expla- nation. A number of studies have shown that, statistically, housing has come to replace occupational class as the most important of the social structural determinants of voting alignments since the 1960s. For example, in 1983, Rose and McAllister reported that the Conservative lead over Labour was 18 per- centage points among unskilled manual owner-occupiers, but it was –23 points among council tenants in the same class. This sharp difference between home-owners and council tenants was replicated across all classes (1986: 61). Such differences remained equally distinct in 1997, with Labour 15 points behind the Conservatives among home-owning unskilled manual employees, but fully 16 points ahead among their council tenant counterparts. The evi- dent impact of the housing sector provoked many observers to suggest that the Thatcher governments' controversial 'right to buy' policy of selling coun- cil houses at discounted prices to sitting tenants in the 1980s was designed to undermine a key component of Labour's core support (that is, working-class council house tenants). The possibility that such 'partisan social engineering' (Dunleavy and Ward 1981) might have been influential seems obvious, although Anthony Heath and Geoff Garrett have argued that much of the apparent impact of the sale of council houses was weakened by what they call a process of 'selective mobility', whereby purchasers were already relatively right-wing and pro-Conservative prior buying their homes from local author- ities. That said, their conclusion is that the policy may have deprived Labour of around 0.5% of the popular vote between 1979 and 1987 (Heath with Garrett 1991: 129 [see also Chapter 4]).

The production sector cleavage first seemed plausible during the 1970s, when public sector trade union militancy was at its peak, and when it seemed to some observers that such militancy could be exercised with impunity due to the relative security from redundancy enjoyed by public sector employees. This lent confidence to the belief that high wage costs could ultimately be passed on to the taxpayer. During the 1980s and 1990s, however, the boot was transferred firmly to the other foot, with many in the public sector being politicized by the real wage cuts, redundancies, changing conditions of serv- ice, privatization and/or marketization of services which occurred. Either way, these arguments stack up to a reasonable prima facie case for the existence of a distinct cleavage between public and private sector employees. What does the evidence suggest?

By 1983, Dunleavy had noticed that unionized non-manual employees in the public sector were much more likely to favour Labour than their private sector counterparts; that is, they gave Labour a two percentage point lead over the Conservatives, whereas the latter favoured the Conservatives by forty points (Dunleavy and Husbands 1985: 132). By 1992 Labour led the Conservatives by fourteen points among unionized non-manual employees in the public sector, but trailed by seventeen points among those in the private sector. This implies that, whereas consumption sector sectoral influences seem especially significant for the working class (private property owners being more inclined to support the Conservatives), production sector effects have apparently had greater impact on the middle class (public sector employment inclining its members more towards Labour). That said, the overall electoral significance of production sector effects should not be exaggerated; compared to most other social background factors (including class and housing), they have always been far weaker (Webb 1992a: 190). Moreover, by 1997 the production sector effect had all but disappeared thanks to a remarkable swing to Labour among private sector employees; thus, while the public sector favoured Labour by 1992, the private sector followed five years later, leaving the party with a virtually identical lead over the Conservatives among private and public sector non-manual union members (see Table 2.4). Whether this is merely a transient reflection of the exceptional nature of Labour's catch-all success in 1997 remains to be seen. For the time being, however, it seems reasonable to conclude that consumption sectors are a far more significant influence than production sectors on electoral behaviour in contemporary Britain.

TABLE 2.4   *The dwindling influence of production sectors, 1983–97*

Election	Private sector	Public sector	Private-public difference
1983	−40	+ 2	42
1987	−44	−14	30
1992	−17	+14	31
1997	+27	+28	1

Note:
Figures report the size of Labour's lead over the Conservatives among non-manual union members.

Sources:
Dunleavy and Husbands 1985: 132; Heath et al. 1991: 93; British Election Surveys.

Geographical cleavages

Between the 1950s and 1980s, evidence suggested that British electoral behaviour was becoming increasingly divided geographically. While some commentators interpret these geographical distinctions between certain regions of the country as centre–periphery cleavages (see, for instance, Field 1997), it is important to stress that such divisions do not conform exactly to Lipset and Rokkan's original meaning of the term.

Ron Johnston, Charles Pattie and their various colleagues are among the best-known electoral geographers to have traced evidence of the much-discussed 'North/South divide' in British voting behaviour. For instance, between 1979 and 1987 they discovered that, while the Conservative vote fell by 0.6% on average, this decline was considerably steeper North and West of an imaginary line drawn between the river Severn and the Wash, while the party's support actually grew in most areas South and East of this line (Johnston and Pattie 1989). There is persuasive evidence to suggest that this has much to do with the different socio-economic profiles of these regions. Thus, during the 1980s the Conservatives enjoyed greatest electoral benefit in the most prosperous regions of the country (suburban London, South East, East Anglia, East Midlands and rural West Midlands). Interestingly, however, it seems that the North/South cleavage peaked in 1987; while distinct differences in electoral support still characterize these two parts of Britain, they diminished during the 1990s (Curtice and Park 1999: 127). This pattern of change raises two questions: what are the causes of the North/South cleavage and what explains the apparent weakening of this cleavage during the 1990s?

It is tempting to regard the North/South divide as an economic centre–periphery cleavage which was precipitated by the Thatcher governments' economic and industrial policies. After all, these governments were resolute in their determination to withdraw industrial subsidies and (allied with the attempt to adhere to a strict monetarist policy between 1979 and 1983) this effectively accelerated the decline of the industrial heartland of Northern Britain. Such economic restructuring resulted in a dramatic increase in unemployment in the regions affected and coincided with the high-point in regional voting differences. And yet, as already implied, the onset of these geographical voting patterns predates Thatcherism by some considerable time. Michael Steed and John Curtice have shown that, while the earliest post-war elections displayed remarkably uniform two-party swings across the country as a whole, things were already beginning to change by 1955 (Steed and Curtice 1982). In fact, not only were the first signs of the North/South divide beginning to appear, but a quite independent urban–rural cleavage was also manifesting itself. That is, even within the most prosperous and Conservative parts of the country, the party fared significantly less well in the cities. These twin trends towards both regional and urban–rural distinctions can to some extent be explained by a mix of social and political factors. First, census data show that the south in particular, and rural Britain in general, were both increasingly populated by middle-class voters after 1960. This middle-class flight from cities left urban centres more working class than hitherto. In short, the changing class profiles of the regions and cities left their mark on patterns of support. Second, this was reinforced by the growing impact of constituency class environments reported by William Miller (1978; see also Note 12). That is, middle-class voters left in predominantly working-class inner-city neighbourhoods became more likely to vote as their neighbours did, while the rural workers tended to vote increasingly like their middle-class neighbours. Third, there was evidence of a growing 'third-party' effect which exaggerated regional differences in support for the major parties. That is, where the Liberals and their successors mounted serious challenges after 1964, it tended to be at the expense of the weaker of the major parties – which is to say, the Conservatives in the North and Labour in the South. Similarly, the SNP especially weakened the Conservatives in Scotland (Curtice and Steed 1982). The most widely disseminated type of explanation, however, relates to the economic situations of different geographical locations (Johnston et al. 1988; Heath et al. 1991: 112); and, since economic differences between these locations predate Thatcherism (even if they were exacerbated by it), such an explanation is compatible with the gradual emergence of geographical cleavages from the 1950s on.

To reiterate, however, this evidence of economic centre–periphery and urban–rural cleavages is not consistent with Lipset and Rokkan's classic model. Whereas the modern post-war geographical divisions discussed seem to be based primarily on contemporary socio-economic and political developments, it will be recalled that Lipset and Rokkan's cleavages derived from quite different historical processes. Thus, their classic urban–rural cleavage revolved around a conflict between the landed gentry and urban industrial/commercial interests, while centre–periphery cleavages had more to do with the attempt by nation-building elites to suppress the political autonomy of culturally distinct outlying regions. The economic and political explanations of Britain's changing electoral geography which we have encountered so far do not imply a re-emergence of archaic conflicts, even where 'peripheral' ethnic identity is clearly a factor, as in Scotland. This is why writers such as McAllister and Rose (1984) have argued that there is no such thing as an authentic regional cleavage in modern Britain; their view was that voters in Scotland were not more likely to oppose the Tories because they were Scottish per se, but rather because they were more likely to be working class or to have experienced the ill-effects of economic dislocation.

Not all observers have concurred in this view, however. In the 1980s, for example, William Miller insisted that the British electorate was 'de-nationalizing', and pointed out that 'when large numbers of voters deserted the Labour and Conservative parties in 1974, their choice of alternatives differed sharply according to whether they lived in Scotland, England, Ireland or Wales' (1983). In reviewing a century of electoral behaviour, he argued that the Welsh had long been distinct from the English, whereas the Scottish only began to emulate the Welsh bias towards the left after 1959. More pertinently, he confirmed Curtice and Steed's claim that authentic regional distinctions remained even after controlling for the socio-economic profiles of regions. That is, even within social classes the Scots and the Welsh were significantly more inclined to be anti-Conservative than the English were in 1979; given that Welsh and Scottish nationalist causes suffered setbacks in the general election of 1979 and in the recent referenda on devolution, this is a particularly significant point. Moreover, in the context of overwhelming public support for Scottish devolution which we encounter two decades later, it is becoming harder to sustain the view that there is no longer an element of cultural nationalism guiding the behaviour of the contemporary Scottish electorate (and still less is this true of Welsh voters, as we saw in Chapter 1). In summary, then, this seems to imply that Britain's geographic patterns of voting behaviour correspond to two types of cleavage: (a) socio-economic divisions (both urban–rural and 'North/South') which gradually developed between the 1950s and 1980s, and (b) authentic centre–periphery tensions based on cultural and ethnic identities.

We have noted that the North/South divide appears to have attenuated somewhat (though certainly not disappeared) since 1987. Why so? Johnston and Pattie initially reported evidence of this after the 1992 election, as voters in the South and Midlands swung more heavily to Labour than elsewhere, while the Conservatives did a little better than average in Scotland and some parts of the North of England. This seemed to reflect the fact that, after 1989 (and for the first time since 1979), recession and rising unemployment had affected the generally prosperous South and Midlands more than they had northern Britain; moreover, the Conservatives had suffered particularly in the constituencies where the disastrous poll tax had been highest, and most of these had been in the South (Pattie et al. 1993). Yet in 1997 the North/South cleavage eroded further in spite of relative economic recovery in the South. This weakens the continuing utility of economic explanations. Instead, the answer seems to lie in the impact of party strategy. Specifically, a conscious effort by New Labour's strategists to overcome its 'southern discomfort' (Radice 1992) means that the party endeavoured to shed its associations with declining industrial groups and communities; thus, the abandoning of Clause IV socialism (see Chapter 3), the distancing of the party from the unions, and the concerted effort to eradicate the image of Labour as a party of high taxation can all be seen as part of the attempt to build a new appeal to the southern middle classes. Research suggests that this strategy of 'modernization' did indeed succeed in bringing the party 'differential benefit in the south' (Curtice and Park 1999: 134).

Overall, what does the research on geographical cleavages imply for the opening up of the electoral market? First, since the 1950s at least, the country has experienced the emergence of both urban–rural and centre–periphery cleavages which are rooted primarily in social and economic distinctions. This is almost certainly the best way of understanding the growing regional electoral disparities within England. But on top of this, there is evidence that an authentic politico-cultural centre–periphery cleavage reinforces (perhaps even outweighs) socio-economic concerns in Scotland and Wales. Such factors by no means render the class cleavage unimportant, but they most definitely cut across it. This in itself does not imply a long-term opening-up of the electoral market of course; on the face of it, these cleavages would seem to correspond to long-term processes of realignment which might well 're-freeze' patterns of electoral support in Britain. However, the reversal of the North/South divide in the 1990s suggests that a new pattern of stable alignment around this cleavage has not been generated after all; in particular, geographical patterns of support do not appear so concrete that they are invulnerable to the effects of party strategy. To this extent, then, the electoral market is undeniably 'open'.

The New Politics cleavage

A third post-1945 development which must be addressed in considering the possible emergence of new cleavages relates to new issues and values believed by some commentators to cut across traditional patterns of alignment. Chief among these is the post-materialist values cleavage associated with the name of Ronald Inglehart (1971; 1977; 1990; 1997). Inglehart attempts to explain, among other things, the widely noted changes in attitudes toward authority, hierarchy and traditional social morality which have characterized most Western societies since the 1960s. He does this by reference to the notion of post-industrial society; this idea has been used by a number of writers, though not all deploy it in precisely the way that Inglehart does. Common to most accounts of post-industrialism, however, is the underlying assumption that advanced industrial societies have reached an epoch-changing stage of socio-economic development. A variety of features typify this post-industrial stage of development including: the growing predominance of service over manufacturing and agrarian sectors within the sphere of economic production; the emerging importance of education, research and information technology; and a new pattern of social values. It is Inglehart's explanation of this latter aspect of post-industrial society which has proved highly influential within contemporary political science.

Inglehart's theory of 'culture shift' across Western democracies is built on two fundamental premises: first, people are assumed to value most highly those human requirements which are most scarce (the scarcity hypothesis); and second, their enduring basic values largely reflect the material conditions prevalent during their 'pre-adult years' (the socialization hypothesis). Taken together, these twin hypotheses are held to imply that the absence of war and the unprecedented spread of material affluence since the 1950s have produced new generations of citizens who place less emphasis on the material achievements which older generations had been unable to take for granted, while aspiring to a new range of non-material 'quality of life' goals. This understanding of post-materialism is rooted in the psychological theories of Abraham Maslow (1954), who proposed a hierarchy of human needs, starting with those fulfilling the requirements of basic subsistence (water, food, shelter), and progressing to higher-order social and psychological wants (identity, participation, self-esteem, self-actualization). This logic explains why people shift priorities to the second type of 'quality of life' issue when their basic physical security seems relatively assured. This quality of life agenda is fairly eclectic and takes in issues of democracy and participation, racial and gender equality, and personal liberty and autonomy. The post-materialist issue par excellence, however, is environmentalism. Concern for the quality of the environment exemplifies the view that (at least sometimes) economic growth and affluence can and should be sacrificed to the dictates of protecting nature and the human ecosphere. Inglehart and various associates have spent years marshalling an impressive array of empirical evidence (largely based on social survey data) in an attempt to validate his theory of value change. It is especially pertinent to concentrate on two broad features of this work: first, evidence showing the spread of post-materialist values across advanced industrial societies like Britain's, and second, evidence showing the impact of this 'culture shift' on party systems.

The classic device for measuring 'post-materialist' orientations among samples of citizens is a mini-index of ideological disposition constructed from four, potentially conflicting, policy goals.[14] This measure has been criticized, however (see, for instance, Dalton 1996: 109) and Inglehart has therefore also constructed a more robust index based on 12 questions posed in the *World Values Survey* that he directed in the early 1990s. Interestingly, while it is apparent from research using these indicators that a number of countries have experienced very significant growth in the proportions of their citizens who might be described as post-materialist, Britain does not appear to be among them: less than a fifth fitted such a description in 1990, virtually the same proportion as in 1973. That said, it should be borne in mind that many citizens also display a mixed profile (with some materialist concerns and some post-materialist), and the number exclusively preferring material goals is less than half even in Britain (op. cit.: 96–7).[15]

Does this affect patterns of party support? According to writers like Russell Dalton, the answer is a resounding 'yes'. He has demonstrated clearly that, in Britain, the more post-materialist a voter is, the more likely he or she is to vote for the left; this is broadly confirmed by the evidence in Table 2.5 which shows post-materialists favour Labour over either the Liberal Democrats or Conservatives. Note also Dalton's conviction that the statistical correlation between post-materialism and electoral choice has grown over time, even as that between social class and party has declined (op. cit.: 189–91). The unspoken implication of this is that the rise of post-materialism at least partially accounts for the decline of class voting; certainly, such a view fits well with the realignment perspective and with Inglehart's own view that post-materialism is generating a 'new left' which cuts across the traditional materialist ideology of the 'old left'. While the latter, based on trade unionism, communism, and social democracy, is still primarily concerned with questions of economic growth, equality and security, the former is motivated by the New Politics agenda to which we have alluded. Dalton goes so far as to claim that

TABLE 2.5   *Value priorities and party support in the UK, 1997*

Party	Post-materialists	Mixed	Materialists
Labour	54.2	49.2	41.9
Liberal Democrat	29.0	14.8	17.8
Conservative	12.3	29.1	36.0
Other	4.5	6.9	4.3
Total	100	100	100

Note: p<.01, Cramer's v = .16 (n = 963).
Source: British Election Survey 1997.

the influence of values-based voting exceeds that of class-voting in countries like Britain, though it must be said that this assertion is not based on a true multivariate analysis which simultaneously tests for the independent impact of class and post-materialism on electoral choice. Consequently, such a bald claim has to be treated with the greatest caution.[16]

Furthermore, the capacity of the post-materialist cleavage to generate a thoroughgoing realignment of British party politics is limited by a number of related factors. First, a vital component of the institutional context – the simple majority electoral system – constitutes a high barrier to gaining electoral representation which virtually precludes the chances of new parties based on post-materialist values from achieving a parliamentary breakthrough. (This goes some way towards explaining the very different electoral fortunes of the British and German Green parties, for instance). Second, the chances of realignment rather depend on the strategic responses of established parties. In Britain, both major political parties and the Liberal Democrats have developed environmental policies which reflect the concerns of post-materialist voters, although we have seen that Labour remains much the most attractive to such citizens. Again, however, this process of adaptation (slow and partial though it may well be) by the established parties to the emerging agenda of New Politics helps prevent electoral breakthroughs by new parties. Given that, to some extent or other, it encompasses all of the established parties – including the Conservatives – it also helps limit the potential for realignment of groups of voters between existing parties. For instance, some Conservative sympathizers concerned about the dangers of pollution may have found just enough in Mrs Thatcher's own environmental programme of the late 1980s to prevent their defection to another party. In short, it is hard to state unequivocally that the established parties can be divided into materialist and post-materialist organizations. Finally, as Alan Ware (among others) has pointed out, many of life's post-materialists are disinclined to indulge in party political forms of engagement:

> Political parties resembling the ones that arose in response to class conflict were regarded with suspicion – partly because of doubts about what they might achieve

and partly because of a commitment to forms of participation that were believed to be impossible within the hierarchies characteristic of parties. Participation should be direct and leaders should be instructed by followers. Politics was to be conducted through social movements, not parties. (Ware 1996: 230)

To the extent that this is true, it clearly inhibits the direct impact of post-materialist values on existing party politics. However, even if it does constrain the realigning potential of New Politics, we should not overlook the dealigning potential which remains. That is, if post-materialists are less inclined to commit themselves to political parties than many other citizens, preferring instead to work through single-interest groups and broad social movements, and if there are more post-materialists in the electorate than hitherto, then it follows that a greater proportion of voters will be dealigned in the sense of being abstainers or floaters. Such individuals only offer support which is contingent on their assessments of short-term factors relevant to specific elections. Overall, this implies a potential (if limited) opening up of the electoral market-place over time.

The European dimension: an emerging cleavage?

As we see in greater detail in Chapter 6, there are reasonable grounds for supposing that issues relating to European integration might have come to cross-cut existing lines of party differentiation during the 1990s, and this raises the prospect that they have the potential to realign patterns of electoral support. The traditionally low political salience of European issues was replaced after 1987 by their growing prominence on the agenda of British politics, and their capacity to provoke internal tensions within both major parties – but especially the Conservatives – has been plain for all to see. The European dimension was a leading factor in the Conservative Party's leadership contests of 1990, 1995 and 1997, and was critical to a number of high-profile parliamentary party rebellions and even a few defections between 1992 and 1998. Moreover, it seems clear that the weight of public opinion began to swing against further European integration after the early 1990s (Evans 1998). The combination of increasing issue salience, shifting party strategies, intra-party dissent and changing public opinion begs the obvious question of whether Europe might have fostered a degree of electoral realignment.

The short answer to such a question appears to be that it has, but only to a limited extent so far. Research conducted by Geoffrey Evans (1999) reveals a number of interesting developments in this respect. First, it is evident that by 1997 voters' attitudes on Europe cut right across their positions on the main dimension of party ideology (socialism versus capitalism). This confirms in principle the realigning potential of the European dimension of party competition. Second, the major parties' supporters seem to have made similar attitudinal odysseys to the parties themselves on Europe, with Conservative voters becoming predominantly Eurosceptic and Labour voters becoming far more positive about integration; indeed, Europe is now an issue which serves to distinguish the centre-left generally (meaning both Labour and Liberal Democrat supporters) from the right (Conservatives). Third, and most interesting, Europe may well have played a role in generating class dealignment; specifically, that is to say, the further decline in class voting between 1992 and 1997 is 'interpretable as, at least in part, a consequence of party realignment on Europe' (Evans 1999: 219). In particular, Evans suggests, New Labour's key target converts among the educated middle classes are precisely the most pro-European group of voters, which helps explain why the party's supporters are now firmly in favour of integration. This research does not directly show that these middle-class voters swung to New Labour *because* of the party's position on Europe; it is possible that many among them had other considerations in mind. Nevertheless, these findings are fascinating and carry the obvious implication that Europe could act (indeed, could already be acting) as a source of electoral realignment. In so far as this is true at all, the magnitude of the effect appears to be minor to date, but the potential of the European dimension of party competition to stimulate further electoral change should not be overlooked.

Dealignment

The view that dealignment – the decoupling of voters from their long-term and habitual attachments to specific parties – is taking place in Britain is implicit or explicit in a number of commentaries on electoral change. More precisely, there are at least three main types of explanation of electoral change which imply dealignment rather than realignment. These are: the view that electors are undergoing a process of 'cognitive mobilization', which threatens to render political parties functionally obsolete in some respects; the notion of class secularization, according to which voters' class identities and values are gradually weakening as classes lose their cohesion; and the feeling that factors deriving from the performance of the parties themselves, including their strategic machinations and policy failings, are generating partisan dealignment. Let us consider these in turn.

Cognitive mobilization

According to this view the expansion of higher educational provision and mass access to television constitute the twin elements of a new 'cognitive mobilization' which facilitates the political independence of electors (Barnes and Kaase 1979). That is, voters become more able to assess information about public affairs without having to rely on party cues (thanks to the role education plays in developing their intellectual skills) at precisely the time that they have far greater access to independent sources of non-partisan information (from the broadcasting media). In one sense, the cognitive mobilization argument constitutes part of a broader critique of modern political parties which we shall revisit during the course of Chapter 9. This critique proposes that parties are gradually losing their functional relevance for modern democratic politics in a number of ways and are consequently undergoing a process of 'decline'. Among other things, it is contended, this shows up in the growing number of sophisticated voters with access to non-partisan sources of political information; such individuals can be independent of parties and can even choose to act through single-interest groups rather than parties should they prefer. Thus, in the context of a sophisticated and rational electorate, the interest groups and mass media come to replace parties in fulfilling key political functions such as political communication and interest articulation.

To assess the significance of the view that cognitive mobilization is producing a more 'rational', autonomous and sophisticated electorate, it is important to introduce one of the best known debates in electoral research: that between the partisan identification and issue voting schools of voting behaviour. Whereas the partisan identification model is, as we have already seen, derived from sociology and psychology, issue voting models draw their inspiration from the 'rational choice' paradigm originally created by economists. Many have been persuaded by the view elaborated by writers such as Mark Franklin (1985) that issue voting models have become more appropriate in accounting for voting behaviour in Britain as an increasingly sophisticated and rational electorate has broken free of the bonds of childhood socialization and habitual group and party ties. On what basis do they sustain such a claim? To understand this, we first need to return to the partisan identification model itself.

The Michigan model cast doubt on the view of the voter as a rational and sophisticated actor who (a) has a set of definite and enduring (or 'crystallized') public policy preferences, (b) clearly and correctly understands the positions of the various parties or candidates on these issues, and (c) then votes accordingly. Indeed, doubts about voter rationality in democratic systems have a long heritage, going back at least as far as Max Weber who argued that the average citizen had little capacity for evaluating public policies, though he or she could play a valuable role in selecting and legitimizing leaders (Held 1996: 168–73). In his classic critique of modern democracy *Capitalism, Socialism and Democracy,* Joseph Schumpeter adopted a similar position and bluntly stated doubts about voter rationality. For instance, he questioned how far it was possible to attribute a rational and independent political will to the citizenry, and he pointed to the lack of political interest that many display: 'Without the initiative that comes from immediate responsibility, ignorance will persist in the face of masses of information, however complete and correct'. Consequently, he suggested that:

> the typical citizen drops down to a lower level of mental performance as soon as he enters the political field. He argues and analyses in a way that he would readily recognize as infantile within the sphere of his real interests. He becomes a primitive again. His thinking becomes associative and affective. (Schumpeter 1952: 262)

Angus Campbell and his associates who created the Michigan model discovered that only around one-half to two-thirds of American electors actually seemed to have clearly crystallized attitudes about issues they were familiar with. Still less did these people correctly perceive party differences on such issues. Moreover, even where a link between issues and voting was found, the Michigan team pointed out that party loyalty itself might be a *cause*, not a consequence, of attitudinal formation. 'The identifier who sees his party take up new issues is likely to be influenced thereby' (Campbell et al. 1960: 97). There were two potential problems, both providing evidence of 'irrational' behaviour. First, a voter might be *persuaded* to alter his or her own issue position in order that it be congruent with that of a party or candidate with whom there was a prior identification. Secondly, voters who favourably identify with a given party or candidate might even *project* their own issue positions on to that party or candidate, regardless of the latter's actual policy attitudes.

The first detailed consideration of these types of argument in relation to Britain was undertaken by Butler and Stokes in the 1960s. They were sceptical about issue voting being widespread in Britain. In the first place (as in America), they discovered that British voters' attitudes were rarely consistent over time (Butler and Stokes 1974: 280–1). Moreover, the electorate as a whole appeared to display a remarkable lack of consistency across related issues – a point reiterated by commentators like Patrick Dunleavy in the 1980s. Thus, Butler and Stokes seemed to indicate that the cognitive development of the British electorate was too limited to take seriously the notion of rational issue voting (1974: 320). However, the first significant challenge to this view was issued by James Alt, Bo Sarlvik and Ivor Crewe in an important article published in 1976. They claimed that:

> most people appear to display a considerable grasp of the issues and where the parties stand on each . . . it appears that, the conventional wisdom notwithstanding, the great majority of the British electorate have both partisan preferences and realistic perceptions of the parties' policies. (Alt et al. 1976: 284)

Moreover, they argued that people were capable of recognizing differences between themselves and 'their' parties over issues, and were even inclined to withdraw their support if those differences were considered significant enough. This was especially true of those voters with weaker partisan identities. It still begged the question of why significant numbers of voters (especially those with strong partisan attachments) behaved 'irrationally' (that is, voted in spite of, rather than because of, their issue preferences), but Alt, Crewe and Sarlvik undoubtedly had a point in suggesting that many people 'who disagree with their party are to a large extent aware that they are doing so' (1976: 289).

Allied to growing evidence of the partisan dealignment and volatility of the British electorate, the arguments of Alt et al. encouraged a widespread reappraisal of Butler and Stokes's view of voting behaviour this side of the Atlantic. Ironically, in view of the title of their magnum opus (*Political Change in Britain*), the real strength of the Butler and Stokes's model lay in explaining behavioural stability, but the focus of research now began to shift to the question of electoral change, which is precisely where attitudinal models were most helpful; they offered insight into comparatively short-term changes in electoral behaviour. Issue voting models, it should be said, are far from monolithic; various models have been developed and it is instructive to consider briefly one or two of the most influential examples.

The earliest of attitudinal models was that proposed by Anthony Downs in his seminal book *An Economic Theory of Democracy* (1957). The Downsian model was strictly rationalistic, instrumental and individualistic, and assumed that voters were able to calculate their personal 'incomes' in terms of the quantities of utility that they would individually derive from the implementation of alternative party programmes. They would then vote accordingly in order to maximize their personal utility. In practice this is, of course, a highly simplistic account of reality. Nonetheless, Downs' model had the merit of representing a serious attempt to work out how voters would vote if they *were* rational according to these criteria. As such, it amounted to an important step along the path towards the development of attitudinal models; moreover, as we see in Chapter 3, it still offers a useful benchmark against which to judge parties' strategies in competing for votes. More typical of subsequent issue voting models was Hilde Himmelweit's 'consumer model', which assumed that the voter knew his or her own mind with respect to a range of potential policy alternatives, and that she or he then sought out the party programme which best matched these preferences. Like a shopper in the market place, the voter could develop partisan 'brand loyalties' to some extent, but this did not equate to partisan identification in the sense of the Michigan model since electors were thought to approach each election like shoppers returning to the market place in search of new products (Himmelweit et al. 1981: 11–16).

So is the social psychology of British voters altering fundamentally as cognitive mobilization enables a greater proportion of them to become 'more rational'? If so, this might explain why some researchers claim to have discovered an increase in issue voting since the 1960s (Franklin 1985; Rose and McAllister 1986). Overall, however, the evidence fails to support their contention. Issue models such as Himmelweit's have encountered criticism on several counts, the first of which is that they simply have not performed well in explaining recent general election outcomes in Britain. Heath and his associates, for example, pointed out that the clear victor of the 1983 general election, the Conservative Party, actually held no clear lead over the Labour Party on any of the five issues that electors felt were most important during the campaign (1985: 91–6). In 1987 Ivor Crewe estimated that, if voters had supported the party they considered best able to handle the issue most important to them, Labour should have won 2 percentage points more of the vote than the Conservatives, rather than 11 points fewer (Crewe 1988). And in 1992 David Sanders noted that Labour was strongly favoured by the electorate on the three issues most frequently picked as being important by electors (the NHS, unemployment and education), and estimated that, had people voted exclusively on the basis of issue preferences, Labour would have polled around 44% of the vote to the Conservatives' 33% (Sanders 1993: 194–7). Again, this estimate bore no resemblance to the actual election outcome.

A second problem of issue voting models has already been alluded to – the question of whether voters really hold 'genuine political attitudes'. As we have seen, Butler and Stokes in the 1960s suggested that they did not. Their work derived in turn from that of Philip Converse (1964) and was subsequently supported by Dunleavy and Husbands (1985), who pointed to logical inconsistencies in voters' attitudes across related policy areas (the problem of low attitudinal 'constraint'), while Lievesley and Waterton (1985) again confirmed that many voters had unstable policy preferences, even across comparatively short periods of time. These criticisms clearly undermined claims of growing voter rationality since they implied that few citizens were ever in a position to match party programmes to crystallized policy attitudes. Such criticisms, however, have been countered in two ways. First, by showing that the apparent instability of voter attitudes was grossly exaggerated by the effect of poor questionnaire design in some of the early studies (Heath and McDonald 1988); and second, by redefining what we mean by 'voter rationality'. For instance, Ian Budge and Dennis Farlie have argued that most voters have a limited but meaningful sense of issue awareness; they tend to understand the broad issue stances of parties in given issue areas. Often, issue areas are effectively 'owned' by parties in that there is longstanding and widespread voter comprehension of their positions on these issues. Thus, welfare policy is generally an electorally positive issue area for socialist parties, as law and order is for conservative parties. This voter awareness becomes significant as different issue areas become salient in given election campaigns. Some areas remain almost permanently salient (for instance, economic performance) whereas others are far less frequently so. Moreover, Budge and Farlie argue that an individual's long-term loyalty to a party is likely to owe more to an 'abiding fixation' with certain issues rather than to partisan identification in the sense of the Michigan model (1983: 36, 41). These arguments help render issue models realistic and workable, since perceptions of an issue's importance count for more than detailed policy preferences. A degree of rationality emerges in voter behaviour, without necessarily satisfying the stringent conditions of cognitive sophistication laid down by Schumpeter. However, useful as such arguments are in salvaging the place of rationality in the behaviour of the British voter, they do not necessarily imply any *change* in his or her social psychology.

This brings us to the third and most critical difficulty with claims of increasingly rational issue voting in Britain. Heath and his colleagues have demonstrated persuasively that, while rational issue assessments certainly do make an impact, it is doubtful that their importance has grown over time. While accepting that the connection between voting and issue attitudes was statistically stronger in the 1980s than hitherto, they argued that this had more to do with the changing political and social circumstances of the period than with the changing social psychology of the electorate. In particular, the fact that far more voters came to regard the major parties as ideologically polarized in 1983 and 1987 (see Table 2.6) in itself generates a stronger statistical association between attitudes and vote.[17] It is therefore necessary to control for the effect of ideological distance between the major parties – for instance by comparing levels of issue voting in years when perceived ideological distance was virtually identical (such as 1964 and 1979). When this is done, these writers concluded that issue effects were no stronger in the latter year than the former. Indeed, the most interesting point that emerges from this analysis is really that 'contrary to received wisdom, issues were rather important in 1964' (Heath et al., 1991). In other words, the rationality of the British electorate was seriously underestimated in some of the early studies. In fact, it seems that rather less has changed in the social psychology of the British voter than some writers have been inclined to suggest. Rational issue voting seems to have played a constant part, and the expansion of higher education and the mass media have done little to alter this. In short, this evidence makes it hard to believe that generalized partisan dealignment has occurred in Britain as a result of cognitive mobilization.

TABLE 2.6   *Perceived policy differences between the parties*

Election year	Good deal of difference	Some difference	Not much difference	Don't know
1964	46	24	26	4
1966	42	26	28	3
1970	32	27	37	3
Feb.1974	33	30	35	2
Oct.1974	39	30	30	1
1979	46	29	22	2
1983	82	10	6	2
1987	84	11	4	1
1992	55	31	12	2
1997	33	42	23	2

Source: Evans et al. 1999: 97.

Class secularization

Class secularization is a term employed by David Robertson (1984: 86) and later embraced by Anthony Heath and his colleagues to refer to the process by which social classes are held to have lost their physical cohesion, along with their ideological and cultural distinctiveness (Heath et al. 1991: 63). This decomposition of class communities is taken by many commentators to imply simultaneous processes of class and partisan dealignment in so far as it 'opens up' the electorate. Indeed, processes of cleavage decomposition are virtually portrayed as historically inevitable in some accounts:

> Any given set of issues that provokes a particular pattern of social cleavage and party alignment will inevitably wane in salience over time . . . voters who are two or three generations removed from the issue conflicts which precipitated the original alignments should show little further commitment to these issues as they are resolved or lose their relevance. (Flanagan and Dalton 1985: 10)

This, it is suggested in some quarters, is the fundamental reason underlying the electoral vicissitudes of parties which have traditionally depended upon specific clienteles; for example, the instability of social democratic party support in Europe noted by observers (such as Maguire 1983) might conceivably be a consequence of the decomposition of the class cleavage. This is of obvious relevance to the case of Britain. The precise sociological mechanisms involved in class secularization are usually held to derive from various types of social mobility which serve to fragment classes (especially the working class). Indeed, such mobility (whereby people born into one social class move to another in adult life) has grown thanks to the replacement of manual jobs in the declining manufacturing sector by non-manual positions in the service sector. This has affected class voting in two ways.

In the first place, it has done so directly as all the evidence shows that, as a group, those who have been upwardly mobile from the working class into the middle class vote neither like the class they have departed nor like the one which they have joined. The 1992 British Election Survey data illustrates the point perfectly. While 58% of the static working class (that is, those born into and remaining within the manual sector) supported Labour, and only 17% of the static middle class did so, 31% of those who had experienced upward mobility from manual to non-manual status voted for the party. Crucially, social mobility has grown steadily since the 1960s. In 1964, 33% of voters had experienced social mobility (assuming a simple manual/non-manual class scheme), while 38% had done so by 1992; the vast majority of these experienced upward mobility, moreover. Those using more sophisticated class schemes claim even higher absolute levels of social mobility (Heath et al. 1991: 44). The fact that more voters are socially mobile than hitherto is bound to have weakened the relationship between class and vote, therefore.

Beyond this, it is possible that social mobility has produced a blurring of class identities and lifestyles in so far as there are far more citizens who are 'cross-pressured' in terms of their class characteristics; such individuals are typically less partisan than those with more uniform sets of class characteristics. Rose and McAllister, for instance, have spoken of 'a block of voters who are caught in the middle by conflicting pressures':

> The ideal-type manual worker, who left school at the minimum age, thought of himself or herself as working class, belonged to a trade union, and was a tenant, is

a small minority of the working class today . . . The ideal-type middle-class person, who has some further education, owns a home, thinks of himself or herself as middle class, and would not belong to a trade union, is also very much in a minority. More than five-sixths of the British electorate today is mixed in social position, having some stereotype working class and stereotype middle class characteristics. (1986: 99)

Gordon Marshall and his colleagues have discovered evidence to support this in the shape of attitudes of cross-class couples; in such cases partners have different occupational class designations, and it is not unreasonable to assume that the numbers of these households will have expanded with the growth of social mobility. The political and social values of such couples on inequality, distributional justice and partisanship differ perceptibly from those of class-homogeneous couples (Marshall et al. 1988: 134). This blurring of identities and values might be assumed to carry over to subsequent generations, moreover.

Finally, it should be noted that growing spatial mobility may well compound the effects of the class mobility already discussed. Advanced industrial societies are associated with high levels of urbanization and residential mobility, both of which serve to break down the narrow homogeneity and social solidarity of small, single-class communities. Therefore, there exist fewer communities which effectively propagate and reinforce clear-cut class identities and values. This is a phenomenon that, in the opinion of some sociologists, has fostered an excessively 'privatist' outlook by many within the working class. For instance, Eric Hobsbawm has written of the replacement of solidaristic forms of community consciousness by 'the values of consumer-society individualism and the search for private and personal satisfactions above all else' (Hobsbawm 1981).

However, the class secularization thesis has provoked considerable dissent. Marshall et al. contended that, notwithstanding the impact of social mobility, ideological differences based on class culture persisted into the 1980s at least (1988: 182), while Goldthorpe and Payne found little real evidence that such mobility was rendering the class structure more 'open' (1986). Crucially, Heath has suggested that, at most, a 'modest process of class secularization' might have occurred but argued that this could not have reduced the social or ideological cohesion of classes to anything like the extent necessary to explain the rapid and discontinuous pattern of changes in class voting witnessed since 1970 (Heath et al. 1991: 64). To the extent that class secularization affects patterns of class voting, it should only be expected to do so in a gradual manner given the generally slow nature of social change. Instead researchers such as these have argued persuasively that the sudden downswings in class voting, which occurred at elections such as those of 1970, 1979 and 1997, have far more to do with the political strategies and performances of the major parties – a theme which merits closer consideration.

Changing party performance

The view that the performance of the parties themselves may trigger dealignment can be subdivided into two distinctive approaches: *policy failure* arguments and *party strategy* arguments. The policy failure perspective emphasizes the significance of the major political parties' inability to deal effectively with certain chronic national policy problems. The roots of this position may be traced back to the 'governmental overload' literature which abounded in the 1970s and which explored the notion that countries such as modern Britain were becoming 'harder to govern' as the political system became overloaded with mutually irreconcilable demands (see, for instance, King 1976b; Brittan 1977; Birch 1984). Where no party has appeared capable of solving such policy problems it is plausible to suppose that this could have generally undermined the electorate's trust in all established governing parties.

The issue with the most obvious potential to effect this kind of generalized partisan dealignment is the seemingly perennial question of Britain's relative economic decline, which became increasingly vexed after the 1970s. Until then, Britain had shared in the post-war growth and modernization that so characterized most industrial economies during the decades following 1945. This changed rapidly in the early 1970s. A number of factors combined to produce this change, including the collapse of the Bretton Woods system,[18] which exposed Britain to greater economic uncertainty, and the oil-shocks of 1973, which torpedoed the economic aspirations of the governments of the day. By 1976, Britain was facing a severe foreign exchange crisis and was obliged to apply for a loan from the International Monetary Fund (IMF). The result was a shift in economic policy away from Keynesianism, and the establishment of a more market-orientated economic strategy – prosecuted with particular enthusiasm by the post-1979 Thatcher governments. This approach, whatever its other merits, was demonstrably incapable of coming to terms with the problem of growing unemployment. The widespread perception of weak economic performance almost certainly undermined the confidence of large parts of the electorate in both major parties. Indeed, doubts about the effectiveness of party government may also flow from policy failures in areas of government responsibility other than the economy. This is a theme to which we return in the course of Chapter 9, and there we find evidence that more than one-third of electors doubted the capacity of any party to 'do much' about unemployment and inflation in the early 1990s, while two-fifths felt similarly with respect to crime, and more than a half concluded that it really did not make much difference which party governed (see Table 9.1, items e–h).

That said, it is equally possible that party strategies are an alternative source of this diffuse sense of indifference about who governs. For example, programmatic convergence between the major parties might be expected to undermine strong partisan identities and even patterns of class voting. That is, to the extent that voters perceive a tendency for these parties to become

increasingly indistinct from one another in terms of their major policy proposals, it would not be surprising if large numbers of them concluded that it
simply did not much matter who they voted for, or even whether they voted at
all. (This line of argument, it should be noted, bears upon influential interpretations of party transformation which we shall be considering in Chapter 8.[19])

In this respect, specific evidence exists of a connection between the programmatic strategy of the Labour Party and class dealignment after 1970: 'as
Labour moves to the centre, the class voting parameter declines' (Evans et al.
1999: 94). In essence, this research shows that during periods when the
Labour Party has shifted its ideological position from left to centre, it has been
deserted by significant numbers of working-class supporters; this helps
explain the sudden drop in relative class voting in 1970, 1979 and 1997 (see
Table 2.3, Alford index and 'Heath' odds ratios). So, in as much as general
partisan dealignment is a close correlate of class dealignment, we have a persuasive explanation of one of its major causes after 1970. This goes as follows:
class dealignment is largely accounted for by working-class voters deserting
Labour since 1970; their support for Labour has always been contingent on
the party delivering the kind of policies which they deem to be in their interest; therefore, when they perceive Labour to favour policies designed to
appeal more to the middle class, they are less likely to support it. (For a more
elaborate account of a similar argument, see Webb 1992a: ch. 5.) Labour's ideology since the 1960s has not been constant, and neither has it shifted in a
simple linear direction (as we shall see in Chapters 3 and 4), but whenever the
party has de-emphasized its appeal to the working class this appears to have
stimulated class and partisan dealignment.

Interestingly, these findings are buttressed by previous research into the
causes of *apartisanship* and *anti-partisan sentiment* in Britain (Webb 1996). These
can be regarded as different aspects of partisan dealignment. This can be
comprehended if one conceives of a linear spectrum of attitudes towards
parties running from partisan commitment, through apartisanship (indifference towards parties) to anti-party sentiment (active and generalized hostility
towards parties) at the other:

Partisan → Apartisan → Anti-party

In these terms, dealignment is largely comprised of 'apartisanship', but a
small number of electors (around 2%) seem to be genuinely 'anti-party'. From
the perspective of this chapter, this study revealed a number of interesting
findings. First, class voting was confirmed as a correlate of strong partisanship, which implies that class dealignment must indeed co-vary with partisan
dealignment. Second, voters unable to distinguish important ideological differences between the major party alternatives were significantly less likely to
maintain strong partisan identities or even to care which party won the election. This confirms the findings of Evans et al. (1999) about the importance of
party strategies (that is, their policy programmes). Third, though less importantly, perceptions of poor economic policy performance showed a significant

relationship with active hostility towards major parties. For instance, respondents perceiving a weakening of the national economy over the decade running up to 1992 were significantly more likely than those who felt it had got stronger to regard the major parties with hostility or indifference. Finally, the main indicator of cognitive mobilization in the model (level of educational attainment) proved not to have the kind of effects that writers such as Barnes, Kaase and Dalton would lead us to expect. Educational attainment simply had no significant bearing on a person's strength of partisanship or feelings of hostility towards the major parties. This tends to confirm the view expressed above that cognitive mobilization appears to have little impact on partisan dealignment in Britain. In short, these findings imply that what Evans et al. (1999) call 'top-down' factors, such as party strategies and policy performances (especially the former), carry most weight in explaining class and partisan dealignment.

Conclusion

During the course of this chapter the literature on electoral change in Britain has been reviewed with the aim of establishing that elections in the country are indeed competitive. The old orthodoxies of the 1960s, which emphasized a frozen cleavage structure and stable patterns of partisan alignment, seemed to imply a relatively 'closed' electorate in which scope for genuine competition was highly restricted. This degree of closure was associated with the sectarian cleavage in Northern Ireland and with social class in mainland Britain, and suggested that the parties' electoral strategies were mainly designed to mobilize groups of loyal 'identifiers' rather than to compete for undecided voters. Yet we have seen enough evidence of partisan erosion, class dealignment and electoral instability since 1970 to be confident that the system is neither 'frozen' nor so rigid as to preclude intensive and 'open' competition for votes. In truth, there almost certainly never was an entirely closed electoral market in the UK; at the very least, serious electoral competition has always been conducted in marginal constituencies. But since 1970 the evidence of electoral change suggests that competition has increased in line with an expansion of the market for votes.

   In seeking to understand the nature and causes of the change the country has witnessed, we have uncovered evidence of both realignment and dealignment; indeed, it is difficult to distinguish clearly the empirical boundaries between these two analytically distinct phenomena. On the whole, the case for realignment carries less weight, but is most apparent in the emergence of new socio-political cleavages based on sectoral or geographical locations and ethnic identities. Even here, though, the weakening of production sector and North/South divide effects during the 1990s undermines a sense of realignment. While post-materialist values may motivate significant numbers of electors, it seems as likely that these have contributed to dealigned behaviour as to realignment. It should be said, however, that European integration may

yet come to engender a degree of electoral realignment around what would
be a new cleavage. Evidence for dealignment is, on the whole, rather more
impressive. It is evident principally in the erosion of strong partisan attachments, which in turn can be traced largely to the factors which underlie the
decline of class voting, such as the strategic behaviour of parties themselves.
On the other hand, we have seen that there is little good reason to believe that
dealignment owes much to a dramatic change in the psychology of the ordinary voter; voters have long been motivated by a blend of expressive partisan
predispositions and a capacity for rational reflection on the political issues of
the day (which implies that the British electorate has always been partially
closed and partially open to the effects of party competition). Instead, partisan dealignment (and therefore the extension of electoral competition) can be
understood in terms of the scheme laid out in Figure 2.2.

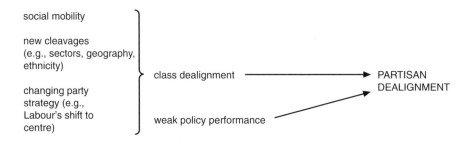

FIGURE 2.2   *The opening up of the electoral market place*

In Figure 2.2, partisan dealignment is explained by a combination of the
factors situated in the space to its left. These principally include class dealignment and weak policy performance; cognitive mobilization has been
excluded as there is no convincing evidence that it has contributed significantly to partisan dealignment. To the far left of the diagram are those factors
which have produced class dealignment (party strategies, new cross-cutting
cleavages and social mobility). To a considerable extent these factors reflect a
phenomenon outlined in Chapter 1: the growing heterogeneity of British society. This is directly evident in the development of new cleavages, and it
complicates the parties' task of devising coherent programmes which can
successfully aggregate the demands of varied social interests.

As we also saw in Chapter 1, a corollary of electoral change has been the
growth of minor party support, and this too has confronted the major parties
with new competitive pressures since 1970. In many constituencies throughout mainland Britain, for instance, the Liberal Democrats and their
predecessors became a factor in the electoral equation after 1970 simply
(though not only) because they fielded candidates where they had not done
so before. Thus, in 1970 the Liberals fielded 332 candidates but they increased

this sharply to 517 in February 1974 (Heath et al. 1991: 17). Although this fact alone certainly did not ensure that Liberals became real contenders for victory in most or even many of these constituencies, it did mean that voters located there were offered new choices and it inevitably came to affect the balance of competition between other parties. The Liberal Democrats are now serious challengers in many seats, and their rise since 1974 has served to weaken one or other of the major parties in these constituencies (especially the Conservatives in the 1997 election [Berrington and Hague 1997: 59–60]).[20] Similarly, the SNP has offered Scottish voters a new option, one which many voters north of the border have been happy to avail themselves of. The effect of this has been to exacerbate Tory decline in Scotland and to produce a fascinating variety of constituency competitions involving four parties. For instance, a good many of Scotland's seats are now dominated by intra-left rivalries between Labour and the SNP.[21] The emergence of Plaid Cymru has had a similar (albeit more modest) effect in Wales, and even in Northern Ireland intra-sectarian competition has intensified within the Unionist and Nationalist blocs (see Chapter 1; see also Aughey 1994: 168, 173–4).

As a counterpoint to this theme of growing dealignment and competition, it should be said that such dealignment cannot be assumed to be permanent. For instance, given that it is partly triggered by aspects of party behaviour such as programmatic strategy and policy failure, we cannot overlook the possibility of its future reversal. Changing voter perceptions of parties' policy competence, heightened levels of programmatic polarization and even the advent of electoral reform permitting electors meaningful choices between a new set of party alternatives might all serve to foster renewed levels of partisan commitment and stable alignment within the electorate. On the other hand, none of these things are guaranteed; moreover, while the introduction of proportional representation (see Chapter 9) could conceivably serve to re-establish partisan attachments, it could also further intensify the competitive efforts of parties, in so far as they would be compelled to extend their efforts across all constituencies. No major party could continue to concentrate most of its resources in marginal constituencies alone; far fewer votes would be 'wasted' under PR and it would become important to maximize support in each and every constituency. This implies the need for more truly national campaign efforts by all parties.

So, we have seen that parties do indeed compete at elections, and that electoral change since 1970 almost certainly implies a more open electoral market and increasingly complex patterns of competition (especially at constituency level). But all this begs a rather obvious and significant question: just *how* do parties compete?

Notes

1   Northern Irish politics, it should be said, is interesting and unusual from the perspective of electoral competition; as we saw in Chapter 1, it constitutes a *sui generis*

party system in which there is virtually no direct electoral competition between Protestant-Unionist and Catholic-nationalist blocs of parties, given unusually high levels of social segmentation. This does not mean that there is no meaningful competition in the province at all, however, for intense party rivalry exists *within* each bloc.

2   For the sake of completeness we should add that Lipset and Rokkan's scheme of cleavage development makes much of one other kind of religious conflict, though it has no relevance to Britain. This is the state–church tension which has afflicted a number of European countries where Roman Catholicism remained strong after the French Revolution of 1789. The secular republican elites who took over France after 1789 sought to reduce the power and privilege to which the church had been accustomed (especially in the field of education) and, not surprisingly, met with resistance. Very similar church–state tensions developed nearly a century later on the other side of the Alps as the new Italian state was born during the Risorgimento. Wherever it occurred in Europe, this type of situation spawned what Rokkan and Lipset called 'parties of religious defence'. However, lacking an established Catholic church, Britain's modern party system has not been structured by this kind of state–church cleavage.

3   This measure implies that, over time, increasingly large net changes must occur if 'significant' trends in electoral support are to be discovered. Thus, by 1997, we would have to find a net change of 13 percentage points in the 1945 party shares of the vote for there to have been a 'significant trend'. In fact, no British party has enjoyed or suffered such a considerable change (the Conservatives being 9.1 points down on their 1945 performance, Labour 5.5 points down, and the Liberal Democrats 7.7 points up on the 1945 score of the old Liberal Party). This seems to point us to the counter-intuitive conclusion that there has not been a significant degree of electoral change in the UK since 1945.

4   The familiar two-party swing (or 'Butler swing') which has long been cited in analyses of election results in the UK takes into account the change in aggregate support earned by any two parties in the system. More often than not the two parties concerned are the Conservative and Labour parties (as in Table 2.1). It is given by the formula:

$$\frac{([C2–C1] + [L1–L2])}{2}$$

where C1 is the percentage of the vote won by the Conservatives at election 1 and C2 the percentage won by them at election 2, while L1 is Labour's share at election 1 and L2 its share at election 2. For instance, if the Conservatives lost a net 3% of the vote from one election to the next, and Labour gained 5%, then the two-party swing would be:

$$\frac{([–3] – [–5])}{2} = –4$$

that is, a net 4% swing from Conservative to Labour. By convention a positive figure denotes a swing to the Conservatives and a negative figure a swing to Labour (see Denver 1989: 18). This measure was most valid when the major parties in Britain absorbed 90% or more of the vote across the country. However, the Pedersen Index has the advantage over the traditional two-party swing of summing the net changes for *all* parties, and is therefore now a better measure of systemic change, given the growing significance of minor party support since 1970.

5   Note that Heath has questioned the validity of this time-series on the ground that the wording of the relevant question in the British Election Study questionnaire changed in 1974 (when a jump in the numbers deciding in the campaign period is apparent). Thereafter, there is no real trend in the series. For him and his co-authors, therefore, 'there is a serious danger that the change is artifactual' (Heath et al. 1991: 14).

6   It must be borne in mind that much of the evidence of electoral change which we shall encounter is based on an analysis of individual-level data, whereas Bartolini and Mair approach the subject through an examination of aggregate levels of party support. It is by no means unusual for political science to uncover paradoxes whereby aggregate- and individual-level analyses can both be perfectly competently conceived and executed and yet appear to tell contradictory stories.

7   Unless otherwise stated, all figures cited in this paragraph are based on my analysis of British Election Surveys 1964–97.

8   Heath and his colleagues argued that the apparent fall in class voting that occurred between 1979 and 1983 was 'in fact almost wholly spurious, an artefact of the inadequate manual/non-manual dichotomy', which was 'wholly inadequate for studying the social bases of politics since it ignores important divisions which have little to do with the colour of a man's or woman's collar'. Consequently, they preferred their own more complex fivefold class scheme comprising a salariat, routine non-manual workers, petit bourgeoisie, foremen/technicians and the working class (Heath et al, 1985: 30–4). Ivor Crewe responded by insisting that there remained certain advantages to employing the simple manual/non-manual distinction; in particular, in constructing measures of class voting which compare the behaviour of the middle and working classes, using the salariat as an indicator of the former (as Heath did) meant ignoring fully 40% of the sample (that is, the groups referred to by Heath as petit bourgeois, routine non-manual and foremen). By contrast, the manual/non-manual dichotomy enables one to base one's findings on the entire sample (Crewe 1986: 623–4).

9   The main methodological dispute focused on the measurement of class voting, which will be reviewed shortly. The second methodological issue of note concerned the baseline year against which most previous (and indeed many subsequent) studies compared rates of class voting. Heath argued that, in part, the appearance of class dealignment reflected the unfortunate fact that detailed academic election surveying only commenced in Britain in 1964: 'The mistake of recent commentators is that they have taken 1964 as their baseline. As we now see, this was a rather unfortunate choice since it marked a peak in relative class voting (as measured by the odds ratio). The adoption of a longer time perspective clearly calls into question claims about any secular trend towards class dealignment' (Heath et al. 1985: 34).

10 This could be achieved by subtracting the percentage of manual workers voting Conservative from the percentage of non-manuals doing so.

11 In fact, both Ivor Crewe and Elinor Scarbrough criticized Heath's preferred version of the odds ratio (Heath 'B' in Table 2.3) on the grounds that this did not properly account for third-party voters; when recalculated in order to allow for

such factors, it becomes apparent that the odds ratio tells a story of class dealignment (see 'Scarbrough' in Table 2.3). Table 2.3 reveals that only Heath's preferred measure suggested a pattern of 'trendless fluctuation' in class voting at the time *How Britain Votes* was authored. In any case, the Heath team seem to have conceded subsequently that a degree of class dealignment has taken place (Heath et al. 1991: 78); indeed, as we see below, they offer very persuasive explanations of the decline of class voting.

12   It should perhaps be said that, notwithstanding the undoubted weakening of class voting at the individual level, evidence from the 1970s suggested it had strengthened at constituency level. People, apparently, were pulled towards voting in line with their 'class environment'; thus, in predominantly working-class constituencies, non-manual electors were more likely to vote Labour than the national norm, while in middle-class areas, manual workers were more Conservative than normal (Miller 1978). In short, this paradox illustrates perfectly the 'ecological fallacy' of drawing inferences from one level of analysis to another; it does not, however, weaken the basic position that individual-level class dealignment creates the potential for a more open electoral market.

13   Note that these are by no means the only social group factors which might cut across the orthodox two-party, two-class pattern of alignment, but they are the only ones which currently have the potential to affect large proportions of the electorate. A good illustration of this is provided by the impact of race on electoral behaviour in Britain. A voter's race has an enormously significant impact on his or her party choice, and it certainly outweighs the influence of class among ethnic minority citizens. Thus, Labour won at least 80% of the support of each of the country's main ethnic minorities in 1997, and even garnered 76% of the votes of upper-middle-class black and Asian voters (Saggar and Heath 1999: 114). However, if one bears in mind that only 5.5% of the population is comprised by these ethnic groups, and, moreover, that some of these groups fail to register and/or turn out to vote at a high rate (ibid: 107), it is apparent that the aggregate-level impact of race on voting cannot be great yet (see also Saggar 1998). Nevertheless, one should not overlook the fact that the impact of race constitutes an element of the growing social heterogeneity discussed in Chapter 1. As such it can be regarded as a small but significant force for realignment which serves to cut across the class cleavage.

14   Respondents are asked: 'If you had to choose among the following things, which are the two that seem most desirable to you? (a) giving the people more say in important political decisions; (b) maintaining order in the nation; (c) fighting rising prices; (d) protecting freedom of speech.' Those who select (a) and (d) are deemed to be post-materialists, while those selecting (b) and (c) are materialists; anybody else is regarded as ideologically 'mixed'.

15   Note that BES data suggest little change in the overall proportion of post-materialists in the electorate by the time of the 1997 general election. Using the simple four-item scale originally devised by Inglehart, some 17% of the BES sample proved to be of post-materialist orientation, while 46% were materialist and the remainder mixed (n = 1190).

16   Note that such a multivariate analysis is offered in Chapter 4; specifically, Table 4.3 reports that post-materialism has no significant effect on electoral choice.

17   Heath et al. explain that 'if the Labour and Conservative parties move away from the centre, voters with centrist attitudes will switch to centre parties, while those who vote Labour or Conservative will now be more extreme subsets of the

electorate. In effect, Labour and Conservative voters will now be more polarized in their attitudes, and this means that the usual statistical measures will show a stronger relationship between attitudes and voting for these two parties' (1991: 33).

18   The international agreement reached at Bretton Woods (USA) in 1944 sought to aid post-war economic recovery by maintaining stable and predictable currency exchange rates. It collapsed in 1971 when the central currency of the agreement, the US dollar, could not maintain its international value (Robbins 1994: 214, 301).

19   Otto Kirchheimer's famous 'catch-all' model (1966), for instance, proposed that by the 1960s some west European socialist parties already felt obliged to modify their ideologies in order to develop an electoral appeal beyond their traditional working-class clienteles. Strategic shifts of such a nature were driven fundamentally by the perception that the class structures of advanced industrial societies were changing; given the gradual shrinking of manual working classes in industrialized societies, left-wing parties were compelled to consider modifying their programmes if they wished to be electorally successful. Indeed, in *How Britain Votes* Heath et al. revived the notion that Labour might have suffered electorally by the shrinking of the working class; they argued that those who interpreted Labour's electoral slump in the decade following 1974 as class dealignment overlooked the simple, but highly significant, fact of the shrinking of the working class (1985: 35–9). Table 2.7 illustrates how the salariat has grown relative to the size of the working class since 1964.

TABLE 2.7   *Class composition of the electorate, 1964 and 1997*

Class	1964	1997
Salariat	18	30
Routine non-manual	18	22
Petit bourgeois	7	9
Foremen/technicians	10	7
Working class	47	33
Total	100	100

Sources: British Election Surveys 1964–97.

20   In 1987 Alliance candidates came second in 261 constituencies (behind Conservative candidates in 223 cases) and in 1992 the Liberal Democrats finished runners-up in 154 constituencies (the Tories winning in all but 9 of these seats [Curtice and Steed 1993: 334]). By 1997, the Liberal Democrats were runners-up in just 104 seats of which 73 were won by Conservative candidates. The reduced number of second-places for the Liberal Democrats was in large part a function of their success in actually winning far more contests (46), of course.

21   In 1992 Labour and the SNP occupied the top two places in 34 (47%) of Scottish seats, and by 1997 this figure had risen to 42 (58%).

3

HOW PARTIES COMPETE 1:
IDEOLOGICAL REPUTATIONS

CONTENTS

As we have seen, British political parties engage in an intense struggle for votes and power. They are far more than passive victims of electoral flux; to a significant extent, they respond to and shape the electoral vicissitudes on which their fortunes ride. It is the aim of this and the following two chapters to consider how they do this. Broadly speaking, there are two somewhat different political science perspectives on the question of how parties compete. The first is associated with formal models of party competition and emphasizes the strategic use of ideological appeals to electors. The second approach is based on the idea of political marketing. This has fascinated academics and journalists alike in recent years, and assumes that parties start by seeking to know their electoral markets (largely through increasingly sophisticated forms of public opinion research) and then shape their 'products' accordingly. These products comprise packages of policies, politicians and general organizational images (akin to industrial firms' corporate images [Scammell 1995; Farrell and Webb forthcoming]). Although party ideology is by no means irrelevant to the political marketing approach, there is also room for emphasis on imagery and presentation; policy is generally seen as adaptable to the demands of the electoral market. By contrast, the party competition approach usually assumes party ideology to be more (though by no means entirely) inflexible and stresses the importance of parties' enduring 'policy reputations'.

In reality, it is almost certainly true that both approaches can contribute to our understanding of the ways in which parties compete for votes and power in modern Britain. On many issues parties do develop enduring policy stances; though such policies may vary somewhat over time, they generally only do so within certain limits. That said, in recent years Labour at least has shown a growing willingness to explore these limits in response to opinion research, and all parties have become increasingly sophisticated in the presentation of their policies and candidates. In Chapter 5 we focus on political marketing by considering party and leadership images, and the importance of the mass media in the creation and dissemination of such images. But the traditional starting point for accounts of party competition lies with the shaping of electoral appeals through ideological and policy stances, which is the theme of this chapter and the next; here we concentrate on the enduring ideological reputations which define the main parties, while Chapter 4 examines in greater detail the connection between programmatic change and the competition for votes.

Ideology and party competition

Why are enduring ideological reputations important to parties competing for votes? In order to understand, it is necessary to begin with Anthony Downs' pioneering work on party competition, *An Economic Theory of Democracy* (1957), a classic example of the rational choice paradigm which has become so influential within contemporary political science. Downs offered

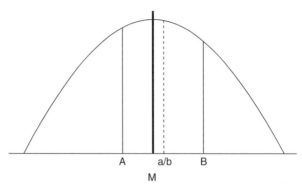

Note: 'M' represents the position of the median voter on a given (left–right) dimension of voter preferences and party competition. 'A' and 'B' represent the ideological locations of the only rival parties competing for electoral support; 'a/b' is the point exactly halfway between these locations.

FIGURE 3.1   *The Downsian model of centripetal two-party competition*

an integrated theory of voting and party competition, in which both electors and political parties were assumed to be rational utility-maximizing actors. Voters will prefer the party which they calculate to be most likely to enact a programme of maximum personal benefit to themselves, while parties are assumed to be internally unified vote-maximizing actors. If voters opt for the party they believe to be nearest to their own policy preferences – the logical implication of their desire to maximize personal utility – it behoves office-seeking parties to adopt policies which will maximize their electoral appeal. Given also the considerable time and intellectual complexity involved in making a detailed appraisal of policy issues and party programmes, many voters are assumed by Downs to make use of broad ideologies. Ideologies provide a guide to the world of policy, while obviating the need to understand policy details. Moreover, assuming that parties and voters understand ideological competition in terms of a single dimension of belief (typically a left–right dimension), and that parties are constrained not to 'leapfrog' over each other on this dimension, we are in a position to understand the inferences which Downs drew from the model.

Figure 3.1 portrays a situation of two-party competition. Where should a party locate itself in order to maximize its vote? The answer depends on the aggregate distribution of voter-preferences (ADP). In this particular figure (in which the horizontal axis represents position on a single left–right ideological dimension, and the vertical axis measures the number of voters preferring a given ideological location), electors' ideological preferences are normally distributed; that is, there is a single peak to the ADP curve, with most voters congregating around the middle of the ideological spectrum and rather fewer at the extremes. Logically, either of the parties A or B wishing to maximize its vote should seek to locate itself as closely as possible to the median voter M (that is, the voter 'in the middle' of the distribution, with as many to the right as to the left of him or her). In Figure 3.1, the point a/b represents an ideo-logical position exactly halfway between the two parties; party A will secure the support of all voters to the left of a/b, while party B will win the support of all those to the right. Since A is slightly closer to M than B is, it will win a majority of the votes. Famously, Downs demonstrated that – over time – any party system conforming to these features should experience convergence on the median voter as both parties seek to maximize votes: a pattern often referred to as one of centripetal competition.

Clearly, the adaptation of party ideology to the distribution of voter pref-erences is central to this model. To this extent, it does not seem so different from the political marketing approach. However, most formal models of party competition add the key stipulation that parties should not be allowed to leapfrog over each other in ideological terms, which limits strategists' room for manoeuvre. What justifies such an assumption? The answer is that voters are more likely to trust politicians who appear to have consistently held policy beliefs. A radical socialist politician who switches to a fervently free market brand of politics would surely leave many voters gasping with incredulity. So rational and unified parties are deemed not to have complete freedom to shift policies; they must, to some extent, be constrained by past policy positions if they are to retain credibility in the eyes of the electorate. In short, parties have an incentive to develop enduring policy reputations (Laver 1997: 136).

In fact, comparative research has confirmed that the 'no leapfrogging' assumption is largely borne out by the facts (Klingemann et al. 1994: 246). Historically, however, political parties have not always been associated with enduring systems of political belief. When Edmund Burke first proposed that political parties should be organized around 'some particular principle in which they are all agreed' in 1770 (Burke 1906), it was considered a radical notion. Hitherto, as in many European countries, parliamentarians gave their allegiance mainly to leaders who dispensed the most attractive patron-age inducements. However, Burke – like all supporters of the constitutional settlement of 1689 – was concerned by the attempt made by George III to extend his powers of patronage so as to buy a permanent majority in the House of Commons. Burke suggested that the best way to counteract this was through the establishment of permanent coalitions of MPs loyal to ideas; such men would not be susceptible to the King's patronage. Furthermore, with the onset of mass democracy, it no longer remained possible for MPs to 'buy' the support of the few who were eligible to vote in parliamentary elec-tions; a new kind of mass appeal had to be forged, and this could really only be done on the basis of some relatively clear system of political ideas and goals. Indeed, as Klaus von Beyme says, 'over the longer term only par-ties based on an ideology have succeeded in establishing themselves' (1985: 29). Given that this is so, it is clearly imperative to examine the enduring ide-ological reputations which the main British parties have established for themselves.

Conservative party ideology

Across Europe as a whole, the programmes of Conservative parties have probably been subject to greater change than those of most other major party families during the democratic era (von Beyme 1985: 48). This is because Conservative parties tended to emerge in order to oppose the liberal demand for democratization; once this had been conceded, however, it was not immediately obvious what the basis of their appeal to a mass electorate might be – unless they were prepared to make substantial adjustments to their traditional thinking.

It is also interesting to observe that Conservative parties are prominent in few western European countries – and nowhere are they as strong as in Britain. They survive as significant political forces in the Nordic democracies, Spain and Greece, but elsewhere they have suffered in the second half of the twentieth century for two reasons. First, many traditional Conservative parties were discredited either by their direct association with, or by their tacit acceptance of, fascism and national socialism. Second, and partly in consequence of this, traditional conservatism has often been overtaken by more popular centre-right party formations since 1945 – especially by Christian democracy (and by Gaullism in France). The British Conservative Party is, therefore, almost unique in its extraordinary prominence: a testament to its unrivalled capacity for adaptation. One might almost describe Conservatism as a dominant ideology within British society. But what is this ideology?

British Conservatism is notoriously difficult to pin down in terms of a comprehensive, systematic value system. Indeed, it has often been referred to as a *non*-ideological phenomenon given its apparent pragmatism and mistrust of abstract grand designs. As one distinguished authority on modern Conservatism has said, its exponents prefer to speak of the attitudes, principles or even dispositions which characterize their political outlook:

> The distinction is an important one, for to have a particular disposition is to have a feeling about the way things should be: the implication is that it is inherent and natural. Conservatives feel comfortable with such natural dispositions and as such feel little need to articulate them; they are personal and they are part of the way of the world. (Norton 1996: 68)

Conservatism's primary goals appear to have been: first, the protection of the established social, economic and political order; and, second, the retention of political power (an obvious precondition of the first goal). That said, there is more than one way to 'protect the established order', and Conservatives have concluded that it may often prove necessary to accept change, for 'a state without the means of some change is without the means of its conservation' (Burke 1968: 106). Consequently, Conservatism resembles – as Sir Ian Gilmour once put it – 'an archeological site on which successive civilisations have left layer upon layer of structure and remains' (cited in Barnes, 1994: 315). In short, Conservatism is flexible and rather disparate in terms of its specific policies and has taken something from each era of political development – but, underlying it all, there are certain recognizable and steadfast principles. These derive particularly from the writing of thinkers such as Edmund Burke and David Hume and from the strategy of great political leaders like Benjamin Disraeli. The following is a brief and by no means original checklist of key conservative principles (see also Scruton 1980; Norton and Aughey 1981; Willetts 1992; Barnes 1994).

Scepticism about human ability

Conservatism first emerged in Europe as a reaction to the values of the eighteenth-century Enlightenment. This Age of Reason emphasized the potential for human understanding if only mankind could throw off the shackles of ignorance and superstition, and place a new faith in scientific and objective knowledge. Central to this view was the conviction that reason could enhance social understanding, and the belief that human progress was contingent on the social and political engineering that it made possible.

Conservatives took their cue from sceptical philosophers like David Hume who utterly rejected the precepts of rationalism. Like Hume, Burke was unimpressed by the claims of those who argued for notions of abstract natural rights (most notably the French revolutionaries of 1789), preferring instead the view that such rights as men had were those derived from age-old custom and conventional wisdom. This rejection of abstract rights and social engineering flowed from a deep scepticism about the potential of the human mind and spirit. Conservatives argued that the world was too mysterious and complex a place to be understood fully; and humans were morally as well as intellectually frail: not only was mankind incurably ignorant, but it was equally prone to moral backsliding. Such arguments were often coined in terms of Man's 'original sin', though this theological rendering of the argument was not strictly necessary. In essence, as Michael Oakeshott put it, Conservatism 'is a philosophy of imperfection' (cited in Barnes, 1994: 321), and as such it undermines belief in the projects of social reformers who claim that reason is on their side. There are a number of specific repercussions of this general argument, as we shall see.

Traditionalism

In general Conservatives prefer the old and venerable to the new and innovatory. In a sense, this is predicated on a utilitarian argument; ethics, customs, laws and rights are based largely on people's needs in a given set of historical circumstances, and the very longevity of established practices and traditions must be regarded as evidence of their continuing utility. This explains why writers like Hume and Burke preferred 'prescriptive rights' – rights established by practice over a period of time – to 'natural rights' conceived in the abstract.

Value of 'prejudice'

This point follows from the foregoing two; the individual is incurably ignorant, but the community is wise in its traditions and therefore the individual
is able to call upon this collective wisdom when guidance about personal
action is required. Burke used the term 'prejudice' to stand for this collective
wisdom, though it seems odd now given the exclusively pejorative connota-
tion of the word today. Clearly, Burke did not regard it as such. It is worth
bearing in mind that what he meant by 'prejudice' might be better rendered
into modern usage by terms such as 'culture', 'social mores' or even 'common
sense'.

   Thus, he argued, although the individual can never hope to understand the
mysteries of life, he or she can at least know how to act in given situations, if
prepared to draw upon 'the general bank and capital of nations and of ages' –
that is, the social norms and conventions that have evolved and which can be
'of ready application in the emergency' (Burke 1968: 183). These 'prejudices'
are not based on casual or chance opinion, but rather on experience and practical reflection, and as such embody the evolved wisdom of the community.
Moreover, not only do such conventional mores guide the individual's personal conduct, they further serve to bind the community as a whole by
providing a common world-view for all its members.

Organic view of society

Conservatives regard society as a complex and mysterious whole, more akin
to a living organism than to an artificial device of human contrivance. It is to
be understood as something which has evolved gradually over time, and
something which reflects the heritage of previous generations; indeed, Burke
and others spoke almost mystically of society as a sort of informal contract
between generations past, present and future (op. cit.: 194–5). Because society
is a complex organism, however, we should be inherently cautious of trying
to change it, for it is difficult to know a priori exactly what it is 'safe' to
change. Certain institutions and practices are felt to be lynchpins of society,
though it is not always easy to identify these 'latent causes'. For this reason,
the danger of destabilizing the entire social edifice is always uppermost in the
Conservative mind. This is not to say that all change should be resisted;
Conservatives recognize that changing situations and societies require political systems and institutions that can adapt, but they prefer change to evolve
gradually through the natural supersession of one custom by another.
Legislative reform may be required, but it should be as limited as possible and
occur only where clearly dictated by the requirements of utility.

Hierarchy, leadership and authority

The organic society is by no means to be understood as an egalitarian one.
The classic Conservative conception of society is one of a harmonious hierarchy of different classes and groups, each with its own role to play in the

greater scheme of things. At the apex of this social order should be a political elite which is offered advice and deference by the rank and file, and which in turn provides authoritative and strong leadership. Though initially opposed to democratization, Conservatism adapted by favouring elitist models of democracy such as that described by Joseph Schumpeter in his classic work *Capitalism, Socialism and Democracy* (1952). Schumpeter advocated a 'real' model of democracy in which an essentially passive citizenry legitimized the rule of elites by periodically selecting between competing teams of political leaders. As LS Amery observed in his *Thoughts on the Constitution* (1947) 'Britain has government of the people, for the people, with, not by, the people' (cited in Barnes 1994: 317). Beyond this belief in hierarchical forms of human organization, Conservatives also exhibit a related commitment to social discipline and general respect for authority. One well-known manifestation of this is the Conservative predilection for 'strong' law and order policies.

Nation and empire

Edmund Burke made much of the national character of the English people (a classic case of over-assimilation, you might suppose, given that he was not strictly one of them), a theme often repeated by subsequent Conservatives (Burke 1968: 181–5). Benjamin Disraeli developed the theme of national unity into one of imperial unity, a notion with enormous popular resonance for all social categories. The way in which the colonies rallied to Britain's cause in 1914 and 1939, and the importance of imperial trade during the economic depression of the 1920s only cemented the sense of importance that Empire had for Conservatives. Yet it is probably this theme more than any other which has had the greatest capacity to foment internal dissensus within the Conservative Party. This was true during the debate over Corn Law repeal during the 1840s, as it was during the debate about tariff reform launched by Joseph Chamberlain in 1903; it resurfaced as tension over the speed and extent of de-colonization in the 1950s; and most recently it has wrought immense internal damage to the party over the issue of national sovereignty and European integration (see Chapter 6).

Remember this

Appeasing the masses

Disraeli was also the founder of a Conservative tradition of social reform on behalf of the masses, the objective of which was social unity. Again this agenda of reform was driven partly by the need to adapt to the requirements of the democratic era. In the 1930s Harold Macmillan was the most prominent of the 'One-Nation' Tories and even went so far as to claim that Toryism had always been a form of 'paternal socialism' (Barnes 1994: 330). This interpretation seemed relatively secure during his own period at the helm of the party (1957–63) and for some time subsequently, but it became far more questionable during the 1980s. In truth, the Conservative Party has always harboured doubts about state welfare, particularly where it has been seen as a device of redistribution and socio-economic equalization – never intrinsically a Conservative goal – or where it has been perceived as a threat to personal responsibility and incentive. From Burke onwards it is possible to find strains of such argument in Tory writings; during the 1950s such themes were particularly associated with Conservative government ministers like Iain MacLeod and Enoch Powell, while they clearly became a far more prominent part of the party's ideological profile after Margaret Thatcher's accession to the leadership.

Limited economic intervention

This theme became both prominent and controversial inside the Conservative Party after the mid-1970s, but it is worth emphasizing that while most Conservatives have argued for the market economy and accepted the inequalities it brings, this does not necessarily make them all proponents of laissez-faire. After all, the social origins of the party go back to the landed elites who benefited from the Corn Law tariffs which sustained a high price for wheat. Though it was a Conservative prime minister (Sir Robert Peel) who eventually repealed the Corn Laws in 1846, there have always been Conservatives willing to argue for various forms of economic regulation. In this sense, one might suggest that there have always been economic 'wets' and 'dries' in the Conservative Party (as the interventionists and free marketeers respectively came to be known in the 1980s). The balance of power between these tendencies generally ebbs back and forth over time, though it is clear that it tilted heavily in favour of the advocates of neo-liberal economics after 1979.

Contemporary Conservative dilemmas

British Conservative Party programmes seem to be inherently flexible and fundamentally driven by the urge to occupy power and sustain unequal property relations. Compared to other European parties of the centre-right, the British Conservative Party in its most recent guise has been unusually right-wing. This is readily apparent if we refer, for instance, to the location of the party on the 'expert judgement scales' first constructed by Michael Laver and W. Ben Hunt in the late 1980s.[1] This primarily reflects the shift in the party's economic and social policy under Mrs Thatcher. Yet here lies a paradox within British Conservative ideology, for some have suggested that the policy shifts embodied by Thatcherism may be better regarded as radicalism than Conservatism. This idea is provoked by the evident zeal for market-oriented reform of the public sector which Thatcher's governments demonstrated. At a deeper level, the paradox encapsulates a longstanding tension between the traditionalist and laissez-faire strands of thought espoused by the party. Anthony Giddens expressed this well in arguing that the 'cult of the market', which was so apparent in Thatcher's brand of Conservatism, actually undermines much that is traditional about a society:

'For nothing is more corrosive of established traditions, habits and forms of social cohesion, just as Marx pointed out, than the wholesale cultivation of market relations (Giddens 1994).

Giddens is by no means alone in arguing that unfettered market competition produces mobility across established geographical, industrial and social boundaries – and thereby erodes the established order of things (see also Gray 1994). It may well be argued that there is something inherently contradictory about a political philosophy which tries to promote the virtues of unregulated market forces while insisting on the continued importance of authority, a strong state, and traditional social mores. This should not be taken to indicate the inevitable implosion of British Conservatism; the party's long history of successful adaptation has been based on the ever-changing blend of its various components. But it does highlight a persisting fault-line between 'Burkeans' (who emphasize tradition, community and evolution) and 'Peelites' (who favour individualism, enterprise and market-led reform), which occasionally destabilizes the Conservative Party (Garner and Kelly 1998: 60). While the libertarian strand clearly took precedence after 1975, it would be unwise to dismiss the possibility of a revival, in some form or other, of the traditionalist and paternalist wing. Indeed, Michael Laver's analysis of updated expert scales suggests that the Conservatives might have already moved back towards the centre by the time of the 1997 election,[2] and in the aftermath of this defeat there were signs that some of the party's leading figures (including John Patten and David Willetts) were prepared to argue for a revived emphasis on community values (op. cit.: 68). However, when Deputy Leader Peter Lilley questioned the place of the market in providing public services such as education and health, he provoked a furious internal squabble from those perceiving it as an attack on the achievements of Thatcherism (Young 1999; *Guardian* 1999). This confirmed the precarious balancing act which Conservative Party leaders must sometimes perform, although a sense of the continuing shift in the party's emphasis away from Thatcherism was evident in new commitments to public spending on health and education, and in William Hague's declared intention not to have the Tories 'caricatured any longer as a party that wants to destroy these things' (White 1999).

Labour and the social democratic tradition

Given its eclectic political background, it is not surprising that the early Labour Party lacked a clear ideological profile. It drew upon a melange of traditions; broadly speaking, these can be divided into socialist and labourist influences, though there were various significant subdivisions, especially within the former camp. Given the predominant position of the trade unions within the party in the 1900s (collectively they accounted for 94% of the initial affiliated membership), it is obvious that they should have had a profound influence on the doctrine and ethos of the developing party. While it would be misleading to suggest that a monolithic 'union ideology' ever

existed, many commentators have suggested that a distinctive union outlook
has nevertheless permeated the Labour Party, typified by a 'labourist'
approach to maximizing working-class gains within the economic structures
and processes of capitalism, and within the political channels of parliamen-
tarism (Leach 1991: 134). Labour's socialist strand drew on a number of
sub-traditions including: Marxism (embodied in HM Hyndman's Social
Democratic Federation, one of the party's founder-affiliates); Christian socialism (hence former party General Secretary Morgan Phillips' oft-cited
observation that Labour 'owes more to Methodism than to Marxism'); and
Fabian social democracy (exemplified by the middle-class intellectual radicalism of Sidney and Beatrice Webb). While these various ideological streams
have all constituted identifiable elements of Labour's doctrine and ethos[3]
throughout the twentieth century, the party as a whole is frequently regarded
by political scientists as an exemplar of the European tradition of social
democracy.

Writing in the middle of the 1970s, William Paterson and Alastair Thomas
defined social democracy as 'a belief that social and economic reform
designed to benefit the less privileged should be pursued within a framework
of democracy, liberty and the parliamentary process'. In particular, they
emphasized the broad consensus which existed on five central tenets of
European social democracy: political liberalism, the mixed economy, the welfare state, Keynesian economics and a belief in equality (Paterson and Thomas
1977: 11). The first time that the party formally adopted a programme in
which these elements were present was at the end of the Great War, when a
new policy statement (*Labour and the New Social Order,* drafted by the Webbs
[Labour Party 1918]) committed the party to the pursuit of full employment
with a minimum wage and a maximum working week, public ownership and
democratic control of industry, progressive taxation and the expansion of
educational and social services. Labour had to wait a considerable time before
it finally won the parliamentary majority (at the great electoral landslide of
July 1945) which enabled it to enact this programme. Under the leadership of
Clement Attlee, the Labour governments of the next six years set about building on the wartime experience of state intervention to construct a new
political consensus based on a mixed economy, a much more extensive
system of social welfare (including a National Health Service), and a commitment to the pursuit of full employment. The expansion of the public sector
through the creation of a new set of nationalized industries (taking in the
Bank of England, coal mining, electricity, gas, iron and steel production, the
railways, and airways) was central to the Labour government's conception of
how it should fulfil the famous commitment (set out in Clause IV of the party
constitution) to seek 'common ownership of the means of production, distribution and exchange'.

However, while the Labour governments of 1945–1951 embodied the faith
that the British state could combine freedom with planning of resource distribution, this assumption was strongly challenged in the 1950s. This was
most apparent in the writing of the country's foremost social democratic

intellectual of the period, Anthony Crosland. In works such as *The Future of Socialism* (1956) he articulated a vision of reformist socialism which directly challenged 'Clause IV socialism'. While he recognized that public ownership of industry could be justified in order to combat excessive monopoly power, consistent under-investment or the failure to utilize a resource in the best interests of the community, Crosland was equally keen to stress its dangers: 'A change from private control to state control is socialist only if that control is democratic; a transfer from private bureaucracy to public bureaucracy in no way furthers the aim of socialism' (1975: 5). Not surprisingly, therefore, he saw the mixed economy as essential to the success of social democracy, 'for . . . complete state collectivism is without question incompatible with liberty and democracy' (op. cit.: 2). In particular, he acknowledged the importance of offering material incentives to both working-class and middle-class individuals alike if output and productivity were to grow; as David Marquand has observed, this revealed a 'utilitarian conception of man and society', even if Crosland and his disciples rejected classical market liberalism (1988: 19). Planning, selective state investment and manipulation of aggregate demand could all enhance economic performance, but the market and its incentive structures were the indispensable bases on which to build.

Economic growth itself was vital to social democratic strategy at this time for, as Crosland pointed out, without it, equality could not be achieved without a 'curtailment of liberty' which would bring 'intolerable social stress' (Crosland 1975: 6). In the context of continuing growth, it would be possible to distribute any marginal increment in the national product in favour of society's less privileged members. This was a strategy for gradual social levelling without threatening the absolute material position of the wealthy. In the absence of continued growth, however, the only egalitarian option left involved redistribution of the existing product, which clearly did affect their absolute material prosperity. It was presumably in this prospect that Crosland perceived the curtailment of liberty and the potential for 'intolerable social stress'. In view of the primacy of growth as a strategic objective, it is obvious that the failure of economic growth which suddenly assailed the world economy in the 1970s was bound to provoke a critical reappraisal of the social democratic approach. Following Labour's electoral defeat in 1979, revisionist social democracy seemed for a while to be submerging beneath the cumulative onslaught of criticism launched by both the Thatcherite right and the radical left. Even during its heyday, revisionist social democracy had always drawn fire from the New Left on the grounds that it refused to break with dehumanizing modes of capitalist production (see Anderson 1961, for instance). In addition, however, by the late 1970s Labour's own left-wing was becoming increasingly critical of social democracy's failure to deliver economic growth and full employment. The result of this was the transitory prominence of a more radical form of socialism, embodied in the *Alternative Economic Strategy* (AES).

The AES (CSE-LCC 1980) drew its intellectual inspiration from sources such as the Cambridge Political Economy Group which, for some time, had been arguing for the need to focus greater attention on foreign trade as a key variable in overall macroeconomic strategy. In particular, the Cambridge economists were associated with the view that import controls were crucial if the depressing post-war stop-go economic policy cycle was to be avoided in the future; otherwise, any reflation of the economy would simply result in a huge influx of consumer imports (1974). An equally significant influence on the AES was the work of Stuart Holland, who argued that modern capitalism was characterized by the twin developments of 'mesoeconomic power' and multinational capital (1975). While the former consisted of firms with the power to circumvent government policies through their domination of sectoral markets, the latter comprised firms with a capacity to shift capital across national borders. In effect, both developments represented a challenge to the economic sovereignty of UK governments (Hill 1998: 25–6). The influence of the AES on Labour's policy was most evident in the 1983 general election manifesto, which included commitments to: a major programme of nationalization; the abolition of wage controls; the introduction of import controls; withdrawal from the EEC; national planning incorporating control of prices, credit and investment; controls on international capital movements; expanded state holdings of corporate equity through the National Enterprise Board; and planned reflation in order to restore full employment (Labour Party 1983). In short, this manifesto proposed a degree of state intervention in economic affairs which Labour had not practised since the days of post-war rationing and control.

However, in the aftermath of the electoral debacle of 1983 (in which Labour achieved its poorest national result for half a century) power began gradually to swing once more within the party. A new leader from Labour's 'soft left', Neil Kinnock and a new deputy-leader from the 'consolidationist' right, Roy Hattersley (McKee 1991) represented this new balance within the Labour Party, and over the course of the next few years they set about jettisoning most of the AES and sought to revive Labour's social democratic credentials. In the aftermath of another election defeat in 1987, a thoroughgoing review of party policy was initiated and this confirmed a shift back to the ideological centre-ground during the 1990s.

Markets, freedom, modernization and Europe: the emergence of a 'Third Way'?

> In our view, the economic role of modern government is to help make the market system work properly where it can, will and should – and to replace or strengthen it where it can't, won't or shouldn't. (Labour Party 1989: 6)

This is the economic philosophy which the Labour Party boldly espoused in the introduction to the final report of the policy review, *Meet the Challenge, Make the Change*. This document left little doubt that Labour was once again wholly embracing a mixed economy in which the market would play a fundamental role. Nevertheless, it was recognized that, left to its own devices, the market would generate both social and economic disadvantages which it should be the task of the state to rectify. Inevitably, therefore, intervention would remain legitimate in areas such as social security, health, social services, environmental protection and education.

However, Labour's policy review also argued that the state should become an 'enabling' mechanism which would play an active role in smoothing the operation of markets. From this perspective, it became the task of the state to facilitate the process of adaptation by individuals and firms to changing market conditions by, for example, providing education and (re)training. Indeed, central to Labour's analysis was now the contention that the British state had traditionally not done enough to make firms and individuals sufficiently adaptable to market conditions. This was hardly an original approach, given that 'claims about Britain's educational deficiencies have been a staple of explanations of the alleged failings of British industry since the late 19th century, and an important component of declinist histories of Britain' (Tomlinson 1999: 13); nevertheless, it is clear that Labour became an earnest advocate of the need to build a 'skills culture' which would underpin a 'talent-based economy'. Indeed, Kinnock's successor as party leader, John Smith, once referred to education and training as the 'new commanding heights' of the economy (Webster 1993: 1), while Tony Blair placed education at the forefront of the 1997 election manifesto – defining it as his 'passion'.

Nothing better symbolizes Labour's willingness to re-embrace the market in the 1990s, though, than the way in which it dropped its traditional insistence on public ownership of major utilities (gas, water, electricity, public transport, postal and telecommunication networks). Though this emerged as a de facto policy shift after Kinnock's policy review, it was exemplified by Blair's dramatic and unexpected decision (on assuming the leadership in 1994) to rewrite Clause IV of the party constitution. Where once this promised common ownership of the means of production, distribution and exchange, it now commits the party to the creation of 'a community in which power, wealth and opportunity are in the hands of the many and not the few'. It is hardly surprising, therefore, that in New Labour's lexicon, the 'public ownership' of utilities has been replaced by their 'regulation'. Parallelling this has been a virtual re-prioritization of the party's core values, given the prominent assertion that 'at the core of our convictions is a belief in individual liberty' (Labour Party 1992: 7). This is not to deny a continuing espousal of the virtues of equality, but this tends to be stated in terms of the need to create opportunities for individuals and groups to compete fairly and effectively in the modern world, and is occasionally even couched in the traditional Tory rhetoric of 'one-nation' communitarianism.

It is important also to emphasize how far Labour has evolved from the stark anti-Europeanism of the AES. Throughout the 1960s and 1970s, the British Labour Party displayed divisions on Europe which closely coincided with general left–right cleavages within the party. While the right saw in the EEC a way of arresting Britain's relative economic and political decline, the left regarded it as a capitalist club which purveyed liberal economic orthodoxy and threatened to restrict the capacity of national governments to implement socialist policies. A major factor behind the departure of the schismatic SDP wing of the party in 1981 was the anti-Europeanism inherent in the AES. However, for Labour – as for social democrats across Europe – the experience of the French *Parti Socialiste* during the early 1980s (in combination with its own catastrophic election defeat in 1983) was salutary. The French experience demonstrated the virtual impossibility of operating national economic policy in isolation from the rest of the industrialized world, and many left-of-centre observers concluded that the European Community offered the best hope of launching coordinated economic strategies which would enable governments to regain greater control over market forces. Many erstwhile Eurosceptics in the party (and, it should be said, in the trade unions) were further persuaded of the merits of Europe by the impact of EC Commission President Jacques Delors in creating a 'social dimension' to the integration project. In addition, the growing disharmony of the British Conservatives on European integration made it tactically advantageous for Labour to adopt a more favourable position. By 1992 clear majorities of the PLP and ordinary party members favoured further integration; for instance, while three-quarters of the Labour Party's MPs and prospective parliamentary candidates (PPCs) wanted 'more integration', some 16.6% desired a 'fully integrated' European Union (n = 344).[4] Similarly, 77% of the new PLP felt that the government should 'move towards a single European currency' in 1997 (Kellner 1997: 24). Thus, Labour had become a party fully committed to the EU by the 1990s; on assuming office, the new government immediately signalled a Euro-positive stance by signing the Social Chapter of the Treaty on European Union (thus overriding the previous government's opt-out on this provision), and agreeing to the extension of Qualified Majority Voting in the Council of Ministers, and further co-decision rights for the European Parliament. In addition, the Cabinet embraced European Monetary Union in principle, though British participation was to remain contingent upon the achievement of appropriate economic conditions and popular endorsement through a referendum.

All this confirmed that Blair's New Labour clearly accepted the imperatives and constraints imposed by the global capitalist market place; the role of government, from this perspective, is to manage capitalism and its effects as effectively as possible rather than to replace it. Quite the best overall interpretation to place on Blairism has proved contentious. Does the renewed emphasis on the mixed economy and institutional reform mean that it has effectively re-embraced Croslandite social democracy (Smith 1992)? Perhaps, though some critics have argued that Crosland would never have abandoned public ownership, redistribution or full employment to the extent that 'post-revisionist' New Labour has (Shaw 1994: 103–7). An alternative designation which has been widely discussed suggests that New Labour represents a genuinely innovative 'Third Way' between 'old-style social democracy' and Thatcherite neo-liberalism (Giddens 1998). As such, Anthony Giddens argues that it remains broadly within the social democratic tradition, but seeks to adapt to a world that has changed fundamentally since Crosland's day. In particular, it seeks to confront 'five dilemmas' facing contemporary social democracy: globalization; individualism and the retreat from tradition; the eroding differentiation between left and right; the challenge posed by democratization to traditional modes of political agency; and the incorporation of ecological issues into a social democratic agenda. To Giddens, Third Way politics retains 'a core concern with social justice, while accepting that the range of questions which escape the left/right divide is greater than before' (op. cit.: 65). Overall, he suggests, Third Way social democracy can be regarded as a philosophy of the 'radical centre', which should be prepared to forge new alliances in order to sustain an agenda of economic, institutional, welfare and civic reform.

There is a further possibility, however, which flows from the criticism that a term like 'the Third Way' both 'diminishes and undersells' the significance of New Labour's true identity; in reality, it has been contended, 'the Third Way turns out to mean the revival of liberalism inside a Labour body' (Marr 1998: 21). In its evident distaste for group conflict, its willingness to embrace free trade and financial deregulation, its emphasis on institutional reform and devolution, its belief in community, personal responsibility, education, liberty, cooperation and progress, it can be argued that New Labour strongly resembles a form of radical liberalism which predates the emergence of socialism in Britain. This is a fascinating and not implausible interpretation, consistent with the notion that Tony Blair's Labour Party is a movement of the 'radical centre'. Michael Freeden has lent it further weight by pointing out that Blair openly associates his beliefs with icons of British liberalism like Lloyd George, Hobhouse, Beveridge and Keynes (1999: 43). If accurate, it suggests that the ideological blend of liberalism, labourism and socialism which was the hallmark of the original Labour Representation Committee has resurfaced, with the former currently preponderant.[5] However, the real force of this argument only becomes apparent once we examine modern Liberal Democrat ideology.

Liberal Democrat ideology

After 1789, the desire of the commercial and industrial classes across Europe to challenge the political and economic privileges of traditional elites led to the emergence of political liberalism. British liberalism was a part of this process, encompassing nineteenth-century campaigns for voting rights, religious toleration and the removal of economic restrictions which favoured landed elites (most notably the Corn Laws). From these origins, liberalism has much more recently blended with social democracy in the form of the contemporary Liberal Democrats. However, for Liberal Democrats, as for Liberals before them, a bitter irony lies in the fact that they have contributed enormously to the ideological content of British party politics without reaping the benefit of national governmental office in the post-war era.

The contemporary Liberal Democrats are more radical than many of their European counterparts, being notably further left than most on issues of economic management. What is more, it is important to understand that this position has been inherited as much from their Liberal progenitors as from the Social Democrats, something which becomes clear when reviewing the historical development of liberal thought in Britain.

Emergence of social liberalism

The historian Michael Brock has suggested that nineteenth-century liberalism was distinguished by three core traits. First, it was 'hopeful rather than fearful' (1983: 16). That is, where the Conservatives feared the consequences of reforms (such as the introduction of democracy, repeal of the Corn Laws, government intervention in the market, or Irish Home Rule), Liberals were altogether more confident about the likely impact of such initiatives. Second, liberalism set great store by freedom and detested coercion, which was apparent in the pursuit of more open economic markets and Roman Catholic emancipation. Third, it embodied a sincere Enlightenment faith in the power of reason to overcome ancient prejudices and to generate progress and social harmony. This explains why Liberals favoured the extension of education and political rights to the masses, and why they believed in the power of enlightened and rational reform to improve the human condition.

After 1880 a 'new' kind of liberalism emerged in Britain – a liberalism in the tradition of JS Mill, LT Hobhouse and JA Hobson – which was notably more inclined to pursuing egalitarian reforms and employing interventionist methods. This 'social liberalism' contrasted with the 'classical liberalism' that had predominated throughout most of the nineteenth century, and which had essentially consisted of a defence of political rights for individuals and the pursuit of laissez-faire principles in economic matters. Social liberalism complemented (and in some ways supplanted) the political and economic liberalism which had preceded it. This new phenomenon was evident in several ways.

A new emphasis on social justice

This was illustrated by the willingness of Liberal-led governments under Herbert Asquith (1908–16) and David Lloyd George (1916–22) to introduce various welfarist and popular relief measures (most notably the introduction of graduated income tax in the 1909 'people's budget', the national insurance schemes of 1911 and the old age pension provisions of 1908). Several decades later the practical tradition of liberal welfarism was exemplified by William Beveridge, author of the wartime report *Social Insurance and Allied Services* (1942) which was widely credited with establishing the founding rationale of a comprehensive post-war welfare state. But why should liberals pursue such policies?

The answer lies in the core liberal principle of individualism. Liberals since JS Mill have valued this as a means (to social progress) and as an end in itself; that is, they believe in the ideal of the fulfilment of each individual's personal potential. This positive conception of liberty is widely regarded as moving beyond the negative conception of classical liberalism – that is, of freedom as the mere absence of external restraint (Berlin 1969). Social liberals recognize that the goal of self-actualization is effectively hampered by the gross inequalities of industrial society. Freedom from wanting for the basic requirements of life are vital if people are to be able to develop their individual capacities, which implies the need for systematic state action against poverty and disease, plus the provision of an effective system of mass education. One of the most influential early apologists for this position was the philosopher TH Green, who argued that men could not be truly free until they were able to develop their moral, intellectual and cultural capacities as members of communities: 'it is certainly within the province of the state to prevent children from growing up in that kind of ignorance which practically excludes them from a free career in life' (1888: 374; cited in Barker 1978: 14). Similarly, LT Hobhouse's influential study of *Liberalism* (1964) argued that redistributive action by the government was justified by a notion of freedom which embraced 'not just civil and political freedoms but also liberation from social and economic impediments' (cited in Jones 1996: 65). Hence we are confronted by a brand of liberalism with a social conscience, which is very different to the social Darwinism of Herbert Spencer's classical individualism.

Willingness to intervene in the market

This follows from the preceding point. The demise of laissez-faire liberalism flowed from the recognition by many liberals that the market was not always fair or efficient in its effects. The liberal economist JA Hobson had condemned the waste and instability of unregulated capitalism in *The Crisis of Liberalism* (1909), arguing that greater state regulation of the market economy was required (so long as intervention served to enhance personal liberty). However, the most enduring example of social liberal economics remains John Maynard Keynes's *General Theory of Employment, Interest and Money* (1936). While rejecting public ownership and socialist planning as illiberal, bureaucratic and inefficient, he recognized that capitalism was prone to great instability and high levels of unemployment. He argued that there was much the state could do to counteract such problems through fiscal and monetary policies designed to manage levels of aggregate demand. Keynes had already contributed to the radical economic agenda of Lloyd George's Liberal Party, and endorsed its plan for a Board of National Investment expounded in *Britain's Industrial Future* (Liberal Party 1928), commonly referred to as the 'Yellow Book'. In the post-war era, the model of economic intervention advocated by Keynes became government orthodoxy in Britain and overseas.

Social liberalism and social democracy

Despite the evident common ground it shares with reformist social democracy, apologists for social liberalism maintain that it constitutes a distinctive phenomenon. In truth, the distinction between the two creeds is now very blurred, though social liberals have always been more sharply critical of certain aspects of socialism. For instance, they argue that socialists have tended to overlook the very real value of the market in creating wealth, providing incentives to human creativity and initiative, and providing opportunities for the expression of freedom and choice. Moreover, while Liberal governments enacted some of the earliest legislation sympathetic to trade unions in Britain, unions have essentially been regarded by liberals as defensive organizations which pursue sectional interests. While it is certainly possible to work with such bodies on specific policies, Liberals contend that they should not constitute the basis for a political movement whose goal is the national interest as a whole. Indeed, Liberals have consistently rejected the espousal of class conflict as a means of social progress.

Nevertheless, since the late 1800s there has existed in Britain a form of liberalism that has frequently seemed undeniably close to reformist social democracy (commencing with Fabianism) in outlook and programme. Indeed, in the view of commentators such as Peter Clarke, these two traditions are virtually indistinguishable. He cites Keynes in support: 'Why cannot they (Labour's social democrats) face the fact that they are not the sectaries of an outworn creed . . . but heirs of eternal liberalism?' (cited in Clarke 1983: 39). Clarke takes his thesis further, moreover, in arguing that social democrats within the Labour Party actually espouse a doctrine which is incompatible with socialism. He agrees with Keynes that the roots of social democracy lie in historic liberalism rather than socialism, and argues that the socialist emphasis on public ownership of industry and trade union power is no more palatable to social democrats than to liberals. As a result, alliances between social democrats and liberals are 'natural, consistent and sensible', and it is one of the great political tragedies of the twentieth century that 'tactical pressures and historic party loyalties' have generally conspired to keep them apart. Historically, progressive social liberalism has prospered during the rare periods of alliance between these two forces (for instance, 1903–1918) and suffered when they have opposed each other.

It is surely no coincidence that Clarke penned these arguments during the early 1980s, shortly after the Social Democratic Party had been formed (as the result of a schism within the Labour Party) and when interest in a political alliance with the Liberals was great; nevertheless, such views are grounded in historical research, and serve to draw attention to the close proximity of social democracy and liberalism in the context of British party politics. The relevance of this point endures with the formation of the Liberal Democrats in 1988, which cemented the alliance of all but a few Liberals and Social Democrats, while the emergence of New Labour only serves to rekindle interest in the issue. As we have seen, there are those who argue that the Third

Way amounts to a revival of social liberalism, and it is hard to dispute their case. In particular, there can be little doubt that New Labour and the Liberal Democrats share virtually identical positions on things like the appropriate roles of state and market, the primacy of individual liberty and self-actual-ization, the need for state action to alleviate the negative consequences of markets, the importance of community and civic virtue, the dangers of class conflict and over-mighty trade unions, the need for institutional 'moderniza-tion', and so on. Indeed, we see below that New Labour appears to have shifted to the right of the Liberal Democrats on some of these issues by the time of the 1997 election. Moreover, the ideological congruence of the two parties was demonstrated by unusually close levels of political cooperation between them at both national and sub-national levels before and after the election (see Chapter 1).

The modern Liberal Democrat agenda

Contemporary Liberal Democratic policy has developed and added to the key social liberal elements of personal development, social justice and Keynesian economics. Most of these new themes derive from the policy work of the old Liberal Party during the leaderships of Jo Grimond (1956–67) and Jeremy Thorpe (1967–76). Grimond took over the leadership at a time when the party's fortunes were at an historically low ebb (they had garnered 2.7% of the national vote in 1955, retaining just 6 seats in the Commons) and, as Thorpe once acknowledged, Grimond's 'great achievement was to give the Liberal Party intellectual credibility'. He managed to do this by establishing a wide-ranging long-term review of party policy, in the course of which the Liberals attracted considerable interest for their willingness to engage with innovative ideas. This has left an indelible mark which still characterizes today's Liberal Democrats. So, apart from the key elements of social liberal-ism already discussed, what are the main features of contemporary Liberal Democrat ideology?

Industrial democracy and cooperation

Grimond's party advocated forms of employee representation on the board of industrial corporations in the early 1960s, though it should be said that the roots of this idea can be traced back further in the Liberal tradition. For instance, in 1916 the Liberal minister JM Whitley first advocated joint works councils, and Herbert Asquith himself publicly supported the idea in 1920. In 1928 the Liberal 'Yellow Book' advocated schemes of local industrial democ-racy. Liberal espousal of such schemes fundamentally reflects the fact that Liberals have, as mentioned above, traditionally found class conflict anath-ema; industrial democracy represents a means of class conciliation – a middle way between the interests of capital and labour. More generally, Liberals baulk at the notion of structured social conflict and behaviour which suppresses the individual's scope for manoeuvre and expression. Today's Liberal Democrats advocate partnership in industry, including profit-related pay and share-ownership schemes, with guaranteed rights of employee participation in decision-making at enterprise level (Brack 1996: 103).

Devolution, regionalism and localism

A major theme for the modern Liberal Democrats and their predecessor parties has been the empowerment of local communities. The philosophical basis for this lies partly in the classical liberal desire to avoid the accumulation of (potentially over-mighty) state power at the centre, and partly in a commitment to civic virtue and political participation. For instance, both JS Mill and TH Green argued that participation was central to the individual's moral and intellectual development. Moreover, this emphasis on decentralization and participation resurfaced within Liberal politics during the 1970s in the guise of the new strategy of 'community politics'. Endorsed by the Liberal Party Assembly in 1970, community politics was initially conceived as an attempt to bolster the increasingly powerless individual in the face of large-scale organizations. This pursuit of new kinds of democratic involvement was intended to apply both inside and outside the sphere of political institutions. In practice, considerable emphasis has been laid on the building of Liberal (and Liberal Democrat) power within local government and on the development of new community structures such as neighbourhood councils. The theme of decentralization was also espoused by the SDP during the early 1980s (see, for instance, Owen 1981), though it had not hitherto been characteristic of social democrats within the Labour Party. In recent years, there have been various examples of Liberal (Democrat) commitment to sub-national power, from the consistent criticism of the Conservatives' centralization of the state between 1979 and 1997, to support for Scottish and Welsh devolution. Not surprisingly, the party's own organizational structure is self-consciously federal (see Chapter 7).

Constitutional reform

In its consistent advocacy of constitutional reform, the modern party echoes nineteenth-century Liberal campaigns for voting and other citizenship rights. This commitment to constitutional reform derives from core values such as individual liberty and the belief in democratic civic engagement. After the 1997 general election, Labour and the Liberal Democrats cooperated formally (via the establishment of a special Cabinet sub-committee) on the implementation of some of the Liberal Democrats' long-standing demands for reform, including devolution, freedom of information legislation, and reform of the House of Lords. At the time of writing, other components of their agenda for constitutional reform remain far less likely to be enacted, including a written constitution with a supreme court, the replacement of the House of Lords with an elected Senate of regional representatives, and electoral reform for Westminster elections (though see Chapter 9 on the latter).

Emphasis on education

Education has long been of central importance to the Liberal view of the world since it is so obviously crucial to the development of individual capacities. Calls for state provision of quality education for the masses can be found in the writings of Liberal thinkers since JS Mill. In this sense, we might conclude that the commitment to educational values is in itself derived from the conception of positive liberty and the drive for social justice which is consequent upon it. Yet this only partly explains the modern Liberal Democrat obsession with education. There are at least two other justifications which surface in modern Liberal Democrat rhetoric, one of which is also typical of social democracy. First, education is seen as important to the development of a skilled and adaptable workforce that will better enable the country to compete in the global economy. This is a supply-side argument which is often used by social democrats, both inside and outside the Labour Party, in the context of debate about Britain's relative economic decline (Tomlinson 1999). Second, a more classically liberal rationale for education is that it is a vehicle of social mobility and therefore a means by which to overcome class structuration (and division) in British society. It is not surprising, therefore, that since the 1960s Liberals have opposed early selection in public education (for instance, via the 11-plus exam) and have argued for more teachers and smaller class sizes. Indeed, one of the most distinctive features of recent Liberal Democrat manifestos has been the high profile the party has sought for its emphasis on greater investment in state education, even at the cost of raising taxation.

Ethnic and European integration

The general liberal preference for the integration of different social groups once again reflects the desire to ameliorate any kind of structured division in society. All such cleavages, whether ethnic- or class-based, threaten to submerge the individual and destabilize society. They may also be a source of deprivation or discrimination. It is not surprising, therefore, that the Liberal Democrats and their predecessors have consistently criticized signs of racial bias in immigration legislation proposed by either of the major parties. They have also been strong and consistent advocates of greater British involvement in a system of European cooperation. This commitment to European integration further reflects a long-held liberal preference for international cooperation in economic and political affairs. In 1945, Liberals first publicly argued for a new European Community with British involvement; in 1956, they called for an economically integrated common market; and since the 1970s they have always backed the 'European option' – whether that has meant campaigning for a 'yes' vote on the EC referendum of 1975, support for the Single European Act and Treaty on European Union (Maastricht), or European Monetary Union.

Environmentalism

The Liberals were the first of the established parties to adopt the new environmental agenda. This first became evident in the 1960s, especially within the new generation of Young Liberals, many of whom fit the intellectual and social stereotype of Inglehart's post-materialists. In 1979 the Liberal Assembly 'declared that economic growth as conventionally defined was neither indefinitely possible nor desirable' (Brack 1996: 107). In recent years the Liberal Democrats have distinguished themselves by proposing innovations such as road pricing (that is, the use of the market mechanism to relieve vehicle congestion on key routes), and Pollution Added Tax (PAT) as a way of overcoming 'externalities' – the real costs of pollution to society as a whole which are not picked up by individual producers; PAT is designed to ensure that 'the polluter pays' these costs. In addition, the party has advocated environmental policies such as tradable emission licences for industry, the phasing out of nuclear power, a new government ministry with responsibility for environmental protection, and greater investment in energy conservation and public transport.

Overall, the Liberal Democrats clearly represent the continuation of the left-of-centre social liberalism which has been prominent in Britain for more than a century. Research suggests that the party's membership has a coherent set of beliefs which can be identified with this tradition: a significant achievement considering the relatively recent and painful merger between Liberals and Social Democrats (Bennie et al. 1996). An interesting feature of modern Liberal Democrat ideology is the extent to which it is prepared to stress policy dimensions which have generally been marginal to competition between the major parties – witness the emphasis placed on constitutional reform and environmentalism. This notwithstanding, one of the most significant strategic problems now facing the party is the similar ideological space it occupies to New Labour. Sympathizers have often lamented the way in which Liberal/Liberal Democrat ideas have been 'stolen' by rival parties (for instance, on Europe, devolution, education and training, industrial democracy, consumer protection, environmental protection, bill of rights and constitutional reform). Whether or not this is fair comment – and one should not overlook the fact that all is fair in love and party competition – we shall see in the next chapter that the crowding of centre-left ideological territory can make the game of party competition difficult for the Liberal Democrats, though it can also present occasional opportunities for cross-party cooperation (as we saw in Chapter 1).

Conclusion

To close this chapter, it is useful to provide a 'map' which summarizes the main ideological traditions found in British party politics. This map requires an understanding of two ideological dimensions rather than one. These dimensions effectively relate to two kinds of left–right distinctions which have characterized the history of political conflict in liberal democracies (Finer 1987). The origins of the first lie with the conflict of values expressed in the Great Revolution of 1789 in France (whence the terms 'left' and 'right' derive in a political sense). This event generated enduring conflicts between those who favoured maximizing individual liberties and citizen rights, and those who preferred the security of traditional values, which were generally more restrictive and authoritarian. Authors have used a variety of terms for this ideological dimension, but here it will be referred to as either the liberty/authority or 'social morality' dimension. The second kind of left–right conflict largely reflects the classic division over the role of the state in managing the economy – interventionism or laissez-faire? Since this is so closely bound up in twentieth-century politics with the argument between socialists and capitalists, it also takes in issues of welfarism, trade union rights and redistribution, and can be referred to as the socialism–capitalism dimension.

Figure 3.2 portrays six ideal-type party ideologies, four of which fall squarely into the quadrants of our two-dimensional map. The first of these might be referred to as *Clause IV socialism*, which – at the risk of simplifying – can be deemed authoritarian-left in essence. Clause IV socialism places the community above the imperatives of personal liberty, and advocates state intervention in economic and social domains, while emphasizing the social responsibilities of individuals. In contrast, *social liberalism* occupies the libertarian-left quadrant. As we have seen, this philosophy embraces state interventionism, but as a means to the ends of individual liberty and self-

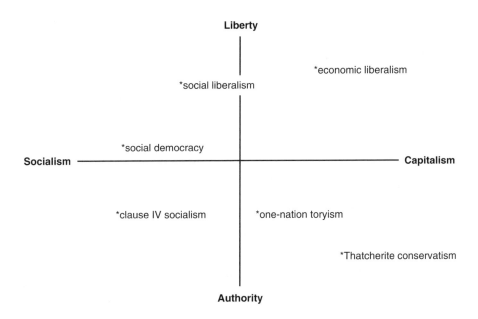

FIGURE 3.2   *A two-dimensional map of party political ideal-types in Britain*

actualization. In the libertarian-right quadrant, we find *economic liberalism* – the unrestricted possessive individualism of the type associated with Herbert Spencer or Friedrich von Hayek. Finally, in the authoritarian-right quadrant we find *Thatcherite conservatism* which espouses a blend of free markets, traditional mores and social discipline.

In addition to these, there are two further ideological categories which we have discussed in the context of British party politics. These lie closer to the boundaries between quadrants, the first being *social democracy* (between socialism and social liberalism), which is a revision of the Clause IV socialism especially associated with Labour prior to 1950 (though still present to a significant extent thereafter). Social democracy, as we have seen, places greater emphasis than Clause IV socialism on the need to protect individual liberty and restrict the public sector, though it does not prioritize liberty and markets to the extent social liberalism does. The other phenomenon is *One-Nation Toryism*. Curiously, this lies not on the boundary between the two Conservative stereotypes of Thatcherism and economic liberalism, but rather, between Thatcherism and Clause IV socialism. With the former it shares a commitment to tradition and authority, but its paternalistic concern for social harmony allows greater scope for intervention in economic and social policy. It therefore has little in common with economic liberalism.

All of these ideological types except economic liberalism lie on a roughly curvilinear axis of party competition which runs from social liberalism in the north-west of the diagram, through Clause IV socialism in the south-west to Thatcherism in the south-east. We shall be discussing this curvilinear space in the next chapter, but for now it is interesting to observe that its significance for British party politics is confirmed by the analysis of both voter-preferences and intra-party politics; while the former shows 95% of electors lying within it (see Figure 4.6 in the following chapter), the latter reveals that 90% of MPs belong to ideological clusters lying within it (Webb 1997: 96; see also Table 6.2 below). In reality, the boundaries between the various ideological stereotypes are not always easy to identify, but each party comprises an ever-changing blend of two or more of these ideological elements, and as the internal power balance between them shifts, so the overall programmatic emphasis of the party moves. (Note that a more detailed discussion of intra-party politics is provided in Chapter 6.) In essence, the Conservatives operate largely in authoritarian-right territory, driven by the interplay of One-Nation Toryism and Thatcherism, though economic liberalism has a minor influence on the party. By contrast, Labour tends to shift between libertarian-left and authoritarian-left territory as a result of the changing balance between Clause IV socialists, social democrats and social liberals. The Liberal Democrats are generally located in similar ideological space, though the greater influence of social liberalism usually renders them a little more right-wing and a little more libertarian than Labour.

These then are broadly the ideological domains within which the main parties reside, but how far do they adjust their programmes in order to maximize voter support? This is the question to which we now turn.

Notes

1   These scales were derived from questionnaire responses provided by a sample of political scientists with research expertise in party politics or public policy. The respondents came from 25 different countries and each sought to locate the main parties in their respective systems on a series of policy dimensions. Laver and Hunt then reported the average location of the various parties on each attitudinal scale, according to such expert judgements (Laver and Hunt, 1992; see also Ware 1996: 32). The original survey was conducted during 1989, but the expert scales have since been updated for a number of countries, including Britain after the 1997 election (Laver 1998).

2   The Conservatives appeared to have shifted significantly to the left on economic and social policy between 1989 and 1997, though they remained comfortably the most right-wing party in the system (Laver 1998). Note that Ian Budge's content analysis of election manifestos confirms the impression of many experts that the Conservatives moved to the left on state intervention and economic policy in 1997 (1999: 16–17).

3   For a fascinating and insightful rendering of the distinction between 'doctrine' and 'ethos' in the context of the Labour Party, see Drucker 1979; 1982.

4   The data sources for these figures are the Labour Party Membership Survey (1989) and the British Candidate Survey (1992).

5   In fact, Freeden goes further than this in suggesting that it additionally draws on conservatism; at first blush this seems surprising given New Labour's insistence on 'modernization', and yet the emphasis on productivity and material well-being, the notion of social responsibility and 'zero toleration' of social deviance, the desire to reconstruct stable family units, and the need for strong leadership all resemble conservative thinking (1999: 48). However, this is not to say – as Freeden concedes – that New Labour's thinking in these respects is drawn directly from conservatism; indeed, themes like economic growth, social responsibility and community values are all present in strands of liberalism and socialism too, so it may be that reference to conservatism serves to complicate the understanding of Labour's ideology unnecessarily.

4

HOW PARTIES COMPETE 2:
PROGRAMMATIC ADAPTATION

CONTENTS

Having established the broad ideological identities of the main national parties, it is important to examine how these are utilized in the process of party competition. The foregoing discussion of party ideologies points to the (admittedly rather trite) conclusion that the Conservatives are a right-wing party, while Labour and the Liberals/Liberal Democrats have been left-of-centre formations throughout much of the twentieth century. But exactly how far left and right are they? And how have their precise ideological locations varied over time? Even more to the point, how have the various parties been located in relation to the voters' Aggregate Distribution of Preferences (ADP) at any given election? It is important to establish answers to these three questions if any formal test of models of party competition is to be attempted. Although a strict comparison of the ADP and party ideologies is all but impossible on the available data, we can employ a variety of data sources to build up a highly suggestive picture of what has happened.

Ideological dimensions and party competition

How can one measure the precise location of party ideologies? Two techniques have generally been utilized by political scientists. The first is the expert judgement scales we have already encountered. The most obvious practical drawback with this approach is simply that such data are of limited help in assessing party ideological change since the time-series are not yet very long; as we have seen, Laver and Hunt's scales only give us British party positions for 1989 and 1997 (refer again to Chapter 3 note 1). The second technique is, therefore, of greater help. This relies on a quantitative analysis of the content of party election manifestos in order to assess the varying emphases given to competing ideological themes. The Comparative Manifestos Project, initially directed by Ian Budge, has systematically analysed election manifestos since 1945 by measuring the space devoted to each issue; these measurements indicate the importance of each issue to the respective parties. Manifesto statements are coded according to a common scheme, and can be regarded as left-wing or right-wing, libertarian or author-itarian, materialist or post-materialist, and so on. It therefore becomes possible to gauge whether, for instance, left-wing statements outnumber right-wing statements and, by comparing manifesto data over time, to obtain a sense of how parties have shifted ideological location from one election to another.

How many ideological dimensions should be employed in order to under-stand British party competition in these terms? Although there is no doubt that a completely comprehensive account of all issues which have made it onto the British political agenda over time would have to be multi-dimen-sional, scholars generally seek to offer explanations and descriptions which are as simple (or 'parsimonious') as possible. In fact, as noted in Chapter 3, it has become increasingly common for comparative political scientists to focus on two dimensions of belief: those concerned with the socialism/capitalism and the liberty/authority dualisms. So how far do British party manifesto statements conform to these two dimensions of 'core' ideological belief (Heath et al. 1993)?

Table 4.1 reports the percentages of British election manifestos since 1964 devoted to each dimension.[1] It is readily apparent from this that the social-ism–capitalism dimension is overwhelmingly prominent compared to the libertarianism–authoritarianism one in Britain. This is essentially true for each of the main three parties; only the Liberals in 1979 came close to devot-ing as much attention to issues of liberty and authority as to issues of socialism and capitalism, but in general they too have given far more empha-sis to the latter. Indeed, overall the parties have given nearly four times more space in their election manifestos to socialist/capitalist themes as to lib-erty/authority questions. This being the case, there are good grounds for regarding the simple Downsian conception of a single dimension of ideolog-ical competition as appropriate in the case of modern Britain. This is doubly true since the majority of electors – not to mention party activists and elected representatives – tend to conceive of party competition in Britain in terms of a single left–right dimension; this is attested to by the clear importance of this ideological dimension in the ideological model of voting tested later in this chapter (see Table 4.3). Further confirmation of this is provided by evidence of the issues voters regard as most important at election times; since 1964, the

TABLE 4.1   *Emphases given to core ideological dimensions in British election manifestos since 1964*

Election	Socialism/capitalism				Liberty/authority			
	Con	Labour	Liberal*	Total	Con	Labour	Liberal*	Total
1964	37.9	32.4	48.9	39.7	4.6	3.2	8.2	5.3
1966	39.9	44.7	31.2	38.6	6.2	8.1	3.6	6.0
1970	39.9	41.0	43.8	41.6	16.3	8.7	19.2	14.7
February 1974	45.3	59.0	46.5	50.3	13.3	4.5	12.2	10.0
October 1974	40.0	45.2	49.4	44.9	12.0	8.5	4.2	8.2
1979	60.8	53.7	32.9	48.4	7.8	9.8	29.3	15.6
1983	48.3	54.4	48.8	50.6	14.1	7.7	9.2	10.3
1987	45.4	49.0	41.1	45.2	18.2	12.3	20.0	16.8
1992	50.1	63.6	34.8	49.8	19.9	7.9	9.8	12.5
1997	40.7	43.5	47.8	44.0	17.3	13.5	16.2	15.7
Average	**44.8**	**48.7**	**42.5**	**45.3**	**13.0**	**8.4**	**13.2**	**11.5**

Note:
All figures refer to percentages of manifestos devoted to relevant ideological dimension.
* 'Liberal' figures for 1983/1987 refer to Alliance manifestos, and for 1992/1997 to Liberal Democrat manifestos.

Source: Comparative Manifestos Project data.

only issues *not* relevant to the socialist–capitalist dimension which have appeared among the three most commonly cited as important for the country have been related to defence and foreign affairs – and even so they have always figured less prominently than classic socialism/capitalism issues (Webb 1992a: 169). It is therefore appropriate to discuss party competition in a single dimension, before moving on to consider the two-dimensional picture.

Party movements in one-dimensional space

Figure 4.1 presents a single dimensional picture of shifts in ideological location since 1964. Each party's position on the socialism–capitalism dimension is given by calculating a simple index which totals the percentage of a manifesto expressing right-wing themes, arguments or proposals and subtracts from this the percentage of left-wing statements.[2] The more that right-wing themes outnumber left-wing themes, the more positive the index's value and the further right the party's location on the figure. As we would expect, Labour adopts a position to the left of the Conservatives throughout the period since 1964, and the Liberals/Alliance Liberal Democrats consistently adopt a position between the two major parties. While the ideological gap between Labour and the Conservatives appears roughly constant in the decade following the election of 1964 (with both parties shifting first right a

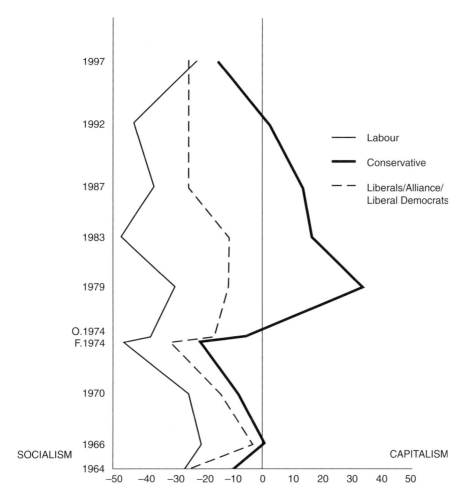

FIGURE 4.1   *Party movement in one-dimensional space since 1964*

little, then left), a gulf opens up thereafter, with the Conservatives lurching sharply right in 1979 and Labour to the left in 1983. By 1987, this gulf – or era of polarized party competition as it is often referred to – was beginning to narrow once more. By 1997 all three of Britain's main political parties had converged closely upon each other, thanks to movement from both major parties, especially Labour.[3] This pattern accords closely with orthodox accounts of party programmatic development in the period; until 1979 the major parties shared a 'consensus' over the need for Keynesian demand management, a mixed economy and expanding welfare provision, but Margaret Thatcher's Conservatives ruptured this consensus in the late 1970s, while Michael Foot's Labour Party took a radical left-wing cue from the AES in the early 1980s. Thereafter, Labour embarked on its long migration back to the 'radical centre', as we have seen.[4] It is interesting to recall, moreover, that voters were broadly aware of the polarization of major party ideologies during the 1980s; whereas fewer than half the electorate perceived 'a great deal of difference' between Labour and the Conservatives between 1964 and 1979, more than four-fifths felt there was in the elections of 1983 and 1987, but this figure declined appreciably again during the 1990s (refer again to Table 2.6).

An important facet of this which is often overlooked in the discussion of party competition is the constricted ideological space in which the Liberal Democrats and their progenitors have often manoeuvred. Their basic problem becomes clear if one considers Figure 4.2. This reveals the paradox that, in a three-party situation, the party locating itself closest to the median voter will not necessarily win most votes if it lies between its two rivals in ideological terms. This argument depends on neither of the others adopting positions which are too extreme; as long as each remains in reasonably close proximity to the median voter's ideological position, the space in which the centre party can trawl for votes becomes very constricted. Thus, in Figure 4.2 we observe the position of the median voter (M) and of the three competitor parties, A, B and C. Clearly, the centre party A lies closest to the median voter, but neither B nor C are especially distant. Following the Downsian logic that voters will prefer the party closest to them, party B will secure the support of *all* voters who lie to the left of the position equidistant between itself and A (indicated by the line a/b on Figure 4.2). Similarly, party C will secure the support of all voters to the right of the position a/c, which is halfway between itself and party A. Consequently, although A lies closest to the median voter, its ideological appeal is restricted to the tranche of voters between lines a/b and a/c. Party A's electoral prospects would be enhanced, however, if either

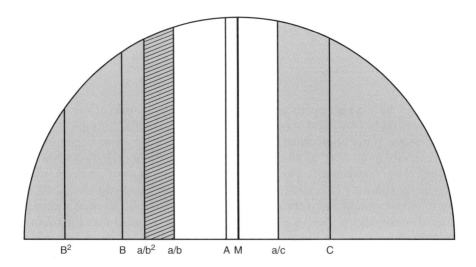

FIGURE 4.2   *The constriction of centre party ideological space*

(or both) of the other parties should – apparently contrary to Downsian logic – decide to forsake their advantage and shift to a more extreme ideological location. Ceteris paribus this would leave an additional group of voters now closer to A. If, for example, the left-wing party B should move to position B^2, then it would only win voters to the left of the new halfway point between itself and A (position a/b^2). So long as the overall distribution of voter preferences (ADP) has not shifted, then B has clearly diminished its own appeal, but has bestowed the support of all those voters in the hatched area (a/b^2)–(a/b) on party A.

Such generosity may not be expected within the strictly rational world of a Downsian model, but it does sometimes occur in real life – and Britain during the early 1980s appears to be a case in point. As we have already seen, by 1983 Mrs Thatcher's new-look Conservatives had swept to power with programmes which were notably more right-wing, while Labour had been seduced by the radicalism of the AES. This obvious polarization of major-party competition seemed to fly in the face of Downsian logic. Of course, it is conceivable that the ADP had shifted one way or the other in this period, thus justifying a shift in programmatic appeals. This is an issue to which we will return, but for now it is worth noting that it was certainly not possible for *both* major parties to be following a vote-maximizing strategy in this period of programmatic polarization – one or the other had to be losing touch with the electorate, and perhaps even both. In these circumstances, the pincer-like constriction which was normally exerted on the centre party was relaxed, allowing the Alliance parties an unusual opportunity to expand their joint electoral appeal; it was almost certainly no coincidence that the centre parties gained their highest ever level of post-war electoral support at the 1983 general election. This is not to propose a single-factor explanation of the centre parties' electoral record in Britain, but it seems to confirm that a Downsian approach provides us with a helpful baseline. That said, something which suggests the model does not offer a full account of how parties compete is Labour's status as 'the centre party' in 1997; this is evident in Figure 4.1 and is implicit in the claims of the party leadership itself and sympathetic commentators such as Giddens. The foregoing analysis suggests a potential danger to Labour in maintaining such a strategy in the long term, yet the shift to the centre did not prevent the party from enjoying overwhelming electoral success in 1997. Evidently, parties do not compete for votes by policies alone.

Party movements in two-dimensional space

What if we take into account the second major dimension of ideological conflict, that of liberty versus authority? Although we have seen that neither parties (in their manifesto statements) nor electors (in their perceptions of the most important issues facing the country) seem to place anything like an equivalent weight on this dimension, it should not be disregarded altogether. It is something which political scientists have been increasingly concerned to take account of in recent years, and it is by no means a simple correlate of the socialism–capitalism dimension. It is certainly possible for parties or citizens to combine preferences for liberty and socialism or authority and capitalism, yet quite contrasting patterns – that is, of authoritarian socialism and libertarian capitalism – are also conceivable. In other words, the two ideological dimensions may well be quite independent of each other.[5]

That said, one of the most intriguing recent perspectives on party competition in Western democracies stresses an interconnection between them. Herbert Kitschelt has argued that contemporary Western citizens' political preferences are shaped by a combination of social and economic factors:

> Reliance on profits or interest as a source of income, work in the private sector and especially in internationally competitive corporations predispose people to more capitalist orientations on the first dimension. A high level of education, client-interactive and symbol-processing task structures and female gender predispose actors towards libertarian orientations on the second dimension. (Kitschelt 1993: 304)

He goes on to suggest that the transformations to which modern societies have been subject will produce an increase in both capitalist and libertarian inclinations among citizens; even more pertinently, 'such societies create more market and work experiences that combine socialist-libertarian or capitalist-authoritarian predispositions rather than socialist-authoritarian or capitalist-libertarian experiences' (op. cit.: 305). The implication of this is that parties will have to compete for votes along a line that runs diagonally through two-dimensional ideological space, bounded by a left-libertarian extreme at one end and a right-authoritarian extreme at the other (see Figure 4.3).

So how have British parties presented themselves in two-dimensional space? Interestingly, the evidence of the manifesto data suggests that, perhaps unwittingly, the relationship between the main three national parties has generally remained stable over time. Figure 4.4a–j uses these data to plot the two-dimensional locations of the parties since 1964,[6] and tends to show a fairly persistent 'triangle', with Labour and the centre parties usually located in more left-wing and libertarian territory than that occupied by the Conservatives. This is true in all elections except those of 1966, 1970 and 1997. In 1966, Labour was a little more authoritarian than either of its main competitors, whereas the Liberals adopted a slightly more authoritarian position than the Conservatives at the following election. 1997 produces the most unusual pattern, however, with the Liberal Democrats now both more libertarian and more left-wing than Labour. The parties generally differ less on the libertarianism dimension – perhaps because it is less central to their beliefs – than on questions of socialism and capitalism.

Similarly, Figure 4.5a–c shows that the major parties have varied their appeals far more over time with regard to the socialism–capitalism dimension; that is, their spatial 'range' is far greater from east to west than from north to south on the diagram. This again confirms the importance of the

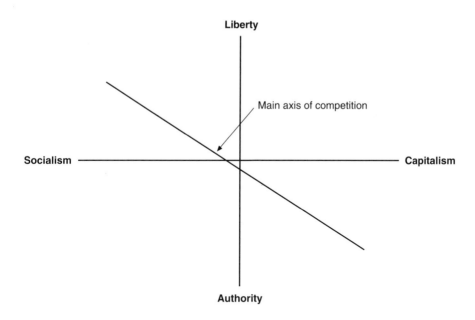

Source: Kitschelt 1993: 309.

FIGURE 4.3   *Kitschelt's model of party competition in two-dimensional space*

socialism–capitalism dimension to processes of party competition. The Liberals, however, have been as likely to alter their emphasis with respect to the second dimension. In 1970, for instance, they actually gave more emphasis to authoritarian messages than to libertarian messages, whereas they placed huge stress on libertarian themes in 1979.

Interestingly, the constriction of centre party ideological space remains evident even when we shift from one dimension to two. Although mapping the ideological territory of each party becomes more complicated when viewed in two dimensions, the same principles apply.[7] The upshot is that Liberal/Alliance/Liberal Democrat territory generally appears to be squeezed between that of the other two parties, even in two dimensions. More often than not, they have 'owned' the ideological space between the major parties on the left–right dimension and to the north – or libertarian – end of the moral policy dimension. Once again, however, it is apparent that the Alliance benefitted from the opening up of ideological space in both an 'east–west' and a 'north–south' sense in 1983, though the major parties began to constrict the Alliance's territory slightly in 1987. In 1997, of course, Labour took the ideological centre-ground from the Liberal Democrats.

The final point worth emphasizing about a two-dimensional conception of party competition in Britain is the one which best demonstrates its value. So

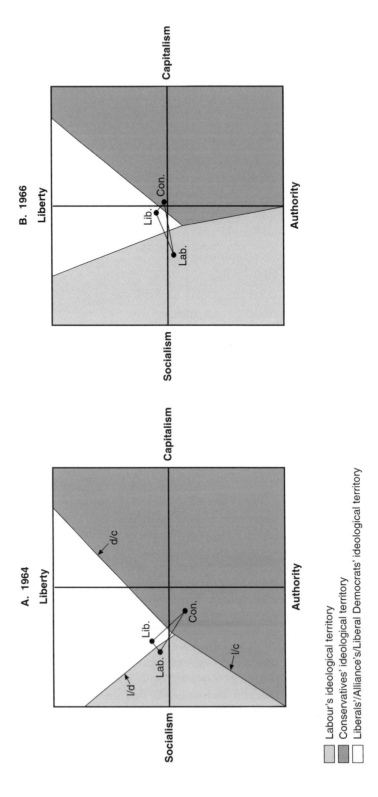

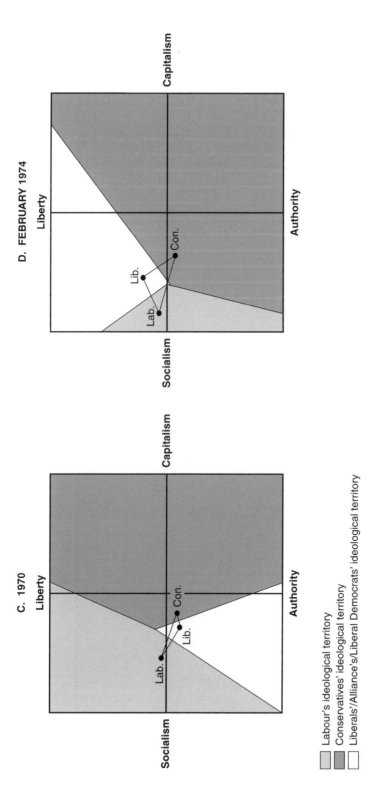

C. 1970

D. FEBRUARY 1974

Labour's ideological territory
Conservatives' ideological territory
Liberals'/Alliance's/Liberal Democrats' ideological territory

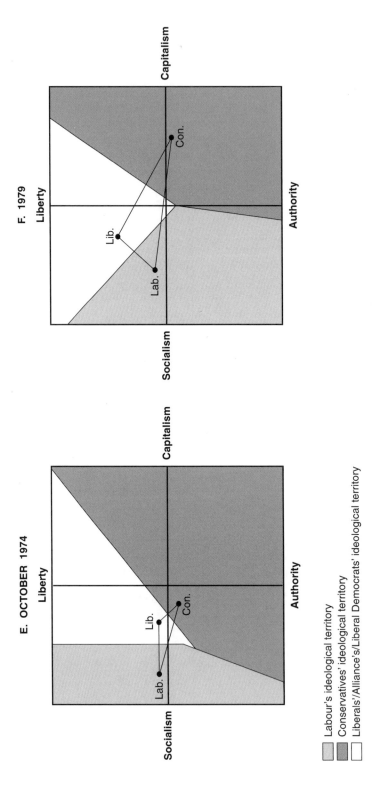

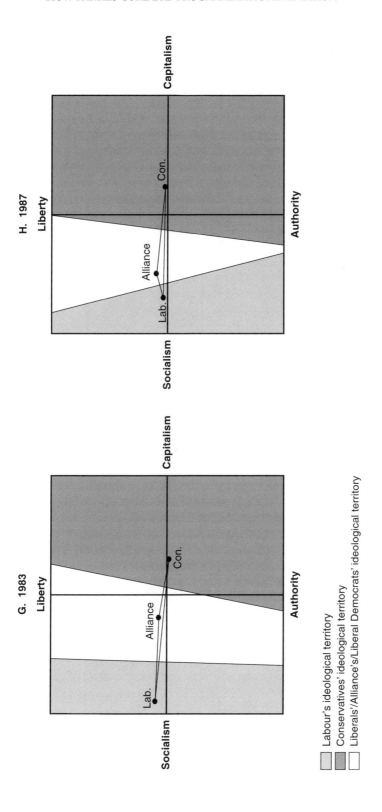

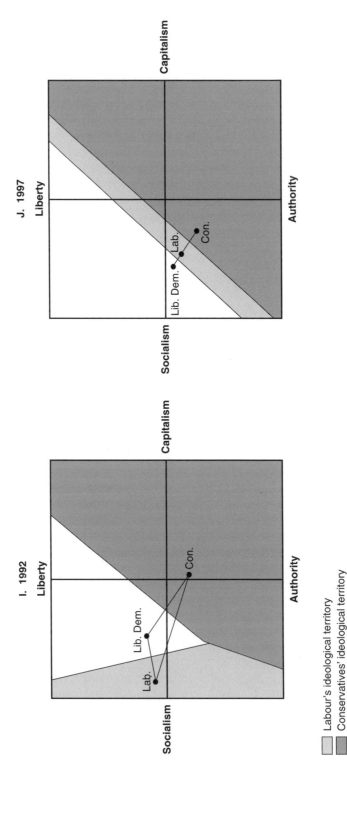

FIGURE 4.4a–j   *British party competition in two-dimensional ideological space, 1964–97*

far it has added little to the understanding achieved through a one-dimensional analysis; we have done little more than confirm that the centre parties have generally been squeezed by the major parties, although the polarization of major party programmes briefly opened up new territory to them in the 1980s. However, the two-dimensional approach – or, rather, Kitschelt's interpretation of it – implies that when a party shifts to the right on the socialist–capitalist dimension, it should simultaneously move in an authoritarian direction on the social morality dimension; conversely, if a party moves to the left, then it should also adopt a more libertarian profile. Is there any evidence to suggest that British parties actually operate this way?

Figure 4.5 indicates a number of occasions when parties did shift programmatic emphases in such a way. Labour apparently offered the electorate manifestos which were simultaneously more libertarian and more left-wing in 1970, February 1974, 1983 and 1992, whereas they made diametrically opposite adjustments in 1966, 1987 and 1997. This leaves October 1974 and 1979, both elections in which Labour's programmatic emphases became less left-wing but more libertarian, though the shift in the latter direction was by no means great in either case. The Conservatives moved in a left-libertarian direction in February 1974, 1983 and 1987, while they shifted towards capitalism and authority in October 1974, and then further right again, but with little net movement on social morality in 1979; 1992 appears to be the most anomalous strategic move from a Kitscheltian perspective, since the party became simultaneously more left-wing and more authoritarian. For the centre parties, left-libertarian shifts were recorded in February 1974, 1987 and 1992,

(a)

Labour Party

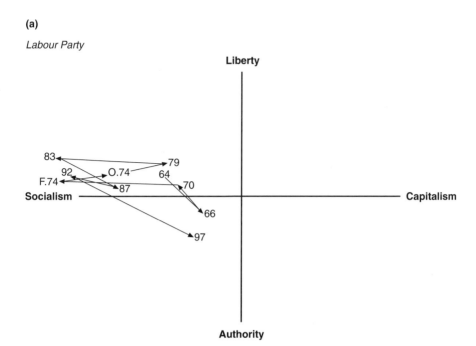

Authority

(b)

Conservative Party

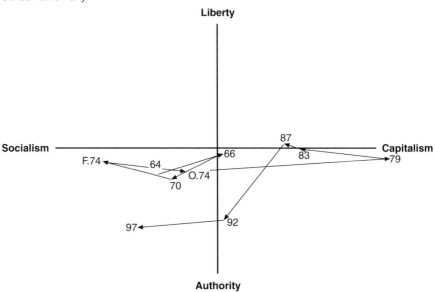

(c)

Liberals/Alliance/Liberal Democrats

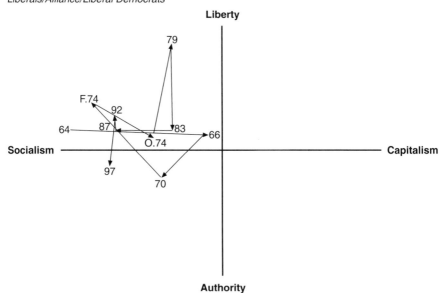

FIGURE 4.5a–c   *Changing party manifesto emphases in two-dimensional space, 1964–97*

while right-authoritarian movements were apparent in 1966 and October 1974. The old Liberal Party, in fact, confronts us with the most obvious contradictions of Kitschelt's advice on modern party competition; in 1970 it made a notable move in favour of socialism and authority, while in 1979 it shifted in precisely the opposite direction.

Overall, parties often do move in the way Kitschelt advises. While they may not be doing so consciously, the increasingly sophisticated opinion research which they commission (see Chapter 5) undoubtedly implies that they are generally aware of the distribution of voter preferences.[8] However, other factors should be borne in mind when assessing the relevance to Britain of Kitschelt's model. First, the model is based on the sociology of advanced industrial societies, and this makes the counter-examples dating back to the 1960s and probably even the 1970s irrelevant. Second, it would in any case be unrealistic to expect all programmatic adjustments to be made in a perfectly linear fashion according to Kitscheltian logic; sometimes movement may be apparent along one ideological dimension, sometimes along the other. In broad terms, though, the two-dimensional perspective on party competition seems persuasive. For instance, in his well-known book on the subject (*The Free Economy and the Strong State*), Andrew Gamble argued that the Thatcherite revolution within the Conservative Party entailed not only a radical commitment to the cause of deregulated capitalism, but also a firm restatement of the traditional Tory virtues of authority and discipline (1988). Indeed, strong law and order policies, with powerful and well-rewarded police, soldiers and judges, were seen as necessary by Thatcher's Cabinet if the free economy was to develop, for impediments such as recalcitrant trade unions and profligate state sectors had to be brought under control (Norton 1996: 60). It is interesting too to observe that Labour's path back to the 'radical centre' consists not only of a rediscovery of the market, but also of the need for social discipline. Although one should not overlook the agenda of constitutional reform (which includes a new freedom of information act and the incorporation into UK law of the European Convention on Human Rights), New Labour has spent considerable effort expounding themes such as: the need to be 'tough on crime and tough on the causes of crime'; providing a new 'fast-track' scheme of administering justice to young offenders; introducing legislation against nuisance neighbours and curfews for children; establishing a total ban on the use of handguns in the country; and re-embracing certain forms of teaching which emphasize order in the classroom (Freeden 1999: 46). In general, New Labour has placed considerable emphasis on the need to rebuild a sense of community and has, quite deliberately and without irony, adopted the language of traditional Tory 'One-Nation' politics. Implicit in all of this is the need for individual self-discipline and an awareness of social obligations and responsibilities. In short, the impression given by the programmatic shifts referred to is that, whether by design or coincidence, the major British political parties have since the 1970s broadly attempted to move in left-libertarian (Labour in the early 1980s) or right-authoritarian directions (the Conservatives in the years of Thatcherism, Labour in the 1990s).

That said, the final point to consider about Kitschelt's model in a British context is that if the parties do not always appear to move along a diagonal axis of party competition in two-dimensional space, this may reflect the fact that popular preferences are not distributed in a simple linear fashion. Kitschelt's is a comparative model appropriate to advanced industrial society in general, but it is unlikely to fit each national case well. In fact, Figure 4.6 suggests that voter preferences in Britain are not distributed in two-dimensional space exactly as the general model predicts.[9] It is readily apparent from Figure 4.6 that the bulk of voters in 1997 were distributed across the libertarian-left, authoritarian-left and authoritarian-right, while very few were located on the libertarian-right. In view of this, it is hardly surprising that none of the main parties have ever located themselves in this quadrant of two-dimensional space (refer again to Figure 4.5). Moreover it implies that, in reality, *British party competition is not linear but curvilinear;* that is, given the distribution of voter preferences, parties are not restricted to moving in left-libertarian or right-authoritarian directions along an imaginary Kitscheltian axis, but have the further option of shifting into left-authoritarian territory where there exists a considerable share of the electoral market. This helps explain why, for instance, the Conservatives could move in a left-

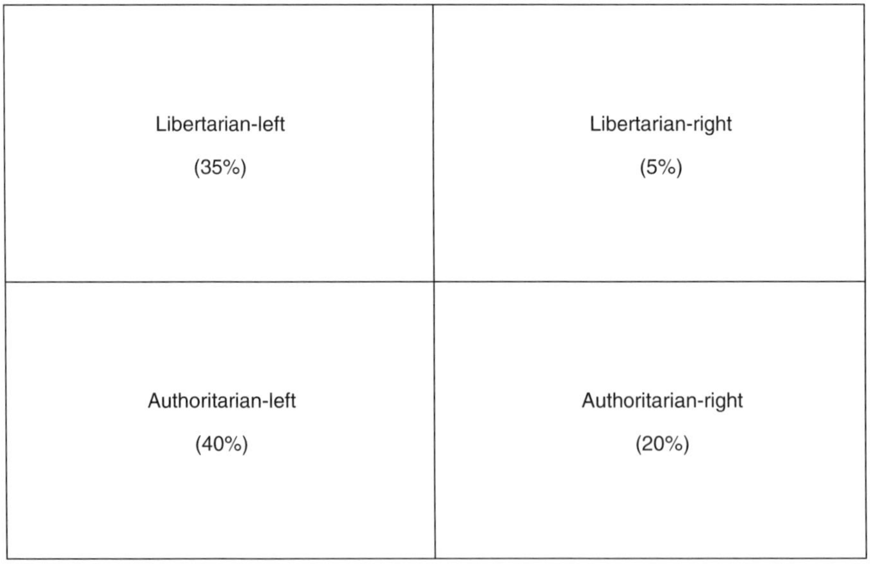

Libertarian-left (35%)	Libertarian-right (5%)
Authoritarian-left (40%)	Authoritarian-right (20%)

Data source: BES 1997 (n = 2731).

FIGURE 4.6   *The distribution of voter preferences in two-dimensional space, 1997*

authoritarian direction in 1992. As we saw in Chapter 3, moreover, virtually all the main ideological traditions in mainstream British party politics can be located within this curvilinear ideological space.

The connection between party ideology and voter preferences

The main parties' ideological traditions and manifesto developments have been examined on the assumption that they are central to the competition for votes, but this is only credible if we can demonstrate two things. First, evidence should exist that voters have ideological convictions which influence their electoral decisions. This can be gleaned from an analysis of individual-level data sources, such as surveys of the electorate. Second, there should also be evidence that parties have profited or lost from the relationship between their programmes and the ADP in the manner suggested by formal models of party competition. This is a matter of aggregate-level data analysis and it is to this that we turn first.

Which parties have been closest to the median voter's ideological location? This question is clearly central to any assessment of party competition, but it runs up against an awkward problem: party and median voter positions have never been measured on directly comparable scales. This means that we are forced into a less precise, though nonetheless suggestive, discussion of trends in public opinion and the connection between these trends and movements in party programmes.

There is no doubt that the second half of the 1970s witnessed significant shifts in British public opinion, and it is equally certain that the Conservatives were well placed to exploit this change of mood. In the decade following 1974 Ivor Crewe noted 'a spectacular decline in support for the collectivist trinity of public ownership, trade union power and social welfare' (1985:138), even among Labour supporters. Thus, between 1974 and 1979 there was a virtual doubling in the proportion of voters favouring more privatization of state-owned industry, while the percentage regarding trade unions as 'too powerful' increased from two-thirds to three-quarters, and the numbers feeling that the provision of state welfare had 'gone too far' increased from one-third to one-half of all electors. These developments are reflected in Table 4.2, in which positive entries in the cells indicate a preponderance of right-wing attitudes over left-wing attitudes and negative figures indicate a preponderance of left-wing attitudes; by 1979, the electorate had plainly turned against the collectivist trinity. In the context of this, the Conservative Party's sharp move to the right at the same time (and particularly its evolving agenda of privatization, trade union emasculation and welfare retrenchment) was clearly in tune with the popular mood.

By 1983, however, the shock of the recession of 1980–81 (in which a third of the country's manufacturing capacity was eliminated) was enough to re-orientate voters' minds on the issue of welfare benefits, and by 1987 there were clear signs that the allure of privatization and the assault on trade unions was

TABLE 4.2   *British electors' attitudes towards the collectivist trinity, 1964–97*

Year	Public ownership	Union power	Benefits
1964	−7.8	22.3	–
1966	−6.5	38.6	–
Feb.1974	−3.6	41.8	–
Oct.1974	−10.3	59.1	11.0
1979	23.1	60.3	33.1
1983	25.5	45.2	−9.9
1987	14.8	33.6	−10.1
1992	−0.3	−28.9	−29.3
1997	−13.4	−48.6	–

Note: All figures are 'Percentage Difference Indices' calculated as follows:

Public ownership – percentage in favour of more privatization minus percentage in favour of more nationalization.
Union power – percentage feeling that unions have too much power minus percentage feeling they have too little power.
Benefits – percentage feeling that welfare benefits have gone too far minus percentage feeling they have not gone far enough. The question on welfare benefits does not appear on the BES in 1997, nor prior to October 1974.

Sources: Norris 1996: 165—8; BES 1997.

waning. Indeed by 1992 there was, for the first time in the time series, a majority perception that unions were not powerful enough and a rejection of further privatization, both trends being consolidated by 1997. In retrospect, it seems clear that the electorate as a whole felt these aspects of the Thatcherite revolution had gone far enough by the 1990s; indeed, Crewe and Searing have even referred to Thatcherism as a 'crusade that failed' to engender an enduring shift in popular attitudes (1988).

Thus far, shifting voter preferences have been discussed in one dimension only, but Figure 4.7 summarizes the electorate's mean location in two dimensions. It is important to reiterate that these locations are measured in a completely different way, and using a different scale, to party ideological locations.[10] Nevertheless, the impression given is highly suggestive, for it seems evident that the ADP shifted so as to locate the average voter in classic Conservative territory – that is to say, in the authoritarian-right quadrant which is the domain of both Thatcherites and One-Nation Tories – in 1979, and there it remained until 1997, even though it began to snake back towards the territory occupied by the Opposition parties after 1983. By 1997 the electorate's centre of ideological gravity had returned to the authoritarian-left quadrant in which it had resided in 1974. On this evidence, it does not seem surprising that the Conservatives managed to win elections between 1979 and 1992, nor that Labour should have been victorious in 1974 and 1997.

Nevertheless, it seems odd, on the face of it, that the Conservative governments of Margaret Thatcher and John Major maintained their right-wing

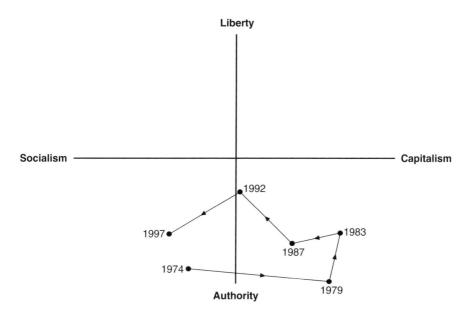

FIGURE 4.7   *Shifting two-dimensional location of the mean voter, 1974–97*

thrust in public policy after 1987, even when it was apparent that the electorate as a whole was losing sympathy for such an approach. The
privatization programme continued (after a brief respite occasioned by the
stock market crash of October 1987) and, while new trade union legislation
and welfare reform became more limited, Britain experienced other innovations such as the introduction of quasi-markets in the public sector. In narrow
vote-maximization terms, this almost seemed to bespeak a perverse contempt
for the distribution of public opinion – unless, that is, the Conservatives felt
confident of their ability to persuade voters to adopt the party's own policy
preferences. This raises the further issue of the autonomous capacity of political parties to shape the voters' ADP.

The endogenous impact of party competition on voter preferences

Thus far, the discussion has assumed the ADP to be a fixed component of the
model of party competition, with parties playing a purely reactive role
(Downs 1957: 46–7). Thus, voter preferences are said to be 'exogenously'
determined (that is, resulting from factors external to the model of party competition itself). However, although such an assumption simplifies matters, it
is highly unrealistic and has been subject to challenge. Patrick Dunleavy and
Hugh Ward (1981) have argued persuasively that political parties are far from
the passive victims of exogenously determined voter preferences portrayed
by Downs, but retain a very real capacity for shaping voter attitudes. That is,

they can adopt preference-shaping strategies as well as preference-accom-modating strategies. Indeed, awareness of this capacity was accentuated after 1979, as commentators suggested that the Tories had sought to introduce policies which would undermine some of the key structural bases of Labour's electoral support. According to Dunleavy and Ward, governing parties are in an especially powerful position to achieve this. They outline two preference-shaping strategies in particular which might conceivably affect the ADP.

The first they refer to as *partisan social engineering*. To understand this it is necessary to have some conception of what might induce voters to adopt core beliefs in the first place. It is reasonable – especially in the light of evi-dence that social cleavages impact on party systems (see Chapter 2) – to suppose that, for many people at least, core values will be derived from their social interests and experience. Most obviously in the case of Britain we would expect that for many voters, core political values will reflect the impact of their class background. Thus, it would seem rational for those lower down the socio-economic scale to adopt socialist (or at least social liberal) values, while we might expect those in relatively advantaged positions to prefer unfettered market capitalism, with low taxes and a limit on redistributive action by the state (Robertson 1984). Similarly, it is reasonable to assume that those working or consuming within the public sector might have different core preferences to those whose interests are more bound up with the private sector (Kitschelt 1993: 305).

This being so, partisan social engineering aims to expand the size of those social groups likely to favour governmental policy and/or to shrink those groups likely to oppose the government. The best example of such an approach in recent times is provided by the Thatcher governments' 'popular capitalism' measures (for instance, the sale to tenants of publicly owned hous-ing and the mass flotations of equity in state-owned corporations); many observers have claimed that such policies were designed to alter decisively the economic interests of some of Labour's most traditional supporters, and thereby change the structural constraints on patterns of party competition.[11] If true, this would constitute a highly significant piece of strategic and long-term thinking by a party seeking to shape the electoral market. But is there evidence to support the contention that popular capitalism shifted voter pref-erences to the advantage of the Conservatives?

Housing tenure is, by and large, the strongest single social structural pre-dictor of electoral choice in the UK. Between 1979 and 1990, more than 1.5 million local authority owned homes were sold to tenants at generously discounted prices, increasing from 60% to 65% the proportion of home-ownership in the national stock of housing. The effects of the privatization programme were even broader; even the most conservative estimates suggest that the number of shareholders in the country more than tripled from 1983 to 1987, and there were further significant sales of public assets after then. In many cases new shareholders gained from the consistent undervaluation of the shares which they bought, enabling them to make large and quick profits on their investments. Geoffrey Garrett has tested the hypothesis that these policies, along with the massive decline in union membership and power after 1979 (also in large part attributable to the effects of Conservative partisan engineering), affected voting behaviour. He discovered that leaving a trade union (while retaining employment) or purchasing a council home or shares in a privatized company after 1979, all made voters either significantly more likely to vote Conservative or, at least, less likely to vote Labour. On aggregate, he estimated that these effects could have boosted the Conservative Party's share of the vote by as much as 1.2% in 1992; assuming these effects to have been evenly distributed throughout the country (a considerable but a necessary simplification), this could well have made the difference between majority and minority governing status (Garrett 1994: 118–21).

The second type of preference-shaping strategy available to governing parties which might bear upon the distribution of core values is that of *context management*. Dunleavy and Ward (1981) suggested that the government of the day managed to induce a mass upsurge of national chauvinism by its conduct of the Falklands War in 1982, and exploited this patriotic fervour to turn a record slump in government popularity into a commanding lead in the opinion polls in the run-up to the general election held a little more than a year later. If true, this provides a key example of the way in which the 'objective situation of the polity as a whole' can be altered so as to change voter perceptions of the government. More precisely from our point of view, it shows how context management techniques were exploited to make more salient than usual the social morality dimension of core belief; one effect of the Falklands episode was to enhance the place of authority and discipline in the name of the national community, and to emphasize national traditions and loyalties generally over other all other imperatives. This emphasis on community over individual and on authority over personal liberty was almost certainly only a short-term phenomenon, but it may have helped transform the Conservative Party's electoral fortunes when they were at a low ebb. Thus, even if the ADP was not actively shifted in favour of authority, the short-term salience of the second dimension of core belief was almost certainly enhanced, and this alone would have been enough to assist the Conservatives given the traditional populist authoritarianism of the British people (refer again to Figure 4.7 for confirmation of this point).[12]

A more common way in which governments seek to manage the national context of politics is through economic management. As we see in Chapter 5, there is strong evidence confirming that voter perceptions of both personal economic prospects and the general performance of the national economy influence their views of the parties; indeed, given the weakening impact of the class cleavage, electors are likely to rely increasingly on such assessments in guiding their behaviour. It is therefore not surprising that governing parties generally regard effective management of the economy as critical to their prospects of re-election; other things being equal, the more prosperous voters feel themselves to be, the more likely they will be to vote for the status quo at an election. Interestingly, however, research suggests that while the self-perceived economic circumstances of voters only exert a limited *direct* influence on electoral choice, they also wield a significant *indirect* impact through their influence on voter ideology: 'Voters who sense that they are economically hard done by, tend in turn to become more left-wing in ideological orientation – presumably a reflection of the fact that leftist parties have traditionally positioned themselves as the champions of the dispossessed' (Sanders and Brynin 1999: 237). This confirms that management of the economic context by governments seems to carry the clear potential to shift the ADP.

Dunleavy and Ward's preference-shaping argument represents a major corrective to the orthodox view of party competition derived from Downs and expounded in many formal models. Perhaps its most valuable feature is that it highlights an asymmetry which exists within processes of competition between parties. With access to state resources and a greater or lesser degree of control over legislative action, governing parties are relatively free to shape voter preferences; by contrast, opposition parties lack these vital advantages and are more likely to be constrained to follow a strategy of accommodating existing voter preferences. This must not be exaggerated, however; even opposition parties can find ways of catalysing a shift in the ADP, especially when incumbent parties run up against policy difficulties. For instance, the Conservatives in opposition may have played an important role in sparking such a shift against Labour's 'collectivist trinity' during the late 1970s. Although it may seem somehow inevitable that trade unions, increasing social expenditure and nationalized industries would have all lost popular support at that time, it is also very likely that the critique of these things developed by the then Opposition – and the alternative it purported to offer the electorate – played a vital role in effectively shifting the ADP to the right.

A mixture of preference-accommodating and preference-shaping strategies is always available to political parties, but the likely success of these various approaches depends on the particular political, social and economic circumstances of the time. In addition, it is probably safe to assume that governing parties will usually benefit from their control of the state and will thus be more autonomous than their opponents to shape voter preferences. That said, no governing party can assume it is omnipotent in this respect; though far from static, there may well be very definite limits to ideological change in the electorate – and such change as occurs may be slow. The example of the poll tax serves to demonstrate how even a governing party in a seemingly strong position can suffer by pushing through radical but fundamentally unpopular policies (Butler et al. 1995). Indeed, in general, core political beliefs by their very nature should not be expected to change radically for most people – at least not in the short term – unless the individual's critical socio-economic interests change. Perhaps we should continue to think, therefore, of preference-accommodation as providing the basis of party competition, while strategies designed to reshape voter preferences constitute a secondary weapon in the party armoury. It falls to party leaders to make the crucial judgements about when they might lead the electorate and when they should follow it.

Ideology and voting behaviour

We have seen then that British parties have developed distinctive, though not completely static, political values, and that they have almost certainly gained and lost votes at the aggregate level through programmatic shifts. The final component of our examination of the role that ideology plays in the business of party competition is to seek evidence that voters do indeed have ideological principles *and* that these principles affect the electoral decisions they make.

A number of studies of the British electorate have drawn attention to the significance of voters' underlying political values. This does not refer to issue voting models, which are primarily concerned with the impact of specific policy questions salient in the short-run context of particular election campaigns and which, as we saw in Chapter 2, have a distinctly limited ability to explain electoral choice. Rather, the focus is on general underlying political dispositions which are stable and enduring facets of the voter's political personality. As such, they are 'structural' components of the vote, akin to (and possibly derived from) the socio-economic interests which serve to foster long-term partisan predispositions (Heath et al. 1991: 174–5). Though voters' underlying political values may not be completely unchanging, clearly defined beliefs should not be easily shed and may even sustain a partisan loyalty in the face of negative short-term issue effects.

The orthodox view developed in the 1960s was sceptical about the capacity of voters to think in general ideological terms. Well-known studies in America by Philip Converse (1964) and in Britain by David Butler and Donald Stokes (1974) concluded that most citizens were incapable of sustaining consistent attitudes or thinking clearly in terms of concepts like 'left' and 'right'. By the middle of the 1980s, however, a revival of interest in the impact of underlying political values was evident among British political scientists. By far the most elaborate attempt to account for this impact was made by Elinor Scarbrough (1984), whose ambitious and fascinating study went beyond the scope of most other studies in the field. Thus, where others used terms like 'ideology', 'principles', 'underlying values' and 'core beliefs' almost interchangeably, Scarbrough was far more specific: her interest was in the role of ideology understood as an 'ideational whole', or a single dimension of belief in which all attitudes can be derived from an integrated and coherent view of the world. She sought evidence of such thinking, and claimed that less than 30% of her electoral sample was ideologically 'confused' or 'incoherent' – even in the demanding terms she prescribed (1984: ch. 9). This suggested a far higher level of ideological thinking within the electorate than most previous research had indicated; moreover, she found that these ideological mindsets had a considerable impact on actual voting behaviour. In total, she argued, ideology seemed to influence the majority of voters; that is, 39% of ideologues voted for the party one would expect on the basis of their ideological profiles ('directional ideological voters'), while a further 16% failed to do so, but expressed a definite antipathy towards parties of opposite ideological complexion to themselves ('immunity ideological voters').

Richard Rose and Ian McAllister (1986) were not interested in the notion of ideology as an 'ideational whole', since this represented 'the ultimate in closed thinking'; their view was that voters were now increasingly free of structural constraints such as class (and class ideology) in making electoral decisions. Nevertheless, they did not propose that such decisions could be made entirely on the basis of contingent short-term factors; indeed, underlying 'political principles' played a central role in their model, for:

> A theory of unprincipled electoral competition implies that parties will alter policies and personalities in a continuing effort to catch the votes of an electorate open to the most ephemeral and transitory campaign influences. (1986: 116)

The political principles to which Rose and McAllister referred were 'underlying judgements and preferences about the activities of government'; they understood such principles to be durable and to guide voters' interpretations and choices over a range of more specific policy issues. Their empirical analysis suggested that around a quarter of the variation in individual voting behaviour in the 1980s could be attributed to the effect of these underlying political principles (op. cit.: 130).

An essentially similar understanding of ideology in an electoral context was developed by Heath et al.; for them 'the fit between the general character of the party and the voter's own general ideology' best accounted for electoral choice (1985: 99). In recent years, Heath and others have developed attitudinal scales which have allowed them to explore both main dimensions of belief (Heath et al. 1993; see also note 9). These scales offer the most robust measures of two-dimensional voter ideology currently available, and are of great value in testing the overall connection between ideology and voting behaviour. Table 4.3 reports the results of a logistic regression model in which party preference is seen as a function of the voter's location on these two ideological scales and post-materialism, while controlling for the influence of social background.[13] This model is applied to each of the main parties in turn, and confirms nearly all expectations: being socialist or libertarian makes a voter significantly more likely to vote Labour, while favouring capitalism or authoritarianism makes a voter significantly more likely to vote Conservative. Location on the socialist–capitalist dimension does not appear to influence Liberal Democrat support significantly, but a libertarian disposition does. Even more notable is the clear evidence that position on the socialism–capitalism scale is – as must have been suspected by now – generally far more important to electoral choice than position on the social morality scale, at least for the major parties' voters; the relative size of the logistic regression coefficients confirms this (see columns headed 'B' and 'R' on Table 4.3).[14] By contrast, post-materialism appears to have no significant effect on voting behaviour (see column headed 'sig'). Bear in mind it is not being suggested that these underlying political values are the only important influences on voting behaviour, but these results clearly suggest they provide us with a good baseline on which to build our understanding.[15]

TABLE 4.3 *Logistic regression models of ideological voting in Britain, 1997*

Variable	Labour vote/other vote				Conservative vote/other Vote				Liberal Democrat vote/other vote			
	B	S.E.	Sig	R	B	S.E.	Sig	R	B	S.E.	Sig	R
HOUSING	.56	.18	***	.06	-.86	.27	***	-.06	-.67	.25	***	-.06
SECTOR	.06	.13	ns	.00	-.18	.15	ns	.00	.12	.14	ns	.00
ETHMIN	-2.28	.42	***	-.11	1.88	.52	***	.07	1.40	.62	**	.04
CLASS	.55	.12	***	.09	-.56	.15	***	-.08	-.12	.14	ns	.00
POSTMAT	-.18	.21	ns	.00	-.48	.30	ns	-.02	.29	.21	ns	.00
GRADUATE	.05	.19	ns	.00	-.50	.24	**	-.03	.23	.20	ns	.00
SOCIALISM	-1.67	.11	***	-.30	2.40	.14	***	.36	-.25	.11	**	-.05
LIBERTY	-.44	.11	***	-.08	.96	.13	***	.15	-.41	.12	***	-.08
REGION	.59	.12	***	.10	-.77	.15	***	-.11	-.67	.14	***	-.11
Constant	9.52	.99			-13.55	1.26			-2.15	1.31	ns	
Model chi-square	498.307 (***)				690.030 (***)				76.390 (***)			
Cases correctly predicted	71.4% (n = 2190)				82.1% (n = 2190)				82.1% (n = 2190)			

Notes:

B   – unstandardized logistic regression coefficient
S.E.   – standard error
Sig   – significance of regression coefficient
R   – standardized partial regression coefficient
***   – significant at .01
**   – significant at .05
*   – significant at .10
ns   – not significant

For each of these models, the *independent variables* are coded:
Housing;   1 = local authority tenant, 0 = other
Sector: 1 = public sector employee, 0 = other
Ethmin: 1 = ethnic minority, 2 = other
Class: 1 = manual, 0 = non-manual
Postmat: 1 = post-materialist, 0 = other
Graduate: 1 = graduate, 0 = other
Socialism: 1 = socialist, 5 = capitalist
Liberty: 1 = libertarian, 5 = authoritarian
Region: 1 = Scotland, Wales, northern England, 0 = other (not N. Ireland)
Dependent variables are coded: 1 = Labour vote/Con. vote/Lib.Dem. vote, 0 = other vote.
Data source: BES 1997.

Conclusion

This chapter has argued that, in trying to comprehend how political parties compete for votes, basic ideological strategy provides us with a solid baseline. This is far from the whole story, but it constitutes a fundamental element of the plot. It is perfectly rational for parties to regard programmatic adjustment as an important part of the competitive process given the evidence that ideological values play a significant role in shaping the electoral decisions of British voters. Their shifting programmatic emphases since the 1960s confirm that Britain's main parties have carved out enduring 'policy reputations' or core ideological territories for themselves and, although they move within these territories, there is seldom any 'leapfrogging' over each other (though 1997 may well have provided a rare instance in respect of Labour's move to the centre). We have seen that there are good grounds for relying on the simple Downsian unidimensional approach to analysing party competition in Britain, since the main parties both emphasize and vary their appeals far more in respect of the main socialism–capitalism dimension than any other. That said, looking at British party competition in two-dimensions is also useful in so far as it shows the curvilinear space in which the bulk of the electoral market is situated and within which the main parties generally compete. For much of the period since 1945, the Labour-Conservative duopoly has made the logic of centripetal competition seem highly apposite, in that parties departing from such logic (as Labour did in 1983) have generally been punished by the British electorate. As a result, centre parties have suffered from the problem of 'constricted' territory in which to launch their electoral appeals, though they obviously benefited during the period of major-party polarization during the 1980s. Nevertheless, parties are more than mere response mechanisms stimulated by the vagaries of aggregate voter preferences; there are good grounds for supposing that they can, to a certain extent, shift the ADP although voters' underlying political values are essentially long-term structural components of their political behaviour and it is not easy to produce dramatic changes within them. In all, then, party ideology is an important element of the story, yet as David Sanders says, 'there is much more to voting decisions than the ideological closeness of the average voter to a particular political party' (1999: 201). So what other factors must parties take into account when competing for votes?

Notes

1   1964 has been used as the starting point for analysis in order to provide a temporal coincidence between the study of party ideologies and voter preferences; although information on manifesto content goes back to 1945, detailed data on voter preferences only begin with the British Election Study of 1964.

2   '*Left-wing*' statements include the following variables in the Comparative Manifestos Data set: Per403 – Need for market regulation; Per404 – Need for eco-

nomic planning; Per405 – Need for corporatism; Per406 – Need for protectionism; Per409 – Need for Keynesian demand management; Per411 – Importance of modernizing technology and infrastructure; Per412 – General need for direct government control of economy; Per413 – Need for nationalization of industry; Per415 – Positive references to Marxist analysis; Per503 – References to social justice and equality; Per504 – Favourable mentions of welfare state expansion; Per506 – Need to expand or improve educational provision; Per701 – Positive references to labour groups; Per705 – Positive references to underprivileged minorities; Per706 – Positive references to assistance for non-economic minorities and groups. *'Right-wing'* statements include: Per303 – Need for efficiency and economy in government; Per401 – Positive references to free enterprise; Per402 – Need for incentives; Per407 – Need for free trade; Per410 – Need for greater productivity; Per414 – Need for traditional economic orthodoxy; Per505 – Need to limit spending on welfare state; Per507 – Need to limit educational spending; Per702 – Negative references to labour groups; Per704 – Positive references to middle class or professional groups.

3   For a similar, though not identical, interpretation of these manifesto data, see Budge 1999: 4–6.

4   Note how Figure 4.1 confirms that prior to Thatcher, the consensus, if such it was, was forged around left-of-centre themes. Though we might expect any new consensus to form in more right-wing ideological territory now, Figure 4.1 does not immediately appear to suggest this is so. However, it must be borne in mind that the policy context of the 1990s is very different to that of the 1960s; for instance, to favour the status quo on the public/private sector mix carried radically different implications in the latter decade given the privatization programmes conducted after 1980. One cannot conclude, therefore, that the major parties have *not* shifted to the right in net terms; the data are simply unclear in this sense.

5   This is confirmed by the results of a factor analysis performed on simple attitudinal scales first created and described by Heath et al. (1993). Each of these scales is constructed from survey responses to a set of six questions on related themes, one measuring location on the socialism–capitalism dimension, the other measuring location on the libertarianism–authoritarianism dimension. Principal components analysis of the scale items using BES data from 1992 and 1997 shows that they load on to two distinctive attitudinal factors (results available from author).

6   The liberty–authority dimension scores are generated by subtracting the percentage of authoritarian statements in a manifesto from the percentage of libertarian statements. *'Libertarian'* statements include: Per602 – Negative references towards the national way of life; Per604 – Negative references towards traditional morality; Per201 – Positive references to personal freedom and human rights; Per202 – Positive references to democracy and political participation. *'Authoritarian'* statements include: Per601 – Positive references to the national way of life; Per603 – Positive references to traditional morality; Per605 – Positive references to strong law and order.

7   For instance, looking at Figure 4.4a, voters lying closer to Labour than to the Liberals, taking both dimensions into account, are situated on Labour's side of the line l/d which bisects the line running directly between the two parties. The same principle applies with respect to the lines l/c (which separates Labour and Conservative territories) and d/c (which distinguishes Liberal and Conservative space). Note that only two, rather than all three, of the lines bisecting the parties

appear on Figures 4.4g (1983), 4.4h (1987) and 4.4j (1997), which reflects the fact that differences between the parties on the liberty–authority dimension were relatively muted in these years. In effect, party ideological distinctions could be adequately understood in terms of the socialist–capitalist dimension alone on these occasions. For a detailed account of two-dimensional maps of party competition, see Laver 1997: 129.

8   Although (as Chapter 5 shows) it seems likely parties are increasingly well informed about the state of public opinion, an interesting attempt to account for competitive strategy when they lack precise information is provided by Ian Budge. He suggests that, in such circumstances, British parties are overwhelmingly likely to follow a 'past results model'; that is, if a previous ideological shift was associated with vote gains, a party will maintain its location or continue to shift further in the same direction, whereas a previously unsuccessful strategy will produce a change of ideological direction (1994: 461–6).

9   Voter locations in two-dimensional space are measured with the attitudinal scales devised by Heath et al. (1993), and described briefly above. Using BES 1997 data, these scales have been re-created, standard reliability tests producing Cronbach's Alpha coefficients of .67 for the socialism–capitalism scale and .59 for the libertarianism–authoritarianism scale. Though it is possible to generate these scales with 1992 BES data, the necessary component variables do not exist in previous data sets, so it is not possible to obtain a fully accurate picture of the way in which voter preferences have changed in two-dimensional space through time (though Figure 4.7 provides a rough estimate of such movements).

10   There are few data available which allow researchers to map accurately and consistently the two-dimensional location of the British electorate over time. However, for Figure 4.7 classic 'synoptic' indicators (Heath et al. 1985: ch. 8) of each dimension have been used. Attitude towards nationalization is used to tap the socialism–capitalism dimension, while attitude towards abortion taps the social morality dimension. (These are just about the only synoptic values which appear throughout the time-series since 1974.) The overall position of the electorate is produced by calculating the percentage difference index of each. For the former dimension this is given by subtracting the percentage of respondents favouring more nationalization from the percentage favouring more privatization, while for the social morality dimension it is given by subtracting the percentage of respondents feeling that availability of abortion on the NHS has 'not gone far enough' from the percentage feeling it has 'gone too far'.

11   It should be noted that the effect of this piece of partisan social engineering was almost certainly reinforced by the simultaneous 'adjusting of social relativities' in favour of homeowners. That is, at the same time that the government was creating opportunities for more citizens to become homeowners through the subsidized sales of council properties, it was increasing the attractiveness of becoming a homeowner by reducing subsidies to remaining tenants, and maintaining tax breaks for homeowners until the late 1980s. In effect, the relative position of core Tory supporters was improved with respect to that of core Labour voters (Maor 1997: 219). Similar effects can be deduced from the tax breaks afforded in the same period to those paying fees for private education or taking out private pensions or health insurance policies.

12   Note that context management is generally used by governments in a more prosaic way, which we shall be examining in the course of the next chapter. That is, governing parties have regularly exploited their power (such as it is) over the

levers of economic control in order to coincide a general election with a consumer boom. This strategy does not necessarily result in changes to the core political values of voters, but it does bear upon the important issue of governing competence.

13 Logistic regression is a statistical technique for assessing the partial and overall influence of multiple causal factors on dichotomous dependent variables. In this case, the dependent variables are respectively Labour vote/other vote, Conservative vote/other vote and Liberal Democrat vote/other vote. The overall goodness of fit of these models can be assessed in a number of ways; here we rely on the significance of the *model chi-square* (which tests for the null hypothesis that the independent variables in the model jointly fail to improve our prediction of the dependent variable's value), and on the overall number of cases in the sample whose voting choices are correctly predicted by the model. The impact of each individual independent variable on voting choice is assessed by reference to three coefficients: the *unstandardized logistic regression coefficient (B)*, which can be interpreted as the change in the log of the odds on a respondent voting for Labour rather than another party (or Conservative rather than another party, and so on) associated with a one-unit change in the independent variable; the *significance of B* (based on a test of the null hypothesis that the value of the B is 0); and the *partial correlation coefficient (R)*, which ranges in value between –1 and +1 (a positive value indicating the increased likelihood of a Labour/Conservative/Liberal Democrat vote associated with a one unit increase in the value of the independent variable). For a technical introduction to logistic regression refer to Goodman 1972, Norusis 1994, or Menard 1995.

14 It has been noted that 'ideological considerations exerted less of a constraining influence on voters' decisions to vote Labour in 1997 than in any previous election since 1964'. Even so, the link remained statistically significant overall (Sanders 1999: 194–5).

15 Note that the relative importance of left–right ideology over other influences on voting choice is confirmed by other research (Sanders and Brynin 1999).

5

HOW PARTIES COMPETE 3: IMAGERY, MEDIA AND POLITICAL MARKETING

CONTENTS

At the outset of Chapter 3, it was suggested that the products which the main political parties in Britain seek to market consist essentially of blends of policies, leaders and 'corporate images'. Now that we have examined in some detail the role played by changing policy programmes, it is time to turn to the impact of politicians and general party images. Specifically, this chapter focuses on a number of interconnected questions: why, and to what extent, do general party reputations for qualities such as competence, probity and cohesion matter in the competition for votes? Similarly, why, and to what extent, do the images of individual party leaders matter? How, and to what extent, do the mass media affect these images and party competition more generally? And how do the parties seek to communicate and market their images and policies? Each of these issues is closely connected with the phenomenon of political marketing, a subject which has commanded growing attention in recent years and on which we shall focus in due course. First, however, it is necessary to explore in turn the significance of party reputations, leadership images and the mass media.

General party images: the importance of establishing credibility

It is seldom sufficient for parties to compete for votes solely on the basis of their programmes of policy. While it is most unlikely that a party will have much chance of winning an election in a country like Britain if its overall ideological location is patently divergent from that of the median voter, citizens will evaluate not only the objectives and content of the policies on offer but also the likelihood of those policy objectives ever being delivered. Indeed, such evaluations may well become critical when it is difficult to perceive clear ideological differences between the major parties. In making these evaluations voters will consider both the possibility that parties will break their promises once elected and the actual capacity – irrespective of intentions – of politicians to deliver their promised policies or goals when in power (Laver 1997: 99). Voter judgements about the trustworthiness of parties will be influenced by their reputations for probity and veracity, while evaluations of party capacities to achieve their governing objectives will take into account reputations for competence and party cohesion. Overall, assessments of a party's probity, veracity, competence and cohesion combine to define its *credibility* in the eyes of the electorate, something which can be critically important to its electoral prospects. Any party lacking credibility for one or more of these reasons will undoubtedly find its support undermined; establishing credibility is therefore an important component of party competition.

Probity and veracity: can parties be trusted?

How far can voters trust parties to keep their promises? In reality, there is – contrary to the oft-repeated claims of cynics – little evidence to suggest that the veracity of parties is a serious problem in Britain. The simple truth is that, by and large, the parties tend to do as they say they will once elected (which is not necessarily to say that the consequences of their actions will be as positive as promised). Colin Rallings found that more than 70% of all manifesto pledges were implemented by governments winning office between 1945 and 1979 (1987: 13), while Richard Rose's detailed analysis of party government in the 1970s concluded in similar fashion that parties 'act consistently with the manifesto model of governing' (1980: 65). Longer-term analysis by Hans-Dieter Klingemann and his colleagues, though methodologically quite different, confirmed essentially the same argument; party governments (especially Conservative governments) in the UK tend to direct resources towards spending programmes in a way which is generally consistent with their manifesto pledges (Klingemann et al. 1994: 70–1; see also Chapter 9).

This is not surprising, on reflection, for party leaders have a very real incentive to redeem their pledges to the electorate; should they be seen to fail in this respect, they will quickly lose credibility and all future policy initiatives will be discounted accordingly in voters' reckonings. Indeed, recent history suggests the electorate may be quite unforgiving if it *does* gain the impression that a party cannot be trusted on its policy promises. For instance, having made much of the supposed danger of high taxation under a prospective Labour government in the 1992 general election campaign, the Conservatives were returned to power only to introduce substantial tax increases of their own within a year. The Opposition, unsurprisingly, went out of its way to point out the government's record of 'broken promises on tax', and evidence suggests that the message found its target: following the 1993 budget, three-quarters of respondents felt they had been 'misled' by the Tories on taxation (Denver 1998: 24). Worse still, the problem broadened from taxation to one of general credibility for the party, as 73% of voters concluded that the Conservatives could not be trusted to keep their promises by 1997; by contrast only 16% took such a dim view of Labour and just 11% of the Liberal Democrats.[1]

Related to the question of a party's veracity is its general reputation for *probity*. Probity is broader than veracity, though it encompasses it. The majority of electors are probably hard-headed enough to understand that politicians will from time to time act in an entirely self-interested and perhaps even corrupt way, but this may not damage a party fatally if most perceive such behaviour to be isolated, occasional and of no serious consequence to the general interest. It may be rather more dangerous, however, if such standards are regarded as pervasive. A party with a poor reputation for probity may come to be perceived as untrustworthy, unprincipled, opportunistic and unlikely to act in the public interest. Again, the Conservatives between 1992 and 1997 suffered a serious loss of reputation for general probity. A common theme of both Opposition criticism and media fascination during this period was 'Tory sleaze', a phenomenon which encompassed transgressions, both alleged and real, related to sexual peccadilloes, irregularities in party funding, the buying of influence within parliament, links with 'boardroom greed' and the abuse of ministerial power. As a result, between three-fifths and three-quarters of voters came to see John Major's party as 'sleazy and disreputable' (Denver 1998: 26–38; Farrell et al. 1998).

Economic competence, voting and party competition

Nevertheless, assessments of the veracity and probity of politicians will probably not trouble British voters so often as the question of whether they are *competent* to implement policy pledges. Assessments of competence to govern will depend on both the 'intrinsic feasibility and coherence of packages on offer' and, crucially, on recollections of previous performance in office (Laver 1997: 99–100). Nothing better illustrates the impact of perceived governing competence on voters in Britain than the field of economic management. The condition of the economy is almost certain to bear directly upon the lives and ambitions of most citizens, and there is an obvious prima facie case for supposing that competence to manage the national economy will figure prominently in the electoral ruminations of voters. Consequently, this is something which parties often place at the centre of their competitive strategies, and something which merits particular attention.

Since the 1970s the academic literature on the impact of economic affairs on voting behaviour has burgeoned, and not only in Britain. While there is a multiplicity of models specifying the precise ways in which economic factors impact on the electorate, most – if not all – either explicitly or implicitly assume that voters assess the competence of rival parties to manage the economy. Indeed, in many ways the economy is a competence issue par excellence, in that the main parties agree on the desirability of key economic objectives (stable prices, low unemployment, high growth, low real interest rates, a stable currency and balanced external trade flows), but each seeks to convince electors that it is the most competent to achieve those ends. This is consistent with the simple 'punishment-reward' (Fisher 1996a: 175) notion of economic voting; according to this, voters are assumed to reward a government which is perceived as competent in managing the economy, while they will punish one which is not. Politicians have most probably long since assumed that this was the case, though it was only in the 1970s that political scientists began to investigate the truth of the matter systematically.

The pioneering study was that conducted by Goodhart and Bhansali (1970), in which it was confirmed that government popularity could be predicted by just two basic indicators of economic performance, namely levels of unemployment and inflation. This seemed to illustrate perfectly and in a simple fashion the significance of economic competence for parties in power, but it was not long before their approach was shown to be simplistic rather than merely simple. William Miller and Tom Mackie, for instance, demonstrated that government popularity is habitually cyclical – as is implicit in colloquial notions of 'mid-term blues' – and this cycle may derive from a host of factors other than economic performance; in other words, the cycle itself was explanation enough and the apparent correlation between economic performance and government popularity was spurious (1973). Over time, however, critical reflection such as this resulted in greater methodological and theoretical sophistication, and subsequent research confirmed that the economy *was* a significant factor in the electorate's eyes. In the 1980s, researchers began to incorporate voters' subjective perceptions of economic performance into their models, and these were found to be especially powerful predictors of party support (though, of course, subjective perceptions and objective measures of economic performance are not unrelated [Sanders et al. 1992]). The best known subjective economic variable was developed by David Sanders and was known as aggregate personal economic expectations (henceforward APEE – indelicate though it may sound). APEE is central to an aggregate level model which has generally performed well in explaining monthly variations in the level of popular support for the government; that is, such variations have been shown to reflect strongly the feelings of voters about their own economic prospects during the period since 1979 (Sanders 1991). This is interesting for it brings to our attention the distinction in the literature between sociotropic and egocentric evaluations of economic factors. Both are subjective perceptions, but whereas the former relate to the overall state of the national economy, the latter focus on the voter's own economic circumstances. APEE, in these terms, is a prospective egocentric evaluation. Strictly speaking, therefore, it does not measure a party's reputation for economic competence; rather, it is logical to expect sociotropic evaluations to capture this more directly since voters will be assumed to perceive the government's (in)competence to be responsible, to a significant extent, for the prevailing state of the overall economy. Nevertheless, it is likely that egocentric evaluations are to some extent connected with broader perceptions of governmental competence in the economic sphere; this is because evaluations of one's personal economic prospects are likely to depend crucially on variables such as the rate of interest (of vital importance in a country in which an unusually high proportion of the population have mortgage repayments to make) and taxation levels (Sanders 1996: 207). These, along with inflation and job security, are all economic variables which British party politicians have habitually claimed an ability to control, and there can be little doubt that many voters will often (though not necessarily always) hold governments responsible for them. Thus, in broad terms, one of the factors influencing a voter's assessment of his or her personal economic prospects will be his or her view of the government's capacity to run the economy competently; the more competent the government, the better one's personal circumstances are likely to be. Seen in this light, APEE might constitute a direct cause of government popularity, but general economic competence will be influential at a further remove, thus:

General assessments of economic competence → Personal economic evaluations → Vote[2]

In short, a party's reputation for economic competence is almost certain to be central to its electoral prospects. Consequently, parties can be expected to expend considerable effort in boosting or sustaining their own reputation in this regard, while seeking to impugn those of their opponents at every opportunity. This, indeed, has been a key feature of competition in Britain in the contemporary era, and both major parties have benefited and suffered in these reputational terms over the past twenty years.

It is probably true that for much of the post-war era, and certainly for the period between 1979 and 1992, the Conservatives have held a distinct advantage over Labour when it comes to the reputation for governing competence, especially in the economic domain. As Anthony King says, this reputation was fed by Britain's history of financial crises, the four most serious of which after the Great War all occurred when Labour was in power, in 1931, 1949, 1967 and 1976 (1998: 185). These all turned in part on Labour governments' struggles to protect sterling in the face of problems in external trade. In 1976 the government of James Callaghan was humiliated by the International Monetary Fund, which dictated a reversal of economic priorities as a condition of providing loans to protect the national currency. But this was not the worst of it, for Labour's reputation for governing competence was damaged virtually beyond repair by the 'winter of discontent' in 1978–79, when public sector strikes destroyed the Callaghan government's incomes policy and brought misery to many ordinary citizens. These events not only contributed directly to the outcome of the forthcoming general election (May 1979), but generated an enduring legacy of general governing incompetence. By contrast, the Conservatives, as King says, 'knew how to run things'; they were widely perceived to understand how business and government worked, and how to maintain financial order. This proved an incalculable electoral advantage for the Tories during the three further election triumphs which ensued. For instance, David Sanders has demonstrated how the close electoral contest of April 1992 probably swung the Tories' way late in the campaign as voters grew fearful that Labour's supposed incompetence would damage their personal economic prospects. Moreover, he observed that:

> these doubts about Labour's economic competence spilt over into the non-economic sphere as well . . . in every issue area apart from homelessness, the percentage of respondents favouring the Conservatives rose (on average, by just under six points) and the percentage favouring Labour fell (on average, by three points). (Sanders 1993: 208)

However, the obstacle confronting Labour was lowered drastically after 1992 by the Conservatives' own dramatic loss of reputation. In part, as we have already seen, this turned on the question of whether they had misled the electorate in the 1992 campaign on the taxation issue. But at least as significant were the events of 16 September 1992 – 'Black Wednesday' as it quickly came to be known. This was the occasion when the Tories were ensnared in the kind of currency crisis to which Labour had been prone historically. In June 1990 John Major, then still Chancellor of the Exchequer, had succeeded in persuading a reluctant Margaret Thatcher that sterling should enter the Exchange Rate Mechanism of the European Monetary System (ERM) at a relatively high rate against the German Deutschmark (£1 = DM2.95). Though it was hailed as a central plank of the government's economic strategy in the election manifesto, by the late summer of 1992 sterling was coming under increasing pressure on the international currency markets as UK exports languished. This pressure came to a head on Black Wednesday when Major (now Prime Minister) and his Chancellor Norman Lamont fought desperately to stave off the inevitable spectre of devaluation. Billions of pounds were borrowed and spent on supporting sterling, while the rate of interest was raised from 10% to 12%, and then again to 15%, in the space of a few hours. But to no avail. Amid a welter of bitter Tory recriminations against German central bankers and politicians, Lamont eventually capitulated by withdrawing sterling from the ERM and allowing the currency to find its own (much lower) level on the currency markets. While the technical detail of the episode was beyond most observers, few citizens had any difficulty in perceiving gross incompetence in the way the government handled the issue. In a single day, the Conservatives' enduring reputation for economic competence had been reduced to tatters, and the Opposition took pleasure in pointing the fact out as loudly and as often as it could manage (aided by much of the national media). The Shadow Chancellor Gordon Brown, for instance, lost no time in declaring that the Tories had forfeited 'all claim to economic competence and credibility', and the evidence undoubtedly suggests that the electorate took little persuading. While the Conservatives had retained a 13-point lead over Labour on the question of which party was best equipped to handle the country's economic difficulties in April 1992, and still held a 5-point lead in early September, Labour took an 18-point lead in October (Denver 1998: 20). It extended and retained this substantial lead over the Conservatives right through to the election of May 1997. Moreover, this competence rating correlated closely with a general preference for Labour in the opinion polls. In short, Black Wednesday demonstrates incontrovertibly the importance of reputations for governing competence which parties develop; these images can be vital in the game of party competition and may even rival general ideological location in times of relative ideological convergence by the major protagonists.

Reputations for party cohesion

Before turning to the impact of individual party leaders, there is one further type of general party reputation which merits attention – the reputation for cohesion. Though no party in the democratic world is monolithic, a party's currency can be seriously devalued in the eyes of the electorate if it is seen to be dangerously divided. This is so for at least two reasons. First, a legislative programme cannot be regarded as credible by voters if they sense that the party lacks the minimum degree of internal cohesion necessary to enact the policy promises made. Second, a party's general competence to govern may be questioned by voters who feel that it lacks the cohesion even to devise clear policies on certain matters. For instance, just such a perception almost certainly damaged the governing Conservatives badly in the contest for office in 1997. There can be no doubt that the issue of European integration came to divide the parliamentary Conservative Party during the 1990s, both on the backbenches and frontbenches (see Chapter 6). Few observers of the 1997 election campaign doubted that the frequently aired differences within Conservative ranks contributed to the party's heaviest twentieth-century defeat at the polls (Norton 1998: 95–6); it is certain, moreover, that those responsible for devising and implementing the party's election campaign strategy felt that the media's fascination with in-fighting over Europe suppressed the prominence of issues and themes they would have preferred to place at the forefront of the political agenda (such as economic recovery). As a consequence, many argued that, while the issue of Europe per se mattered little to most electors (Norris et al. 1999: 128), the evidence of party disunity which it conjured up left many disillusioned with the governing Conservatives. Again, the ERM fiasco seems to have been a turning point for the Tories' party image in this respect: whereas just 26% of respondents surveyed considered the party divided in May and June 1992, fully 77% did by the end of the same year. This public perception of disunity was maintained right through to the election of May 1997, moreover. By contrast, Labour's old image as a party prone to ideological conflict was eroded during the same period until barely one-third of respondents viewed it as divided (Denver 1998: 27).

Leadership reputations and implications for party images

So, a party's reputations for probity, competence and cohesion help to determine its overall credibility and can be safely assumed to figure prominently in the electoral reflections of the British voter. Less frequently considered by political scientists, but rarely overlooked by journalists and politicians themselves, are the personal reputations of party leaders. Acres of media coverage may be devoted to the personalities and abilities of party leaders (Seymour-Ure 1997: 90–6), yet academics have remained curiously detached. In part this oversight reflected a general conviction, at least in the 1970s and 1980s, that structural determinants of the vote (such as social background and ideological predisposition) counted for far more, and in part it reflected the feeling that leadership evaluations were often caused simply by prior partisanship. That is, for many voters, partisan affinities were assumed to affect the way in which they perceived the respective merits of party leaders. Until recently, therefore, few academics engaged in detailed studies of the independent impact of leaders' images.

That said, Butler and Stokes demonstrated as long ago as the 1960s that voters could be 'cross-pressured' by favouring leaders from parties other than the one they generally preferred. While it was true that partisan identity generally tended to count for more than leadership evaluations (something which is broadly confirmed at the aggregate level by the victory of parties whose leaders were personally less popular than their counterparts in 1945, 1970 and 1979), it was also notable that the incidence of electoral defection from preferred party was greater among cross-pressured voters (1974: 364). That is, voters preferring party A, but rating the leader of party B higher than the leader of party A, proved less likely to vote for A than voters preferring both party A *and* its leader. This suggested a prima facie case for a limited, but authentically independent, leadership effect on voting behaviour. It was the 1980s, however, before political scientists in Britain grew more interested in the electoral impact of leaders, and they did so for a number of reasons. First, the evidence of partisan and class dealignment after 1974 generally induced researchers to investigate the impact of short-term influences on electoral choice; like issue effects, leader effects (which plainly vary from election to election) had to merit renewed investigation in these terms (Newton 1993: 149). Second, there emerged a growing perception that British parliamentary elections were generally becoming more 'presidential' in their growing emphasis on the direct contest between party leaders (Webb 1992b: 276). Third, and relatedly, influential models of general party transformation such as Kirchheimer's 'catch-all' model (1966) and Panebianco's 'electoral-

professional' model (1988) emphasized the growing autonomy of party leaders from the grass roots (see Chapters 7 and 8).

In general, the research conducted on leader effects since the 1980s has,
despite its methodological variety, concurred in the view that such effects are
modest but significant (Graetz and McAllister 1987; Stewart and Clarke 1992;
Mughan 1995). A good example is provided by Bartle et al.'s study of the 1997
general election. They borrow the notion of a 'funnel of causality' from
American electoral research (Miller and Shanks 1996) in which leader effects
are deemed to influence individual voters only *after* the impact of factors
such as social background, ideological predisposition and evaluation of party
performance in managing the economy. While this inevitably minimizes the
statistical impact of leadership evaluations, they nonetheless found that overall assessments of who would make the best prime minister impacted
significantly on individual voters (Bartle et al. 1997: 21). Perhaps more significantly, they point out that while the effect of leadership evaluations on
individuals may be relatively slight compared to other factors, the *aggregate*
impact on the electorate as a whole could still be considerable. This would be
the case if the distribution of such evaluations was clearly skewed in favour
of one leader over another. Thus, although a pro-Blair evaluation significantly increased the probability of an individual voting for Labour in 1997,
this fact alone would have made little difference to the overall election outcome if the majority of voters had preferred John Major (or even, perhaps, if
the electorate had been split equally between the two men). However, the
individual-level impact coupled with Blair's clear personal advantage over
Major (an 18-point lead on the eve of poll) probably helped Labour. In fact,
Bartle estimates that Labour gained 273,000 extra votes across the 640 constituencies in mainland Britain as a result of leadership effects and, assuming
these were equally distributed across all constituencies, some six Labour MPs
'may well owe their seat to favourable evaluations of Tony Blair' (op. cit.: 25).
In the context of an election in which Labour achieved a 179 seat majority
over all other parties, this hardly seems earth-shattering news, but one could
certainly imagine scenarios in which half a dozen seats might determine the
overall outcome of the election; close contests such as those of 1950, 1964 and
February 1974 could have turned on the impact of leadership effects of similar magnitude to those reported in 1997 (though, of course, it should not be
assumed that leadership effects always *will* be of similar strength from one
election to another).

Bartle and his colleagues make a further point about leadership effects
which serves to take us back into the territory of more general party reputations. That is, quite apart from the narrowly conceived leadership effects we
have been exploring up to now, a leader's impact can also lie further back in
the 'funnel of causality' by virtue of his or her effect on general party image.
Thus, Labour's general reputation improved markedly between the elections
of 1992 and 1997, and we might plausibly suppose that this in no small measure reflected the impact of Tony Blair on the party. For instance, under Blair not
only did Labour's reputation for competent leadership improve, but the

party's images in respect of 'extremism' and internal disunity were also significantly enhanced (King 1998: 203). The question of how 'extreme' Labour was seen to be – a potentially serious issue in the context of an electorate with normally distributed core values and centripetal party competition – partly reflected Blair's determination to shift the party into centrist ideological space, but it also hinged on the leader's particular style of party management. That is, Blair quickly demonstrated his ruthlessness at imposing party discipline and continuing the work started by Neil Kinnock in marginalizing the radicals in his party. Similarly, while the importance of a party's reputation for cohesion has already been discussed, it is worth adding that such a reputation will again reflect in no small measure the managerial skills of the leaders. Thus, while John Major was often depicted as indecisive and vacillating in the face of his recalcitrant colleagues, Blair was viewed as utterly determined to impose a uniform party line. As Philip Norton has said of Major, he was essentially a 'balancer' who sought to maintain some kind of equilibrium between the various intra-party groups, but his many critics viewed such an approach as disastrous – and frequently said so in public (Norton 1998: 96). By contrast, a priority of Tony Blair's from the moment he assumed leadership of the Labour Party was party unity, 'and both the shadow cabinet and the PLP were run in a strictly controlled manner from 1994 onwards' (Seyd 1998: 66).

So, to summarize the overall argument so far: a number of factors influence electoral choice and parties competing for votes seek to exploit these factors to best advantage. While their ideological locations constitute the strategic foundations of party competition, reputations matter as well. In particular, the credibility of a party's policy statements and its general competence to govern will concern voters, and voter assessments of these qualities will depend on their opinions of the general trustworthiness, veracity and probity of parties, and on their judgements about a party's capacity for cohesive and disciplined action. Furthermore, leadership images may well be expected to have a special bearing on the overall reputation of parties. It is not surprising, therefore, that modern vote-maximizing and office-seeking parties are concerned to market their corporate and individual leaders' images in increasingly sophisticated ways. But it is crucial to note that when political parties in advanced industrial democracies seek to communicate their ideological positions and party images to the public, they do not do so in a direct and unmediated way; rather, information about parties and politicians is channelled largely via the mass media. Thus, a party's public image will very likely depend critically on how it is portrayed in the media. This prompts an important question to which attention must be devoted: do the media affect voters and, if so, how?

The role and impact of the media

Pippa Norris reports research suggesting four possible 'avenues' of influence through which the media can affect public opinion: through providing information about political issues and candidates, and thereby enhancing voters' cognitive understanding of politics; through defining the contemporary agenda of issues which are debated; through framing responsibility for policy successes and failures; and through influencing the final electoral choices which voters make. The first three of these avenues may help shape the final avenue of overall choice; indeed, a causal sequence is implicit, with one 'avenue' of influence leading logically to the next (Norris 1996: 216). But to what extent do these avenues of influence operate in Britain?

First, can the media enhance voters' cognitive understanding of politics? Evidence gathered during the 1992 and 1997 general election campaigns confirms that a person's level of political knowledge is significantly associated with high levels of attention to news broadcasts, especially to 'high brow' current affairs programmes (Norris 1996: 218–19) and quality 'broadsheet' newspapers (Norris et al. 1999: 104). But in stating this superficially impressive fact we immediately run up against a problem which dogs research in the field of media effects, that of causality. Thus it might well be that attention to quality media output on political affairs directly enhances an individual's cognitive understanding of the issues involved, but an equally plausible explanation for the relationship is that those who are already most politically interested and knowledgeable are more likely to consume such material. Recent research suggests the latter alternative may well be a true assessment; even so, it remains possible (probable even) that 'in the long-term we might expect a virtuous cycle as those who regularly keep up with current affairs will be more likely to be interested and knowledgeable' (op. cit.: 96). In other words, the most avid consumers of current affairs output may already be well informed, but how are they to maintain this political knowledge if not through paying close attention to the news? This implies that political education of this type is a function which parties must share with the mass media; indeed, it is probable that they are the junior partners in this educational process, for most citizens report non-partisan TV channels as their primary source of political information now (Gunter et al. 1994). In 1997, two-thirds of British voters claimed to see a TV news programme every day during the election campaign, and one-third claimed to pay 'a great deal' or 'quite a lot' of attention to the political content of such broadcasts.[3]

What of the agenda-setting capacity of the media in Britain? Such effects are crucial to the thinking of party strategists since it has been argued by some commentators that, while it is not always easy to change the minds of electors, it is possible to change what is *on* their minds (McCombs and Shaw 1972). That is, direct persuasion of voters is difficult to achieve since voters are largely assumed to know their own minds about issues which are important to them, so the party's task becomes one of shifting the agenda of political debate to the issues calculated to most favour it. In the language of political science, parties will seek to ensure that the issues which are salient in an election campaign – that is, which are at the forefront of the agenda and weigh most heavily in the considerations of the electorate – are likely to benefit them. Typically, for instance, we would expect Labour to benefit electorally at times when issues such as education and health are salient, since these are issues on which its policies have traditionally been more popular than those of the Conservatives, whereas the reverse is true of defence or law and order issues (Budge and Farlie 1983).

But if agenda-setting battles are an important element of the process of party competition, it should be noted that the parties themselves are not the sole contestants; it is widely assumed that newspapers and the broadcast media themselves are important players in the agenda-setting game since they also bring issues to the fore while pushing others into the background. Surprisingly, however, the research to date suggests that the agenda-setting capacity of the British media is not as strong as might be suspected. While it seems that in America a shift in the media's agenda can influence the electorate's view of which issues are important (Iyengar and Kinder 1987), neither William Miller, in his detailed study of the 1987 election campaign, nor Pippa Norris, in her much briefer analysis of 1992 BES panel data, found firm evidence of similar effects in Britain (Miller et al. 1990; Norris 1996: 221–2). It is true that Norris et al. uncovered experimental evidence suggesting that exposure to television news has a potential capacity to influence the British public's issue agenda (1999: 122), yet on the whole voters seemed to take a very different view to the media of which were the important issues during the 1997 election campaign (op. cit.: 128).

In any case, problems of causality generally plague our understanding of agenda-setting since, even where associations can be found between the shifting agendas of, respectively, voters and the media, it is not easy to say which is cause and which is effect. Do the media simply pick up on and reflect changes in public opinion, or do they actively catalyse such changes? And what of the role of the parties themselves in all this? How successful are they at setting or constraining the agenda? Norris and her colleagues argue that it is probably becoming more difficult for the parties to set the agenda as the press becomes increasingly autonomous; despite the best efforts of the parties to focus on an agenda of policy debate, the media is more and more inclined to concentrate on the campaign itself (the conduct of the campaign, party strategies, opinion polls, candidate personalities, intra-party tensions and so on [op. cit.: 82–4]). Overall, it is fair to say that an increasingly intense battle to set the agenda is fought out between the parties, the media and other actors such as interest groups. The media are to a considerable extent autonomous of the parties in establishing their agenda, but it is not an agenda that coincides closely with what the electorate believes to be important. To this extent, the media's agenda-setting influence may be regarded as surprisingly feeble. More perniciously, however, the failure to reflect the concerns of the electorate may even contribute to widespread dissatisfaction with media coverage of election campaigns (Norris 1998: 138–40).

The third stage in the process of potential media influence involves the framing of responsibility; that is, the media provide a lens through which citizens view the relentless turmoil of political dispute, and it seems logical to assume that they are in a position to influence mass perceptions of which party (if any) deserves the blame for the shortcomings of public policy and which (if any) the credit for its achievements. This reflects the fact that the mass media as a whole seek to perform the function of scrutinizing both government and opposition. Such a task entails the more or less rigorous examination of public policies, both proposed and implemented; implicitly, at least, the attribution of fault for policy shortcomings will often follow from this. The attempt to criticize and attribute blame in this way is most obvious in the openly partisan manner in which some newspapers cover political affairs, but even non-partisan broadcasters operate on the assumption that politicians of all partisan persuasions must be interrogated in a highly adversarial manner if scrutiny is to be effective. Quite whether the tense encounters between party spokespersons and broadcasters which this approach engenders succeed in getting at the truth behind complex public policy questions is beside the point: the media agent in such cases is clearly intent on attributing political responsibility for public policy.

In particular, it should be noted that many of the key reputational aspects of party competition hinge on precisely this aspect of media influence. Engaged and critical debate in the media, designed to frame responsibility for public policy, inevitably provides the voter with a series of cues about the competence, probity and cohesion of parties – not to mention the overall credibility of their policy programmes and qualities of their leaders. Not all voters will be equally attentive to the detail of such media debate, and no single voter will pay equal heed to each and every policy issue under the media's critical spotlight, but few are likely to remain completely untouched by the unending cycle of claim and counter-claim which is reported and analysed by the media. Once again, the question of economic competence furnishes relevant evidence: Sanders et al. discovered that press coverage of economic issues, while not directly affecting aggregate levels of government popularity, could significantly influence aggregate personal economic expectations (1993: 208–9). We have already noted, of course, how personal economic expectations might flow from perceptions of the government's economic competence, and in a separate study Sanders and Neil Gavin confirmed that 'changes in party preferences are strongly related to changes in perceived management competence and that competence perceptions are, in turn, clearly influenced by the overall balance of television news coverage' (Gavin and Sanders 1995: 16). In other words, in helping to frame responsibility for economic performance, the media influence voter assessments of governing parties' competence. John Curtice and Holli Semetko came to similar conclusions about the impact of the tabloid press in 1992: thus, even after objective economic experiences of individual voters were taken into account, they still found 'that pro-Labour tabloid readers were less likely to give a favourable personal or general economic evaluation between 1987 and 1992' (1994: 55). Research findings such as these confirm that the media can affect party reputations through helping to frame responsibility for public policies. There is no doubt that modern political parties well understand this and endeavour to be adept at working through the media in order to frame responsibility.

The final avenue of potential media influence over the electorate is that of direct persuasion in the choice of which party or candidate to vote for. The likelihood of persuasion would seem to be greatest in the case of the largely partisan national press, and indeed it has not been difficult for researchers in Britain to uncover evidence of a statistical association between the newspaper a person usually reads and the political party he or she prefers. For instance, Curtice and Semetko found that 64% of those reading a pro-Conservative tabloid newspaper in 1992 voted for the Conservatives, whereas 60% of those reading a pro-Labour tabloid voted Labour (Curtice and Semetko 1994: 44). Once again, the obvious difficulty with this type of analysis has always been deciding which way causality flows; is the reader of a pro-Conservative paper influenced to vote for the party because of the persuasive effect of the press coverage to which she or he is daily exposed, or does she or he prefer to buy a pro-Conservative paper because of a prior partisan predisposition? In fact, the prevailing orthodoxy in the research literature since the 1960s has been that the latter is more likely to be the case. This has produced what David Denver refers to as the 'filter' model of media effects on voters. According to this, the main effect of the media is to reinforce existing preferences; even where readers encounter media information at variance with their precon-ceptions, the 'cognitive dissonance' which might result can be dispelled by conscious or unconscious attempts to screen out the dissonant information. This might be achieved in a number of ways, including: selective exposure to media messages (for instance, only buying newspapers known to share sim-ilar biases); selective perception of messages (by overlooking the threat to one's beliefs implied by certain messages or even misinterpreting messages in such a way that they seem to support rather than challenge those beliefs); and selective retention of media messages (that is, remembering only those mes-sages which conform to existing beliefs) (1989: 98–9). For these reasons, it would seem that the media cannot really persuade any voter to change party preference, but they may help cement existing voter loyalties.

There have been dissenting voices, however. For instance, Dunleavy and Husbands have argued strongly that 'the relationship seems too close to be attributable solely or even mainly to partisan self-selection into readership' (1985: 114). William Miller and his colleagues discovered some concrete evi-dence to support this claim in so far as the swing to the Conservatives in the period before the 1987 election was most marked among readers of the main pro-Conservative tabloids (Miller et al. 1990: 88). Similarly, Ken Newton demonstrated that significant newspaper effects on vote remained even after controlling for the impact of other political and social variables (1991: 68). More recently, however, Norris et al. have placed these arguments in per-spective by reporting panel study findings more consistent with the old orthodoxy of 'reinforcement, not change':

> By reinforcing partisan preferences the steady pattern of newspaper coverage func-tions, like the influence of class, as a mechanism to help structure voting behaviour. Yet, as shown by the classic case of *The Sun*, the ability of the press to switch their readers' political leanings are (*sic*) extremely limited. (1999: 184)

However, these same authors have unearthed interesting evidence of the persuasive power of television. Employing experimental research designs
unusual in political science, they show that exposure to TV news broadcasts
biased positively towards one or the other of the main political parties produces significant short-term improvements in the subject's perceived images
of those parties (op. cit.: 139). This is interesting, since their research strategy
and method avoid the traditional problems of causality, and because their
findings relate to TV – an area usually considered less likely to have direct
powers of persuasion given the non-partisan nature of the medium. On the
other hand, this research must be treated cautiously, since the attitudinal
effects discussed are very short-term, and it is impossible to be sure how
long they might endure. Moreover, experimental research is always susceptible to the criticism that the subject's behaviour is observed under artificial
conditions not resembling those in the real world.

Overall, it should be clear from this review of the evidence that the media
can influence voters' perceptions of parties and politicians in a variety of
ways, and thereby help shape their overall partisan preferences. Although
evidence of the British media's capacity to change people's party preferences
directly is less than convincing, there is little doubt that they play significant
roles in providing voters with political information, setting political agendas
and framing responsibility. In any case, regardless of the objective impact of
the media, it is plain that party strategists believe the media to be critically
important. This being the case, the implications for vote-maximizing parties
are obvious: they must endeavour to organize themselves and their operations in such a way as to best project their desired images in the media.
Parties well recognize that their own capacities to educate, set agendas, frame
responsibility and persuade voters are shared with the mass media. Thus, in
order to cultivate their desired public reputations, parties are obliged to
engage in a four-sided struggle for influence with: rivals for office; non-partisan interest groups; and the media. Each protagonist is jealous of its own
autonomy: in particular, the parties seek as much influence as possible over
media coverage of politics, wishing always to place the most favourable possible 'spin' on news items, while media representatives – except where
blatantly partisan – will attempt to resist charges of bias or manipulation by
politicians. Thus, party competition is about far more than strategic shifts in
ideology calculated to maximize voter appeal; it is also about the day-to-day
business of projecting and protecting images and reputations in the face of
withering attacks by party political opponents and media critics. This
explains why contemporary British political parties often seem obsessed with
the twin arts of media presentation and political marketing.

Party competition and the emergence of political marketing

Much academic attention has been devoted to the development of election
campaigning in Britain since the 1980s (see especially Franklin 1994;

Scammell 1995; Kavanagh 1995; Rosenbaum 1997; Scammell 1999), reflecting widespread interest in the evolution of campaign methods and styles. Prior to the era of mass access to television (around 1960), election campaigns were characterized by limited (and relatively late) preparation; the use of traditional party bureaucrats and volunteer activists; direct communication with electors through public meetings, rallies and canvassing (plus indirect communication via partisan newspapers); and relatively little central coordination of campaigning across the country. Televisualization of campaigning gradually altered this traditional model, mainly by producing a far greater emphasis on indirect communication with voters via TV, but it was really only after 1979 that the modernization and professionalization of campaigning took a 'quantum leap' forward in Britain (Scammell 1995: ch. 2). By 1987, both major parties had adopted a model of campaigning which differed from the traditional approach in a number of important respects, including: careful campaign preparation centred around the role of specialist campaign committees established well in advance of the election; greater exploitation of media and marketing professionals; a 'nationalization' of campaigning with resources and coordinating power concentrated at the centre; greater emphasis on the party leader; and television as the dominant channel of communication. During the 1990s, campaigning techniques continued to develop with the arrival of new telecommunications technology (especially cable and satellite technology, and the Internet) helping to generate innovations such as the 'narrowcasting' of specific campaign messages on targeted groups of voters.

   More generally, the advent of the 'permanent campaign' has rendered the influence of marketing professionals so pervasive that the adaptation of party messages to suit target constituencies has reached new heights. Specifically, it can be said that campaigning, at least for the major parties, has evolved into fully fledged *political marketing*. Though often used as a form of shorthand for modern advertising and promotion techniques, writers like O'Shaughnessy (1990), Scammell (1995) and Wring (1996a, 1996b) have argued that there is more to it than this; rather, it entails a qualitative shift in the strategic influence of marketing professionals such as opinion researchers. While there is nothing particularly new in British parties using professional pollsters to gauge public preferences,[4] hitherto the product remained sacrosanct in so far as the underlying strategic aim was to 'sell' the existing package of policies and leaders. The adoption of a political marketing approach implies that consumer demand is now privileged; it is the product rather than the market which is regarded as malleable, as the emphasis shifts to the satisfaction of consumer wants (Scammell 1995: 8–9). This seems to imply a model of party competition which is overwhelmingly preference-accommodating rather than preference-shaping, and it is possible that Labour's 'leapfrog' into the ideological centre-ground in 1997 confirms that genuine marketing of political parties has arrived. What else, other than the influence of market research, would have induced Labour to move so far out of its traditional ideological domain? On the other hand, 1997 might be thought of as some kind of

aberration reflecting a particular set of historical circumstances, rarely – if
ever – to be repeated. After all, both orthodox party competition theory and
empirical research suggest there are limits to the malleability of the product;
rational party strategists must recognize that party programmes can only
retain credibility if they adapt within the bounds of enduring ideological reputations. In fact, the need for credibility is also of paramount importance
from the perspective of political marketing theory (Scammell 1999: 729). It is
likely, then, that even though modern parties will draw increasingly on
market research in devising competitive strategies, they will conform to the
need for credibility. Indeed, Scammell prefers (surely correctly) to see political marketing as a complement to programmatic strategy:

> In reality, political marketing and its associated opinion research rarely pick the
> details of policies; rather, the 'marketing approach' sets the parameters, suggests
> the stance and tone of policy, and recommends shifts of emphasis to play up or
> down parts of the already selected programme. (1995: 10)

This still implies, however, that political marketing experts have taken on a
strategic significance for the major British parties. Indeed, it is abundantly
clear that the major British parties have evolved into highly professional,
market-oriented organizations which are geared to the needs of virtually permanent campaigning. In a number of ways these transformations bring to
mind Angelo Panebianco's model of the 'electoral-professional party' (1988:
264). Although no British party conforms absolutely with each detail of
Panebianco's model, in its essentials it is broadly instructive: major parties in
the country are driven by the desire for electoral success and deploy the latest
in coordinated professional campaign sophistication in order to achieve their
goals (Webb 1992b). In Chapter 7, we see that such a transformation also carries implications for the distribution of power within parties, but here we
concentrate on developments in the main parties' approaches to campaigning
and communications.

Labour

The party which now best exemplifies a highly professional and media-ori-
ented approach to political marketing is undoubtedly Labour, though it was
not always thus. For many years, the best that professional expertise had to
offer was eschewed by the party; in part this flowed from sheer financial
necessity, since Labour has rarely been in a position to match the Tories for
resources, but in part it also reflected a principled distrust of sharp-suited
marketing professionals. This sentiment was never so prevalent within the
Conservative Party, and Labour has therefore faced the greater challenge in
adapting to the electoral-professional requirements of an era of extended
party competition. The disastrous 1983 election campaign – weak in terms of
party, leadership and policy images, and amateurishly organized – marked
the nadir of Labour's post-war electoral fortunes, and it most clearly embodied the problems that the party faced in adapting to the new era. Between

1983 and 1987, Labour took the first steps towards electoral-professional adaptation under the leadership of Neil Kinnock. After another election defeat, the pace of reform picked up and continued after the subsequent defeat of April 1992, finally coming to triumphant fruition in May 1997. To be sure, this success was also built on policy adaptation, as we have seen, but the significance of the party's marketing operations should not be understated. It is clear that this process of adaptation (or, rather, transformation) has been quite deliberate and self-conscious. The painful experience of four consecutive general election defeats and nearly two decades of exclusion from national office engendered a determination on the part of one leader after another (Kinnock, the late John Smith and then Tony Blair) to effect the reforms which they believed to be necessary. Furthermore, the impact of a number of key party strategists, advisors and professional consultants, such as Peter Mandelson, Philip Gould, Patricia Hewitt, Deborah Mattinson, Charles Clarke, Chris Powell and Alistair Campbell has now been well documented (see, for instance, Hughes and Wintour 1990; Webb 1992b; Shaw 1994; Scammell 1995; Kavanagh 1995), and indeed, frequently parodied, so emblematic has it become. The professionals' impact on policy development (as well as presentation), organizational centralization, the standardization and professionalization of campaigning, and even the party's relationship with its affiliated trade unions, is plain to see. Their influence over policy and strategy has usually been the most controversial aspect of this, going back to the role played by Labour's Shadow Communications Agency in the Policy Review process of 1987–89 (Hughes and Wintour 1990; Shaw 1994). While it may be true that no British pollsters have ever achieved the political influence of their counterparts in America (Kavanagh 1995: 142), it is widely acknowledged that focus group research conducted by Philip Gould became increasingly important during the 1990s. In particular, this is credited with helping forge Labour's strategic goal of targeting potential swing voters in 'middle income, middle Britain' for the 1997 election (Seyd 1998: 60).

In the 1997 election campaign, the professionalization of Labour's political marketing reached new heights. This reflected not only the harsh lessons taught by repeated electoral failure, but a willingness to learn directly from the campaigning approach of sister-parties overseas, especially the Democrats in the USA. While too much can be made of the 'Clintonization' of New Labour – senior staff were well aware that much that was normal to US campaigning would not export well to Britain – there is no doubt that it influenced new approaches to activities such as fund-raising and telephone canvassing (Braggins et al. 1993).[5] The party shifted its media and campaign operations away from the national headquarters in Walworth Road (southeast London) to a large open-plan office development at Millbank Tower on the Thames embankment, and within a short distance of Westminster and various news media offices.[6] The Millbank operation incorporated purpose-built media facilities and was staffed by more than 500 employees, many of whom were on secondment (from affiliated trade unions) or were temporary; post-election, central staffing was quickly trimmed to 179. In addition to those on the payroll, the efforts of some 360 volunteers were coordinated from Millbank. Operations during the campaign were organized horizontally around a number of 'task-forces' with specific responsibilities.[7] Thus, Labour's central campaign staff were certainly significantly greater in number than at previous elections, and their work was structured in a carefully devised fashion and planned well in advance. Moreover, orchestration of the national campaign was probably greater than hitherto, with regional and local figures kept meticulously 'on-message' through a variety of personal, computer and telephone links. One of the innovations of Labour's 1997 campaign which attracted a certain amount of media attention was the computer program *Excalibur*. This was a resource that was deemed vital to the party's 'rapid-rebuttal' capability; in essence, it was a comprehensive database of up-to-date material on political issues and personalities, which the party could plunder whenever it needed to provide a swift response to its adversaries' attacks. The intention was, therefore, to neutralize such attacks as quickly as possible, and thereby protect the credibility and reputation of party leaders and policies. The centrality of election campaigning to New Labour's entire style of organization and operation was underlined when the party chose to shift its national headquarters from Walworth Road to Millbank on a permanent basis in the autumn of 1997.[8]

The Conservatives

The Conservatives have generally effected a far smoother transition to the age of political marketing, although in recent years they have clearly been surpassed by Labour. In fact, readiness to adopt the latest in campaigning and communication techniques is not in itself a new feature of the party. As Richard Cockett says:

> The record of the party's use of advertising and communications techniques for publicity is, therefore, one of extraordinary innovation – certainly compared to that of the other British political parties. Belying its name, the party had always been prepared to embrace the most modern publicity methods and techniques to gain political advantage. (1994: 577)

Nonetheless, the arrival at the helm of Margaret Thatcher in the 1970s generated a qualitative shift in the party's exploitation of modern campaigning techniques. In particular, the role of experts such as the Saatchi and Saatchi advertising agency attracted an enormous amount of attention after 1979, and this is widely regarded as having heralded a new age of professionalization in British political campaigning (although, as we have seen, it took Labour the best part of a decade to follow suit). Although the Conservatives had used advertising professionals before, Saatchis were unique in being the first to assume full-time control of all aspects of publicity and opinion research, and in being heavily involved between elections. This enabled them to work with the leadership on long-term campaign strategy. As Scammell puts it, 'they effectively transformed the role of marketing specialists in

British politics from technicians to strategists' (1999: 733). Their sustained relationship with the party was later supplemented by the introduction of new public relations and marketing approaches to the staging of annual conferences, direct mailing of targeted supporters, telephone canvassing and computer-aided communications (op. cit.: 576). The election of 1987 provides interesting evidence of the Tories' advantage over Labour in marketing at that time; even though Labour's new Director of Communications, Peter Mandelson, was revolutionizing campaigning, opinion research still made little impact on his party's policy or strategy in 1987 (O'Shaughnessy 1990). However, the same could certainly not be said of Margaret Thatcher's Tories: a qualitative research study entitled *Life in Britain* played a decisive role in persuading Thatcher to adopt a radical manifesto (including commitments to further privatization, rent reform, educational change and the poll tax) in the belief that this would demonstrate the party had not run out of policy ideas after eight years in office (Scammell 1995: 119–22). Under John Major in 1992 and 1997, the influence of the marketing experts was maintained over issue terrain and campaigning style (op. cit.: 242). There is no doubting the party's continuing commitment to the techniques of modern political marketing.

The Liberal Democrats

No other parties in Britain have taken the art of professional political marketing as far as the major two parties, not least because of the cost implications. Labour and the Conservatives are considerably wealthier than any other party and can spend far more on their election campaigns; in 1997, the Conservatives spent £28.3m nationally and Labour £26m, while the Liberal Democrats' campaign cost just £2.3m (Neill 1998: Table 3.10). This imposes obvious constraints on investment in advertising, opinion research and professionalization. For instance, in 1997 the Liberal Democrats were unable to devote many resources to fixed sites at which election posters could be displayed, although they did attempt to compensate for this by use of mobile 'poster vans' which they moved around the country to key seats (Bonham-Carter 1997: 3). In total, the party spent just £300,000 on advertising during the campaign, compared to the £14.4 million which the Tories devoted to all forms of advertising and the £5.7 million spent by Labour.

Despite this funding gap, even the Liberal Democrats are showing signs of a growing sophistication and professionalization in their marketing operations. Three features of recent campaigns demonstrate this. First, the party has become notably more inclined to invest resources in opinion research. For the 1997 election, this was started years in advance of the expected polling day and focused particularly on target seats where the party felt its best chances of electoral success lay. Second, the party ran a more coordinated national campaign. This was judged vital both to the strategy of targeting resources and efforts onto selected seats and to the goal of keeping all contributions to the party's campaign 'on message'. A new national 'Communications Centre' was established at the national party headquarters in Cowley Street

(Westminster) and this was the engine that drove the coordinated campaign. Its work, moreover, was supported by a network of regional media coordinators. For Jane Bonham-Carter, a key figure in the party's campaign team in 1997, this resulted in a 'highly centralized campaign with a strong central command':

> Press releases, responses to events and sound bites, consistently hammering home these facts, were coordinated through the Communications Centre, as was the briefing of spokespeople. This meant that there were no competing groups within the party attempting to control the message. (op. cit.: 1)

The third feature of contemporary Liberal Democrat campaigns which shows how they have moved some way towards professional political marketing is the party's growing willingness to focus on the leadership. In Paddy Ashdown in 1992 and 1997, its strategists were convinced that they had a highly marketable electoral commodity, and the leader's personal campaign was judged crucial to the overall party campaign. Accordingly, Ashdown started a series of regional visits to target seats a year in advance of the expected 1997 election and a Party Election Broadcast was devoted entirely to an 'unashamed' attempt to highlight the leader's personal virtues (Holme and Holmes 1997: 10). In short, while it would be an exaggeration to suggest that the Liberal Democrats conform closely to the electoral-professional model, there is no doubt that they are professionalizing their approach to political marketing.

Conclusion

This draws to a close the assessment of how parties compete. We know that underlying party ideologies play a key role in this process, and that the reputations which parties and their leaders maintain for qualities such as competence, trustworthiness and cohesion also enter into the equation, since these things help determine credibility. Given also that each of these factors impresses itself on the electorate through the lens of the media, modern British parties inevitably take pains to market themselves in a highly professional and sophisticated way. Expertise in media skills is especially highly valued, as the ubiquity of the parties' 'spin-doctors' seems to bear witness. However, there is almost certainly more to modern political marketing than mere advice on the presentation of leaders and policies; professional market research has demonstrably wielded strategic influence over the parties' programmatic developments.

Confirmation of the importance to party competition of the factors discussed in Chapters 3, 4 and 5 is provided by Table 5.1, which reports the results of logistic regression analysis of voting behaviour in 1997. These are multivariate models which test the impact of various independent variables on the likelihood of an individual voting Labour, Conservative or Liberal

Democrat. Using BES data, the models seek as far as possible to incorporate variables which represent the variety of influences we have reviewed; they are similar in construction to the ideological models of voting tested in Chapter 4 (see Table 4.3), but take in a far greater array of causal influences. Naturally they once again include ideological dispositions (socialism/capitalism, libertarianism/authoritarianism and post-materialism) and control for the impact of key socio-economic cleavages (class, sectors, region, ethnicity and education); in addition, however, they take into account a range of party and leadership images which reflect some of the factors discussed in this chapter.[9] This model is tested in respect of three dichotomous dependent variables – Labour vote/other vote, Conservative vote/other vote and Liberal Democrat vote/other vote.

Overall, the models in Table 5.1 are statistically significant; that is, taken together the independent variables significantly improve predictions of voting decisions (see model chi-square significance levels and the high percentages of correctly predicted cases). Moreover, in all three models most of the individual predictor variables make a significant impact on voting choice, and in precisely the way that we would expect. The most notable feature is that the socialism/capitalism scale ('socialism') still proves to be the strongest single predictor of Labour and Conservative voting (see column headed 'R'), though it does not significantly influence the decision to vote for the Liberal Democrats (see column headed 'sig'). The libertarianism scale ('liberty') is a significant factor in all three models (especially the Liberal Democrat one), but post-materialism ('postmat') is confirmed as a generally weak ideological influence (though it just about contributes significantly to Labour's support). On the whole, the direct impact of social group factors is comparatively modest, although region figures as a prominent influence in all three models and class affects decisions to vote Labour or Conservative, but not Liberal Democrat. Interestingly, party and leadership images play a large part in each of the models: the perception that the Conservatives could not be trusted to keep their promises ('conpromise') looms relatively large in every case, which clearly confirms the importance of credibility to processes of party competition. Labour's credibility ('labpromise') also figures highly in the Labour and Conservative models, and party capacities for strong government are plainly associated with electoral choice. The importance of economic competence is attested to by the significance of both sociotropic and egocentric evaluations in the major party models ('economy' and 'pee' respectively), but even more striking is the prominence of leadership assessments in all models; opinions of John Major clearly impacted strongly on the decisions to vote Labour or Conservative, while Paddy Ashdown's leadership seems to have been a big factor in persuading electors to support the Liberal Democrats. It is always conceivable that these effects are to some extent artifactual; for instance, respondents' views about who would make a good prime minister might simply be a tautology for general *party* preferences; however, in the light of other researchers' findings (see above), it certainly does not seem unreasonable to conclude that leadership images matter.

TABLE 5.1 Multivariate logistic regression models of voting behaviour, 1997

Variable	Labour vote/other vote				Conservative vote/other vote				Liberal Democrat vote/other vote			
	B	S.E.	Sig	R	B	S.E.	Sig	R	B	S.E.	Sig	R
HOUSING	.38	.19	*	.03	-.47	.32	ns	-.01	-.61	.26	**	-.05
SECTOR	-.01	.14	ns	.00	-.06	.19	ns	.00	.12	.15	ns	.00
ETHMIN	-1.91	.43	***	-.10	1.04	.54	*	.04	1.42	.66	**	.04
CLASS	.46	.14	***	.07	-.40	.18	**	-.05	-.21	.15	ns	.00
POSTMAT	-.38	.22	*	-.02	-.06	.36	ns	.00	.15	.22	ns	.00
GRADUATE	.09	.21	ns	.00	-.64	.28	**	-.05	.32	.21	ns	.02
SOCIALISM	-1.18	.13	***	-.20	1.57	.17	***	.24	.12	.13	ns	.00
LIBERTY	-.33	.12	***	-.05	.83	.16	***	.13	-.31	.13	**	-.05
REGION	.61	.13	***	.10	-.90	.18	***	-.13	-.68	.15	***	-.11
ECONOMY	-.47	.13	***	-.08	.99	.17	***	.15	-.11	.15	ns	.00
PEE	-.71	.18	***	-.08	.66	.21	***	.08	.14	.18	ns	.00
ASHDOWN	-.20	.15	ns	.00	-.54	.18	***	-.07	1.16	.21	***	.14
MAJOR	-.67	.13	***	-.11	1.24	.18	***	.18	-.09	.15	ns	.00
BLAIR	1.62	.41	***	.08	-.56	.29	*	-.03	.46	.32	ns	.01
LDSTRONG	-.23	.14	*	-.02	-.67	.19	***	-.09	.70	.15	***	.12
LABSTRONG	1.29	.22	***	.13	-.44	.22	**	-.04	-.91	.20	***	-.11
CONSTRONG	.03	.16	ns	.00	.37	.18	**	.04	-.33	.17	*	-.04
LDPROMISE	.60	.25	**	.04	.09	.28	ns	.00	-.20	.28	ns	.00
LABPROMISE	-1.33	.23	***	-.13	1.08	.24	***	.12	-.11	.23	ns	.00
CONPROMISE	1.04	.18	***	.13	-1.61	.18	***	-.23	.60	.20	***	.07
Constant	4.70	1.12	***		-8.51	1.36	***		-4.61	1.44		
Model chi-square	187.278 (***)				410.395 (***)				133.492 (***)			
Cases correctly predicted	80.0% (n = 1246)				87.5% (n = 2187)				82.6% (n = 2187)			

Notes:

B – unstandardized logistic regression coefficient
S.E. – standard error
Sig – significance of regression coefficient
R – standardized partial regression coefficient
*** – significant at .01
** – significant at .05
* – significant at .10
ns – not significant

For each of these models, the (independent variables) are coded:

Housing: 1 = local authority tenant, 0 = other
Sector: 1 = public sector employee, 0 = other
Ethmin: 1 = ethnic minority, 2 = other
Class: 1 = manual, 0 = non-manual
Postmat: 1 = post-materialist, 0 = other
Graduate: 1 = graduate, 0 = other
Socialism: 1 = socialist, 5 = capitalist
Liberty: 1 = libertarian, 5 = authoritarian
Region: 1 = Scotland, Wales, northern England, 0 = other (not N. Ireland)
Economy: 1 = believes Britain's economy is doing well, 0 = other
PEE: 1 = pessimistic about financial prospects for household, 0 = other
Ashdown: 1 = believes Ashdown would be good as PM, 0 = other
Major: 1 = believes Major would be good as PM, 0 = other
Blair: 1 = believes Blair would be good as PM, 0 = other
Ldstrong: 1 = believes Lib.Democrats capable of strong government, 0 = other
Labstrong: 1 = believes Labour capable of strong government, 0 = other
Constrong: 1 = believes Conservatives capable of strong government, 0 = other
Ldpromise: 1 = believes Lib. Democrats break promises, 0 = other
Labpromise:1 = believes Labour breaks promises, 0 = other
Compromise:1 = believes Conservatives break promises, 0 = other

Dependent variables are coded: 1 = Labour vote/Con. vote/Lib.Dem. vote, 0 = other vote.
Independent variables are entered in two blocks; in step 1, all social background and ideology variables (socialism, liberty, post-materialism) are entered, while the party and leadership image variables are entered in step 2.
Data source: BES 1997.

Overall, then, these models broadly confirm the significance for voting behaviour and party competition of the range of factors identified in Chapters 2–5: ideology, social location, leaders, and the competence, cohesion, trustworthiness and credibility of political parties.

Nevertheless, while it is heartening to note that these conclusions are broadly consistent with formal theories of party competition, there is no doubt that such models greatly simplify reality. Nowhere is this more clear, perhaps, than in the classic Downsian assumption that parties are unitary actors. While it is important, as we have seen, that they should approximate unified organizations as closely as possible if they are to be taken seriously by voters, all parties are effectively coalitions of actors. A feature of the trend towards electoral-professionalism is that leaders seek to enhance their power within the party; this is important if they are to maximize their strategic room for manoeuvre in playing the game of party competition. However, parties are sometimes far from stable coalitions, which is why the subject of intra-party politics merits far closer scrutiny than it has so far been accorded. In the following chapters, therefore, attention shifts to the internal life of British political parties.

Notes

1 Data source, BES 1997 (n = 2725). See also King 1998: 191 for similar evidence which corroborates these findings.
2 Sanders himself has articulated the relationship between voters' general assessments of governmental economic competence and their personal economic expectations in similar terms. Thus, in discussing the impact of the ERM crisis of 'Black Wednesday' (16 September 1992), he suggests that the crisis which, as we shall see, severely damaged the Conservatives' reputation for economic competence, was associated with a 'huge decline in economic expectations' (Sanders 1997: 11).
3 Data source, BES 1997 (n = 2731).
4 It is clear from sources such as Kavanagh (1995: ch. 6) that the major parties commissioned private surveys as long ago as 1959. However, until relatively recently polling was essentially sporadic, there was considerable resistance to their findings in both parties, and neither party necessarily knew how best to make use of the research. In short, it did not constitute authentic political marketing.
5 Author's interview with senior Labour Party staff member, Millbank, August 1999.
6 The Millbank operation borrowed directly from the US Presidential campaign structure employed by Bill Clinton in 1992. Moreover, individual experts from Clinton's team, such as pollster Stan Greenberg and spokesman George Stephanopolis, were seconded to Labour in the months preceding the 1997 campaign (Braggins et al. 1993; Kavanagh 1997).
7 There were 13 election task-forces, covering: election coordination, campaign message and delivery, leader's tour, finance and administration, party (that is, members), media, policy, key campaigners, regions, key seats, projection (that is, visual presentation), rapid response, logistics (covering computing and IT needs).

8 These insights into the Millbank operation derive largely from interviews with Labour Party staff, October 1997 and August 1999 (see also Farrell et al. 1997).

9 Specifically, variables are included in these models which measure: sociotropic perceptions of economic performance ('how well is the British economy performing?'); egocentric economic expectations ('how well do you expect your household to do in the next year?'); leadership images ('how would Blair/Major/Ashdown do as prime minister?'); assessments of how far parties can be trusted to keep their promises; and evaluations of their capacity to deliver 'strong government' (the nearest to an indicator of perceived party cohesion in the BES data set).

6

CONFLICT AND COHESION WITHIN PARTIES

CONTENTS

'there is little we can understand and discuss as long as the assumption remains that the party underworld is all alike, all made of one and the same stuff. The first step is, then, to identify the diverse nature of fractions' (Sartori 1976: 106).

Few who have investigated intra-party politics could disagree with Giovanni Sartori's observation that, 'as with icebergs, it is only a small part of politics that rests above the water-line'. It is certainly true that students of British party politics have long had occasion to examine factional conflict, and have often been drawn to the periodic bouts of disharmony which have characterized the Labour Party's first century (see, for instance, Haseler 1969; Hatfield 1978; Jenkins 1979; Kogan and Kogan 1982; Seyd 1987). Yet over the past few years, attention has switched to other parts of the party system, for at least two reasons.

The first and more general reason derives from carefully researched evidence suggesting that the behavioural cohesion of parliamentary parties has been declining for some time (Norton 1975; 1978; 1980; 1994a; Norton and Cowley 1996). Norton draws on this evidence to argue that there have been three broad phases of legislative behaviour since 1945. Initially, there was a lengthy period of 'quiescence' which lasted until 1970, and which was marked by extremely high levels of backbench discipline and efficacious mechanisms for assuaging discontent 'in private' (that is, through party committees and whips). This, however, was followed by a decade in which public dissent became steadily more apparent; Norton speaks of a 'sudden and unprecedented growth in cross-voting' in the Commons, and points to government defeats caused by backbench rebellions as a feature of all three parliaments between 1970 and 1979. Finally, he refers to a post-1979 'watershed' after which formal party structures of discipline and constraint appear to have been rendered decreasingly effective (1994a: 57).[1]

The second and more specific reason for the growth of academic interest in intra-party politics in Britain has been the growing propensity of Conservative MPs to air their differences in public. The most dramatic example of this has been the internecine and passionate conflict generated by the question (or rather, the various questions) of European integration. This has fascinated the media and the citizenry alike, and stimulated a rash of new academic studies of the nuances of Conservatism in Britain (see, for instance, Baker et al. 1993a; 1993b; 1994; 1995; Garry 1995; Sowemimo 1996; Taggart 1996). Many of these authors would at least implicitly agree with John Garry's view that the question of European integration 'was by 1991 the most potent policy division operating within the Conservative party' (1995: 185).

These developments have served to readjust our focus more generally on to the politics of intra-party conflict and cohesion in Britain. For too long we have tended to live with the residue of the classic but anachronistic Westminster model of party competition, which stressed the de facto dominance of the executive over the legislature and the near-monolithic unity of parliamentary parties. Yet Britain is no different to most other democratic party systems in sustaining a significant sub-party dimension to its political life, and in reality it was ever thus. Indeed, taking a long-term view, we discover that highly cohesive parliamentary parties only emerged at Westminster in the wake of the Reform Act of 1867 (Cox 1987: ch. 3). But even during the midst of Norton's era of post-war 'quiescence', Richard Rose was able to state with conviction that 'the realignment of policy groups within and across party lines has been as significant, if not more significant, than shifts in government caused by general elections' (1964: 36). He argued that only the general elections of 1906 and 1945 had actually precipitated major shifts in governmental policy during the twentieth century, to which we might now add the election of 1979, though this only serves to reaffirm the point. And if further evidence is required that within-party politics can be as significant as between-party politics in Britain, we need only reflect on the consequences of major splits which have occurred during the development of the Westminster party system: the list of such divisions includes the Conservatives during the 1840s and after 1900 (over questions of tariff reform); Labour in 1931 (over economic policy responses to the Depression), 1951 (on rearmament) and 1981 (the SDP schism); the Liberals in 1886 (over Ireland) and during the interwar era (over the leadership question). Each of these instances of factionalism wrought terrible damage on the governing prospects of the party affected; the *shortest* period of exclusion from national office endured by any of these parties following the conflicts listed was 13 years (Labour after 1951). Recent history underlines the point: Labour's divisions in the early 1980s

(see Kogan and Kogan 1982) undoubtedly contributed hugely to the emergence of a generation of more assertive and electorally dominant
Conservatism. More recently, we have seen that perceptions of Conservative
disunity may also have damaged the party in the 1997 election campaign
(Chapter 5).

In short, the politics of all democratic systems – even 'two-party' Britain –
is in a very real sense the politics of coalition, for all parties are to some extent
marriages of convenience between different types of political actor. The harmony and stability of such marriages, therefore, become central to our
understanding of party politics. In the light of this, the purpose of this chapter is to explore a number of key questions relating to intra-party cohesion
and conflict in Britain: To what extent do parliamentary backbenchers influence the development of governmental policy? How factionalized are British
political parties? And what bearing does intra-party politics have on matters
of cross-party cooperation and realignment?[2]

The influence of the parliamentary backbenches

It has become almost trite to observe that parliaments throughout the Western
world are 'in decline' in so far as they have ceded powers to political executives. Westminster more than anywhere else seems to exemplify this, with the
domination of the legislature by the executive – Bagehot's 'efficient secret' of
the British constitution – and a concomitantly high level of party discipline
within parliament. From this perspective, parliamentary parties are almost
entirely subservient to the needs of the elites occupying the executive offices
of the state. In terms of Michael Mezey's widely used classification,
Westminster constitutes an excellent example of a (non-policy initiating) *reactive* legislature, rather than an *active* assembly (such as the US Congress) with
extensive powers to introduce legislation (1979: 36).

Nevertheless, some have contended that parliament amounts to considerably more than the compliant lap-dog of the core executive. In fact, there are
a number of means, both formal and informal, by which backbench parliamentarians can exert influence on government. Most dramatically,
parliamentary parties are occasionally able to bring about the resignation or
dismissal of members of the government who have lost their confidence. A
government's own backbenchers are crucial in this respect, the most striking
example in recent years being provided by the political demise of Margaret
Thatcher; the most heroically styled Conservative premier post-Churchill
gradually incurred the doubts of more and more of her own backbenchers
over leadership style, policy judgement and her status as an electoral asset,
until her position became untenable after the first ballot of the party leadership contest of November 1990. Similarly, open rebellion by a significant
proportion of a governing majority's own supporters can bring about the
amendment or even collapse of proposed legislation. As we have already
seen, the incidence of backbench rebellion appears to have grown since 1970,

and such behaviour almost certainly conditions a government's thinking about the parameters of future policy development. The scope for backbench intimidation of governments is likely to be all the greater when parliamentary majorities are comparatively small (or better still, non-existent), a point amply illustrated by the problems encountered by the administrations of James Callaghan (1976–79) and John Major (1992–97). All of this goes to illustrate Anthony King's view that, whereas a government can usually withstand the attacks of the Opposition, it 'cannot always shrug off attacks from its own backbenchers' (1976a: 214).

A further means by which backbenchers can exert pressure upon their leaders is through the system of party whips. As observers have long been aware, the whip system is a two-way affair in that it not only exists to impose discipline on wayward rank and file members of parliamentary parties, but also serves as a conduit for relaying backbench sentiment back to the leadership. The whips do their job partly through an informal process of soundings and meetings with backbenchers, and partly through formal parliamentary party committees. For instance, whips are able to glean considerable information about the present state of backbench feeling from regular attendance at the weekly meetings of the Conservative 1922 Committee and the Parliamentary Labour Party, as well as at the various subject and regional committees which the major parties maintain in parliament (Norton 1994a; 1994b). Backbenchers can also bring informal influence to bear on governments through private meetings with ministers, though the effectiveness of this channel depends on factors such as the seriousness of the problem, and the seniority and number of MPs involved (Brand 1992: 34).

Backbench MPs also have at their disposal a number of parliamentary devices which afford them the opportunity of publicizing criticisms of government. These procedures – such as Early Day Motions (EDMs), Adjournment Debates, parliamentary questions, Ten-Minute Rule bills and Consolidated Fund bills – seldom, if ever, lead directly to the passage of legislation, but they do enable MPs to place or keep certain issues and arguments on the agenda. Even more influential in this sense are the proceedings and reports of the parliamentary select committees which were introduced in 1979. Although these committees have built-in government majorities, they are increasingly likely to capture the attention of the media. In 1993, for instance, nothing could prevent the Conservative majority of the Home Affairs select committee issuing a report on the funding of political parties which was broadly sympathetic to the position of the government, but the process of gathering information and staging public hearings prior to publication ensured publicity for the views of opposition politicians and experts who were highly critical of the system. This helped ensure that, while placed on a political backburner by the government of the day, the issue refused to die. The select committee's deliberations served as the focal point for a highly contentious debate which resurfaced when the new government commissioned a fresh inquiry in 1997 (see Chapter 9).

Finally, of course, backbench MPs can introduce legislation through the device of the private member's bill. The success of such initiatives will depend on the parliamentary timetable for a session, and the nature of the proposed legislation; it is particularly important that such bills have little or no capacity for stimulating partisan conflict if they are to avoid being crushed at the hands of the parliamentary majority. Despite the evident constraints imposed upon a parliamentarian aspiring to introduce a successful private member's bill, some significant additions to the statute books have been made in this way; a notable example of innovation in post-war social policy is provided by David Steele's bill of 1967 which legalized abortion in the country.

Through these devices and their general importance in sustaining and opposing governments, backbench parliamentarians emerge as protagonists who play three major roles on the stage of national politics: they legitimize the rule of the political executive (by ensuring that only governments and ministers who retain the confidence of parliamentary majorities maintain office); they help shape the political agenda (especially through their connections with the mass media, their participation in select committees, and their powers to propose EDMs and adjournment debates, etc.); and they occasionally exert independent influence on the development of public policy. This influence is limited given Westminster's identity as a 'reactive' legislature, but there is evidence to suggest that it is nonetheless tangible. Jack Brand (1992) argues that it varies by policy area. For instance, while it has generally been very restricted in defence policy, it has been difficult for the core policy community (that is, the group of ministers, civil servants, experts and interest representatives who generally formulate national policy) to keep rank and file MPs out of the highly politicized area of education. In general, Brand argues that all policy communities are, to some extent or other, 'leaky' and that parliament plays a crucial role in opening up these communities to the influence of wider networks of actors concerned with the issues at hand. Two factors seem to be of particular importance in enabling backbench MPs to break into a policy community: expertise and fundamental partisan belief.

Even in areas in which relatively few parliamentarians feel comfortable with the technical detail of policy (such as defence or the economy), some inevitably will and they may be able to exert influence. Here Brand cites the example of the late Sir Gerald Nabarro, the flamboyant Conservative backbencher who became an influential expert in certain aspects of taxation (op. cit.: 28). Note that this factor may also go some way to explaining the widespread involvement of backbenchers in the detail of education policy, given the large proportion of MPs (especially on Labour's benches) with a background as professional educationists.[3] The second factor enabling backbenchers to exert influence over the policy community is their commitment to core partisan beliefs. This factor can operate even in sectors where it is otherwise rare for MPs to involve themselves in the detail of policy formulation. Thus, Labour prime minister Harold Wilson was able to refuse President Lyndon Johnson's invitation to send British troops into Vietnam in 1967 partly on the grounds of the anticipated reaction of his own backbenchers; that is, while few of them would have claimed the status of defence or foreign policy experts, Wilson nevertheless recognized that the PLP as a whole was unlikely to tolerate direct military involvement in south-east Asia. In short, the parliamentary party sets the broad ideological parameters within which the leaders can operate.

Overall then, while it is certainly true that after the Great Reform Act of 1832 the autonomy of backbenchers was greatly eroded by the growing domination of the legislature by the executive (Cox 1987: ch. 6), it is nonetheless clear that they remain more than mere lobby fodder. They can use their access to information, media and government, and their democratic credentials to (de)legitimize government, help shape the political agenda, establish the boundaries of governmental action and occasionally break directly into policy-making communities. This potential for influencing and constraining government must always be understood in the context of intra-party conflict and coalition-building, however. In other words, the issue of factionalism must be addressed.

Factionalism and the conceptual dimensions of intra-party politics

How factionalized are British political parties? The answer to this question depends on precisely what we mean by the term 'faction', of course. The literature on intra-party politics, much of which is essentially comparative, is extensive and provides valuable conceptual cues. It is interesting to note that one of the recurring themes in this literature is the pejorative sense in which sub-party groups in general and factions in particular are often regarded. This may rest in part on the feeling that a faction is something which 'tries to control its parent body while avoiding being accountable to the outside community' (Graham 1993: 145–6). Belloni and Beller go further:

> Factions tend to be viewed from the vantage point of parties – often to explain party weaknesses, disintegration of unity, corruption and opportunism among party leaders. Competition between parties is often lauded for providing leadership and political alternatives, but no such assessment is made of factional competition. (1978: 5)

In view of this, it is hardly surprising that contemporary electoral analysts generally assume it to be electorally damaging for a party to be perceived as less 'united' than its competitors (see, for instance, Curtice and Semetko 1994: 52–3, 60–1; Heath and Jowell 1994: 204). Somewhat paradoxically, however, it may be unlikely that we will find such internal unity in the context of a relatively unfragmented party system, for Sartori suggests that 'the number of ideological fractions (his generic term for intra-party groups) is inversely related to the number of parties'. That is, assuming a more or less constant number of ideological groups in the active political population, it should follow that:

> if there are enough parties to accommodate them, the fractional division will tend
> to coincide with the party division; at the limit, each fraction becomes a party.
> Conversely, the larger the discrepancy between numerous ideological fractions
> and few parties, the more we shall have parties divided into fractions. (1976: 102)

It has long been recognized, of course, that the electoral system in Britain
generally operates as a very considerable barrier to minor party representation in parliament. While this almost certainly constrains the effective
number of parliamentary parties, it must be equally sure that it obliges
many voters, activists and perhaps even politicians to select major party
options which are less than wholly consonant with their own political
values and attitudes. This reaffirms that the major parties are broad coalitions of varied social interests and ideological persuasions. It is virtually
inevitable, therefore, that intra-party conflict will occur between groups
dedicated to prioritizing their own values and preferences. But what sort of
groups? At least four different types of intra-party group can be distinguished in the literature, three of which (faction, tendency and
non-alignment) derive from Richard Rose's work (1964),[4] while the other
(single-issue alliance) owes its intellectual paternity to David Hine (1982).
These groups are defined by a mixture of ideological, organizational and
behavioural characteristics.

Rose argues that a *faction* should be regarded as a group which displays at
least four defining features. First, it should be self-conscious. Second, it must
persist through time, so that it is more than just an ad hoc combination of
politicians in agreement on a particular issue at a particular moment. Third,
it seeks to further a broad range of policies, which again distinguishes it from
the ad hoc single-issue coalition. Implicit in this account is the fourth and in
some ways most crucial characteristic, moreover, which is the presence of a
significant organizational infrastructure. This is necessary to ensure that faction members establish a clear identification with the faction and act with a
measure of discipline and cohesion over time; indeed it is no exaggeration to
say that faction leaders expect loyalty of their members:

> These expectations are a form of discipline operating socially and internalized by an
> individual. To abandon a faction is to risk appearing publicly as a renegade, as well
> as causing tension in the personal relations of the defector with his associates. The
> existence of recognized lines of conflict can become the cause of policy disagree-
> ments, as factional opponents transfer old enmities to new issues. (Rose 1964: 37)

Hence, Rose suggests that a faction displays not only a cohesive attitudinal
profile (which shows the relevance of ideology in defining a faction), but also
organizational characteristics like leadership, officers, and a communications
network. Moreover, although Rose was primarily interested in parliamentary
structures and activities, it may be that factional organization extends into
extra-parliamentary arenas (such as the national executive, party conference
or network of local party bodies). David Hine calls this extra-parliamentary
aspect of factionalism 'coverage', as though it were a distinct analytical

dimension, although it is simpler to regard it as a particular facet of the general organizational dimension of intra-party politics. We might summarize by declaring that a faction, in the sense described here, virtually amounts to a party within a party.

A *tendency*, by contrast, is a significantly less organized and cohesive body than a faction. Rose sees a tendency as 'a stable set of attitudes, not a stable set of politicians' (op. cit.: 37).[5] Like a faction, it is based upon a more or less coherent ideological position, and may take in a range of policy issues, but it lacks the discipline, consciousness, organization and behavioural cohesion of a true faction. Again, we see from these features that a tendency is defined in terms of ideology, degree of organizational development and extent of behavioural cohesion. Because tendencies lack stable support over time, individuals may shift from one tendency to another according to particular issue preferences; there will be no discernible political cost incurred by politicians behaving in such a fashion. Thus, to the extent that a party is generally characterized by tendencies rather than factions, we would expect it to lack clearly demarcated lines of intra-party alignment.

Non-alignment refers to the status of politicians who identify with the party as a whole rather than any internal group. This may result from a genuine lack of concern with internal disputes compared to the weightier business of opposing politicians from other parties, or it may reflect a calculated decision to avoid identification with specific sub-party groups in order to win the trust of the entire party. Non-alignment is a real option for politicians, and the non-aligned represent 'a slack resource' to be mobilized by one side or another during periods of intense internal conflict. The term implies a flexible ideological position and no organizational infrastructure.

The final type of sub-party grouping we can identify from the literature is implicit in Rose's work, though it is only rendered explicit by David Hine (1982: 12). The *single-issue alliance* cuts across normal lines of intra-party conflict and alignment, and is distinct from both faction and tendency in terms of the scope and duration of its activity. However, this tells us nothing of the degree of organization, discipline or cohesion that it might come to display; if, for instance, we accept that the various questions of European integration so prevalent in Britain during the 1990s can properly be described as constituting a 'single' issue, then there can be little doubt that it is an issue which has inspired some notably cohesive and well-organized behaviour by parliamentarians, often in the face of intense pressure from the official party whips. In this context, one thinks particularly of the Conservative Eurosceptic alliance associated with bodies such as the Bruges Group and Fresh Start; the response of those pro-European Conservatives who founded the Action Centre for Europe and the Positive European Group; and the resolute defiance of those backbenchers who opposed the 1994 European Finance Bill (Sowemimo 1996: 79). Neither should we overlook the potential that single-issue alliances might have for creating a lasting impression on patterns of intra-party alignment; such groups may catalyse an enduring intra- or cross-party realignment if they begin to resonate across a range of related issues, and if their organizational networks persist. Indeed, it is not inconceivable that the internal machinations of the Conservative Party on Europe will have such an effect in the long term, though this is by no means certain at the time of writing. Like the issue of Tariff Reform in the early 1900s, tensions over Europe may constitute little more than a transient phase of conflict when viewed by future historians of party politics; on the other hand, it is not yet out of the question that European integration will become so pervasive – and indeed, so pernicious to the Tory cause – that it links together a network of issues in such a way as to generate an enduring realignment of forces within the party, and even across the party system itself. Note that, were this to happen, the single-issue group would be transformed into an authentic and enduring faction during the process of realignment.

We may summarize this part of the discussion as follows. Factions and tendencies are both characterized by more or less coherent attitudinal profiles, but distinguished from each other by differences in organizational development and behavioural cohesion. The non-aligned lack distinctive attitudinal, organizational or behavioural profiles. Single-issue alliances lack ideological breadth compared to factions or tendencies, but may display relatively high levels of organizational development and/or behavioural cohesion on the issues which unite their members.

A final point worth making about intra-party politics is that the *motivations* for conflict may vary. Sartori points this out by reminding us of David Hume's distinction between 'factions from interest and factions from principle' (1976: 76). We have suggested that factions and tendencies both display relatively distinctive attitudinal profiles, yet apparently ideological groups such as these may include followers whose underlying motives are to support leaders who can dispense material rewards (a spoils faction) or access to office (a power faction). In reality, power and spoils motivations may well become somewhat commingled, and neither has been absent from British party politics in the twentieth century, though commentators tend to speak as if intra-party conflicts in the country are generally based on bona fide ideological differences. If we think of the tensions which split the Asquithian Liberals from Lloyd George's wing of the party during the interwar period, for instance, it is quickly apparent that patronage and power lay at the root of the key differences between these factions-cum-parties. Not that factionalism based around the appeal of charismatic leaders need always be unprincipled in nature, as the rise of Bevanism in the 1950s' Labour Party demonstrated (Jenkins 1979).

So, how can this conceptual framework be used to study intra-party conflict in modern Britain? For one thing, it illuminates the fact that the main parties are not necessarily comprised exclusively of one type of sub-party unit. There is no logical reason why a single party should not be an amalgam of factions, tendencies, single-issue groups and non-aligned politicians and activists, and no reason why a mixture of ideological, power-seeking and material motivations should not underlie this blend. This becomes clear if we consider the (surprisingly few and outdated) general studies of intra-party politics in Britain which have drawn on the framework. If we go back to Richard Rose himself, from the vantage point of the early 1960s he declared that while the Conservative Party was 'pre-eminently a party of tendencies' (which he labelled 'reaction', 'status quo', and 'amelioration and reform'), Labour had been 'since its foundation a party of factions' (1964: 40–1); he identified a left-wing faction within the party, and implied that the social democratic right was capable at least from time to time of transforming itself from a mere tendency into an organized faction (for instance, under the helmsmanship of Gaitskell during the 'Campaign for Democratic Socialism' episode [Haseler 1969]). In the late 1980s, Jack Brand argued that 'until recently, the majority of MPs in both parties have not been adherents of factions', but he suggested that by 1983 this had changed in the case of the Labour Party, with members joining one of three genuine factions (two on the left, one on the right [1989: 148]). Among Conservative MPs Brand identified two factions, a right-wing one based around the 92 Group and a very small left-wing group associated with the Lollards. Writing at about the same time, Philip Norton ignored the distinction between factions and tendencies in analysing Thatcher's Conservatives, but he did distinguish a 'party faithful' group – which corresponded closely with what Rose intended by the term 'non-alignment' – and he stated that in general Conservative groupings were 'now organised around such activities as putting forward their own slates of candidates for the annual elections of officers for backbench committees' (1990: 55). This level of organizational development might be taken to imply a relatively high – and possibly increasing – level of factionalism within the Conservative Party.

Clearly, the conceptual framework supplied by Rose and Hine is of direct value in answering the question of how factionalized the main British parties are. The upshot of previous research seems to be that Labour is generally more prone to factionalism than the Conservatives, but the latter have been seriously riven by conflict between single-issue alliances over Europe in the 1990s. If anything, however, the orthodox view of Labour expounded by Rose (and implicitly supported in works like Hatfield 1978; Kogan and Kogan 1982; and Seyd 1987) seems anachronistic in the context of a New Labour Party famed for its discipline and cohesion (see also Chapter 7). There is an obvious need for more up-to-date analysis of general intra-party politics in Britain, and this is the purpose of the remainder of this chapter. Nevertheless, it is important to note the limits of the analysis which follows. First, no attempt will be made to identify the underlying motivations of intra-party groups. This is virtually impossible to achieve in a study of this nature, given the problem of ideological 'camouflage' which self-interested factions and individuals may display. It is therefore assumed that, while internal party groups in Britain may be self-interested to some extent, ideological motivations are central. Second, the analysis is restricted primarily to the attitudinal, and secondarily to the organizational aspects of intra-party politics; while it would be fascinating to measure connections between these dimensions of intra-party conflict and the actual *behaviour* of politicians (for instance, in parliamentary divisions), this is impossible given the nature of the survey data we shall be using.[6]

Analysing intra-party politics in two-dimensional ideological space: data and method

Studies of intra-party politics in Britain have drawn on a variety of data sources and methodological approaches. In the 1960s and 1970s, for instance, Hugh Berrington and various associates pioneered the analysis of Early Day Motions among parliamentarians (Finer et al. 1961; Berrington 1973; Leece and Berrington 1977). By contrast, Ivor Crewe and Donald Searing made use of in-depth interviews with MPs (1988) while Philip Norton (1990), in his study of Conservative Party alignments at the end of the 1980s, drew on three different kinds of source material: division lists from the floor of the House of Commons which recorded cross-voting by Conservative Members between 1979 and 1989; the membership lists of specific internal party group organizations such as the Selsdon Group, No Turning Back and the 92 Group; and a miscellany of public and private policy statements made by the Members themselves. In his brief study of both major parties Jack Brand concentrated on the membership lists, activities and policies of specific sub-party organizations from Labour's left-wing Tribune and Campaign groups through to the Tories' 92 Group (1989). Incidence of parliamentary rebellion, public statements and closed questionnaires have all been employed in the various studies produced by the Baker team (Baker et al. 1993a; 1993b; 1994; 1995), while Taggart (1996) drew upon 'semi-structured interviews' with MPs and Garry (1995) on a postal survey of MPs.

The approach adopted in this chapter is somewhat different to most of those outlined above. Here we shall be exploring the attitudinal profiles of intra-party groups by making use of survey data (specifically, the British Candidate Survey 1992 [BCS] and the British Representation Survey 1997 [BRS]). These are valuable and detailed surveys of a representative sample of MPs and Prospective Parliamentary Candidates (PPCs). The analysis which follows proceeds in two broad steps; first, statistically and substantively discrete attitudinal clusters will be distinguished within the various party elites, and following this the internal party group affiliations of these clusters will be examined. Whereas the first of these steps provides insight into the attitudinal dimension of intra-party politics, the second goes some way towards informing us how far cohesive attitudinal groups within British parties are rooted in some kind of formal organizational infrastructure.

Such an approach has its limitations, it should be said. For one thing we cannot pretend to identify the precise membership of each intra-party group in a comprehensive way (as Norton and Brand can), since we are only working with a sample of the parliamentary elite. Moreover, the data only give limited information about the formal group affiliations of cluster members; thus, there are no indications as to which groups are most important to a respondent, which most actively seek to impose discipline on their members, and which seek to channel members' beliefs or mobilize their commitment through programmes of political activities. Thus, analysis of the behavioural dimension of factionalism is more limited by data constraints than analysis of the attitudinal dimension. This is regrettable, because attitudinal cohesion is at best a necessary though not a sufficient condition of factionalism proper in British parliamentary parties. Nevertheless, such an approach does have value. In particular, it permits us to describe very precisely the variation and location of intra-party groups in ideological space. This in turn facilitates an appreciation of the relative proximity of intra-party groups *across* party boundaries – a fascinating point for those interested in the potential for long-term realignment and cross-party coalition-building in British politics.

It makes sense to investigate the attitudinal basis of intra-party alignments in a manner consistent with the analysis of party programmes and electors' values articulated in the earlier chapters of this book. That is, the two-dimensional space with which the reader should now be familiar is equally appropriate to the study of intra-party politics. Once again, we are able to construct the attitudinal scales utilized in Chapters 4 and 5 ('socialism' and 'liberty' in Tables 4.3 and 5.1),[7] using them this time to measure the ideological locations of MPs. But how can cohesive attitudinal groups be identified with these scales? An appropriate statistical technique for achieving this is cluster analysis. This will enable us to identify homogeneous groups (or clusters) of MPs by measuring their Euclidian distances from each other on the two attitudinal scales. This may sound like an obscure formulation to readers who are not quantitatively minded, but in reality it is quite simple. (Technical details of the cluster analyses conducted in this chapter can be found in the appendix to the book.) Unless specified, the discussion which follows concentrates on the cluster analysis of BRS data from 1997, though it is important to emphasize that these results are remarkably similar to those for the BCS data of 1992; in particular, a virtually identical model of six different groups of MPs who cluster both within and across party lines emerges as the best for both datasets.[8]

British parliamentary elites in two-dimensional space

Tables 6.1–6.3 report the main findings of the cluster analysis. The first thing to note is that the schedule of distance coefficients (Table 6.1) suggests a six-cluster model could be appropriate, in so far as there is a notable change in the value of the coefficient when shifting down to a five-cluster solution; this implies that a five-cluster model forces together individuals who are actually quite different to one another. The remaining criteria all confirm that the six-cluster solution is a more than acceptable model of attitudinal clustering for the British parliamentary elite.

TABLE 6.1   *Distance coefficients for final stages of cluster analysis, 1997*

Number of clusters in stage	Coefficient	Change from previous stage
6	1.04	0.03
5	1.40	0.36
4	1.40	0.00
3	1.64	0.24
2	2.29	0.60
1	5.50	3.28

N = 257.
Data: BRS 1997.

Thus, analysis of variance confirms that this model is good at explaining variation in both attitudinal scales (see Table 6.2); differences between cluster means are significant for both, and the Eta^2 coefficients indicate that the six-cluster model explains over 90% of the total variation on the socialism scale and nearly two-thirds of all variation on the libertarianism scale. The mean standard deviation for each of the clusters in this model is .30, which suggests, in the context of scales running from 1–5, that the clusters are reasonably cohesive. (Note that all of these results are extraordinarily similar for the 1992 BCS data, as reported in Webb 1997.)

TABLE 6.2   *Location of clusters on attitudinal scales: cluster means and standard deviations of preferred model (six-cluster), 1997*

Cluster designation	Percentage of cases (n)	Mean (SD) on socialism scale	Mean (SD) on libertarianism scale
Libertarian far-left	19.1 (49)	1.47 (0.24)	2.34 (0.35)
Libertarian left	20.2 (52)	2.07 (0.25)	1.79 (0.28)
Conventional left	23.0 (59)	2.32 (0.31)	2.64 (0.25)
Libertarian centre	17.5 (45)	2.87 (0.24)	2.02 (0.38)
Conventional right	8.6 (22)	4.14 (0.36)	3.27 (0.26)
Libertarian right	11.7 (30)	4.30 (0.36)	2.46 (0.29)
Overall sample	100.0 (257)	2.59 (0.98)	2.34 (0.52)
Eta^2	–	.92 (p=.00)	.65 (p=.00)

Note:
Significance statistics represent the probability of the null hypothesis – that all cluster group means within the population are the same – holding true.

Data: BRS 1997.

TABLE 6.3   *Ideological designations of scale locations*

Socialism scale	Scale location	Libertarianism scale
Far-left	1.00–1.49	Ultra-libertarian
Left	1.50–2.49	Libertarian
Centre	2.50–3.49	Conventional
Right	3.50–4.49	Authoritarian
Far-right	4.50–5.00	Ultra-authoritarian

The nominal ideological designations which have been given to each of the intra-party clusters reported in Table 6.2 require some explanation. Given that each of the scales runs from 1–5, with 1 representing the most left-wing or libertarian position and 5 the most right-wing or authoritarian position, an intuitively reasonable interpretation of cluster mean locations on the scales can be suggested, as Table 6.3 shows. These interpretations depend upon cluster means being rounded up or down to the nearest integer. For instance, any cluster with a mean score between 1.50 and 2.49 on the socialism scale is designated as 'left-wing' since the nearest complete integer to any value within this range is 2; as '2' indicates a left-of-centre position, though not the furthest left possible, on any of the six items comprising the socialism scale, it seems justifiable to regard a mean location near to 2 on the scale as 'left-wing'. Similarly, anything closer to 1 than 2 merits a 'far-left' designation. The label 'conventional' for clusters which appear neither distinctively authoritarian nor libertarian is justifiable primarily in the sense that the mean position of the British electorate as a whole on this scale is 3.16.[9] Thus, conventional opinion at large lies in the indeterminate range of values which is neither definitely authoritarian nor definitely libertarian.

The cluster analysis divides our 1997 sample in such a way that the left constitute nearly two-thirds of cases, while the remainder are right-wing or centrist (see Table 6.2). The three left-wing clusters (libertarian far-left, libertarian left and conventional left) are roughly equal in size and the libertarian centre is only slightly smaller. Unsurprisingly in view of the 1997 election result, the two right-wing clusters (conventional right and libertarian right) are small, jointly comprising a fifth of cases in the sample.

Table 6.4 and Figure 6.1 confirm a pattern of party allegiance for members of these clusters which is much as we might expect. Nearly 95% of Conservative MPs belong to the two right-wing clusters (with over half of the party's decimated parliamentary forces now clustering on the libertarian right), while Labour and Liberal Democrat parliamentarians congregate into the four most left-wing clusters. Not surprisingly, perhaps (despite the relative manifesto locations of the two parties in 1997), Labour politicians are much more likely to be found in the three most left-wing clusters, while Liberal Democrats are most likely to be libertarian centrists. The three clusters nearest the centre of the left–right spectrum (the libertarian left, conventional left and libertarian centre) are the most mixed in terms of

TABLE 6.4   *Cluster membership by party, 1997*

	Libertarian far-left	Libertarian left	Conventional left	Libertarian centre	Conventional right	Libertarian right	Total
Cons.		1.8	–	3.6	40.0	54.5	100.0
		1.9	–	4.4	100.0	100.0	
		n = 1	–	n = 2	n = 22	n = 30	n = 55
Labour	28.7	25.1	29.9	16.2			100.0
	98.0	80.8	84.7	60.0			
	n = 48	n = 42	n = 50	n = 27			n = 167
LD	3.3	26.7	20.2	50.0			100.0
	2.0	15.4	10.2	33.3			
	n = 1	n = 8	n = 6	n = 15			n = 30
Other		20.0	60.0	20.0			100.0
		1.9	5.1	2.2			
		n = 1	n = 3	n = 1			n = 5
Total	100.0	100.0	100.0	100.0	100.0	100.0	100.0
	n = 49	n = 52	n = 59	n = 45	n = 22	n = 30	n = 257

Cramer's V= .51 (p = .00)

Note:
For this and other cross tabulations reported the top figure in each cell represents the percentage of the row category (party) falling in each column category (cluster), and totals 100% when read across the rows. The middle figure in each cell represents the percentage of the column category (cluster) falling in each row category (party), and totals 100% when read down the columns. For instance, 29.9% of Labour MPs in the sample are members of the conventional left, while 84.7% of the conventional left are Labour MPs. The bottom figure in each cell is the raw number of cases.
Data: BRS 1997.

partisan composition, which is interesting as it demonstrates which politicians are nearest to parties other than their own. The libertarian centre is especially mixed, incorporating some 16% of the Labour sample and half the Liberal Democrats; in 1992, 11% of Conservatives also clustered into the libertarian centre (Webb 1997: 98), but the corresponding figure for 1997 is less than 4%. Nevertheless, it remains the cluster most likely to include politicians from all three main parties; prima facie, therefore, we might expect MPs interested in cooperating with other parties or those considering defecting to another party to be most likely to inhabit this cluster.

Defections are comparatively rare in British politics, but they do happen from time to time, usually on an individualized basis, though occasionally en bloc. The latter type of realignment is historically unusual; one thinks, for instance, of the departure from the Liberal Party (and eventual realignment with the Conservatives) of Joseph Chamberlain's Liberal Unionists in 1886. More likely is the less spectacular seepage of disaffected individuals from one

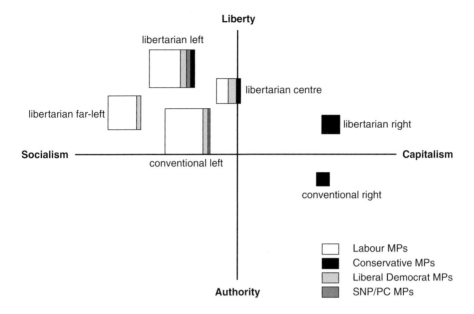

FIGURE 6.1 *Ideological clusters of parliamentarians in two-dimensional space, 1997*

parliamentary party to another. In the 1992–97 parliament, for instance, John Major's embattled Conservative government suffered two such defections; one by Emma Nicholson, MP for Devon North, who joined the Liberal Democrats in December 1995 and the other by Alan Howarth, MP for Stratford, whose departure for New Labour preceded Nicholson's by two months. In June 1998 another MP, Peter Temple-Morris, crossed the floor to join the Liberal Democrats, while the MEP James Moorhouse made a similar journey the following October. Interestingly, these individuals could be attributed ideological profiles placing them on the libertarian centre of British politics.[10] In general, it is probable that the Conservative libertarian centrists include many of the 'wets' who criticized the party's leadership during the 1980s and 1990s (Norton 1990: 49–50). However, one of the few benefits the electoral nightmare of 1997 may have brought the Conservatives was a more attitudinally cohesive parliamentary party, because it swept away a substantial number of libertarian centrists; it is clearly now a more solidly right-wing caucus than in the early 1990s. However, this view does not take into account the impact of the issue which has most polarized Conservative intra-party groups since 1990, that of European integration. This issue dimension cannot be overlooked; indeed, the question of Europe was directly relevant to the defections of Nicholson, Temple-Morris and Moorhouse. What happens, then, to our two-dimensional picture of British parliamentary alignments when we incorporate attitudes towards Europe?

Europe: the emerging third dimension?

Quite whether Europe represents a persisting basis for intra-party conflict and alignment in the way that attitudes toward socialism and liberty do remains to be seen. Could it come to constitute a third dimension of core political belief? Certainly, there has been much speculation about the potential for realignment unleashed by the irruption of the European question. Most of this speculation has centred on the very evident discord which the Conservatives have displayed over the issue. As Norton and Cowley point out, in the 1990s conflict over this issue effectively replaced the economic policy battles between 'dries' and 'wets' which were characteristic of intra-Conservative disputes in the 1980s (1996: 42). Why should Europe be so particularly divisive for the Conservatives?

The answer is that it reveals a tension at the heart of British Conservatism. This is a tension between market rationalism and romantic nationalism. There is a sense of a very old conflict here, going right back to the Enlightenment. As we saw in Chapter 3, classic Conservatism embodied a romantic and irrationalist counter-reaction to the Enlightenment, emphasizing the limits of human reason, and the centrality of national traditions, identities and loyalties. Consistent with this has been the party's characteristic self-portrayal as *the* party of the nation, a critical element of its political and electoral appeal since at the least the time of Disraeli. On the other hand, the exigencies of market rationalism have been prominent in the thinking of many Conservatives, and have been very evident since the 1970s (Barnes 1994). It is logical to associate a belief in the rationality of market allocation with a preference for free trade between nations; both might be defended on the grounds that they enhance prosperity and ensure the most efficient allocation of resources in the long run.

The difficulty with European integration is that it exposes the contradiction between these two elements of Conservatism by decisively favouring one over the other. That is, the goal of European integration represents an obvious threat to the sovereignty of the nation-state, while simultaneously justifying itself largely in terms of market rationality. For instance, apologists for the goal of European Monetary Union (EMU) often make their case in terms of its importance for the realization of the single market, the savings to consumers and producers in currency transaction costs, the benefits to industry of stable currencies and interest rates, the consequent boost to long-term growth rates, and so on. Yet the symbolism of abolishing the national currency, and the loss of national autonomy over economic policy, weigh heavily on the Conservative conscience. What should the true Conservative do: defend national sovereignty or pursue the logic of economic reason in an era of global capitalism? It seems that it is not strictly possible to do both, so the answer must be that it depends upon which of these two objectives the individual values more highly.

In fact, some argue that divisions over Europe are characteristic of a long history of disagreement within Conservatism over Britain's place in the world economy. Matthew Sowemimo, for instance, argues that the first major example is provided by Sir Robert Peel's repeal of the Corn Laws in 1846; by favouring manufacturing over agrarian interests the Peelites effectively privileged economic interdependence and free trade in the international market place. Similarly, he contends Joseph Chamberlain's attempt to restrict free trade to the colonies and to throw a protective barrier around the Empire in 1903 was provoked by the urge to regain national economic sovereignty. Both episodes brought forth an orgy of internal strife and effectively banished the Conservative Party to prolonged periods on the Opposition benches (1996: 81).

When UK membership of the European Economic Community was first proposed by the government of Harold Macmillan in 1962, it became apparent that a significant minority of Conservative (and, it should be said, Labour) backbenchers were unhappy about the idea. Throughout the 1960s and 1970s the number of Conservative MPs rebelling (by either abstaining or cross-voting in Commons debates) against the leadership on EEC-related questions usually amounted to approximately 10% of the parliamentary party (Ludlam 1996: 104).[11] During the 1980s the Thatcher governments often enjoyed a tense relationship with the EC Commission and the leaders of other member-states, usually over questions of the EC budget (and especially over the UK's financial contributions). However, questions of further political and economic integration did not provoke tension until the late 1980s. Margaret Thatcher herself signed the Single European Act of 1986, which not only committed Britain to the creation of a single market, but also introduced Qualified Majority Voting (thus ending the national veto) in a number of policy areas and raised the prospect of EMU as a long-term goal. Thatcher's own disquiet about the path of integration only started to become plain in her notorious speech at the College d'Europe in Bruges in 1988, when she memorably claimed that 'we have not successfully rolled back the frontiers of the state in Britain only to see them reimposed at the European level, with a European superstate exercising a new dominance from Brussels' (1988). Thus, her concerns – and subsequently those of other Eurosceptics in the party – centred on the loss of national sovereignty to the EU and the possibility that it would impose policies that seemed too left-wing from the perspective of Thatcherite Conservatism. The tone of Conservative Euroscepticism became increasingly strident after this, and was especially apparent in the context of European Parliamentary elections and party conferences. This only served to stimulate a backlash from those Conservatives who saw economic integration as a prime means of strengthening the ailing British economy. Intra-party tensions over Europe, moreover, extended to the front-bench itself, and lay behind the conflict which produced the dramatic resignations of Chancellor of the Exchequer Nigel Lawson and Deputy Prime Minister Sir Geoffrey Howe, in 1989 and 1990 respectively, not to mention Thatcher's own removal from the leadership in November 1990 (George and Sowemimo 1996: 251–6). Similarly, differences on Europe have defined subsequent leadership contests (Major v. Redwood in 1995, Hague v. Clarke in 1997) as much as any other issue.

The internal agonies of the Conservative Party only became acute once the Treaty on European Union (Maastricht) came to the forefront of the political agenda in the early 1990s. The extension of Qualified Majority Voting into new areas of EU legislation and the explicit commitment to EMU contained in the draft treaty stirred real antipathy within certain sections of the parliamentary Conservative Party. The prospect of a rebellion against the Major government's attempts to ratify the treaty in parliament loomed as a series of new anti-European ginger groups (the Bruges Group, Fresh Start, the European Foundation) provoked a pro-European response (the Action Centre for Europe, the Positive European Group). This was a particularly ominous development for John Major and his whips, given that the Labour Party was now relatively united on the European question (a considerable change from the situation during the 1970s and 1980s). As a result, the Conservative government suffered a number of parliamentary defeats (for example, on amendments dealing with the Council of Regions and the Social Chapter of the Treaty on European Union) and ended up removing the party whip from eight of its most inveterate Eurosceptic backbench rebels in November 1994. This only brought further humiliation on the government as the expulsions deprived it of its parliamentary majority, and the 'whipless 9' (a colleague having voluntarily resigned the party whip in order to join them) were eventually welcomed back into the fold without offering the least sign of capitulation or contrition.

Sowemimo suggests that a number of different groups can be discerned within the parliamentary Conservative Party on the question of European integration. The 'Thatcherite nationalists' constituted the bulk of the party's Euro-rebels in the 1992–97 parliament, and they seemed to embody the tension at the heart of Conservatism: though attracted to the idea of the Single European Market, their nationalist impulses led them to reject EMU as a condition of its achievement. Moreover, the Social Chapter of the Treaty of Maastricht, with its emphasis on workers' rights, represented an obvious threat to the achievements of Thatcherism. Therefore, members of this group (the most prominent among whom, such as Norman Tebbit, Cecil Parkinson and Margaret Thatcher herself, are no longer in the Commons) were able to support the Single European Act of 1986, but were strongly opposed to Maastricht. The 'neo-liberal integrationists' were (and are) in many respects similar to the Thatcherite nationalists, but differ on the key issue of monetary union. In recognizing the diminishing effectiveness of national monetary controls in an era of global financial markets, they see EMU as an opportunity to regain control at the European level. However, politicians of this ilk (such as Kenneth Clarke, Geoffrey Howe and Edwina Currie) are motivated by the potential economic benefits of integration rather than by the goal of political union. 'Interventionist integrationists' are those Conservative 'wets' like Sir Edward Heath or Tristan Garel-Jones who have consistently opposed Thatcherism, welcomed closer cooperation with Europe, and see it as a means by which neo-liberalism can be thwarted (Sowemimo 1996: 83–8).

Sowemimo is one among many commentators who believes that 'EMU has the potential to split the Tory Party when the day of decision finally arrives' (1996: 94). Whatever policy the party leadership opts for at this time, there would seem to be a risk of further defections – or perhaps even the realignment of an entire bloc of politicians. The probability of this cannot be predicted with any real certainty, but it would seem that much likelier if evidence shows certain core clusters are particularly susceptible to either pro- or anti-European sentiments. Is there any such evidence? Table 6.5 suggests a very sharp difference between the right-wing clusters and the rest on Europe: while the three left-wing clusters and the libertarian centre are all located close to each other in pro-European territory, the conventional and libertarian right lie together at the opposite end of this attitudinal scale. Since these two clusters are entirely populated by Conservative politicians, this confirms that the Tory right is quite distinct from other parts of the parliamentary party system. The only group of Conservative MPs that does not appear anti-European is the now small libertarian centre. Note that each of the main parties is relatively cohesive with respect to Europe, in so far as all of the Labour and Liberal Democrat clusters are similarly located in pro-European space, while all bar the few libertarian centrists among Conservative parliamentarians are anti-European. This was not the case in 1992, when it was clear that Tories were considerably more divided over Europe (Webb 1997: 100).[12] Once again, in fact, the decimation of the libertarian centre has effectively enhanced the ideological cohesion of the Conservative Party in parliament: after 1997 it became an unequivocally right-wing and anti-European body. If anything, this serves to undermine the likelihood of

TABLE 6.5   *Attitude towards Europe by cluster, 1997 (all parties)*

Cluster	All MPs		Conservative		Labour		Liberal Democrat	
Libertarian far-left	3.7	(2.2)	–	–	3.7	(2.6)	3.0	(–)
Conventional left	4.5	(2.4)	–	–	4.7	(2.5)	3.5	(2.6)
Libertarian left	3.5	(1.8)	10.0	(–)	3.6	(1.6)	2.4	(1.3)
Libertarian centre	3.8	(2.1)	4.0	(1.4)	3.5	(2.0)	4.3	(2.3)
Conventional right	9.3	(1.9)	9.3	(1.9)	–	–	–	–
Libertarian right	8.9	(2.6)	8.9	(2.6)	–	–	–	–
Overall sample	5.0	(3.0)	8.9	(2.5)	3.9	(2.2)	3.6	(2.2)
Eta^2	.49 (p=.00)		.17 (p=.03)		.05 (p=.04)		.14 (p=.26)	

Notes:
The dependent variable is an 11-point scale measuring respondent's attitude on EU policy, where '1' represents preference for a policy which is 'united fully with EU', and '11' represents a preference for a government that 'protects the UK's independence from EU'. Main figures are cluster means on this scale. Standard deviations in parenthesis; where no standard deviation is reported, n = 1. Sample n =251.

Data source: BRS 1997.

intra-party strife in Conservative ranks for the foreseeable future and makes William Hague's decision to campaign against EMU at the next general election (announced in October 1997) unsurprising; given the ideological composition of the parliamentary party he was elected to lead in 1997, it is not easy to see how he could very well have done otherwise. This is not to suggest that the prospect of internal conflict over Europe has completely vanished (note that the Conservatives' standard deviation on the European attitudinal scale remains greater than those of the other parties[13]). Neither can it be assumed that things are destined to remain this way indefinitely; for one thing, an electoral recovery at the next general election might bring the revival of the party's pro-European libertarian centre. It seems likely, however, that until such time the Conservatives may be less obviously divided over Europe than in the 1992–97 parliament.

Conclusions: factionalism, intra-party and cross-party alignments

A number of points emerge from this analysis of intra-party conflict and cohesion. First, the Conservatives may continue to suffer from the occasional rebellion or defection over Europe, but it is unlikely that a major schism will occur before the next election. As we have seen, they are now a relatively cohesive right-wing, anti-European parliamentary party. Having already lost the battle over economic policy in the 1980s, it is not surprising that some of the remaining members of the party's libertarian centre in the 1990s (such as Temple-Morris) felt disillusioned enough to defect to Labour or the Liberal Democrats. Though this has not exactly constituted welcome news for the leadership, the alternative strategy of shifting to a significantly more sympathetic position on European integration is palpably more dangerous under present circumstances. Indeed, given the ideological profile of the parliamentary party, it would be a virtually suicidal move for the leadership to make. But even if it were foolhardy enough to attempt such a policy shift, *and* survived the inevitable outcry from the backbenches, the anti-European Tories would be unlikely to defect to the other main parties in their ones and twos, as the pro-Europeans have done. This is because our data shows how, coming predominantly from the conventional and libertarian right, very few Conservative Europhobes would share common ground with other parties in terms of core beliefs or attitudes towards Europe. Ceteris paribus, therefore, other than continuing to voice their opposition from within the Conservative Party, the only way out of such a situation for right-wing Europhobes would be to exit the party and form a new organization of the nationalist right. It is highly unlikely that the present leadership would risk provoking such a reaction.

Second, our analysis of party elites suggests that there is an underlying ideological consonance between Labour and the Liberal Democrats which sustains the idea of developing cooperation between the two parties. As we saw in Chapter 1, such cooperation has grown tangibly over the past decade –

be it in local government, regional government (that is, Scotland), or even Westminster. While there is no doubt that sections of both parties resent the idea of cooperation and coalition, the ideological proximity of the party manifestos (see Chapter 4) is clearly mirrored in the values of the two sets of parliamentarians. This proximity is most apparent in the overlapping memberships of the conventional left, libertarian left and (especially) libertarian centre. This in itself does not point to the inevitability of cooperation, however, since other strategic factors come into the reckoning: indeed, there are those in both organizations who argue that there is not room enough in the system for two parties of the Europhile centre-left. Nevertheless, the cluster analysis sheds fascinating light on the sorts of dilemmas and possibilities facing the likely protagonists.

Finally, what does our analysis tell us about the extent of true factionalism in modern British parliamentary parties? Recall that Rose's definition implied real factions cohered in terms of ideology, organization and behaviour. This chapter has focused primarily on ideological cohesion alone, which at best is a necessary but not a sufficient condition of factionalism. Unfortunately, the nature of the 1997 data set does not permit investigation into direct associations between the attitudes, organization and behaviour of the various intra-party groups. However, previous research on the 1992 BCS data does offer some insight into whether attitudinal groups have distinct organizational bases. Thus, it was evident that members of the Conservative libertarian centre were much more likely to join party bodies generally known to be progressive and pro-European (such as the Tory Reform Group, the Progress Trust or One-Nation Forum) than colleagues in other attitudinal clusters, while the libertarian right was considerably more inclined towards right-wing or Eurosceptic bodies (like the 92 Group, the Bruges Group, No Turning Back, and so on). The evidence on Labour was less clear-cut. Overall, however, there was enough to suggest that a basis for organized factionalism might exist within (a) Labour's libertarian far-left and (b) several of the Conservative clusters, especially the anti-European libertarian right and the pro-European libertarian centre (Webb 1997: 103–4).

Taken together with other evidence relating to the relatively quiescent and disciplined nature of New Labour,[14] and the existence of organized voting in elections of Conservative backbench committee officers (Norton 1990: 55), this suggests that Rose's classic conception of the Tories as primarily a party of tendencies, and Labour as a party of factions, is seriously anachronistic. Of course, no British parliamentary party is entirely factionalized in that there are certainly always large numbers of non-aligned party loyalists. Indeed, it would not do to lose sight of the fact that disciplined and cohesive behaviour at Westminster remains comparatively high, most probably due to a number of institutional factors, including the nature of the electoral system, and the blend of incentives and sanctions which leaders and whips can exploit (Bowler et al. 1999: 6–14). Nevertheless, intra-party strife is something which ebbs and flows with the rhythms of political history, and both major parties are periodically prone to serious factional conflict. While some observers may, as Sartori notes, regard factions as 'the despair of politics' (1976: 105), their inevitability and significance for party politics cannot be overlooked.

Notes

1   It is fascinating to note that this periodization points to the contemporaneous development of behavioural volatility among both party elites and voters after 1970. This suggests the possibility of a connection between the two, a connection explained in Chapter 1 in terms of the growing problems of demand-aggregation faced by parties confronting increasingly complex issue agendas.

2   It might reasonably be contended that it is equally important to ask why cohesive political parties formed in the first place. Such an issue is really beyond the scope of a book whose focus is modern British party politics, but readers who are interested will find Cox (1987) fascinating. Bearing in mind the importance of comparative insights, moreover, works dedicated to the emergence and survival of party politics in general (such as Laver and Shepsle 1999) or specific foreign systems (such as Aldrich 1995) can also be rewarding.

3   BRS data suggest that 25.9% of the PLP in 1997 came from the educational professions, compared to 12.9% of Liberal Democrat and 5.2% of Conservative members (n = 268).

4   Note, however, that Rose himself acknowledges an intellectual debt to Samuel Beer for the formulation of the distinction between factions and tendencies (1964: 37).

5   However, Hine has argued the term 'tendency' must imply some degree of stability of personnel if it is to be identifiable at all. For if a tendency has no identifiable group of personnel, then how is it to be differentiated from the non-aligned members of a party? Hine's preferred definition of a tendency is therefore: 'a group which displays a broad position upon some ideological or value-based continuum (e.g., left, centrist, right) but which lacks clearly defined membership, leadership or discipline, makes few attempts to coordinate activities or extend itself throughout all levels of party organization' (1982: 12). This represents a modest but helpful improvement on Rose's original definition.

6   It is inherently difficult to research direct connections between attitudinal and behavioural aspects of intra-party behaviour, though one recent study suggests that they may be muted. Baker et al. discovered that Conservative backbenchers were highly likely to toe the party line in parliamentary divisions on European policy, irrespective of their personal preferences on the issues at stake (1999: 86–7). This says a good deal for the strength of party discipline, even over the most divisive of issues.

7   Principal components analysis of the 12 attitudinal items concerned shows that they load on to two discrete ideological factors in the expected manner (results available from the author on request). Cronbach's alpha reliability coefficients were .88 for the socialism scale (n = 265) and .51 for the libertarianism scale (n = 259).

8   Readers interested in the details of the BCS 1992 cluster analysis will find the results in Webb 1997. It is worth emphasizing that, although essentially the same six-cluster model emerges in both the 1992 and 1997 analyses, the marginal

distribution of cases across these clusters inevitably differs. This simply reflects the changing strength of parliamentary forces across the period; in particular, Labour's landslide majority in 1997 is reflected in the notable increase in the size of the conventional left in the BRS data (from 3% to 23% of the total sample) and a commensurate shrinking of the conventional right (from 43% to 9%).

9   With a standard deviation of 0.57 (n = 2241); data source: BES 1997.

10 See Howarth's letter resigning the party whip, reported in *The Times* 9 October 1995; Webster 1995; and White 1998.

11 Note that this crept up to 16% of the party when the Heath government permitted a free vote on the original motion supporting EEC membership in 1971.

12 Note that the variables measuring respondent's attitude to Europe differ in the 1992 BCS and 1997 BRS data sets. This makes it impossible to measure accurately change in mean party/cluster locations and cohesion over time; nevertheless, it is clear that the results reported in Webb 1997 (100) suggest a considerably more divided Conservative parliamentary party in 1992. This largely reflects the fact that the libertarian centre – proportionately bigger then – was notably more pro-European than other Conservative clusters.

13 It should be borne in mind that, while this analysis concentrates on the problems which Europe poses for Conservative Party cohesion, it can provoke conflict within the other main parties too, if not to the same extent. For instance, legislation ratifying the Treaty on European Union provoked most instances of backbench rebellion in the PLP in the 1992–97 parliament (Cowley et al. 1996: 21–22).

14 Not that Labour in office since 1997 has been entirely free from internal dissent. For instance, as early as December 1997, some 47 PLP backbenchers rebelled over new government proposals to cut benefits to single-parent households. While this was not a sizeable enough rebellion to threaten the government's overwhelming parliamentary majority, it was an early indication that a very real capacity for intra-party conflict existed within New Labour.

7

MEMBERS, LEADERS AND THE DISTRIBUTION OF POWER WITHIN PARTIES

CONTENTS

We have seen, then, that political parties in Britain (as elsewhere) are far from monolithic institutions, despite the assumptions made to the contrary by many formal theories of party competition. Conflicts within parliamentary party elites only tell us part of the story of the diversity and pluralism which is inherent within parties, however: there is also a need to consider relationships between the various party strata, especially the parliamentary leaderships and grass-roots members. This draws us into a number of questions about the internal life of parties, such as: what roles do grass-roots members play and how much power do they wield within their respective parties? How far are British political parties elitist institutions? How participatory are they? And how closely do leaders and members approximate each other in ideological terms, and how far does this matter in the competition for votes? In essence, then, the purpose of this chapter is to move beyond the parliamentary parties in order to examine the internal distribution of power and its impact on electoral competition.

These issues are crucial to our understanding of modern party politics in the country, and they cannot be fully appreciated without a grasp of some of the classic models of party organization found in the comparative literature on political parties: the relationship between members and parliamentary elites is central to such models. Their conception is intimately connected to the process of democratization which gradually affected European political life from the second half of the nineteenth century on. The origins of British political parties predate this, of course, in alliances of parliamentarians who pursued certain objectives in common. Yet with the gradual extension of the suffrage it became increasingly apparent to these elites that they had to adapt organizationally if they were to survive the transition to a modern form of parliamentary democracy. In particular, they had to extend their political appeal and organizational tentacles beyond the closed world of Westminster and into the newly enfranchised citizenry beyond. This change befitted parties' new role as political mediators between state and society. As Peter Mair has said, many political parties in democratizing societies now sought to develop in such a way that they:

> reflected the public will and provided the crucial linkage between citizen and state. They did so as mass organizations, for it was as mass organizations that they belonged to the society from which they emanated. In effect, and above all else, the twentieth century has been the century of the mass party. (Mair 1990: 2)

Cadre parties, mass parties and British idiosyncrasies

The most widely acknowledged account of just how this transformation of parties took place was provided by the French political scientist Maurice Duverger. In his classic work *Political Parties*, first published in English in 1954, Duverger argued that extension of voting rights triggered the gradual replacement of parties based on groups of parliamentary elites by nationwide organizational networks of citizens who joined party branches in their locality. The older and more elitist type of organization had typically not sought to recruit a large membership: 'its strength does not depend on the number of its members but on their quality' (1954: 18). In particular, 'notables' were important to such a party because of their social standing and influence within local constituencies, as were those with expert knowledge of running election campaigns and the financiers who could bank-roll these campaigns. This elitist organizational ideal-type was referred to by Duverger as the *cadre party*, and its rather restricted form of local organization as the *caucus*. By contrast, he stressed how the *mass-branch party* had a more open membership policy and a more centralized national structure. He regarded the mass party as initially a natural form of left-wing political organization, a 'socialist invention', for two fundamental reasons. First, since political education of the newly enfranchised masses was the primary goal of the left, it was obvious that the integration of as many individuals as possible into the institutional structure of the party was necessary: 'The members are therefore the very substance of the party, the stuff of its activity. Without members, the party would be like a teacher without pupils' (op. cit.: 63).

Second, mass membership had an obvious financial rationale for the left.

Nowhere in Europe could left-wing parties intent on mobilizing the working class hope to attract the support of many wealthy backers, but the aggregated subscriptions paid by a mass of ordinary individuals could clearly constitute a significant amount. Thus, for Duverger, 'the first duty' of the branch was the collection of subscriptions. By contrast, the parties of the right were historically more likely to have their roots in the cadre model, the organizational basis of which was the wealth of parliamentary elites and their backers. Nevertheless, Duverger did acknowledge the probability of 'contagion from the left' as cadre parties would seek to extend their appeal by adopting the organizational methods of mass parties.

The Conservatives

The Duvergerian distinction between cadre and mass parties is a useful starting point for our consideration of modern British party organizations. Clearly, the Conservatives and the old Liberals were historically cadre parties whose origins lay in parliamentary alliances, the provenance of which can be traced back at least as far as the Tory–Whig conflicts of the eighteenth century. Duverger argued that two types of European cadre-caucus party existed by the late nineteenth century: one grouped together aristocrats, industrial magnates, bankers and influential churchmen, while the other represented lesser industrialists and tradespeople, civil servants, teachers, lawyers and writers (Duverger 1954: 20). This description fits the Conservative and Liberal Parties of the period almost perfectly. Equally clearly, however, the effects of 'contagion from the left' eventually became evident in so far as national extra-parliamentary organizations with branch structures came to be adopted by both parties (and of course by the successor party to the Liberals, the Liberal Democrats). Indeed, Table 7.1 suggests that by the numbers criterion alone, no British party has had a better claim to be regarded as a 'mass' phenomenon in the modern era than the Conservative Party.

Nevertheless, the Conservative Party's organizational model has never closely approximated that of an authentic mass party. For one thing, it has made little pretence throughout most of its history of running a democratic organization (though, as we shall soon see, recent internal reforms suggest the need for a partial revision of this judgement). Although Duverger did not suggest that the mass party should be regarded as an exemplar of grass-roots democracy, it can be argued that a degree of internal democracy is inherent in his model since, in return for their vital contributions as members (via the provision of finance and voluntary labour), 'individuals can expect to have at least some control (in theory) over the goals and activities of the party' (Ware 1996: 66). Certainly, it has been the European norm for socialist mass parties to maintain formally democratic constitutions. Rather like the British state itself, however, the Conservative Party has often seemed instinctively hierarchical and secretive. Formally, all authority and policy emanates from the leader, who has traditionally been autonomous of the membership. Indeed,

TABLE 7.1   *Party individual membership in the UK since 1964*
(election years only)

Year	Labour	Conservative	Liberal/Lib.Dem.
1964	830,116	2,150,000	278,690
1966	775,693	2,150,000	234,345
1970	680,191	2,150,000	234,345
1974	691,889	1,500,000	190,000
1979	666,091	1,350,000	145,000
1983	295,344	1,200,000	145,258*
1987	288,829	1,000,000	137,500*
1992	279,530	500,000	100,000
1997	405,000	400,000	100,000

Note:
* Includes SDP membership figures.

Sources: Labour Party NEC Annual Reports; National Union of Conservative and Unionist Associations; Liberal Democrats Information Office; Berrington and Hague 1997: 48.

until recently the membership was formally and legally separate from both the parliamentary party and the party's organizational headquarters. Conservative Central Office (the national headquarters located in Westminster's Smith Square) has generally been the creature of the leader (with its overall director, the Party Chairman, being an appointee of the leader), whereas the National Union of Conservative and Unionist Associations (which shared the Smith Square premises but remained a formally distinct institution) has played the role of federating the local Constituency Associations to which individual members belong. Thus, while Central Office could be regarded as the 'professional' extra-parliamentary organization, the National Union has represented the 'voluntary' wing of the extra-parliamentary party (Garner and Kelly 1998: 76).

The National Union has maintained its own standing rules and staged an annual conference which the party leader and other parliamentary frontbenchers have been invited to address. Local organizations (Constituency Central Associations) have been represented at conference and their basic goals have included (and continue to include) the selection and support of Conservative candidates for public office. Although Constituency Associations have generally endeavoured to 'work closely in coordination with Conservative Central Office' (National Union of Conservative and Unionist Associations 1988: 1), they have not until recently been subject to the authority of the latter. On the other hand, neither the National Union as a whole nor its annual conference have had any formal policy-making rights *vis-à-vis* the parliamentary leadership, although the capacity of Conservative Party conferences to exert informal influence on frontbench Tories may often have been underestimated. It has long been orthodox to regard the annual conference as little more than a glorified party rally, the major function of which was to enthuse activists rather than make policy. Moise Ostrogorski, in his pioneering study of party organizations at the turn of the century, argued that the annual conference was a 'show body' that the parliamentary leadership was able to regard with impunity (1902: 527). Since then a procession of academic commentators have tended to reiterate this basic view, including AL Lowell (1908), Ivor Bulmer-Thomas (1953) and RT McKenzie (1955). Bulmer-Thomas, for instance, argued that the conference of the National Union was essentially 'demonstrational' rather than 'deliberative'; that is, its stress was upon party unity, morale and publicity rather than on policy-making. McKenzie felt that political apathy on the part of representatives, plus the fact that they were not mandated to vote in predetermined ways, helped account for the rather unexciting lack of policy conflict that characterized most Conservative conferences.

That said, in an interesting departure from this orthodox perception, Richard Kelly contends that academics have persistently misunderstood the nature of Conservative conferences because they have judged them from a 'centre-left' standpoint. That is, they fail to imagine that Conservative conferences could have much policy significance unless and until they come to resemble Labour Party conferences (with more provision for a formal programmatic role, greater conflict between delegates, and so on). In fact, Kelly avers that Conservative conferences do play a significant role in influencing policy and that they provide a means by which the membership may exercise such influence – if in a less than obvious way. He reminds us that the Conservative Party actually operates a 'system' of conferences, in that each of its various ancillary bodies (youth and students, women, trade unionists, local councillors, and so on) hold conferences, as do sub-national sections of the party organization (areas and regions). In all, Kelly calculates that something like 60 or more conferences are staged by the Conservative Party during the course of a typical year. If conferences are really so unimportant and achieve so little within the party, why are there so many of them and why do so many senior party figures bother to attend? 'Rallying the troops' and bolstering morale may well constitute part of the answer, of course, but Kelly insists that there is more to it than this. The members have a 'hidden' policy influence in so far as 'senior party figures attend these conferences not only to speak but to listen' (1989: 182). In fact, he claims that there are a number of examples of grass-roots contributions to conferences working their way into subsequent ministerial speeches, and even into government policy. Kelly concedes that it is difficult to demonstrate this sort of process directly, but insists that this does not make it any less tangible.

This means that conference representatives are trusted and reliable indicators of public opinion which the leadership uses to set the parameters of its own policy action: in effect, they have a subtle but influential role to play in the formulation of party policy, in so far as they are responsible for setting the tone of policy development. Conservative Party conferences provide a means by which the mood of the party grass-roots is conveyed to the leadership and this system is, consequently, central to the goal of winning elections. Were the leadership to try and 'stage-manage' the conference system too tightly, it would almost be a 'negation' of its very purpose (op. cit.: 185). Kelly's is a thoughtful and persuasive account of how individual members can exert informal influence over policy-making in the modern Conservative Party, though the formal autonomy of the parliamentary leadership in policy matters betrays its roots as a cadre party. Overall, the blend of formal leadership authority with an active and informally influential mass membership implies that the Conservative Party has constituted an idiosyncratic 'hybrid' throughout much of the twentieth century (Ware 1996: 66).

The impact of the Fresh Future reforms

However, this essentially orthodox account of Conservative Party organization is now in need of considerable revision as a result of a number of far-reaching changes implemented in the wake of the 1997 election defeat. In the October following the general election, the party issued *Blueprint For Change*, a consultation document proposing organizational reform. Significantly, this was issued in the joint names of the Party Chairman, the Chairman of the National Union, and the Chairman of the parliamentary party's 1922 Committee; in essence, the three formally (and formerly) discrete wings of the party sought the creation of a radically new form of organization in which they would merge under the aegis of a codified party constitution. A number of factors precipitated this transformation. First, it should be borne in mind that the shock of electoral defeat (especially when as heavy as that sustained by the Conservatives in 1997) is frequently enough to stimulate a response at the level of organizational change; the Tories did much the same thing after traumatic defeats earlier in their history, with 1945 offering the most obvious example, while Labour (as we shall see) responded in a similar way after the electoral reverses of 1983, 1987 and 1992. Second, the new party leader, William Hague, needed to make his mark on the party yet it was difficult for him to do this at the level of policy reform in the light of the continuing potential for bitter division which beset his party; party organization was, therefore, a somewhat less thorny nettle to grasp (though by no means an entirely uncontentious one), especially perhaps for someone who by profession was a management consultant. Third, there had been for some considerable time a number of internal critics (such as the Charter Movement) who lobbied for the democratization of the Conservative Party, and their arguments carried greater weight in the context of the stormy National Union conference staged that October, at which a number of representatives from the local Constituency Associations recriminated bitterly with the parliamentary wing of the party. The pervading sense that the grass-roots had been 'betrayed' by an irresponsible and unruly parliamentary elite which needed bringing to heel often translated into demands for greater democratization. Fourth, Central Office had encountered considerable financial difficulties in the years between the 1992 and 1997 general elections (see Chapter 8), and yet had generally been frustrated in its attempts to alleviate these problems by gaining access to local Constituency Association funds. This was due to the legal autonomy from the centre of the party's voluntary wing (Garner and Kelly 1998: 95), an obstacle which provided Central Office with an incentive to initiate fundamental reform. Finally, there was quite simply a widespread feeling within (and, indeed, without) the party that it had fallen a long way behind the Labour Party in terms of organization and management, and was patently in desperate need of its own brand of modernization.

Consequently, the party's consultation exercise on reform spawned *Fresh Future*, a proposal setting out 'the most radical changes to our party's institutions since Benjamin Disraeli', as William Hague declaimed in the document's foreword. Interestingly, the document was suffused with the rhetoric of participation and democratization, as Hague declared his bold intention to 'build the single greatest mass volunteer party in the Western world' (Conservative Party 1998: 1). The *Fresh Future* proposals were overwhelmingly endorsed by the party membership (80% in favour) in a vote whose result was announced in March 1998. This amounted to little less than a constitutional revolution for the Conservative Party. For the first time, a 'single and unified' party was created in the sense that its voluntary, professional and parliamentary pillars were drawn together into a single structure. Moreover, the party which had hitherto always operated much as the British state itself had, without any codified set of overarching rules, and with a pronounced penchant for evolving conventions, now embraced a new and binding codified constitution. This constitution can only be changed by a two-thirds majority of a 'Constitutional Convention' (comprising MPs, MEPs, Conservative Peers, and members of the equally novel National Conservative Convention [NCC]); such changes can be proposed by the Board of Management, the NCC, the 1922 Committee or a petition signed by 10,000 party members. The new Board of Management is the 'supreme decision-making body on all matters relating to party organization and management' (op. cit.: 6) and comprises members drawn from the three wings of the party.[1] The Board is obliged to meet at least six times a year, though it is expected to meet on a monthly basis in practice, and it has three permanent sub-committees, with respective responsibilities for candidate recruitment, conference preparation and management, and membership subscriptions.

One of the most striking features of the new party constitution is the disappearance of the legal autonomy of the Constituency Associations. Doubtless they run much as ever on a day-to-day basis, but they are now formally subject to the authority of the central party in a number of ways – a radical departure from established tradition. For a start, new rules for the conduct of the associations are now included in the party constitution, and replace the National Union's old 'model rules' by which most used to abide. The constitution also sets down such details as the minimum number of elected officers for each association, and stipulates that they should submit to the Board of Management an annual report on the association's activities, membership and financial accounts. Complaints about breaches of rules are dealt with by new Area Executives (whose boundaries coincide with those of county and metropolitan local authorities) in the first instance, with the Board acting as a final arbiter of appeal. Most notably, perhaps, the Board has the right to specify a variety of 'minimum criteria' for local association perform-ance in respect of such matters as membership levels, fund-raising and campaigning: those failing to fulfil such criteria can be designated 'Supported Associations' into which the Area Executive can parachute nominees who will run local campaigns and supervise constituency operations. In short, the party centre (and its local representatives) now have hitherto undreamt of rights to gather information about local associations and intervene in the way they are run.

In addition, the Conservative Party's system of conferences is maintained, with the annual party conference, the Spring Assembly and the National Conservative Convention being the most notable. Constituency Associations send representatives to each of these, the NCC dealing mainly with organi-zational issues (its brief being to 'recommend action to the Board to ensure the maintenance of an effective organization throughout the country'[op. cit.: 14]), while the former two bodies debate policy matters. While all associations may submit motions for debate at conference via the Conservative Policy Forum, the party's Committee on Conferences determines the agenda; the status of conference deliberations and decisions, moreover, remains consul-tative rather than binding. In national policy matters, therefore, it is unlikely that anything has changed much with the advent of the *Fresh Future* revolu-tion: *pace* Kelly, Conservative policy development may continue to reflect in subtle ways the influence of the party conference system, but members still lack formal rights of control.

Neither does *Fresh Future* seem to imply a tangible difference in matters of parliamentary candidate selection, where grass-roots members have always exercised considerable autonomy. The National Union's traditional task of maintaining a national list of approved parliamentary candidates has now passed to a sub-committee of the National Board of Management, but it remains the job of Constituency Associations to short-list applicants, and the members themselves make the decisive choice at a final selection meeting. However, it should be said that the members are accorded new rights in the procedures to select candidates for the European Parliament, the Welsh Assembly and the Mayor of London. After short-lists have been produced by regional 'screening committees' (drawn from constituency and area chairs within the regions), members have the right to attend and vote at one of a number of final selection meetings held in their region: given the multi-member nature of the European and Welsh constituencies, moreover, the members' task is to generate a rank-order of candidates (op. cit.: 22–3). This constitutes an undeniable extension of democratic rights to party members; indeed, they can genuinely claim to be better endowed than Labour Party members in this respect (see below).

An even clearer democratization of Conservative Party procedure is appar-ent in the method of selecting the party leader. Prior to the election of Edward Heath in 1965, Conservative Party leaders had always 'emerged' through an

opaque process of negotiation and 'soundings' involving senior party figures. This system resembled a feudal process of king-making in which the
party 'barons' (metaphorically and sometimes literally speaking) anointed
their 'monarch'. Since Sir Alec Douglas-Home became the last leader to
assume the mantle of leadership in this fashion (in 1963), his successors have
been elected by a system of exhaustive ballots of Conservative MPs. Though
the precise rules for election varied over time, when William Hague came to
be elected in July 1997, they stated that a successful candidate needed to win
the support of an overall majority and to achieve a clear margin of at least
15% over any other rival.[2] The new constitution replaces this with a system in
which the parliamentary party only has the right to act as the preliminary
selectorate which, through a system of ballots, reduces to two the number of
candidates; the final choice between these remaining candidates is then in the
hands of the party's mass membership, who cast their votes in a one-member,
one-vote postal ballot. Though it cannot be denied that this provides for leadership election by a greatly increased suffrage, two features of the new system
are worth bearing in mind. First, it is likely to be considerably harder to
depose incumbent leaders than hitherto. Whereas a challenge to a sitting
leader could previously be sparked by a contestant with the declared support
of 10% of the party's MPs, it can now only be triggered by an explicit vote of
no confidence in the leader; such a vote can itself only be called when at least
15% of MPs request it by writing to the Chair of the 1922 Committee. Should
the leader lose this vote of no confidence, however (a simple majority against
him or her will suffice), he or she is obliged to resign (op. cit.: 21). Second, it
must also be recognized that the leader is now leader of the *entire* party,
whereas before he or she was leader only of the parliamentary party. This is
significant in so far as it implies that the leader now gains authority over all
other sections of the party (including, for instance, Conservative MEPs,
Members of the Scottish Parliament and the Welsh Assembly, and of course
the hitherto autonomous membership). Thus, the price exacted of the members for their involvement in the election of the leader is a new kind of formal
homage which they are obliged to accord.

Fresh Future boldly opines that 'the reformed Conservative Party will be an
open and democratic organization . . . owned by its members' (op. cit.: 21),
and the extension of membership rights in matters of candidate and leadership selection gives definite credence to such claims, illustrating once again
perhaps the adaptive capacity of this most enduring of political organizations.
In view of this and its declared aim of becoming a great 'mass volunteer
party', should we now conclude that the Conservative Party is finally transforming itself into a Duvergerian mass party? If so, it would be ironic indeed
in view of the fact that political scientists have generally long been of the view
that the era of the mass party has been superseded (Kirchheimer 1966; Epstein
1967; Panebianco 1988; Katz and Mair 1995); indeed, some have even questioned how general a phenomenon the mass party ever really was, although
its heuristic value is unquestionable (Scarrow forthcoming). In any case, however, the party almost certainly remains a hybrid of sorts, albeit an evolving

one. As we have seen, democratization does not really extend to the critical domain of policy-making within the party, and while the Conservatives (and, indeed, Labour) may aspire to a 'mass' membership, there is little doubt that enrolment has fallen precipitously over the past decade and is unlikely to revive dramatically.[3] It remains safe to conclude that, while the mass party is an anachronism when viewed from a comparative perspective, it never has been entirely apposite in the case of British political parties: as we shall see, this is true of Labour as well as of the Conservatives.

The Labour Party

Compared to many of its European socialist counterparts, Labour has always been a somewhat unorthodox mass party, owing largely to the role played by the trade unions from the time of its inception. For one thing, it was nearly two decades after the party's foundation before individual members were recruited for the first time. Until this time 'members' only existed indirectly and on paper if they belonged to trade unions or socialist bodies which affiliated and contributed financially to the party. Duverger himself recognized this idiosyncrasy, stating that:

> From the financial point of view, the system is a mass-party system, election costs being met by trade unions, collectively. But this collective membership remains quite different from individual membership; it involves no true political enrolment and no personal pledge to the party. (1954: 65)

This reflects the fact that the original Labour Representation Committee founded in 1900 was in effect a federal organization to which its various founders affiliated as corporate entities; it was only *indirectly* through such bodies that the party gained 'members'. Even after Labour started to recruit individual members (via the CLPs) in 1918, the Party's new constitution provided for an unusual brand of democracy which did not regard the individual as the basic unit of the democratic process. In order to understand the Labour Party it is necessary to bear in mind that it was formed by an alliance of affiliating institutions – unions, socialist societies and (eventually) CLPs. The authors of the constitution therefore sought to provide for a quasi-federal structure in which the central imperative was the need to guarantee representation for each affiliating body. Thus it was the affiliating body, rather than the body's individual members, which was represented in the party's policy-making organs.

Nevertheless, once Labour created individual members in 1918, it initiated serious recruitment drives and gave their representatives rights at Conference. This seems to indicate that Labour was intent upon transforming itself into a mass party based on an active and influential membership; indeed, the notion of an active mass membership was to become an official party myth. In reality, however, the individual party members always had to face the fact of the numerically far greater (and therefore, politically more influential) affiliated membership. This is chiefly associated with the affiliated trade unions, although various socialist societies (for example, the Fabians) also affiliate members on the same basis. Each such body has tended to pay an affiliation fee for the number of members that happens to suit its political needs or financial capacities, rather than the number it actually has. Conference votes are accorded to each affiliating organization (that is, union, CLP or socialist society) on the basis of the number of members it has affiliated, and this procedure secured the numerical domination of the unions up to the 1990s since they always had more members than the CLPs.

Historically, the central role that the affiliated unions have played within the Labour Party has almost certainly shaped its attitude towards the individual membership. Indeed, it is hard to disagree with Ware's opinion that 'of all the mass membership parties, the British Labour Party is perhaps the one where membership recruitment has been taken least seriously' (1987: 146). This reflects a difference between Labour and some other major European left-wing parties in so far as the British Labour Party never really sought to 'encapsulate' the indigenous working class within an extensive network of interlinking social, economic and political organizations. This strategy of 'organizing and incorporating within the political party as many of the every day activities of the membership as possible' (Wellhofer 1979: 171) was pursued by parties such as the German Social Democrats or the Communists in Italy and France, with the object of isolating the nascent industrial working classes from the influence of dominant cultures which were Catholic and socially conservative (Barnes 1974). Critics on the British left have sometimes lamented the failure of Labour to provide an all-embracing ideological and cultural home for the domestic working class through this strategy of encapsulation (Anderson 1965; Miliband 1972). In reality, however, the British Labour Party has, throughout most of its history, been content to allow the affiliated trade unions to provide its organizational basis and a notional 'mass membership', rather than foster an army of voluntary individual activists. In this sense too, then, it has not really become an authentic mass party. This is not to deny that it has fulfilled the vital function of integrating a section of the citizenry into the British system of parliamentary democracy, but the party's internal structure and membership strategy have never fully corresponded to Duverger's classic conception of the mass party. This has been reflected in the fact that, until the 1980s, party leaderships did not seem to perceive any great need to provide individual members with participatory incentives (such as rights over policy-making, or candidate or leadership selection).

As with the Conservatives, however, substantial recent changes in the party constitution now give pause for thought. This is not to suggest that the Labour Party has suddenly embarked upon a strategy of encapsulating the working class: nothing could be further from the truth. However, constitutional changes have potentially and actually affected the distribution of power within the party in a variety of ways since 1980, and many of these reforms have been promoted under the label of 'democratization'. This changing balance of power can, as in the case of the Conservatives, be assessed primarily by considering processes of policy-making, candidate selection and leadership election. In fact, it is vitally important to separate organizational changes into these different spheres of party activity, for in so doing it becomes apparent that they have almost certainly not been designed to enhance the power of individual members in making policy, though they clearly boosted the membership's role in choosing candidates and leaders.

Party competition, political marketing and democratization

In reality, Labour's policy-making reforms since the 1987 election have almost certainly been motivated by the desire to enhance the strategic autonomy of the leadership. To understand why, it helps to view developments through the lens of party competition theory. As we know, the simplified logic of most models of party competition assumes that political parties are unitary actors, though in reality, this is seldom true. Thus even if leaders do have a clear notion of the policy positions their parties need to adopt in order to achieve vote-maximizing or office-seeking objectives, they may well be thwarted by the vagaries of intra-party conflict. Similarly, political marketing theory recognizes the potential damage a party can suffer if its own leading actors dispute the 'product': 'It is hard to imagine a parallel in business, of company directors publicly squabbling about their product as the goods are being dispatched to the shelves' (Scammell 1999: 727). Seen in this light, the organizational reforms introduced in an era of intensified electoral competition can be seen as attempts to make Labour 'quasi-unitary' by enhancing the autonomy of the leader at the expense of backbenchers and extra-parliamentary actors: in particular, the leader's capacity to shape policy appeals is maximized. This cannot completely eradicate the threat of intra-party dispute, nor the damage this can do to a party's image, but it strengthens the strategic hand of the leadership. To reiterate, none of this implies that there are no examples of organizational changes which have served to empower members in recent years, but such reforms have rarely enhanced membership power in the sphere of policy-making.

   In seeking to understand the detail of Labour's policy-making reforms, it is necessary to remember that the party's idiosyncratically federal form of democracy has never implied control by the individual membership. Rather, coalitions of parliamentary and union elites have usually dominated: the numerical preponderance of Labour's affiliated membership at annual conference – never accounting for less than 80% of the vote between 1945 and 1990, and often nearer to 90% – explains why. Of course, it would be fatuous to assume that all affiliated trade unions have regularly voted as an undifferentiated, monolithic block, but it is clear that the CLP delegates could (and still can) do little to sway Conference if a few of the largest unions make common cause over an issue. It is widely recognized that the major union leaderships have passively taken their policy cues from the PLP leadership throughout much of the party's history (to the occasional frustration of radical constituency activists), though this was 'always a contingent and not an endemic feature' of Labour's power structure (Minkin 1980: 317). Even where such coalitions have broken down temporarily, the parliamentary leadership has shown that it is quite prepared to overlook parts of the Conference-made programme in drafting election manifestos (Hatfield 1978; Kogan and Kogan 1982). Indeed, since Robert McKenzie's classic work on *British Political Parties* was first published in the 1950s, it has become commonplace to assert that formal differences conceal a high degree of de facto similarity in the internal distribution of power within the major parties. McKenzie's view, reiterated frequently ever since, was that power tended to reside with the parliamentary elites in both organizations, notwithstanding the democratic form of Labour's written constitution (1955).

For a relatively brief period during the early 1980s, the customary balance was disturbed by the confluence of two separate rivers of discontent which flowed against the leadership of the Parliamentary Labour Party (PLP). The source of one was the unhappy state of party-union relations provoked by a decade or more of political conflict over industrial relations and incomes policy (Panitch 1976; Dorfman 1979; Coates and Topham 1986; Taylor 1987). The other sprang from the widespread resentment felt within the party's left-wing over the manner in which the Wilson and Callaghan governments sometimes chose to ignore Conference decisions they did not like, irrespective of the provisions of the party constitution. When this resentment translated itself into a new Campaign for Labour Party Democracy (CLPD), directed largely by the extra-parliamentary left, some of the leadership's traditional allies among the union elites chose to break ranks (Kogan and Kogan 1982). Thus, for a few short years there existed a powerful alliance of CLP and affiliated trade union forces which sought new ways in which to constrain formally the power of the PLP frontbench; in this they were supported by some leftist elements within the PLP. As we shall shortly see, this produced an extension of CLP and union rights in respect of candidate selection and leadership election, but the main CLPD initiative on policy-making proved unsuccessful: specifically, the proposal to place authorship of general election manifestos exclusively in the hands of the party's National Executive Committee (NEC) was narrowly defeated at the 1980 annual conference. Had it succeeded, it would have imposed a considerable restriction on the autonomy sought by PLP leaderships to implement their own strategies of party competition.

After Neil Kinnock assumed the party leadership, he succeeded in raising the leader's policy-making autonomy to new heights. This was apparent in the development of a new system of campaign committees and a highly influential team of advisors and officials which he gathered around himself (Webb 1992b: 269–70), and in the impact of the comprehensive review of party policy which he initiated following Labour's third successive general election defeat in 1987. Through this he ensured that a major switch in the party's policy orientation was effected by a completely innovatory method which marginalized the NEC and its system of sub-committees (Shaw 1994: 110–11). In the wake of this, three further developments were especially significant in respect of Labour's policy-making process in the 1990s. First, the role of the affiliated unions was restricted in a number of ways: the proportion of the Conference vote controlled by the unions was gradually reduced to a maximum of 50%. Furthermore, in 1993 John Smith, Kinnock's successor as leader, fought hard to push through a number of union-related reforms, one of which was the decision to end the 'block vote' (or more accurately, the 'unit vote'): thus, union delegations to Conference were encouraged to split their vote in such a way as to reflect either the distribution of opinion among their political levy-paying members, or their individual conference delegates (Webb 1995).

The second major development affecting Labour's policy-making process in the 1990s was the introduction of *Partnership in Power* (Labour Party 1997b), which constitutes nothing less than a radical recasting of the entire process. Planning for this preceded the 1997 general election, and drew in part upon other innovations, such as the *National Policy Forum* (NPF) which Conference had agreed to establish in 1990. In January 1997, party General Secretary Tom Sawyer issued a consultation document (Labour Party 1997a), which represented the outcome of the 'Party into Power' project. This project derived from consultation between 'senior members of the NEC' and the Cranfield School of Management in 1995; its express purposes were to create new (and by implication, more stable and pacific) relationships between future Labour governments and the rest of the party, to strengthen intra-party democracy, to reorganize the NEC, and to build strong, active and 'healthy' local parties. In essence, Labour's modernizers wished to avoid what they regarded as some of the critical failings of the past: they were particularly haunted by the spectre of highly visible conflicts between Labour governments and key components of the extra-parliamentary party such as Conference and the NEC. At the heart of *Partnership in Power* (the final proposal for reform which was endorsed by Conference in the autumn of 1997) lay the new procedure for making policy.

This is based on the idea of a two-year 'rolling programme' of policy formulation. While it is certainly the case that this allows for input by individual members, local branches and their representatives, the rolling programme approach nevertheless enshrines a powerful role for the leadership. While the first year of the programme is intended to allow consultation and the development of a range of policy options, the second year is designed to narrow these down to final proposals on which Conference votes. In this way, it is hoped by the new system's apologists that:

> If the party has concerns about Government policy these can be and are addressed year-round through informed dialogue with ministers in the policy commissions rather than being stored up for set-piece battles at party conference. (Taylor and Cruddas 1999: 2)

The main institutional vehicle for the leadership in the policy-making process is the Joint Policy Committee (JPC), which comprises members drawn in equal measure from the front bench and the NEC, and is chaired by the leader. The JPC shapes the initial agenda and terms of reference for detailed consideration by the NPF, which comprises 175 members representing all parts of the party (including the CLP memberships), and its first task in year one of the two-year cycle is to establish a number of Policy Commissions and their precise terms of reference. These commissions consist of small numbers of politicians, NEC members and other co-optees. They invite, receive and consider submissions from individual members, officials, politicians, experts, CLPs and other affiliated organizations, before producing reports with comments and proposals for the JPC to consider. The JPC is free to add its own comments and (counter-) proposals before passing it in turn on to the NPF for deliberation, whence it returns yet again to the JPC before the NEC prepares a document including 'all options, alternatives and minority proposals as a consultation paper throughout the party and in advance of the conference' (Labour Party 1997b: 16).

While it is certainly the case that the individual members get opportunities to be heard via submissions to the Policy Commissions and the NPF, policy documents are bounced back and forth between these bodies and the JPC so many times that the party leadership gets ample opportunity to respond to or dilute input it does not favour. Furthermore, having been through this process once, proposals are then subjected to a second year-long round of consultation and modification before Conference gets to vote on the final policy recommendations (see Figure 7.1). Clearly, the intention is to create a system

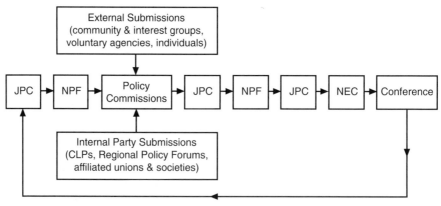

Key: JPC – Joint Policy Committee
     NPF – National Policy Forum
     NEC – National Executive Committee

Source: Labour Party 1997b: 17.

FIGURE 7.1   *Labour's two-year 'rolling programme' cycle of policy-making*

of policy-making which is iterative and consensual, so that Conference might no longer be the venue for highly publicized (or 'gladiatorial') conflicts. So, although the Labour Party Conference remains nominally sovereign, its agenda is fundamentally determined by a process of which the parliamentary elites are likely to remain in control. To be sure, this is not necessarily a system which offers the membership a *less* meaningful policy role than hitherto. For one thing, it would be deeply misguided to regard the old system as a kind of golden age of intra-party democracy in which ordinary activists set the agenda and made inviolate conference decisions which bound the PLP leadership: had this been so, it is unlikely that there would ever have been a CLPD. For another, the leadership might find that the various provisions in the new system for rank and file input serve to delimit the parameters within which policy innovation can take place: indeed, it may even welcome this (in the way that Tory leaders value the indications of grass-roots 'mood' which Conservative conferences provide). However, early though it is to offer definitive assessments of the new system, certain developments already seem to point to enhanced leadership control. Thus, the NPF's agenda is heavily influenced by frontbench politicians, given that initial policy drafts are submitted by ministers. Moreover, senior party officials act as 'facilitators' of NPF discussions and have considerable interpretive power when drafting NPF reports and statements. Finally, the NPF meets in private, which clearly undermines the capacity of party dissidents to mobilize opposition to the leadership (Seyd 1999). To summarize, it seems likely that the leadership has engineered a process by which it sets the agenda of policy debate from the outset, and maximizes its opportunities for guiding the flow of debate by hindering the articulation of public opposition, interpreting the outcome of consultation and framing the proposals which Conference considers. This could not really be said of the previous system in which actors such as the NEC and the Conference Arrangements Committee (whose loyalties to the leadership could not always be guaranteed) played more prominent roles.

The third major change in Labour's policy-making process in recent years has been the advent of plebiscitary democracy. This was first evident in 1995, when Tony Blair used a ballot of individual members to approve the major and highly symbolic change to Clause IV of the party's constitution (see Chapter 3). Though ostensibly democratic, this model of constitutional change clearly served to bypass the CLP conference delegates that Labour's modernizers regarded as too likely to offer resistance. Furthermore, in 1996 Blair introduced another such referendum on what he promised would become the main features of the forthcoming election manifesto. This offered members the chance to give a simple 'yes' or 'no' answer to the question of whether they would support the overall package of key policies likely to be included in the final manifesto. The referendum followed a national series of 'Road to the Manifesto' rallies and events at which the leadership campaigned for its position in the spring and summer of 1996. As in the case of the Clause IV ballot, this position was emphatically endorsed by the membership, but the process itself was not without its critics. Indeed, to many observers the plebiscitarian model of democracy has always suggested the manipulation of gullible masses by cynical elites: in this case, for instance, it might be said that the 'charismatic leader' bypassed the constitutional organs of policy-making, including the party's formal 'legislature', in order to address directly the mass membership – offering it a crude choice between support and opposition for something that was relatively bland and uncontentious to the progressive mind. Radicals could argue that while what was on offer was not necessarily insupportable, there was a real problem in what was *excluded* from the package.

Whatever the merits of such arguments, it is surely not unreasonable to suggest that the 'Road to the Manifesto' exercise was partly driven by public relations considerations: that is, Blair and his advisors were able to claim to the media and the electorate at large that they had a democratically derived programme on which there was an obvious internal consensus. This could be easily, and for Labour happily, contrasted with the many manifestations of civil strife which had broken out inside the Conservative Party by that time. In addition, such overwhelming grass-roots endorsement made it all the harder for internal party dissidents to raise their voices in the run-up to the general election. In effect, therefore, plebiscitarian democracy serves clear party management functions.

There remain the related functions of candidate and leadership selection to discuss, which generally offer a less equivocal picture of growing membership influence over the years. In each area the CLPD successfully pursued key reforms in the early 1980s, and although neither change has survived in its original state, they can be seen as having triggered a continuing concern for intra-party democracy. Prior to 1980, party leaders and deputy leaders were elected solely by Labour MPs, and it was against the rules of the PLP for any challenge to be issued to an incumbent Labour prime minister. In an attempt to elect a leader who would be less likely to earn the disapprobation of the extra-parliamentary party, the CLPD promoted a move to have leaders elected by a new electoral college. This college was initially divided into three sections, with 40% of the votes going to affiliated societies (trade unions or socialist groups), and 30% each to CLPs and MPs respectively. Voting was conducted by delegates at a special meeting of the electoral college (which may or may not coincide with annual conference); delegates from the various affiliated unions, societies and CLPs always voted as units, and were often mandated to vote in a certain way by the bodies they represented. In order to win, a candidate was obliged to win the support of an absolute majority of the college's weighted votes: to date, only the 1981 deputy leadership contest has necessitated a second ballot (in which the second votes of the candidate faring worst at the first ballot were redistributed among the leading contestants). Nominees require the support of 12.5% of the PLP if they are to contest a vacant leadership position, or 20% of the PLP plus a two-thirds majority of annual conference if they wish to challenge an incumbent Labour prime minister.

Following the general election defeat of April 1992, the new leader John

Smith decided to seek a revision of the system. Adopting the logic which his predecessor Neil Kinnock had employed in the 1980s, he argued that the college was unnecessarily complex and accorded the unions too much influence. His preferred model was a 'one-member-one-vote' (OMOV) system in which the leadership electorate would simply consist of individual members. This proved too great a step, however, for a party mindful of its federal roots and of the considerable financial, political and organizational contribution which the affiliated unions continued to make to Labour. The compromise which Smith managed to persuade Conference to adopt, therefore, was one whereby the electoral college remained in place but was reformed. Therefore, in 1993 it was agreed that the balance would be altered so that each section of the college was accorded an equal share of the votes; just as significant, perhaps, was the decision to replace the block or unit voting pattern of delegatory democracy which operated within the affiliated organization and CLP sections with a form of OMOV. That is, the existing practice whereby each union delegation cast an undivided vote (weighted according to the number of members for whom it paid an affiliation fee), was replaced by a direct postal ballot of each union's members.[4] Similarly, the power of CLP delegations to cast block votes on behalf of their local memberships was replaced by a direct postal ballot of the individual members themselves. This idiosyncratic blend of federalism and OMOV did not ensure that each vote cast in the electoral procedure carried an equal weight: how could it when there are never more than a few hundred Labour MPs, but hundreds of thousands of CLP and levy-paying union members, with each section obtaining a third of the total electoral college votes? Nevertheless, it undeniably constituted an extension of intra-party democracy by enhancing the real participatory rights of individual CLP and union members.

A similar story can be told of changes to the procedures for selecting parliamentary candidates. Again, the story of reform here begins with the CLPD, which successfully pursued the introduction of 'mandatory reselection' in 1980. This obliged constituencies with sitting Labour MPs to hold a reselection contest at least once during the life-time of a parliament, and was regarded as vital to the left's attempt to create a PLP of more radical socialist hue. As the political balance of power shifted, however, Kinnock managed to persuade Conference (in 1990) to replace it with a system whereby reselection could only be triggered by a prior ballot of CLP members. The complexion of the 'selectorate' itself has been an equally contentious issue for the party. Traditionally the province of the local party activists (that is, members of CLPs' *General Committees*) whom Kinnock distrusted for their supposed radicalism, in 1984 he proposed – in the name of democratization – candidate selection by OMOV. This idea was rebuffed by Conference, but in 1987 he did succeed in introducing a compromise in the form of 'local electoral colleges' in which up to 40% of the votes were reserved for locally affiliated trade unions,[5] while the remaining votes were cast individually by rank and file party members. This system was always cumbersome and controversial within the party, however, and was replaced in 1993 with straightforward

OMOV for CLP members.[6] The NEC retains the right to intervene in matters of candidate selection and occasionally (and usually controversially) exercises this. Electoral reform, however, has rendered the question of candidate selection contentious once more within the Labour Party, by appearing to generate restrictions on the participatory rights of CLP members. Thus, final selections and rankings of candidates for the European Parliamentary elections held in June 1999 under the new regional list-PR system were made by committees of centrally appointed nominees.[7] The candidate-selection system was different again for the Scottish Parliament and Welsh Assembly given that these were subject to Additional Member electoral systems (see Chapter 1); while 'constituency' candidates were selected by OMOV ballots of the membership, 'additional' candidates for regional lists were selected and ranked by special committees of regional and national party elites, before being approved by regional 'electoral conferences' (Scottish Labour Party 1998).[8] In respect of the additional candidates, therefore, party elites exercised the power of selection.

To summarize, then, the various organizational changes Labour has experienced since the Callaghan government lost power in 1979 suggest a gradual extension of new democratic rights to individual members in matters of candidate and leadership selection, while the leadership has simultaneously sought to increase its autonomy within the sphere of policy-making. The paradox of these apparently contradictory trends is explained quite simply by Peter Mair:

> it is not the party congress or the middle-level elite, or the activists, who are being empowered, but rather the 'ordinary' members, who are at once more docile and more likely to endorse the policies (and candidates) proposed by the party leadership . . . the activist layer inside the party, the traditionally more troublesome layer, becomes marginalized . . . in contrast to the activists, these ordinary and often disaggregated members are not very likely to mount a serious challenge against the positions adopted by the leadership. (1994: 16)

This interpretation is broadly compatible with Angelo Panebianco's conception of the electoral-professional party (1988) – at least, it is when viewed in the light of other developments we have encountered, such as the obvious professionalization of Labour's political marketing operations and the gradual marginalization of the role played by the trade unions within the party. The electoral-professional organization is primarily motivated by electoral rather than ideological imperatives, and characterized by the pre-eminence of the leadership within the party, the centrality of professionals within the party organization, and the party's financial dependence on the state and/or contingently linked interest groups (op. cit.: 264; Webb 1992b). While it is true that this model does not fit Labour perfectly, it is highly suggestive. For instance, Panebianco's general statement about the importance of professionals within the organization can be refined to specify that only certain types of professional expert (namely, pollsters and advertisers) assume strategic importance in the Labour Party (Shaw 1994: 215), but this hardly undermines the basic precept. More problematically, it remains the case that Labour is organically rather than contingently linked to the unions and, in comparative international terms, financial subventions to parties from the state are low in the UK. Equally, however, there has been some change in both these respects: the unions' constitutional role in policy-making and selection has certainly been restricted considerably since 1983, and since the late 1980s Labour's financial dependence on them has diminished; moreover, new party funding laws will increase the value of state subsidies to parties to some extent (see Chapter 8). Therefore, Panebianco's model has become increasingly appropriate. We may summarize by concluding that, whereas Labour once provided an imperfect example of Duverger's mass party, latterly it has evolved in the direction of the electoral-professional party.[9]

The Liberal Democrats

Overall, the Liberal Democrats can be regarded as a comparatively democratic party which offers individual members clear incentives to participate. To a significant extent, the cadre party origins of the old Liberal Party – never quite so obvious anyway as in the case of the Conservatives – have been further diluted by the influence of the SDP after the foundation of the new party in 1988. The Liberal Democrats have a federal structure, though not one which in any sense resembles Labour's: rather, the Liberal Democrats exemplify a more orthodox form of territorial federalism, with distinct 'state parties' in England, Scotland and Wales, and a 'Federal Party' for Britain as a whole. (Unless otherwise specified, the following discussion focuses on the federal party organization.)

Liberal Democrat members have significant participatory rights in matters of policy-making, leadership election and candidate selection. Thus, a national postal ballot of members is used to elect not only the leader of the parliamentary party, but also the Party President (effectively the head of the extra-parliamentary organization). Such elections are an innovation derived from SDP practice; previously, Liberal leaders were elected by a special convention of constituency party representatives (Finer 1980: 83). An incumbent leader can be challenged if he or she loses a vote of no confidence among parliamentary colleagues, or if at least 75 local parties or Specified Associated Organizations (SAOs)[10] request an election by writing to the Party President. Moreover, party members can now send representatives to a conference which is sovereign in defining party policy: the old Liberal Assembly had no such formal power. Policy development may be initiated by either the Federal Conference or the Federal Policy Committee (a majority of whose members are directly elected by conference representatives); policy working groups are then appointed by the FPC to take submissions and produce a consultation paper for dissemination to local parties, regional and state party conferences, before a final draft is put to the Federal Conference by the FPC.

In practice, the FPC drafts general and European election manifestos. Individual members have the right to be heard (with the permission of the Conference Committee) at Conference, and to elect a majority of voting members to the FPC and the party's Federal Executive. Finally, postal ballots of party members are used to select candidates for parliamentary, European and regional elections.[11] Thus, Stephen Ingle does not exaggerate greatly when he states that:

> the Liberal Democrats have built a party which encourages popular participation and makes such participation feasible. (They have) popular participation in the party's policy-making processes, a conference system which enhances popular debate, an administrative structure which not only encourages but requires widespread participation, and finally a system of politics which seeks to empower ordinary people in a thoroughgoing manner which, in their periods of dominance, the major parties have not equalled in fifty years. (1996: 130)

That the Liberal Democrats should be such a membership-oriented phenomenon is perhaps an inevitable development for a party which had few MPs at the time of its birth and relatively little corporate or state financial backing: its members are its lifeblood and need to be offered participatory incentives to maintain their enthusiasm. This was something that was first enshrined in the SDP when it was founded in the belief that it might 'break the mould' of British politics in the 1980s. 'Breaking the mould' was a multifaceted notion: though commentators frequently implied an electoral breakthrough which would enable the party to attenuate the adversarial pattern of party competition and facilitate stable coalition government, there was also a less frequently stressed organizational aspect to the notion. The SDP was to be a party unlike its better-established rivals in so far as it would seek to mobilize an enthusiastic, if hitherto disenchanted, band of citizens. It could only hope to give credence to this promise, however, if it was prepared to offer new opportunities for political influence to individual members. That said, the need to offer incentives to a newly mobilized membership only offers a partial insight into the organizational orientation of the SDP: reaction against the Labour Party, with its history of union interference and militant constituency activism, completes the picture. This explains why, notwithstanding the participatory ethos and constitution of the party, Liberal Democrat leaders still retain considerable autonomy in practice: it is normal, for instance, for party leaders to chair and direct the work of the pivotal FPC (Ingle 1996: 116).

Party strata and 'the law of curvilinear disparity'

We now have some idea of the formal power and informal influence wielded by individual members within parties. But how does this internal distribution of power affect the capacity of modern parties to compete for votes? In order to address this question, it helps to understand that members carry both benefits and costs for an electorally motivated leadership (Scarrow 1996), a notion that we explore in greater detail in Chapter 8. In particular, such a leadership might regard the membership as a resource of continuing significance in the battle for votes, but this benefit must be set against the potential costs of a membership which may not wholeheartedly endorse the policy package which the leadership wishes to set before the electorate as a whole. These costs spring from the widespread perception, shared by many academics, journalists and politicians alike, that grass-roots members are inclined to see themselves as keepers of the flame of ideological purity. Of particular note in this respect is John May's well-known 'law of curvilinear disparity', which is premised on the notion that different strata within political parties have different incentives and motives. While leaders are driven primarily by vote-maximizing imperatives, 'sub-leaders' (a category which includes grass-roots activists) are largely motivated by 'purposive' incentives such as the desire for influence over party policy or candidate selection. Thus, while leaders can be expected to seek out policy positions which approximate those of the median voter as nearly as possible, members may be more concerned to maintain ideologically 'pure' (which is to say radical) positions. A further party stratum of 'non-leaders' includes individuals who are not formally members at all, such as supporters and sympathizers in the electorate; these are hypothesized by May to be the most ideologically moderate of the strata (1973: 135–6). This scenario of systematic ideological disparity between the various party strata creates obvious potential for intra-party tension and difficulties of party management (see Figure 7.2)

In the light of this, it is legitimate to ask just how problematic party members have in fact been for the major party leaderships in contemporary Britain. This question has often been characterized as especially relevant to the Labour Party given the sway which radical CLP activists were often deemed to have held during the intra-party battles of the 1980s – to the apparent electoral cost of the party (Kogan and Kogan 1982). As we have seen, leaders since Neil Kinnock have sought to undermine the influence of these CLP radicals through what Peter Mair calls the 'paradox' of democratizing in order to emasculate the activist stratum. That is, recruiting drives designed to

FIGURE 7.2   *Ideological locations of party strata according to May's law*

flood the local parties with new members who are more representative of the 'ordinary' voter have been complemented by the various reforms designed to give non-activists new decision-making rights in candidate and leadership selection. The dramatic success of the party in attracting new members after Tony Blair was elected leader in 1994 (refer again to Table 7.1), and the resounding support he received in membership plebiscites on Clause IV and the 1997 manifesto, clearly point to the possibility that such a strategy may have worked. But was there ever really any need for it? Have British party activists generally been as radical as May's law implies?

In fact, research into the question of May's law has failed to produce a clear general consensus. While, for instance, accounts of factional struggle in the Labour Party have often pointed to the role played by radical extra-parliamentary activists, and research suggests that there may indeed be significant ideological differences between active and passive members of the party (Seyd and Whiteley 1992: 112), this does not seem to apply equally to the Conservatives (Whiteley et al. 1994: 117). Moreover, even in Labour's case, some writers have suggested that members and delegates are often not the militants they are frequently portrayed to be (Minkin 1980; Harrison 1982). However, the most systematic recent inquiry into ideological disparities in British parties has been conducted by Pippa Norris. Drawing on survey data, she was able to compare the ideological profiles of parliamentary elites ('leaders' in May's terms), local party officers ('sub-leaders'), and other members/party voters ('non-leaders'); contrary to the expectations generated by May's law, she did not discover that the sub-leaders proved consistently the most radical. Indeed, surprisingly perhaps, party elites generally demonstrated the greatest radicalism, with party voters the most moderate and sub-leaders falling between the two in ideological terms; in view of this, we might feel justified in renaming May's 'law' one of *linear* disparity, at least in so far as major parties in Britain are concerned (Norris 1995).

That said, it should be borne in mind that Norris's research does not distinguish backbenchers from frontbench parliamentarians, but groups them together as part of a single stratum of 'leaders'. While this may be appropriate as a strict test of May's law, it does not rule out the possibility that frontbenchers – in a sense the authentic 'core' leaders of major parties in Britain – really are more moderate than both backbenchers and grass-roots 'sub-leaders'; unfortunately, this possibility is hard to test empirically given data constraints. Moreover, Norris's work does at least confirm that members and activists are generally more radical than ordinary party voters, and this implies that the strategies followed by Labour's leaders since the mid-1980s probably have been justified from a purely electoralist perspective. Indeed, it is interesting to note that recent research into the changing ideological profiles of party members since the 1960s lends further support to this conclusion. First, it is readily apparent that there is something quite different about Labour members in 1997: the shift to the right within this group represents an unprecedented lurch in the time-series since 1964 (Webb and Farrell 1999:

figure 3.1 and tables 3.2–3.4). Second, it is hard to resist the conclusion that the massive influx of new members who joined the party after Tony Blair's election to the leadership goes some way towards accounting for this sudden change in grass-roots Labour opinion, though it is also important and interesting to observe that research by Whiteley and Seyd suggests this is not the whole story, for there appear to have been changes in the outlook of those who joined the party prior to 1994 (1998: 20). Third, largely (though not entirely) as a result of this shift to the centre by Labour members, the ideological 'extremism' of major party memberships (compared to the median voter) was smaller in 1997 than at any time since the 1960s. Finally, and not surprisingly in view of this evidence of growing moderation on the part of members, ideological disparities between the party members and ordinary supporters in the electorate diminished considerably in the 1990s (Webb and Farrell 1999: table 3.7).[12]

To summarize, while it seems fair to conclude that empirical research provides no clear basis for accepting John May's general claims about systematic ideological differences between party strata in Britain, we should not overlook the evidence of disparities between party members and voters in the past, and neither should we rule out the possibility that a curvilinear pattern of disparities holds (or has held) once 'core' leaders are distinguished from other parliamentarians. Whatever the truth of this might be, it seems apparent that such disparities as did exist in previous decades between sub-leaders and non-leaders have largely eroded during the 1990s. Overall, this suggests that the 'problem' (from the perspective of an electoralist leadership) of a radical and unrepresentative party grass-roots has – for the time-being, at least – been resolved (and it may have been exaggerated even at the height of CLPD influence in the early 1980s). However, while it is undeniable that membership attitudes became as moderate as any electoralist leadership could reasonably desire in 1997, nothing is forever: issues, agendas and circumstances are constantly in flux, and the (re)emergence of ideological disparities between party strata can never be ruled out.

Conclusion

In general, no political party should ever be expected to conform perfectly to heuristic ideal-types such as the cadre, mass or electoral-professional party models, although valuable insights can be derived from such analytical devices. For instance, none of the main British parties has ever equated fully to a mass party in Duverger's sense, although they did serve the classic mass party functions of political mobilization and integration during the early era of parliamentary democracy. Structurally, the Labour Party most nearly resembled a mass party, although its 'mass membership' was always exaggerated, and the unions rather than the members tended to act as the chief organizational backbone of the party. Despite Labour's recent drive for individual members and the democratization of certain processes, the dominance of the parliamentary leadership continues for the time being. Moreover, while they are less central to the party than hitherto, the major union affiliates are not completely devoid of significance in the somewhat modified form of delegatory democracy which has emerged. The Conservative Party has traditionally been a hierarchical organization whose origins approximated those of the cadre party. Although it has attracted a genuine mass membership in the post-war era, activism rates have probably been lower than among Labour members (Seyd and Whiteley 1992: 88, 95; Whiteley et al. 1994: 68). Moreover, the membership has had little formal influence over policy-making within the party, though its participatory rights have recently been enhanced through the *Fresh Future* reforms. In a strictly numerical sense neither the Liberal Democrats nor their predecessor parties could ever be described as mass membership phenomena, though they have been quicker to accord grass-roots members participatory rights than either of the major parties.

In general, all three of Britain's main political parties have democratized themselves in certain ways, and even flirted with plebiscitary democracy, though few commentators see such reforms as constituting a simple transfer of internal party power from elite to mass membership. To some extent at least, they can be regarded as part of a strategy for containing ideological zealots among local party activists, though research has tended to suggest that ideological disparities between intra-party strata may not have been as great as is often supposed and have particularly eroded in the 1990s. Whatever the truth of this, the desire to maximize strategic autonomy in order to compete in the electoral market as effectively as possible can almost certainly be imputed to party leaderships, whence we may infer the relevance of the electoral-professional model to major party organizations in modern Britain. As ever, though, no abstract model fits empirical reality perfectly: in particular, the members are more highly valued by the parties than Panebianco's ideal-type implies. To appreciate this better, however, it is important to address the importance of members in the wider context of general party resourcing.

Notes

1 The Chair of the 1922 Committee represents the parliamentary party on the Board of Management, while the leader's appointees include the Party Chairman (who presides over the Board), his deputy, a treasurer, the party leader in the Lords and a senior member of the professional staff. The voluntary party is represented by the Chair of the NCC, the President of the NCC, 4 representatives elected by the NCC, further elected representatives of the party in Scotland and Wales, and the Chair of the Association of Conservative Councillors (Conservative Party 1998: 6).

2 Although there was no formal role for the party membership to play in the election of Conservative leaders prior to 1997, it should be said that MPs were expected to consider the views of party activists in the constituencies. Again, this supports Richard Kelly's argument that the influence of the rank and file members within the Conservative Party can only be fully appreciated once one looks

beyond the traditional (lack of) formal rules and procedures. The startling removal from power of a leader who had come to appear an electoral liability (Margaret Thatcher) and her replacement by a colleague who suddenly captured the imagination of the media and the party alike (John Major) in November 1990 certainly owed something to the influence the party membership. As typifies a cadre-type party, the leader owed his or her legitimacy to the support of parliamentary colleagues, but there is no doubt that these parliamentarians were expected to be in touch with the 'mood' in the constituencies. Between the dramatic ballots that decided the outcome of the 1990, 1995 and 1997 leadership contests, there was much frantic consultation in local Constituency Associations, a process in which the media took an almost obsessive interest. It was very apparent that the eventual outcome depended in no small measure on the way in which Conservative MPs responded to these constituency pressures.

3   Note that the party estimated its membership had fallen to less than 350,000 by mid-1998 (MacAskill 1998).

4   Note that only those affiliated union members who agree to pay a 'political levy' over and above their regular union dues are entitled to vote in the electoral college.

5   It is possible for unions and socialist societies to affiliate to particular CLPs as well as to the party nationally.

6   The proponents of OMOV claimed that the local electoral colleges only served to extend the influence of trade unions at the expense of the individual members of CLPs. For instance: 'In the old days, trade union delegates actually had to attend a selection meeting to vote, but the local electoral college makes it possible for branch secretaries to vote by post, and this has increased the scope for union influence exponentially. Many parties have 60 affiliated union branches, many of them with only a few members in the constituency, and in many of them the branch's nomination and vote in a parliamentary selection is on the say-so of one individual' (Linton 1992: 5). Nevertheless, John Smith found the replacement of local electoral colleges by OMOV an immensely contentious issue and only managed to allay enough suspicion that unions were being further marginalized within the party by agreeing that certain members of affiliated unions could form part of the local CLP selectorates. These are the so-called 'levy-plus' members: in addition to regular union subscriptions and the 'political levy', these individuals pay a further modest sum (£3 in 1993) for the right to become full CLP members.

7   Labour's candidate selection for the 1999 EP elections was a convoluted process. OMOV ballots of CLP members were initially conducted in order to generate lists of male and female nominees. However, final selection and ranking of candidates on regional party lists was made by a centrally appointed national Joint Selection Board; this in turn acted on the recommendations of regional selection panels, who comprised 'five members of the NEC, three members from the region (appointed by the relevant Regional Executive Committee/s), one national trade union representative, one ethnic minority member and the party General Secretary' (Labour Party 1998: 8). Final selections and rankings by the Joint Selection Board were subject to endorsement by the NEC and Conference. Thus, while the membership had a role to play, it was essentially in the nominating process, rather than the final selection; teams of local, regional and national party elites fulfilled the latter function.

8   For instance, in Scotland the special selection committees comprised four Scottish Executive Committee members, two NEC members, the Secretary of State for

Scotland and the Scottish Labour Party General Secretary; the regional electoral conferences consisted of 3 representatives nominated by each constituency party within the region (Scottish Labour Party 1998: 8).

9   It should be said that Katz and Mair's 'cartel party' represents an alternative model against which to compare the contemporary Labour Party. Indeed, there is a certain overlap between the cartel and electoral-professional models, but the former is distinguished by a far greater emphasis on the connection between parties and the state. According to Katz and Mair, parties with access to state resources and power have a clear advantage in maintaining their own position and denying such power to others. They suggest that contemporary political systems are often characterized by an 'interpenetration of party and state' and by a degree of 'collusion' by ostensibly competing parties which is in fact designed to facilitate their survival: 'The state, in this sense, becomes an institutionalized structure of support, sustaining insiders while excluding outsiders' (1995: 16). In fact, when considering this thesis in the context of Britain it is interesting to note that it only ever held to a limited extent, and that it was damaged by the era of Conservative dominance between 1979 and 1997. It is true that in 1974 the Labour government introduced the legislation which provided for state financial subventions to parties in Britain – the 'Short Money' that Opposition parliamentary parties receive; but while this might be regarded as the first sign of a defensive 'cartel' strategy designed to help bolster the organizational infrastructure of the major parties, this money remains far from generous in comparative international terms (see Chapter 8). Moreover, since this time there have been a number of indications that this 'major party cartel' is anything but cohesive, with the Labour Party increasingly inclined to take a distinctive view of its interests. For instance, where the Conservatives continued to hold out against calls for the extension of state subventions to parties (largely on the basis of the assumption that the present reliance on individual and corporate donors affords them a relative advantage over all other parties), Labour moved to a position of support (in principle, at least, though see Chapter 8 for details of a subsequent volte-face). Similarly, by the 1990s there were clear signs that Labour was prepared to rethink its traditional rejection of electoral reform, and was becoming increasingly critical of the way in which the Tories exploited the patronage potential of the quangocracy. In short, it is doubtful that a 'cartel' could ever really be said to exist in Britain. If anything, Conservative dominance produced a cartel of Opposition, as Labour and the Liberal Democrats came to develop a shared agenda of institutional reform, incorporating *inter alia* electoral reform, devolution and the state funding of parties. Of course, it is not inconceivable that, with the shoe firmly on the other foot now, Labour and the Liberal Democrats might in time evolve into 'cartel parties' in their own right, but for now it is too early to say.

10   The SAOs are ancillary bodies such as the Liberal Democrat Parliamentary Candidates Association, the Liberal Democrat Agents Association, Liberal Democrat Youth and Students, Liberal Democrat Women, the Association of Liberal Democrat Trade Unionists, the Association of Liberal Democrat Councillors, and the Liberal Democrat Ethnic Minorities Association.

11   While Liberal Democrat members are undoubtedly afforded a considerable role in the selection of candidates, it should be said that there remains an element of elite intervention. For instance, while all members living within a region have the right to participate in a postal ballot to select European parliamentary candidates, the Joint States Candidates Committee (JSCC) has the right to decide which

candidate should be placed first in a regional list. This is by no means an insignificant power, given that the Liberal Democrats won 9 seats overall in 1999, and in only one region (the south-east) did they gain more than one.

12   Note that the available data on which this research was based did not permit us to distinguish between active and non-active members; as a surrogate for a true test of May's law, therefore, we compared the attitudinal profiles of party members and party voters. Admittedly, this only provides an approximate test of the law, yet the results are highly suggestive.

8

PARTY ORGANIZATIONAL RESOURCES

CONTENTS

In the course of Chapter 7 we examined the relative power of members and leaders, but this only presents us with a partial understanding of how the way in which a party is organized can affect its performance as a vote-winning machine. A further, and equally significant, element of modern party organization is its resourcing. What kinds of resource do parties have at their disposal, and how well resourced are they? How are such resources distributed across the organization, and how are they utilized? Are modern British parties better or worse resourced than hitherto? These are the main questions on which this chapter focuses. What follows is a consideration of the three main types of resource which modern parties have at their disposal: members, money and staff.

Resources 1: party members

In Chapter 7, we noted how the main parties have all suffered from membership decline since the 1960s. This has happened despite increasingly strenuous efforts to reverse the trend: only New Labour in the mid-1990s appears to have had any degree of success in this undertaking, and it is not clear that even this will prove to be enduring. This immediately raises interesting and important questions. First, why is it that far fewer citizens are willing to become party members now? And (to place the whole issue in a somewhat different light) why is it that, notwithstanding the evidence of pre-cipitous membership decline, some *do* still feel compelled to join? In addition, there is a further puzzle which needs addressing: why should parties con-tinue to bother to recruit members at all? After all, our review of intra-party power in Britain suggested that members can hinder electorally motivated parties by limiting the strategic autonomy which leaders require to compete for votes. Moreover, given the revolution in political communication which has taken place in the televisual era, it might well be argued that parties no longer require the services of large numbers of volunteer activists. Indeed, such arguments have occasionally been articulated and were first proposed as early as the 1950s (McKenzie 1955: 591; see also Butler and Rose 1960). Before discussing these issues in detail, however, it is necessary to elaborate further on the dimensions of membership decline.[1]

Although in purely quantitative terms the Conservative Party probably was for many a year the closest thing to a mass membership party in Britain, it is evident that it has suffered greatly from membership decline (indeed, probably even more in real terms than Labour, given the habitual over-esti-mation of the latter's individual membership until 1980, of which more below). In 1953, the Conservatives claimed some 2,800,000 members nation-ally; in 1974, the Royal Commission on party finance (Houghton 1976) estimated that this had fallen to 1,500,000; in 1992 Whiteley et al.'s survey put the national figure at approximately 750,000 (1994: 25); by the time of the 1997 general election this had collapsed to 400,000 (see Table 7.1) and subse-quent estimates placed it at less than 350,000 a year after the election (MacAskill 1998). Thus, it seems reasonable to conclude that Conservative Party membership fell by approximately 75% over the final quarter of the twentieth century.

As we saw in Chapter 7, Labour long maintained a myth of mass mem-bership, based largely on the size of its affiliated membership. The distinction between individual and affiliated membership is worth elabo-rating on, since it is so central to understanding Labour Party membership. To become an individual member today, it is necessary either to apply directly for membership of a local CLP, or to apply to the party's national head office at Millbank; individuals joining by the latter method will then be contacted by officers of their local CLP and invited to its meetings. On the other hand, unions affiliated to the Labour Party are also entitled to gather a 'political levy' from those of their members willing to pay it, regardless of whether these people are individual party members or not. This money can be passed on to the Labour Party in affiliation fees, and the levy payers designated the 'affiliated membership'.[2] While trade unions are not obliged to affiliate all those who pay the levy, it is nonetheless clear that the bulk of Labour's claimed national membership over the years has comprised this affiliated element rather than the individual ele-ment. In reality only a small proportion of the affiliated membership has been active on behalf of the Labour Party (and many of these probably because, first and foremost, they happen to be individual party members too). Thus, Labour's affiliated membership has brought money to the party and voting rights to the unions, but it has not brought a mass of committed party activists with it. It is, furthermore, almost certain that many who pay the political levy do so out of apathy rather than out of conviction; that is, they pay the levy automatically unless they can be bothered specifically to 'contract-out'. When it was legally necessary to 'contract-in' in order to pay this levy between 1927 and 1945, affiliated membership income declined significantly (Pinto-Duschinsky 1980: 76). Again this illustrates why individual membership rather than affiliated membership should be regarded as the true indicator of grass-roots commitment in the Labour Party.

Overall, Labour has obviously suffered from a loss of individual members since the 1960s. However, this derives in part from a change in party rules in 1980 which obscures the true extent of membership change; between 1957 and 1980, no local constituency party was permitted to affiliate to the national party for anything less than 1,000 members – although it was widely recognized that many CLPs had far fewer members in reality. This requirement was then relaxed (largely in order to relieve local parties of the financial strain of paying for members they might not actually have), which explains the especially precipitous decline in Labour's individual membership between 1979 and 1983 (refer again to Table 7.1).

Since the late 1980s, however, Labour has made a number of attempts to respond to the evidence of grass-roots organizational weakness. Driven in part by the desire to dilute the influence of radical CLP activists and in part by the arguments of academics like Patrick Seyd and Paul Whiteley about the continuing value of members (of which more below), the 'people's party' has sought to counter its membership losses. Thus, under Neil Kinnock it became Labour's stated goal to generate a genuine mass membership of a million or more individuals. To boost the membership drive, the party reformed the process of joining in a number of ways, creating a national membership scheme and offering affiliated levy-paying trade unionists the chance of becoming individual members at discounted subscription rates.[3] At the same time, annual subscriptions for individual members were increased (from £10 in 1989, to £15 by 1993 and to £17.50 by 1999) as a means of boosting revenue from the individual membership.

While these initiatives have come nowhere near realizing Kinnock's dream of a million individual members, there appear to have been some positive results. Although initially the party seemed merely to have stemmed the 1980s' haemorrhage in individual membership (Wintour 1991: 24; Seyd and Whiteley 1992: 201), by the time of the 1997 general election individual membership had climbed to 405,000, an extraordinary 30% advance on the number claimed by Labour three years previously (310,400). However, quite whether this represents a long-term trend is far from clear; it seems just as likely that it reflects an extraordinary, but essentially transient, surge of enthusiasm for the party in the aftermath of Tony Blair's election to the leadership. Indeed, by the winter of 1997–98 it was already apparent that the trend was beginning to

reverse itself, with membership dropping to 385,000 – a 5% fall
than 6 months (MacAskill 1998).

Overall, while the significance of Labour's recent achieveme
ment should not be underestimated, it is hard to believe that the
will ever come close to realizing some of their leaders' wild
recall Kinnock's target of 1 million individual members, and .
tion of building 'the single greatest mass volunteer party in the Western
world'. This need not necessarily represent a difficulty for the parties, however. For instance, it may be more important that they successfully address
the problem of 'de-energized' memberships (Seyd and Whiteley 1992: 89;
Whiteley et al. 1994: 69): organizationally, they may not actually require more
than a certain number of core activists for local parties to run effectively.
However, before examining the activity and value to parties of such members,
there remains first the puzzling question of just why there are so many fewer
party members in Britain than a generation ago.

Interpreting the decline of party memberships

A useful cue for considering the decline of party memberships in Britain
(and elsewhere) is provided by Susan Scarrow, who speaks in terms of
both 'supply-side' and 'demand-side' explanations (1996: 6–9). Whereas the
former category incorporates reasons why citizens of advanced industrial
democracies such as Britain may not be as inclined to join parties as previous generations, the latter focuses on reasons why parties might no longer
wish to invest time and effort in recruiting mass memberships. The various
supply-side theories which have been advanced largely replicate the explanations of partisan dealignment we encountered in Chapter 2. In essence,
the argument here is that processes of class and (by implication) partisan
dealignment have 'reduced the supply of loyalists from which parties can
recruit their members' (op. cit.: 8). Another supply-side explanation which
may well be closely related consists of the argument that political parties
have been increasingly challenged by single-issue pressure groups as articulators of citizens' interests (Moran 1985: 120). Indeed, in many Western
democracies a vast expansion in the number of such interest groups since
the 1960s has been observed. From this, commentators have concluded
that citizens are largely coming to prefer interest group activity to party
membership as a form of political participation (or simply to opt out of
either form of activity). In fact, this argument is perfectly consistent with
the partisan dealignment interpretation: that is, as political parties struggle
to aggregate coherently the growing diversity of social group interests,
many citizens are disinclined to develop strong partisan affinities, and
instead prefer to act via organizations which focus on issues and agendas
of particular concern to them. In essence, this interpretation implies that
there are further concomitants of the processes which lead to partisan
dealignment in electoral behaviour, including membership decline and the
growth of single-interest group activity (as portrayed in Figure 8.1 below).

Whatever the truth of this, recent evidence certainly indicates that more British citizens are prepared to participate in single-issue group activity than to join a political party: thus, whereas some 13.8% of respondents surveyed in the mid-1980s declared that they had 'got together with other people to raise an issue' in the previous five years and 11.2% had 'supported or worked in an organized group to raise an issue', only 7.4% claimed to be party members and only 5.2% had helped raised funds on behalf of a political party. Even fewer had actually offered their services as canvassers or clerical workers to parties (Parry and Moyser 1990; Parry et al. 1992: 44). These data do not tell us anything about change over time, of course, but evidence which bears upon change can also be cited. For instance, Kees Aarts reports that the proportion of Britons involved in social organizations increased from 48% to 61% between 1959 and 1990 (1995: 232).[4] Similarly, Peter Hall has calculated that 'the average number of associational memberships among the adult population grew by 44% between 1959 and 1990, rising most rapidly in the 1960s but subsiding only slightly thereafter' (1998: 4).

A further supply-side theory which is consistent with the partisan dealignment interpretation is that people have become increasingly disinclined to join political parties as generalized disillusionment with their performance spreads. To recapitulate briefly, the problems that all western governing parties have faced in managing economies and public sector budgets since the 1970s are widely thought to have negatively influenced popular approval ratings, and in Chapter 2 we saw that there was some evidence to support this contention in respect of the UK (Webb 1996). Then again, the supply of willing recruits in advanced industrial society could be affected by the process of cognitive mobilization, since greater access to higher education and non-partisan sources of political information might reduce the relative importance of parties as political communicators and educators (Katz 1990: 144–5). Finally, it is also possible that party membership has fallen as the value of the non-political benefits provided by parties has diminished. For instance, party membership has always been a form of social as well as political activity, and all of the main parties have traditionally recruited from their associated social clubs (the Conservative Clubs, Liberal Clubs and various working men's and trades and labour clubs affiliated to Labour), which provided relatively cheap and congenial sources of entertainment and leisure for members. However, it is quite possible that the attractiveness of such benefits has declined considerably with the expansion of alternative (non-partisan) sources of entertainment and leisure in British society. Certainly, it is clear enough that the number of such leisure clubs has fallen considerably over the years: for instance, the Club and Institute Union, covering both Labour and Liberal clubs, affiliated more than 4,000 different bodies in the early 1970s but currently affiliates approximately 2,600. By contrast, shrinkage in the number of organizations affiliated to the Association of Conservative Clubs has been far more modest (from a zenith of 1,300 during the interwar era to 1,100 today).[5] On the other hand, the erosion of Conservative youth organizations has been a major component of the declining social function of parties in Britain. The once legendary 'marriage bureaux' for the sons and daughters of the middle class comprised as many as 170,000 Young Conservatives in 1951, but fewer than 8,000 by the 1990s (Holroyd-Doveton 1996).

Demand-side explanations of membership decline focus on the reasons why party leaders and managers might come to regard the membership as an increasingly 'worthless asset', as Scarrow puts it (1994). In fact, we have already visited a number of such explanations, implicitly or explicitly, during the course of this book: above, for instance, we noted the possibility that electorally motivated leaders might have cause to conclude that life would be easier without members; certainly it would obviate concern over the kinds of inter-strata ideological disparities which prompted John May to devise his famous 'law'. Furthermore, time and money spent on activities such as recruiting members; hiring facilities and organizing meetings and conferences for them; writing, printing and distributing literature for them; and talking to, arguing with, persuading, cajoling and disciplining their more recalcitrant elements dissipates leadership energy and organizational resources. Might it not be better simply to concentrate valuable resources on more effective forms of direct communication with the electorate? Finally, a rather different demand-side factor which could conceivably enter into the thinking of party leaders in some countries is the availability of state funding which might obviate financial dependence on the membership: in Britain, however, it should be said that public subventions to political parties have not yet become this substantial (as we shall shortly see).

It is fascinating to reflect that a demand-side explanation of membership decline is implicit in what is probably the single-most influential interpretation of party transformation to have emerged since 1945: Otto Kirchheimer's 'catch-all' thesis (1966). It is worthwhile spending some time on Kirchheimer's seminal theory since it has greatly influenced many other writers (Angelo Panebianco, for instance), and bears upon a number of themes we have already visited in this book, including electoral change, ideology and party competition, and shifts in intra-party power. Furthermore, it is generally consistent with the partisan dealignment perspective.

Kirchheimer wrote in the context of the controversial debate about the waning of ideological conflict which engaged social and political theorists during the 1960s. Like a number of observers, such as the American sociologist Daniel Bell, who published his influential study *The End of Ideology* in 1959, Kirchheimer perceived an attenuation of ideological conflict in Western societies. He credited this to the development of more fluid social class situations and the secularization of societies once firmly influenced by organized religion. A major implication of this was that:

> the mass integration party, product of an age with harder class lines and more sharply protruding denominational structures, is transforming itself into a catch-all 'people's' party. Abandoning attempts at the intellectual and moral *encadrement* of

the masses, it is turning more fully to the electoral scene, trying to exchange effectiveness in depth for a wider audience and more immediate electoral success. (Kirchheimer 1966: 185)

Following the initial mobilization of the newly enfranchized masses (approximately 1885–1920 in the UK) and early experience of left-wing government (Labour's minority governments of 1924 and 1929–31), Kirchheimer argued that a new post-war phase was coming to be characterized by parties such as Labour 'trying to hold their special working class clientele and at the same time embracing a variety of other clienteles'. This process involved an amelioration of the 'expressive' function of these parties: that is, the tendency to articulate grievances, ideas and demands on behalf of a specific social constituency. Instead, the party bent on attracting a wider electoral audience must 'modulate and restrain' such expression – hence, the erosion of ideological rhetoric and conflict. Indeed, this process was likely to become contagious given that Kirchheimer expected large and successful catch-all parties to spawn imitators among their main electoral competitors.

Such a model seemed for a while persuasive in the context of a high degree of programmatic consensus between parties like Labour and the Conservatives in Britain, or the Social Democrats and Christian Democrats in Kirchheimer's native West Germany. However, of greater interest to the discussion of membership decline is Kirchheimer's general description of the processes involved in the transition of parties to 'catch-all' status. These processes involved not only ideological change, but also organizational changes affecting the respective positions of party leaders and members. Kirchheimer (1966: 190) specified the following characteristics of the catch-all party:

1 a drastic reduction of the party's ideological baggage;
2 further strengthening of top leadership groups within the party;
3 downgrading of the role of the individual party member;
4 de-emphasis of the specific social class or denominational clientele, in favour of recruiting voters among the population at large;
5 securing access to a variety of interest groups (partly in order to broaden electoral appeal and partly to raise funds).

Quite clearly, each of these features bears upon themes we have already considered in the course of this book: thus, while 1 and 4 are relevant to Chapters 2 (class dealignment), 3 and 4 (party competition via programmatic appeals), characteristics 2, 3 and 5 are especially relevant to Chapter 7 (the changing balance of power between members and leaders, and the marginalization of the unions within the Labour Party). Interestingly, while the issue of ideological change initially tended to capture the attention of scholars, it is the organizational aspect of Kirchheimer's thesis which has probably turned out to have the more enduring relevance. This is exemplified by the work of Panebianco, who has built directly on Kirchheimer's intellectual foundations in devising the electoral-professional model, and whose primary interest lies in party organization rather than ideology (1988: 262–7).[6]

The essential point, however, is that Kirchheimer (and, indeed, Panebianco) can be taken to imply a demand-side explanation for the decline of mass memberships. When the chief function of parties such as Labour was to mobilize the newly enfranchised masses politically, they concentrated on expressing group demands and utilized the group's collective loyalty as a vital resource: thus, an active mass membership was logically essential. As we know, Labour relied on the organizational input of the unions to a considerable extent in lieu of a genuine mass membership, but it nevertheless succeeded in recruiting a significant number of individual members, if only because such membership was an expression of class identity for some voters. Equally, for many recruits, joining the Conservative Party must have been a class-conscious act in the context of Britain's two-class, two-party model of politics. However, the catch-all model implies that with the erosion of the class cleavage the parties' need for members receded. It is true that, strictly speaking, Kirchheimer speaks of the 'downgrading' of the members' role rather than the complete abandonment of a membership organization, but it is surely reasonable to suggest that a reduced demand for members is implicit in his claim that parties came to regard them as 'a historical relic which may obscure the newly built-up catch-all party image' (1966: 190). This interpretation suggests that as the major parties came to approximate the catch-all model after 1960, so they inevitably experienced a loss of members.

But how persuasive is such a view? More generally, which of the variety of factors discussed thus far carries most weight in explaining membership decline in Britain? It should be said straight away that it is very difficult, if not impossible, to conduct a systematic quantitative analysis of the issue. Ideally, we would want to create a statistical model incorporating both supply- and demand-side factors which could pinpoint the most significant causes of membership decline, but this strategy is rendered impractical by the unavailability of reliable time-series data for a number of these variables: in particular, there are too few data-points in the party membership time-series (the dependent variable). Nevertheless, careful consideration of other evidence enables us to draw certain conclusions.

First, we can virtually dismiss the demand-side explanations. For one thing (as we shall see), public subsidies to British political parties have never yet been great enough to warrant the conclusion that income generated through the individual membership can be dispensed with. Moreover, we have already seen that ideological disparities between party strata are probably not so great that leaders need eschew members altogether: in any case, the preferred strategy appears to be to democratize in order to dilute the influence of the radicals. Overall, however, the major argument against any kind of demand-side explanation is simply that there is no good evidence to suggest that British parties *have* reduced their demand for members. Notwithstanding the undoubted impact of the communications revolution in British politics, parties still seem to believe that the membership constitutes a valuable resource in a number of ways (as we shall see shortly). Indeed, both Labour and the Conservatives have undoubtedly sought to boost recruitment in recent years; thus it is clear that Kirchheimer exaggerated greatly in suggesting the parties had come to regard memberships as little more than a 'historical relic'.

This leads to the conclusion that the explanation of membership decline in Britain must lie primarily with supply-side factors. In essence, party membership has declined because fewer citizens are prepared to make the commitment to join and remain involved in party life, rather than because the parties have chosen not to recruit them. It is difficult to be much more specific about the particular supply-side factors which are most influential in the British case, since we are unable to draw on any individual-level research into why people do *not* join parties (though very good evidence now exists about why people *do* join). Nevertheless, circumstantially at least, it seems unlikely that one of the supply-side explanations carries much weight. In Chapter 2, it was noted that cognitive mobilization did not generally constitute a very persuasive explanation of electoral change: relatedly, it should be said here that the growth of higher education is a very improbable cause of membership decline, given that we have individual-level evidence to associate it *with* membership; that is, members of both major parties are generally more likely to be graduates than the average British citizen (Seyd and Whiteley 1992: 32; Whiteley et al. 1994: 43), so it hardly seems to make sense to suggest that the expansion of higher educational opportunities could have contributed to a decline in party membership.[7]

This leaves us with two kinds of supply-side argument which cannot so easily be discounted. The first is the declining value of non-political selective benefits which are bestowed by party membership. Earlier we noted the decline of the parties' networks of social clubs in this respect. In recent years, it should be said, the parties have shown signs of trying to provide alternative non-political selective benefits for their members: Labour, for instance, now offers its individual members discounted deals on personal loans (through the Cooperative Bank), insurance, mobile phones and legal advice (Labour Party 1999). However, it remains a distinct possibility that the parties are less important providers of non-political benefits than hitherto. The second and most plausible explanation of membership decline is that it is a concomitant of the broader process of partisan dealignment which has characterized mass political behaviour in the country since 1970. Thus, the various factors revealed as contributing to partisan dealignment in Chapter 2 are also relevant here. Principally these include class dealignment (which in turn derives from the impact of party strategy, new cleavages and social mobility) and weak policy performance by governing parties. This suggests an overall model of membership decline resembling the one portrayed in Figure 8.1. Here, class dealignment and weak policy performance more or less simultaneously produce partisan dealignment in electoral behaviour, growing single-issue group activity and party membership erosion, while the declining value of party membership's non-political benefits also contributes

[handwritten margin note: Increasing number of new parties / but decline in main membership.]

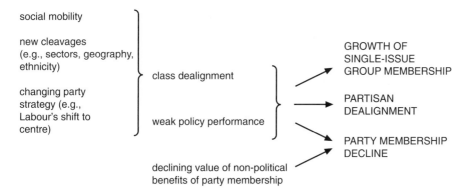

FIGURE 8.1   *A supply-side model of party membership decline*

independently to the latter phenomenon. Note that such a model can be regarded as partially vindicating and partially refuting the catch-all thesis: in so far as it emphasizes the importance of class dealignment, it clearly connects with the overarching theme which prompted Kirchheimer's model; on the other hand, we have already seen that the rejection of any kind of demand-side explanation implicitly runs counter to a specific implication of his thesis.

The value of members to modern parties

We have seen that demand-side explanations of membership decline can largely be dismissed, but why should modern political parties retain an interest in recruiting members? After all, it could be argued that the most efficient way of maximizing leadership autonomy and avoiding the costs of maintaining a membership organization would simply be to return to a model resembling the cadre party: indeed, some commentators have gone so far as to suggest that something akin to this has occurred in some Western democracies (Koole 1996). Yet it is clear that political parties in Britain have generally avoided such extreme conclusions. As we have seen, both major parties (especially Labour) have gone out of their way to enhance their membership recruitment. It must be assumed, therefore, that they continue to regard members as worthwhile resources. Why is this?

Once again, Susan Scarrow helps provide the answer. In her survey of major parties in Britain and Germany, she points to a number of potential reasons why modern parties might still be very concerned to maintain and improve membership levels (1994; 1996: ch. 2). In the first place, even a party interested primarily in electoral success may need to demonstrate that it has a vibrant appeal and a healthy level of internal activity in order to establish its basic legitimacy with the electorate. In other words, impressive membership statistics are in themselves an electoral asset (legitimacy benefits). Secondly, members provide a reliable core of loyal voters: the more a party has, therefore, the greater its 'core' vote (direct electoral benefits). More importantly, however, members should ideally become 'ambassadors' or opinion leaders for the party in the local community, and so multiply its electoral support (outreach benefits). This network of personal representatives in the locality – who may often operate in a purely informal day-to-day manner – could be especially important in helping to establish a new party or to re-establish a party with a damaged reputation. Moreover, it should not be forgotten that – notwithstanding the changes in modern campaign communications – parties do still rely upon local members to do a great deal of necessary voluntary work during an election campaign. Indeed, in recent years some observers have taken pains to argue that constituency campaigns may have a greater impact on election results at this level than has commonly been understood (labour benefits); logically, this is likely to be especially significant for the outcome in close-fought constituency contests (Denver and Hands 1992a; 1997; Whiteley and Seyd 1992; Pattie et al. 1994).

Beyond the electoral benefits that parties might derive from their members, Scarrow argues that there are other attractions. Particularly in parties with pretensions to internal democracy, members could be a potentially valuable source of policy ideas (though this innovation benefit might also restrict leadership autonomy, of course, thus transforming itself into a 'cost'). Relatedly, members can also act as a source of information about public concerns (linkage benefits), although it should be remembered that modern electorally motivated parties have come to rely heavily on professional opinion research in this respect. However, the membership is critically important as a source of party candidates for public office (personnel benefits); this factor is not to be underestimated, for the provision of public officials is a vital function of political parties in liberal democratic regimes, and it is central to the way in which parties penetrate and control the state (see Chapter 9). Finally, members can be a source of financial benefit to parties: indeed, the financial significance of party memberships in the UK has, if anything, been of growing importance in recent years, as we shall see shortly.

So, modern British political parties should (and, according to Scarrow, do) value members for a number of reasons. Yet we know also that maintaining recruitment levels has not proved easy, though this in itself need not be problematic so long as those who are members are committed enough to perform important organizational functions. How active are the members? In recent years, detailed empirical research has afforded observers of modern British parties greater insight into the level and nature of grass-roots members and organization. This research reveals, among other things, that Labour members are far more likely to be politically active than Conservative members (Parry et al. 1992: 116; Seyd and Whiteley 1992: 88; Whiteley et al. 1994: 68). Broadly speaking, between one-third and two-thirds of Labour members claim to take part in these activities on a frequent basis, whereas no more than 28% of Conservatives do (Seyd and Whiteley 1992: 95; Whiteley et al. 1994: 74). The effect of this differential propensity for activism has probably been that the major parties have had similar numbers of activists – even at the time when the Conservatives nominally had far more members (Whiteley et al. 1994:

69) – although the collapse of Conservative Party membership in the 1990s may well have left Labour with a distinct (though possibly temporary) advantage.

The explanation for such behavioural differences may well lie in political outlook. Thus, Parry et al. stress that participation is both valued and practised more highly by those who are left-wing (1992: 194). This coincides neatly with the fact that the Conservative Party is an essentially hierarchical organization which has not until recently placed great emphasis on political participation as a value in itself: the chief role of the membership has been to help select candidates for public office and then ensure that they are returned by the electorate. The political elite is expected to get on with the job of governing, subject to the constraints of remaining in touch with the vaguely defined 'mood' of the grass-roots membership and, indeed, the public at large. By contrast, participation as a valued end in itself is emphasized more in the other parties which have long had formal pretensions to internal democracy; in view of this, it is hardly surprising that Labour's individual members have showed significantly greater inclination to extend their political activism beyond the narrow confines of election campaigning (op. cit.: 114). As Parry and his colleagues put it: 'The Tory campaigners get out the vote. The Labour . . . activists pursue their goals across the participatory landscape' (1992: 236).

The rather more aged profile of the Conservative Party's membership may provide another source of behavioural asymmetry between the major parties; indeed, given the party's low activism rate, this seems to paint a picture of Conservative membership as something of a social activity for the retired.[8] Perhaps this is not surprising given the ample leisure and social facilities that many Conservative Clubs can provide, and the minimal political commitment that is expected of members.[9]

Of concern to both major parties, however, must be the 'de-energization' of local party memberships. Whiteley and his colleagues use this term to describe the surfeit of those reporting themselves to be 'less active' over those reporting themselves to be 'more active' than five years previously; in such terms, some 23% of Labour members surveyed had become 'de-energized', compared to 17% of Tories (1994: 69). In the light of this problem, first reported in the early 1990s, it is fascinating to observe the responses of the parties. Circumstantially, at least, it seems evident that they have taken seriously the advice proffered by Whiteley et al. This advice is largely derived from their 'general incentives' model of membership and activism, which requires brief explanation. Their starting point lies with what has been referred to as the 'paradox of participation'. This paradox stems from the influential work of Mancur Olson, whose *Logic of Collective Action* was written in the tradition of 'rational actor' models (Olson 1965). Implicit in Olson's work was the argument that, even when favouring a party's policies, it would make no sense for rational citizens concerned with maximizing their personal utility to join or become active in that party. This is because political parties typically provide what Olson defined as 'collective goods' – that is,

democratic party competition and public policies from which all will derive
benefit regardless of whether or not they actually participate directly themselves. Since nobody can be excluded from these effects, it makes no sense in
terms of narrowly defined individual 'rationality' to pay the 'costs' of membership and activism; people might just as well 'free-ride' on the backs of
those who are active party workers. In considering British party memberships, Seyd and Whiteley argued that Olson's approach was informative but
too narrow. They consequently prefer what they call a 'general incentives'
model of party activism.

In the first place, there are a number of 'selective incentives' to participate,
which may be related either to processes (as, for instance, when individuals
find that political activity can be interesting and stimulating in itself) or outcomes (the achievement of personal rather than collective goals through party
membership). In addition, Seyd and Whiteley insist that account must be
taken of the way in which people 'think *collectively* rather than individually'
(1992: 61). That is, they go beyond the narrow motivations of individual self-
interest which lie at the heart of most rational choice theories, and argue that
individuals might be moved to participate because of the benefits they believe
policies can bring to certain social groups. Such 'collective benefit incentives'
can be either positive (through working for the introduction of new policies)
or negative (through working for change in present government policies), and
they will be discounted by the individual member's sense of 'political efficacy' (the perception that he or she can make a significant difference by
participating). Seyd and Whiteley also allow for the possibility that people
might be motivated to participate out of sheer altruism or 'expressive commitment' (that is, a sense of loyalty, affection or emotional commitment to a
party), regardless of the costs and benefits involved (op. cit.: 107). Finally, participation could conceivably derive from the pressure of social norms (such as
family influences).

The empirical tests of this model on the major party memberships revealed
that both expressive motives and selective incentives influenced activism,
which seems to confirm the value of an intellectually hybrid model. One of
their most striking findings concerning the importance of selective incentives was that 'middle class, highly educated party members with relatively
high incomes are more likely to be active because of their greater sense of personal efficacy and greater desire to achieve elective office in politics'
(Whiteley et al. 1994: 124): though made in respect of Conservative members,
this observation is essentially true of Labour members too (Seyd and Whiteley
1992: 117).

Seyd and Whiteley proceeded to argue that membership decline and de-
energization flowed from a number of developments which affected different
aspects of this model: while social norms, expressive and altruistic motives
have been undermined by social and geographical mobility, class dealignment and policy failure,[10] selective incentives have been eroded by factors
such as the weakening of local government autonomy in the UK.
Consequently, they advised that parties seriously intent on reviving their

grass-roots might take a number of steps, including the enhancement of membership influence in policy-making via new internal policy forums (think of Labour's national, regional and local forums), the establishment of internal inquiries into party organizational and membership matters (the Conservatives' *Fresh Future* initiative), and the decentralization of powers to local and regional government (Whiteley et al. 1994: 226–38). This latter suggestion is especially fascinating, and potentially highly problematic from the Conservatives' perspective since it is widely acknowledged that state power was centralized considerably during their prolonged sojourn in office after 1979 (Stewart and Stoker 1989; Jenkins 1995). Whiteley and his colleagues suggest that the erosion of local government during this period did much to undermine important selective outcome incentives associated with building individual political careers, and coincided especially with a decline in Conservative Party activism – what was the point of becoming active if one of the main foci of local party activity, local government, was increasingly impotent? Seen in this light, the programme of devolution and the reform of local government introduced by the Blair government after coming to power in 1997 seem pertinent. Equally striking, however, are the unmistakable signs of an extraordinary volte-face by William Hague's Conservatives. At the party's Spring Forum in 1999, Hague made a speech in which he argued that it was 'time to stop trying to defend the errors of past Tory governments, including taking too much power from local government and concentrating it in Whitehall' (McSmith 1999: 2). This implies that the Conservatives are to eschew nearly two decades of centralization in order to re-emphasize an older Tory tradition of local autonomy. More generally, it is clear that British political parties see the value of healthy and active grass-roots, and are alert to the problems posed by the decline and de-energization of local party memberships. While Labour currently appears to be further along the road of recovery, the signs are that the Conservatives take the problem no less seriously now.

Resources 2: funding

Members are not the only organizational resource available to modern political parties, of course. In particular, it is obvious that the question of finance has to be broached in any attempt to appreciate the resourcing of party organizations. It can be argued that, given the size and wealth of the country, British political parties have tended to be rather poorly resourced in comparative international terms (Webb 1995: 309–10). Nevertheless, with respect to both income and expenditure, British parties are considerably better off in real terms than they were a generation ago, as Table 8.1 and Figures 8.2 and 8.3 make clear. These report national head office funding since the year of the first 'television election' in 1959.[11]

In real terms, Conservative Party central income and expenditure fluctuated virtually trendlessly between 1959 and 1983, but climbed considerably in

TABLE 8.1　UK party head office income and expenditure, 1959–97

Year		Cons: money terms	Cons: real terms	Labour: money terms	Labour: real terms	Libs/LDs: money terms	Libs/LDs: real terms	Average: money terms	Average: real terms
1959	Y	1,672,000	20,900,000	498,000	6,225,000	28,275	353,438	732,758	9,159,475
	X	1,180,000	14,750,000	485,000	6,062,500	27,057	338,213	564,019	7,050,238
1964	Y	2,092,000	22,740,040	573,000	6,228,510	82,965	901,830	915,988	9,956,790
	X	2,280,000	24,783,600	583,000	6,337,210	82,784	899,862	981,928	10,673,557
1966	Y	1,976,000	19,760,000	725,000	7,250,000	113,547	1,135,470	938,182	9,381,820
	X	2,450,000	24,500,000	420,000	4,200,000	115,582	1,155,820	995,194	9,951,940
1970	Y	1,860,000	15,493,800	1,034,000	8,613,220	213,630	1,779,538	1,035,877	8,628,855
	X	1,668,000	13,894,440	948,000	7,896,840	96,699	805,503	904,233	7,532,261
1974	Y	2,221,500	12,484,830	1,781,000	10,009,220	87,074	489,356	1,363,191	7,661,133
	X	2,519,500	14,159,590	1,865,000	10,481,300	119,241	670,134	1,501,247	8,437,008
1979	Y	5,292,000	14,394,240	3,113,000	8,467,360	299,101	813,555	2,903,131	7,896,516
	X	5,885,000	16,007,200	3,358,000	9,133,760	252,089	685,682	3,165,030	8,608,882
1983	Y	9,800,000	17,836,000	6,200,000	11,284,000	1,235,035	2,247,764	5,745,012	10,455,921
	X	8,600,000	15,652,000	6,100,000	11,102,000	4,704,000	8,561,280	6,468,000	11,771,760
1987	Y	15,013,000	23,270,150	9,843,000	15,256,650	1,896,640	2,939,792	8,917,547	13,822,197
	X	15,600,000	24,180,000	11,300,000	17,515,000	4,106,000	6,364,300	10,335,333	16,019,766
1992	Y	23,449,000	26,731,860	13,200,000	15,048,000	3,000,000	3,420,000	13,216,333	15,066,619
	X	19,600,000	22,344,000	19,000,000	21,660,000	2,500,000	2,850,000	13,700,000	15,618,000
1997	Y	42,500,000	42,500,000	24,100,000	24,100,000	3,800,000	3,800,000	23,466,666	23,466,666
	X	38,400,000	38,400,000	31,500,000	31,500,000	3,500,000	3,500,000	24,466,666	24,466,666
Change, 1959–97	Y	+2442%	+103%	+4739%	+287%	+13339%	+975%	+3103%	+156%
	X	+3154%	+160%	+6395%	+420%	+12836%	+935%	+4238%	+247%

Notes: X = Expenditure, Y = Income.

All amounts are quoted in sterling; all years selected are general election years. Figures for 1974 are the average for financial years 1973/4 and 1974/5, thus taking in both the general elections of February and October 1974. Figures represent an attempt to total income to and expenditure from all central party funds, including both general and general election funds, where parties make such a distinction. Note that the figures for the old Liberal Party are almost certainly a significant underestimate of the party's true financial position (see Webb 1992a: 867; Pinto-Duschinsky 1980: 182–9). 'Liberal' figures for 1983 and 1987 are aggregated for both the Liberal Party and the SDP.

For real terms figures 1997 price index = 100; 1992 = 87.9; 1987 = 64.7; 1983 = 55.0; 1979 = 36.7; 1974 = 17.8; 1970 = 12.0; 1966 = 10.0; 1964 = 9.2; 1959 = 8.0. These deflators are calculated from Retail Price Indices cited in Central Statistical Office 1963, 1976, 1989, and Office for National Statistics 1999.

Sources:

1959–79 figures: Pinto-Duschinsky 1980; 1983–87 figures: Neill 1998. Ultimately, all these figures can be traced back to Conservative Party Annual Financial Statements, Labour Party NEC Annual Reports, Liberal Party Annual Reports and Liberal Democrat Federal Party Annual Reports.

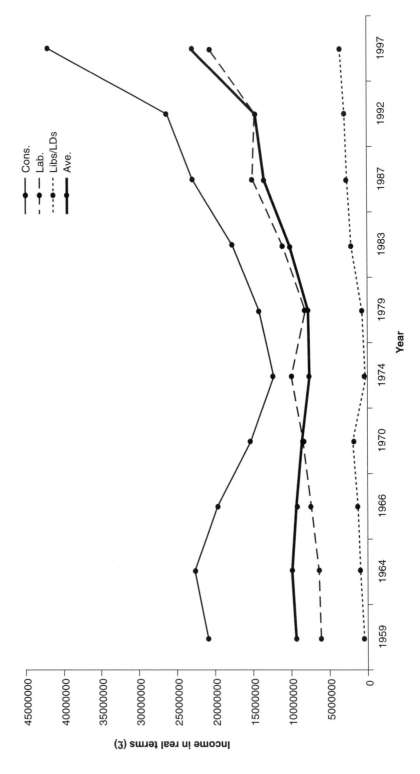

FIGURE 8.2 *UK party head office income, 1959–97*

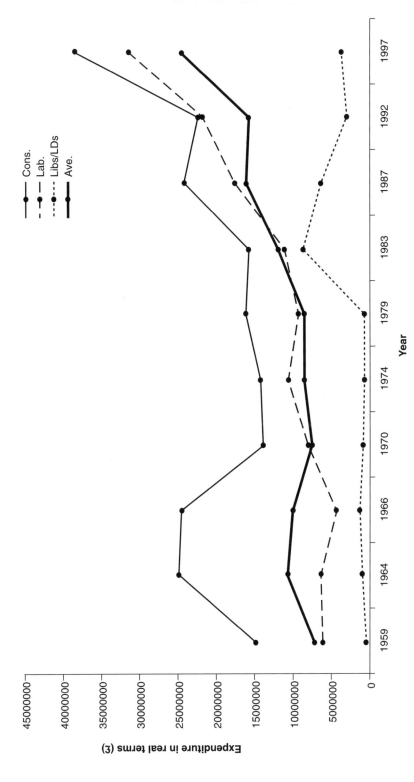

FIGURE 8.3   *UK party head office expenditure, 1959–97*

the decade from 1987–97. The Labour Party has enjoyed an even more emphatic growth in real revenue and expenditure; in fact, as the figures in the bottom row of Table 8.1 make clear, both Labour and the Liberal Democrats have gone a long way towards closing the traditional funding gap between the Conservatives and themselves.[12] Thus, while Conservative central income has doubled in real terms since 1959, Labour's has grown by nearly three times and, even allowing for the incomplete nature of Liberal Party financial data (see notes to Table 8.1), there can be little doubt that the modern Liberal Democrats are wealthier than their precursors. On the whole, therefore, the main British political parties are significantly better funded than hitherto; indeed Table 8.1 (final column, bottom row) suggests that on average central party income has grown by more than one and a half times, while expenditure has increased by nearly two and a half times.

Where do the parties obtain their funds from? Traditionally, this was largely through institutional donations, at least in respect of the major parties; thus, the affiliated trade unions contributed the bulk of Labour's central income via affiliation fees and donations (the latter usually into a special general election fund), while the Conservatives relied largely on donations from private companies. Other parties, the Liberal Democrats and their predecessors included, have always been hampered by their lack of connections with institutional supporters. This picture of institutional support for the major parties reinforced the substance and image of the British party system as an expression of class conflict: the funding supplied by trade unions and business corporations ensured that Labour and the Tories were quite literally the parties of labour and of capital. Since the 1980s, however, this traditional picture has changed significantly in that neither major party now relies on institutional funding to the same extent as hitherto.

In the case of the Tories, it has been estimated that two-thirds of Central Office income was derived from corporate donations throughout the 1950s and early 1960s, but this seems to have fallen to a little over half by the late 1980s, barely one-third by the early 1990s and just one-fifth by 1997 (Pinto-Duschinsky 1980: 139; Fisher 1996b: 158; Neill 1998: 32). The explanation for this change lies in a number of factors. In part, it may be purely contingent on the erosion of business confidence in the Conservative governments of the late 1980s and early 1990s (something which could have been spurred by the impact of the 'prawn cocktail offensive' through which Labour politicians wooed finance capital during the same period). It is increasingly likely, moreover, that potential donors prefer to direct 'political' expenditure towards the burgeoning number of professional lobbyists who can facilitate contacts with all parties. However, it should be said that the Conservatives' declining dependence on corporate donations reflects a degree of success as well as failure, in so far as the party has become more adept at the strategy of eliciting major contributions from wealthy individuals, and in generating revenue through selective financial services, conferences and sales. Indeed, some 80% of Central Office income came from individual donations in 1997 (Neill 1998: 33). The party has not, however, managed to increase the proportion of income it derives from local Constituency Associations: by the mid-1990s, this constituted only 5% of Central Office income (Fisher 1996b: 159–62). It will be interesting to see if the Conservatives' new constitutional arrangements affect this; recall that the *Fresh Future* reforms have abolished the legal autonomy of Constituency Associations from the national organization and Central Office now has the right to stipulate 'performance criteria' relating, among other things, to constituency parties' levels of fund-raising. Although the central party has long prescribed financial 'quota' targets for constituencies, these have never hitherto been binding: it will therefore be fascinating to see how Central Office interprets its new relationship with the Constituency Associations.

Labour has wrought a remarkable reduction in its financial dependence on the trade unions over the course of a little more than a decade. In 1983, some 96% of all central party income (including General and General Election Funds) could be traced to the unions (Webb 1992a: 20–2), but within a decade no more than two-thirds could and by 1997 the figure stood at just 40% (Neill 1998: 31). How has this been achieved? Largely through a determined and conscious effort to professionalize the task of fund-raising, an activity for which the party now employs external specialists on fixed-term contracts.[13] This has proved especially successful in generating small personal donations, Labour claiming to raise some 40% of its funding from such sources by the late 1990s. Some 70,000 members pay a regular monthly subscription, while a further 500,000 make ad hoc donations each year (Neill 1998: 32). A particular success has been the party's 'Business Plan', established in the late 1980s in order to attract individual donations through activities such as fund-raising dinners; within five years of its foundation, this accounted for nearly one-fifth of the Labour Party's central income (Fisher 1996a: 80). After the 1997 election, a new 'High Value Donors Unit' and the '1000 Club' were established, both with the aim of increasing income from relatively large contributors (Neill 1998: 32–3). These changing financial connections demonstrate graphically the transformation of New Labour at the levels of both political linkage and organizational style.

The Liberal Democrats are far more dependent on individual members for funding than either of the major parties. Major institutional donations have been relatively few and far between; in so far as the old Liberal Party is concerned, this is not surprising, for it was essentially a 'non-aligned' organization attempting to operate in the context of a party system in which both ideology and mass behaviour were fundamentally structured by class interest. In the context of a significantly more dealigned political system, however, the position of the modern Liberal Democrats is no longer quite so anomalous; moreover, in terms of party funding they appear less exceptional than their predecessors because their major party rivals have lost institutional support (in relative terms), rather than because the Liberal Democrats have at last gained it. It is not surprising to discover, therefore, that close examination of their accounts reveals that more than 70% of the federal party's income can be traced back to the membership.[14]

The main parties are clearly wealthier in real terms and are more extravagant than they were a generation ago, but do they have enough money to meet their needs? This is a critically important question, for parties must be able to do the jobs required of them by the wider political system. According to Robert Garner and Richard Kelly, British parties face a number of problems in meeting the soaring costs of 'electorally effective activity' (1998: 201–3). First, partisan dealignment means that membership levels and revenue have dropped at the very time when the need for parties to campaign harder in order to persuade a more open electorate has increased. Though broadly true (and certainly in keeping with the underlying argument of Chapter 2 of this book), it should be said that the financial problems of declining enrolment have to some extent been overcome by simply increasing subscription rates in real terms; Labour, for instance, increased its standard membership fee from £1.20 to £17.50 over the 20 years following the election of 1979, a greater than fivefold increase in real terms (the 1979 fee being £3.26 at 1997 prices). Second, parties not only campaign more intensely but also more frequently given the advent of direct elections to the European Parliament since 1979. This 'problem' might appear destined to become all the more acute given the need for regular elections to the new assemblies in London and the regions. Finally, technological innovation has increased the real cost of electoral activity, as parties have sought to adapt to the revolutions in communications and information technology which have taken place since the 1970s; the computerization of party organization and campaigning has required considerable investment in hardware and personnel.

Therefore, it is perhaps not surprising that observers have sometimes lamented the chronic under-funding of the main British parties, notwithstanding the undeniable growth in real income which they have enjoyed. At the time of the inquiry into party funding conducted by the House of Commons Select Committee on Home Affairs in 1993–4, the Conservative Party Chairman Norman Fowler revealed that his party had accumulated a deficit of £19 million; despite shedding Central Office staff, the deficit still stood at £14 million 3 years later, and it was only by dint of a remarkable burst of generosity from donors that the party was able to clear this and build an election fund in time for the 1997 election.[15] Even so, the extremely heavy expenditure incurred in the course of the 1997 campaign meant that the Conservatives went into opposition confronting another larger deficit and staffing cutbacks inevitably followed (Hencke and Ward 1998: 1). Though not so troubled during the 1990s, Labour too has not infrequently run into debt and been obliged to cut back operations and staffing, both centrally and regionally, while the Liberal Democrats plainly have far more meagre resources than either major party at their disposal (Garner and Kelly 1998: 204). It is interesting to note that the former General Secretary of the Labour Party, Tom Sawyer, estimated in his evidence to the (Neill) Committee on Standards in Public Life in 1998 that his party required an average of £20–25 million a year across the course of an electoral cycle in order to function properly, whereas its actual average income during the 1992–97 parliament was just £12.6 million (Neill 1998: 36). For their part, the Conservatives considered their own income of more than £20 million in 1996 inadequate for their needs (Garner and Kelly 1998: 204).

It therefore seems safe to conclude that British parties have regularly struggled to cover the costs of doing their job. Indeed, it is perhaps not too great an exaggeration to say that the British get their party politics on the cheap; certainly, this is true given the size and wealth of the country. Previous research shows Britain placed bottom out of 10 Western European countries in this sense in the late 1980s, generating just 11 pence of central party income per elector (at 1987 prices), compared to £1.60 for Austrian parties (Webb 1995: 308–9). What, if anything, is to be done? A number of inquiries into party funding in Britain have considered this question over the years and their conclusions have varied. One of the most obvious potential remedies is for the state to provide subsidies to political parties. The first Western European state to fund its party organizations was the Federal Republic of Germany in 1959, and it did so precisely on the grounds that additional funds were required to cover the increasing costs of party activity (Linton 1994a: 35). In 1975, state subsidies were introduced in Britain for opposition parliamentary parties; this scheme is still widely known as 'Short money' after the Leader of the House of Commons who piloted the legislation through parliament (Ted Short, subsequently Lord Glenamara). In 1996 a similar, though more modest, scheme (known as 'Cranborne money') was established in respect of the two leading parties in the House of Lords. Short money was introduced in order to enable opposition parties in the Commons to fulfil their parliamentary duties, and it was particularly intended for the provision of research assistance to front-bench spokespersons and staff for Chief Whips' and party leaders' offices. Such aid has come to be regarded as vital if opposition parties are to be effective in holding the government to account. Indeed, in 1998, all parties argued that the Short money scheme required augmenting considerably, and the Neill Committee concurred by recommending that it be increased by as much as three times (1998: 102–3), a proposal accepted by the government (Cm.4413 1999: para. 6.8).[16] The Short and Cranborne schemes, however, remain the only direct financial subventions to political parties provided by the state in Britain.[17]

At least two major inquiries into the funding of parties in Britain have recommended that state aid be extended to central (that is, extra-parliamentary) party organizations. The Houghton Committee on Financial Aid to Political Parties, established by the Labour government in 1975 (Houghton 1976), and the Hansard Society (1982) both concluded that the central parties required direct subsidies from the Exchequer if they were to operate effectively and without becoming chronically susceptible to debt. However, such proposals have never been acted upon by any British government and there is little prospect of this changing in the foreseeable future. After Houghton reported in the mid-1970s, the Conservative Party treasurer (Lord) Alistair McAlpine persuaded his party chairman that Labour had more to gain from the extension of state funding than the Tories did. Consequently – and notwithstanding concerns about the state of party finances – the Conservatives rejected the Houghton Committee's proposals and the Callaghan government felt unable to enact state funding without all-party support (Linton 1994b). The Conservatives have maintained their opposition to state funding for extra-parliamentary parties ever since, though Labour appeared ready to break the bipartisan consensus in the 1990s. At the time of the Select Committee on Home Affairs' report into party funding (1994), Labour spokespersons were prepared to advocate both annual subventions to central party organizations and the reimbursement of election expenses; however, once the party had resumed office and invited the Neill Committee to address the question of party funding, Labour's official position had changed. Though still conceding that 'there is a case in principle for various forms of state aid', the demands of 'fiscal prudence' meant that the time was not right to prioritize the needs of parties. Quite when the exigencies of fiscal prudence *will* permit such a priority is hard to imagine, so it is tempting to conclude that Labour has once again set its face against the extension of state funding to extra-parliamentary party organizations, and perhaps this is not surprising given its apparent success in closing the 'funding gap' with the Tories (refer again to Table 8.1). However, the narrow self-interest of the major parties is not the only reason for the lack of state funding in Britain, since the Neill Committee concurred in the view that it should not be extended to extra-parliamentary organizations. What was its reasoning?

The Neill Committee concluded that a better way of limiting party debt was to impose legal limits on permitted spending in election campaigns. Since the Corrupt and Illegal Practices Act of 1883, individual candidates in local constituency contests have been subject to very tight campaign expenditure limits, but the legal case of *Rex* v. *Tronoh Mines* in 1952 established that such limits did not apply to the national campaign expenditure of central party organizations. This, allied to the advent of televisual communication techniques, explains why the parties have focused ever more effort on their national campaigns, but such campaigns are costly and have fostered a so-called 'arms race' mentality in parties desperate to outspend their rivals. Between 1983 and 1997 the Conservative Party's national election campaign expenditure increased by more than three times in real terms, and Labour's by more than five times (Neill 1998: 43). Therefore, the Neill Committee recommended that no party contesting more than 600 seats in Westminster elections should be permitted to spend more than £20 million (at 1998 prices) on its national campaign (over and above specific constituency campaign expenditure). Given that the Conservatives spent £28.3 million and Labour £26 million in 1997, it seems reasonable to conclude that, should this recommendation be implemented and effectively policed, it could indeed be expected to curb the profligacy of the major parties in election years. The Home Secretary (Jack Straw) was certainly persuaded by the Committee's arguments, proposing to enact the recommendations, and to extend them to European and devolved elections.18

In addition, the Neill Committee was sensitive to the dangers of the 'cartel party' thesis, according to which state funding might 'make the parties, in effect, part of the state' (1998: 92). The cartel thesis, deriving from the work of Richard Katz and Peter Mair, was discussed briefly in Chapter 7 (see Chapter 7, note 9). To recap, this suggests that parties in some countries come to exploit their access to state resources to cement their advantage over others: 'The state . . . becomes an institutionalized structure of support, sustaining insiders while excluding outsiders' (1995: 16). Mair, in particular, has argued that this can have serious repercussions for the popular legitimacy of parties, especially when combined with the impression that parties might be struggling to fulfil some of their traditional political functions (an issue considered at length in Chapter 9):

> On the ground, and in terms of their representative role, parties appear to be less relevant and to be losing some of their key functions. In public office, on the other hand, and in terms of their linkage to the state, they appear to be more privileged than ever. (1995: 54)

In a sense, a similar concern for the legitimacy of parties underlies the point made by Conservative interlocutors who argue that 'forcing taxpayers to contribute to costs of party political activities of which they do not approve would be a very significant step' (Neill 1998: 89). These are persuasive reasons for rejecting the extension of state funding, though perhaps the factor of greatest significance is the lack of firm support from either major party. The position of the Neill Committee is undoubtedly politically prudent in this sense, yet it is not entirely convincing or logical. For one thing, the idea of capping national campaign expenditure is not unproblematic; it is open to legal challenge on the grounds that it inhibits freedom of expression and could also prove very difficult to police. Indeed, one dissenting voice on the Neill Committee made these (and other) criticisms (1998: 121). For another thing, on the face of it, there is a certain inconsistency in arguing that parties are vital mechanisms of democracy which require state support in respect of their parliamentary functions, but not in respect of any other sphere of their activity. Where is the inherent logic in this? One might equally well argue that if political parties are so central to the operation of the democratic system, all citizens have a vested interest in their well-being and effective operation and should be obliged to contribute to their financial needs. Seen from this perspective, the funding of parties can be regarded as a classic problem of collective action (Olson 1965); that is, while all benefit from the operation of a competitive party system, the overwhelming majority of citizens 'free-ride' on the contributions and input of a committed minority.

However, it is not entirely just to damn the Neill Report in these terms, for it redeemed itself to a considerable extent by recommending a system of tax-relief on donations up to £500. In a sense, such a scheme is a kind of public subvention given that the Inland Revenue would be obliged to forego a small amount of tax revenue. Moreover, such a scheme would almost certainly have the virtue of encouraging parties to seek the contributions of small donors; not only is the risk of corrupt exchange between politicians and donors minimal in such cases, but the parties gain a new incentive to boost individual membership recruitment and involve more citizens in political participation (Neill 1998: ch. 8). A system of tax-relief on small donations would, however, be unlikely to provide such a predictable and consistent pattern of party income as direct subventions. Nevertheless, the Neill proposals were undoubtedly innovative in a British context, and would almost certainly have helped secure the resources which parties routinely require. However, the Labour government chose to make tax-relief the one major Neill recommendation which it rejected: estimating a likely revenue loss of £4–5 million per year, the Home Secretary argued that this would be too expensive for both the state and the parties to administer (Cm.4413 1999: para. 6.3). This explanation is less than convincing, given the very small sums involved as a proportion of overall tax revenues. Indeed, it is far more likely that calculations of relative party political advantage weighed in the balance: while the Conservatives and Liberal Democrats both seemed to regard tax-relief in a positive light, Labour's former Director of Finance did not, judging that it would be of little value to his party, but of 'enormous value to our opponents' (Neill 1998: 97).

Overall, the main British parties can be viewed as considerably better off financially than they were a generation ago, but engaged in a constant struggle to stave off the spectre of debt and organizational retrenchment. While they have undoubtedly become increasingly skilled at fund-raising, resources derived in this fashion bring no guarantees of long-term stability (witness the periodic debt crises and staff reductions to which the parties are chronically prone). Nothing better illustrates the relative poverty of British parties than the realization that the combined central party income of the three main organizations in 1997 amounted to just 55% of the income of *one* of Germany's major parties (the Social Democrats) in 1990 (Linton 1994a: 37) – indeed, it is probable that the entire British party system could be run on what it costs to finance a single German party! Moreover, although the state funding which could alleviate this 'shoestring approach' to British democracy is potentially unpopular with voters, it can be argued with even greater force that the current system of voluntary fund-raising has produced evidence of impropriety which is far more damaging to the legitimacy of parties. While the sort of regulatory measures proposed by the Neill Committee and largely accepted by the Labour government should certainly go a long way towards limiting the potential for such damage (see Chapter 9), voluntarily funded parties will nevertheless always remain susceptible to allegations that they can be 'bought' by powerful donors.

Resources 3: staff and policy assistance

What of the personnel who work for party organizations? Although we know of the periodic need which all the main parties have faced to reduce staff numbers, in truth very little is really known (by political scientists at least) about party employees. This shows in the lack of reliable time-series data on staffing levels, though there can be little doubt about the broad picture: it is evident that while each of the parties has increased its establishment of personnel at the central level, the local story has generally been one of substantial decline since the 1960s (see Table 8.2). Again, the Labour Party has experienced the most dramatic growth of central party resources (especially in the decade following the election of 1987).[19] However, even Labour has not been able to prevent the loss of full-time staff working in constituency parties. This trend seems to point to a process of centralization of party resources, accompanied by an overall weakening of local party organization (especially when taken in conjunction with the evidence of membership decline and de-energization which we encountered earlier). This notion of the 'centralization' of resourcing and party management becomes more persuasive when taken

TABLE 8.2 *Party staffing in Britain*

Year	Cons.		Labour		Liberals/Lib.Dems	
	Central	Sub-national	Central	Sub-national	Central	Sub-national
1964	97	580	50	248	19	74
1970	95	431	50	167	12	22
1979	–	350	–	128	17	–
1983	–	–	–	104	20	11
1987	100	291	71	95	25	8
1993	148	240	90	–	–	–
1998	167	221	179	150	35	5
Change 1964–98	+72%	–62%	+258%	–40%	+84%	–77%

Note:
'Sub-national' staff includes both regional office staff (employed by national party headquarters) and party agents (usually paid for by local party organizations). The figures cited for 1993 and 1998 are certainly lower for each of the parties than they would have been during the general election years of 1992 and 1997 respectively; for instance, the Conservatives claim to have employed around 290–300 full-time agents at local level during each of these election years. Since I have been unable to gather central party staffing data for 1992 and 1997, however, the more complete 1993 and 1998 figures have been cited. The main implication of all this is that the general growth in the number of party employees has almost certainly been even greater than this table implies. Thus, Labour sources estimate that, including paid and voluntary staff, as many as 500 people may have been working at the party's national headquarters during the 1997 general election campaign.

Sources:
Conservative Central Office; Labour Party Personnel Department; Labour Party NEC Organization Committee minutes; Liberal Party Annual Reports; Liberal Democrats' Information and Personnel Offices; Finer 1980.

in the broader context of changing styles of political communication. Thus, in Chapter 5 we noted how the development of modern campaigning entailed televisual communication with electors, and does not necessarily require large numbers of locally based officials and an army of volunteer activists. This is not to suggest that local campaigns are viewed as insignificant by the parties or expert observers, but rather that the careful targeting of resources and effort on certain localities is what counts.[20] Nowhere was this more evident than in the 1997 election, when all parties (especially those in opposition at the time) concentrated their efforts on key seats (Kavanagh 1997: 31; Berrington and Hague 1997: 52). The crucial point about this is that such carefully targeted campaign efforts require central coordination of resources and campaign strategies; indeed, the need for all party candidates and spokespersons to be 'on message' at all times has virtually become a caricature of centralized control within modern parties (especially New Labour). In addition, as we have seen, the strict legal constraints imposed on local constituency campaign expenditure also dictate an inevitable centralization of campaign resources.

Fascinatingly there is further evidence of the centralization of Labour Party organization in the sudden increase in the number of regional office staff hired since the 1997 election. To understand the significance of this, it is necessary to grasp the fact that regional offices are essentially provincial outposts of central party headquarters. Though not based in London, regional organizers are (unlike most party agents) not employed by constituency organizations, but rather by the central party and are answerable to it. In the 12 months following the Spring of 1998, the number of staff employed at Labour's ten regional offices increased from 75 to 142, which strongly suggests that Millbank has taken steps to enhance yet further its capacity to coordinate the activities of CLPs.[21] Seen in this light, the running down of local parties in the UK may not be as significant as it initially appears for the overall strength of national party organizations. Parties certainly need resources but, more importantly, they need to deploy them in such a way as to achieve their primary purposes; central coordination is one means by which parties adapt both to technological change and to the loss of staff and members at the local level.

So, it should be said, is the professionalization of staff. The notion of 'professionalization' is, of course, central to the model of electoral-professionalism that was discussed in the context of party campaigning in Chapter 5. There it was taken to imply an increasingly expert approach to campaigning, drawing more heavily on the use and influence of opinion researchers and advertising consultants; however, professionalization could refer equally to the parties' regular pay-roll employees. If this were the case, it would constitute evidence of a further qualitative change through which parties adapt their organizational resources to the context and needs of modern British politics. The paucity of evidence about party staff makes it difficult to assess with confidence how far this might be the case; however, it does appear that a remarkable transformation of the workplace culture occurred within Labour's organization during the 1990s – both centrally and locally. In particular, changes in organizational structure have been accompanied by a growing emphasis on the need for flexibility, competence and adaptability among staff. Thus, while one senior employee spoke of a sense of something akin to 'permanent revolution' in organizational approach, another stated:

> If you can't cope with change, if you can't sort of manage to think, 'oh well, two years down the line we're changing again', then really it's not an organisation for you. It's constantly moving. You adjust structures and you can't be too rigid in the way you do things because the nature of politics is that things are constantly changing.[22]

In large part the impulse for this change of organizational ethos stems from the influence of the former Labour Party General Secretary, Tom Sawyer, and his deputy and eventual successor, Margaret McDonagh. Sawyer's general importance for Labour's transformation since the 1980s has long been recognized (Hughes and Wintour 1990), though his particular impact on organizational ethos is less noted. One unit head at Millbank illustrated this by referring to an incident in the party's former head office at Walworth Road, in south-east London:

> I think it started to come with the appointment of Tom Sawyer as General Secretary: he brought in a fresh approach when he was appointed . . . there was this old tatty chair in the Boardroom at Walworth Road and he had a full staff meeting, and he picked up this chair . . . and said: 'this chair isn't good enough for our organisation. It isn't good enough for our members and it isn't good enough for you as party staff. We need to start treating people with more respect and we need to start looking at ourselves, the way we organise ourselves, and all the rest of it.' And it was . . . all about that chair really. We were shoddy . . . You walk around this building now and you see the way we organise ourselves, the way we are, and there is a different feel . . . you feel like a professional and that you've come to work . . . whereas Walworth Road . . . it was tatty and it did, in a sense, reflect the way we were back then.[23]

Furthermore, it is interesting to note the growing emphasis placed by senior staff on the training and professional development of Millbank employees; one unit head claimed that he would no longer 'recruit people who either don't want to start studying or haven't studied'.[24] Even though Labour is almost certainly more advanced in terms of changes such as these, there are unmistakeable signs that the Conservatives are attempting their own organizational transformation. After 1997 the Deputy Chairman, Archie Norman, sought to reorganize the way in which Central Office worked: in some ways the reported changes seemed to emulate Labour's operations at Millbank, with the introduction of professional fund-raisers, and the horizontal integration of hitherto separate units such as research, campaigning and communications into single open-plan offices. Other changes seem to have less to do with structural reorganization and more to do with an attempt to alter the ethos and culture of the workplace: hence, the introduction of a 'clean desk' policy and meetings at which staff are selected at random to speak about their department's work (Hencke and Ward 1998: 1).

If we consider the overall picture created by the various changes discussed here (and in Chapter 5), the impression is of one major party consciously seeking to professionalize its staffing and operations in a variety of ways, while the other has latterly become aware of the need to adapt similarly. It should be said that the concept of 'professionalism' is, in fact, multifaceted, and it would be wrong to imply that it now suffuses every aspect of the parties' working practices; neither is it accurate to suggest that every party employee displays all the characteristics that sociologists ascribe to a professional, such as expertise, job autonomy, commitment, vocational identification, a code of professional ethics and membership of a professional body which regulates its members (Wilensky 1959; Raelin 1991). Nevertheless, it seems broadly appropriate to conclude that a growing number of Britain's major party staff – especially Labour's at this point in time – can be described as 'professionals in pursuit of political outcomes' (Romzek and Utter 1997: 1263): this is implicit in the growing sense of specialized expertise which party staff exude, their substantial if qualified autonomy, and their commitment to political enterprise.

Apart from staff formally on party payrolls and professional consultants or limited-term fund-raising specialists hired by the parties, we should not overlook the possibility that modern British parties might benefit from professional research and policy assistance provided by independent policy research bodies. Formally, few of these 'think-tanks' (as they have generally come to be known) are linked to any of the parties or have representation within party structures. Informally, however, it is widely recognized that there are partisan and ideological sympathies as well as overlaps of personnel which to some extent connect parties to research bodies. Thus these bodies should not be entirely dismissed when evaluating the overall picture of party resourcing in contemporary Britain. For instance, the Institute for Economic Affairs (IEA, founded in 1945), the Centre for Policy Studies (CPS, founded by former Conservative government minister Sir Keith Joseph in 1975), and the Adam Smith Institute (ASI, 1977) are essentially right-wing think tanks, whose political outlooks were especially sympathetic to the governments of Margaret Thatcher. Less high profile, but broadly right-of-centre, are the Social Market Foundation (1989) and Politeia (1995). Further left, there are long-established research foundations such as the Fabian Society (1884, and the one such body which is formally affiliated to Labour), the Policy Studies Institute (PSI since 1978, though its roots lie in Political and Economic Planning, which goes back to 1931), and the National Institute of Economic and Social Research (NIESR, 1938). Closer to New Labour in recent years, however, have been the Institute for Public Policy Research (IPPR, 1988) and Demos (1994).

Just how influential have these bodies been in shaping party and government policy? This is not easy to assess, but it seems most likely that direct influence is limited in reality. Though often the focus of media attention since the 1970s, close scrutiny of policy development suggests that politicians are only willing to draw on the recommendations of think-tanks when these coincide closely with their own views. In other words, politicians gain intellectual support and credibility by highlighting the work of think-tanks, while the latter gain publicity, occasional research contracts and publication sales in return (Denham and Garnett 1999). Thus, think-tanks are usually a party 'resource' in a subtle sense only. It should also be said that the parties do sometimes recruit individuals to their own ranks from independent research bodies: David Willetts, for instance, moved from the PSI to Conservative Central Office's own Research Department before eventually being elected to parliament and becoming a minister in the Major government, while Neil Kinnock's former press secretary Patricia Hewitt travelled a not dissimilar path into the Blair government via the deputy directorship of IPPR. More recently, Tony Blair has recruited both David Miliband (of IPPR) and Geoff Mulgan (of Demos) to his Downing Street policy unit. In these ways, think-tanks can occasionally act as useful sources of staff and policy assistance for front-bench politicians.[25]

Conclusion

This chapter has reviewed the main types of resource available to modern political parties in Britain, and examined the distribution and utilization of such resources. Those who argue that parties are generally 'in decline' are inclined to suggest that this is demonstrated, among other things, by the 'weakening' of party organizations. The evidence of this chapter, however, does not straightforwardly bear out such a contention. Rather, it shows that, though constantly under considerable pressure to find the resources required, parties are adept at living with resource constraints.

Thus, although the decline of party memberships and the 'de-energization' of some local constituency organizations have been part and parcel of the broader process of partisan dealignment in Britain, the major parties have shown themselves ready to respond to these problems in recent years. While unlikely to reinvent themselves as mass parties (in either a quantitative or qualitative sense), both Labour and the Conservatives are clearly aware of the continuing value of active members, and seem keen to devise selective incentives which might sustain and even revive their memberships. The signs are that Labour has made most progress so far in this undertaking. In any case, one can go some way towards refuting the 'decline of party' argument by pointing out that the centralization and professionalization of staffing and campaigning help counteract the effects of shrinking numbers of local party members. Moreover, it is plain that the very substantial increases in central party funding lend no credence whatsoever to the declinist perspective, even though it can be argued that funding is not yet fully adequate for parties to operate as they should in a healthy democracy. The success which parties

Parties ready to adapt

have had in exploiting new fund-raising techniques and sources of party funding also illustrate once again their capacity to adapt and survive. In short, parties have found themselves under organizational pressure from a variety of changes in their external environment (social, technological, electoral, and so on) and have sought to adapt accordingly. On the whole, they have shown themselves reasonably effective at this, though the struggle to maintain adequate levels of resourcing is an enduring one.

Notes

1   Two points should be made about the nature of the membership figures discussed in this chapter. First, the discussion is restricted to the subject of *individual* members. While Labour's affiliated membership undoubtedly represents a resource of sorts to the party, it has never offered a very meaningful indicator of individual commitment and activism. In any case, numerical changes in the affiliated membership have followed a quite different pattern to those in the number of individual members. Whereas Labour's individual membership, subject to minor fluctuations, followed a broadly downward trajectory between 1960 and 1994, the affiliated membership only began to decline during the early 1980s (thanks largely to a combination of rapidly rising unemployment and legal reforms such as the ending of union 'closed shop' agreements). Second, it must be emphasized that the data available are far from perfect. Neither the Conservatives nor the old Liberal Party regularly reported their membership levels; indeed, both organizations were generally unsure of precisely how many individual members they had across Britain at any given time. The federal nature of the old Liberal Party and the decentralized structure of the Conservative National Union tended to hamper the flow of this sort of information to the centre. From time to time, national membership figures have emerged, but these have only ever been informed estimates based on partial surveys of local parties. One of the clearest implications of the *Fresh Future* reforms introduced by the party in 1998 is that this state of affairs would continue no longer: henceforth, the party would have a national membership structure and a computerized database of members. (Indeed, without this it is hard to imagine how the Conservatives could possibly conduct future leadership elections given the shift to one-member, one-vote.)

2   Equally, however, it should be noted that trade unions' political funds do not have to be spent on affiliation fees or donations to the Labour Party; many trade unions choose not to affiliate to Labour, but maintain political funds which are used for independent political lobbying and campaigning on behalf of members' interests.

3   The creation of the national membership scheme has helped remove de facto barriers to membership, even though it did suffer from various (mainly computer-related) teething problems during its infancy. Prior to the scheme, new recruits could only join via a CLP, and only if already members of affiliated trade unions: these conditions effectively narrowed the range of eligible members.

4   Note that Aarts does not specify precisely what types of organizational membership are involved here, but they include 'traditional interest groups, such as political, social and religious groups, and trade unions' (1995: 231). Although the inclusion of 'political' group involvements might mean party membership is counted in the figures, given that we know the latter has declined greatly across

the period, the clear implication is that involvement in non-party activity must have increased substantially.

5   My thanks to Philip Smith of the Association of Conservative Clubs for his help with these data.

6   The catch-all model is entirely incorporated within the electoral-professional model, but Panebianco adds the centrality of professionals and the likelihood of greater state funding to arrive at his formulation.

7   One should acknowledge the danger of committing an 'ecological fallacy' (that is, using individual-level data to draw aggregate-level inferences) in this argument; nevertheless, it is circumstantial evidence which detracts from the overall likelihood that cognitive mobilization contributes significantly to membership decline.

8   Seyd and Whiteley provide a useful account of the overall social profile of major party memberships in the 1990s. From their research it seems that Conservative members are more likely to be female, to have less experience of higher education, to work in the private sector, to own their own homes and to have run their own businesses or reached a higher occupational status than their counterparts in the Labour Party. They are also considerably older on average (at 62 as against 48 for Labour members). Labour's members can probably be split crudely into two groups: those from a middle-class background, with experience of higher education and employment in the public sector, and those from the party's 'traditional' core working-class constituency (Seyd and Whiteley 1992: 32–3; Whiteley et al. 1994: 43, 45).

9   Until recently, the only obligations Conservative Party members have traditionally been required to make are a vague declaration of support for the stated objectives of the party and an annual financial contribution – and there has been no minimum value for this contribution. The *Fresh Future* reforms change this state of affairs, however.

10 Note the similarity to the explanation of membership decline developed earlier in this chapter, albeit without explicit reference to a formal model such as the general incentives theory.

11 This table concentrates on election years only, since the electoral cycle drives political party resourcing in many ways. Thus, it is clear that central party income and expenditure levels always rise sharply in election years and drop between elections; much the same is true of staffing figures, which explains why Table 8.2 also focuses on election years.

12 This is not true of local party funding, however. On average, local Conservative Associations are still massively wealthier than either Constituency Labour Parties or local Liberal Democrat organizations; thus, research conducted by Justin Fisher reveals that in 1997 the average incomes for the three parties' constituency organizations were £33,305, £8,912 and £6,199 respectively (Neill 1998: 40).

13 Interview with Labour Party personnel staff (Millbank, March 1999).

14 That is, revenue from direct mail (41.4%), the 'state party levy' on the regional organizations (18.4%), and standing orders (10.8%) can all be traced back chiefly to the membership – and it is highly likely that a significant portion of 'further donations' (totalling another 16.8%) also derives from party members (all figures taken from Liberal Democrat Federal Accounts, 1992).

15 Donations increased from £18.8 million to £38.2 million in 1997 (Neill 1998: 31).

16 The government agreed to increase Short Money by a factor of 2.7, with effect from 1 April 1999 (Cm.4413 1999: para. 6.8). The implications of this are illustrated by reference to Table 8.3, which reports the growth of Short money since its

TABLE 8.3   *Allocation of Short money to main opposition parliamentary*
             parties, 1979–97

Year	Conservative	Labour	Liberal/Lib.Dem.
1979	143,335	139,698	29,457
1983	–	296,497	57,150
1987	–	436,669	75,238
1992	–	946,250	199,420
1997*	986,762	–	371,997
2000**	3,377,973	–	1,085,009

Notes: All figures expressed in sterling at current price levels. * May 1997–March 1998.
** Estimated maxima each party will receive in 1999–2000, including £500,000 to the office of
the Leader of the Opposition.

Sources:
Webb 1994: 123; Neill 1998: 101; Cm.4413 1999: para. 6.8.

introduction in 1975. Short money is allocated to opposition parliamentary parties according to a formula which takes into account the number of seats and votes won at the preceding general election; this is then indexed annually to changes in retail prices. The Neill Committee recommended changing this system so that the Official Opposition's allocation is fixed and not dependent on electoral performance (1998: 103–4), but the Home Secretary rejected this suggestion, arguing that the increases in Short money and Leader of the Opposition's funding would be adequate for parliamentary party needs.

17   It should be noted that the state also bears the cost of certain subsidies-in-kind to candidates for elective public office which indirectly benefit political parties. Thus, candidates in European and Westminster (but not local) elections are entitled to free postage for one election communication to every address or elector within a constituency. It is estimated that the cost to the Exchequer of free postage was £20.5 million in 1997 (Neill 1998: 88). Moreover, each candidate in European, Westminster and local elections is entitled to the free provision of rooms in school premises or public buildings for the purpose of holding public meetings 'in the furtherance of his candidature' (*sic:* Representation of the People Act 1983, s 95[1]). In addition, the main parties benefit by not having to pay broadcasting networks for the airtime used in Party Political Broadcasts and Party Election Broadcasts.

18   The relevant draft legislation proposed a limit equal to £30,000 of expenditure for each Westminster constituency contested by a party, giving a theoretical maximum of £19,770,000 for the UK. The limit applies to the 365 days before polling day, and includes all campaign expenditure incurred by a party in that period, including that on local government elections; if (as in 1974) two general elections are held within a single 365-day period, the limit for the second election applies from the day after the conclusion of the first election campaign. For European Parliamentary elections a limit equal to £45,000 per MEP to be returned in a multi-member constituency has been set; this applies to a period dating from 4 months prior to the election day. The devolved assembly election limits also apply to the 4 months leading up to an election (or the period from the

announcement of an 'extraordinary' election), and are set at: Scotland – £12,000 per constituency plus £80,000 per region; Wales – £10,000 per constituency plus £40,000 per region; Northern Ireland – £17,000 per constituency (Cm.4413 1999: paras. 7.14–7.17).

19 In addition to the staff enumerated in Table 8.2, the main parties employ small numbers of personnel (typically between 6 and 10) to service their parliamentary parties. These are generally located in Chief Whips' offices. Party leaders also maintain a number of advisory staff, and individual MPs hire secretarial and sometimes research staff using their constituency allowances.

20 Indeed, there is a growing body of academic work which now confirms how local organizational efforts can have a significant impact on election outcomes at constituency level (Pattie et al. 1994; Pattie et al. 1995; Whiteley and Seyd 1992; Denver and Hands 1997) and there is no doubt that Labour, at least, has taken the work of local party organizations increasingly seriously in recent years. Even so, the strict legal spending limits on local campaigns imply considerable constraints on local parties.

21 Author's interviews with Labour Party personnel staff (Millbank, March 1998 and March 1999).

22 Interviews with author (Millbank, March 1999 and August 1999).

23 Interview with author (Millbank, August 1999).

24 Interview with author (Millbank, August 1999).

25 An interesting twist to the think-tank issue was provided by the Neill Committee, it should be said; mindful, perhaps, that no British party had links with serious research and political education organizations such as the *stiftungen* associated with the main German parties (Poguntke 1994: 187), Neill proposed that a 'Policy Development Fund' (of no more than £2 million per year) be established. The aim would be to provide a modest source of public funding that would be ring-fenced for the purposes of long-term policy development, something which the Committee felt parties found it hard to dedicate themselves to (Neill 1998: 93). This recommendation was accepted by the Home Secretary, who proposed that 'policy development grants' be administered by a new Electoral Commission to parties with at least two sitting MPs (Cm.4413 1999: paras 6.16–6.17).

9

PARTIES AND THE POLITICAL SYSTEM

CONTENTS

We have now considered at length the variety and extent of changes affecting British party politics since 1970. Essentially these entail both programmatic and organizational responses to change in the electoral market, which in turn derives from factors such as the growing heterogeneity of British society. Before concluding our study of party politics in the UK, it is essential that we reflect on the implications of these patterns of change for the broader political system: in short, how well does the party system serve the political system as a whole?

The value of parties to the political system is closely bound up with problems of party legitimacy and 'decline'. A number of critics have claimed that political parties are in a state of decline precisely because they (the parties) fail to fulfil certain requirements which the wider political system makes of them. Those on the left have been particularly prone to see evidence of party decline in this sense. For instance, Martin Jacques has contrasted the erosion of party–society links with the burgeoning non-partisan associative life of the country. In this context, he argued that the established model of representative politics which focuses on the parties at Westminster constitutes something of an impasse for democracy and it needed to be supplemented by the development of new forms of political participation (Jacques 1993). In similar vein Geoff Mulgan, former director of the independent think-tank Demos and a policy advisor to prime minister Tony Blair, once asserted that 'it is hard to see the secular decline of the party reversing' (Mulgan 1994a: 18). According to Mulgan, this decline is associated with a gap between the ethos and practice of democracy, and parties in parliament, he insists, are the culprits in much of this, stuck as they are in the nineteenth century – 'centralized, pyramidal, national with strictly defined rules of authority and sovereignty' (op. cit.: 16; see also Mulgan, 1994b).

As we shall be seeing in the course of this chapter, underlying most of these criticisms of parties is a participationist vision of democracy; from this perspective, the British model of democracy is profoundly disappointing, since it continues to place far too much faith in the stultifying power of party elites. Parties themselves are seen as particularly culpable of failing to stimulate adequate levels of popular engagement with politics. While this, and related themes, will be examined in the course of this chapter, the reader should bear in mind that parties in Britain have not been subject to the intense and widespread criticism that some of their counterparts have faced in other Western countries (such as Germany, Italy or even the USA) in recent decades (see Poguntke and Scarrow 1996). This is not to suggest, however, that the British public is universally satisfied with political parties. Indeed, if parties are falling short in certain aspects of their broad systemic performance, it seems likely that citizens will register some dissatisfaction. Is there any evidence of this?

Popular dissatisfaction with British political parties

How might we gauge levels of popular dissatisfaction with political parties? One of the problems which the political scientist comes up against in addressing this issue is finding robust measures which unambiguously tap mass-level antipathy towards parties. This, for instance, has been a difficulty confronting comparativists working on the theme of anti-party sentiment; on close inspection, the 'admittedly crude' behavioural indicators suggested by Thomas Poguntke (1996) appear quite problematic (for a detailed discussion of these issues, see Webb 1996: 367–9). Similarly, it is not necessarily the case that all of the evidence of low public trust in parties which will be presented in this section is pathological for democracy; to the contrary, one might argue, it is good that citizens show some awareness of the weaknesses and shortcomings of parties and their leaders – just so long as people do not conclude from this that the political system would be altogether better if they simply rid themselves of parties (or, indeed, of democracy itself).[1] But given that some such risk *is* always likely, at least for a few citizens, it is fair to assume that expressions of discontent will always carry with them an element of something unhealthy for democracy; consequently, such indicators are worth reviewing.

So what evidence, if any, do we have of popular disaffection with parties? Clearly, we need to call upon the findings of survey research in order to pursue this question. Unfortunately, it is not easy to find long time-series of

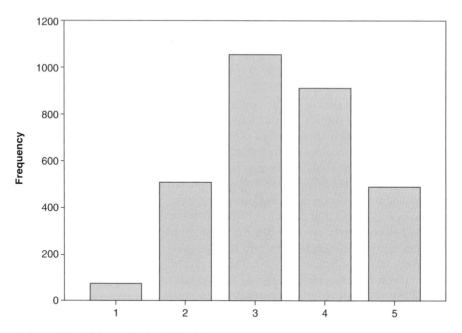

Notes: 1 = Yes, MPs know, 5 = No, MPs don't know.
            Mean = 3.4, standard deviation = 1.0, n = 3027.

Source: BES 1997.

FIGURE 9.1   *Do MPs know what ordinary voters think?*

TABLE 9.1   *Indications of popular dissatisfaction with parties in the UK*

Percentage of respondents feeling that:	1986–87	1991–92	1996–97
a. Parties are only interested in people's votes, not their opinions.	64.4	65.3	63.6
b. Parties can be trusted to put national interest above party interest.	36.8	33.2	22.0
c. Governments can only sometimes, or never, be trusted.	–	–	66.1
d. MPs can only sometimes, or never, be trusted.	–	–	91.5
e. It doesn't matter which party is in power, in the end things go on the same.	–	54.1	44.1
f. No party can do much about unemployment.	33.0	36.0	–
g. No party can do much about inflation.	27.0	38.0	–
h. No party can do much about crime.	34.0	41.0	–

Sources: British Social Attitudes Reports, British Election Surveys.

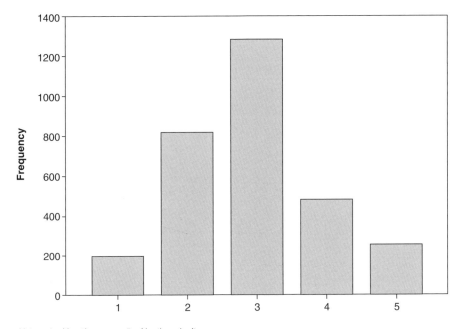

Notes: 1 = Yes, they care, 5 = No, they don't care.
Mean = 2.9, standard deviation = 1.0, n = 3018.

Source: BES 1997.

FIGURE 9.2   *Do parties care what ordinary people think?*

relevant variables, but we can use a variety of sources in order to illuminate
the state of British public opinion at the time of the last three general elections. Table 9.1 and Figures 9.1, 9.2 and 9.3 reveal a number of things about
the popular standing of political parties and party elites since the 1980s.
These suggest three different kinds of problem which British voters have
with political parties. First, a significant number of citizens distrust parties
and party politicians in some respect or other. Two-thirds of the British
electorate has been cynical about the motives of parties since the 1980s
(item a in Table 9.1), and by 1986–87 less than a quarter of voters believed
that parties would place the national interest ahead of party interest (item
b). Similarly, two-thirds expressed doubts about the extent to which party
governments could be trusted (item c), and fewer than 10% were prepared
to trust politicians, a level of disaffection which may in part reflect the
numerous examples of adverse publicity which MPs have attracted concerning their sexual peccadilloes and financial misappropriations during the
1990s. Then again, it might be argued that this reflects badly on individual
politicians rather than parties per se, though quite whether all citizens draw
such a clear distinction is open to speculation. The second problem which
parties appear to have in terms of popular perception is that significant

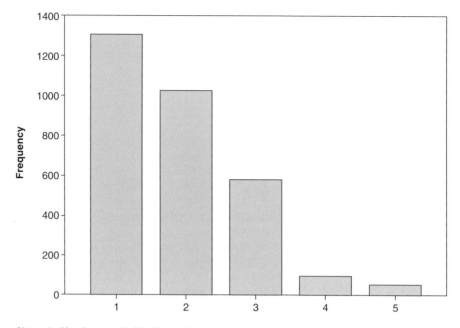

Notes: 1 = Yes, they are, 5 = No, they aren't.
        Mean = 1.9, standard deviation = 0.9, n = 3016.

Source: BES 1997.

FIGURE 9.3   *Are parties necessary for the political system?*

minorities doubt the distinctiveness and effectiveness of party government. Thus, while around half of respondents doubt that it really matters which party governs (item e), between one-quarter and two-fifths doubt the ability of any party to resolve certain persistent policy problems (items f–h). Finally, parties suffer from the widespread perception that they neither know nor care what ordinary voters think (Figures 9.1 and 9.2). Still, there is one comforting piece of news for parties; when all is said and done, the overwhelming majority of citizens find it hard to conceive of a political system which could operate without them (Figure 9.3).

Where might these doubts about contemporary political parties emanate from? Most likely they derive from two broad sources. First, people's respect for and trust of parties is almost bound to diminish to the extent that these organizations reveal themselves to be nakedly self-interested or plainly corrupt. This has become increasingly problematic for contemporary political parties in Britain. There is certainly nothing new in political corruption either in the UK or abroad, yet the 1990s in particular were characterized by multiple instances of alleged and actual 'Tory sleaze' during the Thatcher and Major administrations. These generally related to the sexual behaviour and financial abuses of Conservative backbenchers, though matters occasionally affected government ministers too. And though Labour made maximum political capital of the phenomenon of 'Tory sleaze' while it was in opposition, it was unable to steer entirely clear of the mire itself. For one thing, a number of instances of corrupt practice emerged in areas where Labour was the dominant force in local government (notably Doncaster in South Yorkshire). For another, the party was barely in power nationally before it very nearly found itself hoist with its own petard. In October 1997 Blair met with Bernie Ecclestone, President of motor sport's Formula One Association; this took place less than a month before the Minister of Public Health (Tessa Jowell) announced that the government was seeking to exempt Formula One motor racing from an EU-wide ban on tobacco advertising. What was already an awkward matter for Labour, given revelations that Jowell's husband had been a non-executive director of a Formula One company until earlier in the year, became potentially explosive when Ecclestone admitted that he had donated £1 million to the party in January. Both Ecclestone and Blair denied that political favours had been sought or offered, and the inevitable storm of criticism was weathered as the donation was returned by the party. Similarly, in 1999 Labour came under further pressure when it was revealed that one of its most generous benefactors was none other than Lord Sainsbury, who had been elevated to the position of Minister for Science in 1997 (Hibbs 1999); again, Sainsbury and other party spokespersons denied any conflict of interest,[2] but some of the lustre was worn from New Labour's image by this and the Ecclestone affair.

These kinds of incident do nothing to enhance the general legitimacy of parties, and they must be of particular significance for the spread of popular cynicism and mistrust. What, if anything, can be done about this kind of problem? The temptation to line one's own pocket will always prove too great for some individuals, of course, and no amount of regulation of party life will ever succeed in eradicating this entirely. Nevertheless, it is important to note that the parties have sought to take positive action, primarily in establishing the Committee on Standards in Public Life. Chaired initially by Lord Nolan and latterly by Lord Neill, this Committee has been despatched to provide regulatory frameworks designed to curb the more nefarious practices to which parties and politicians have been prone. Initially, the Committee concentrated on rules for ex-ministers over the acceptance of company directorships, and on declarations (in a Register of Members' Interests) by MPs of their consultancies, retainers and other commercial interests. Of greater interest, however, is the report issued by the Committee on the *Funding of Political Parties in the UK* (Neill 1998), aspects of which have already received attention in Chapter 8. While the Major government always refused to widen the Committee's brief so that it could address the issue of party funding, the Labour government of Tony Blair saw things differently and requested an investigation into the matter once it assumed office. The very substantial report published in October 1998 made a host of recommendations, some of which we have already considered in discussing parties' financial resources. However, in tackling the 'misconduct question', the

Report also addressed issues directly relevant to the propriety and legitimacy of parties:

> Do the ways in which political parties are funded at the moment cause ministers,
> opposition leaders and others to behave in ways that they ought not to behave? For
> example, do party donations by individuals, companies and trade unions, in effect,
> buy privileged access to ministers? Do they influence policy? Do they influence the
> awarding of contracts? Do they influence the awarding of honours? Clearly, they
> should not do any of these things. (Neill 1998: 26)

At the heart of many perceptions of misconduct lies public concern over what
Neill calls the 'inscrutability' of the sources of party funding, and many of the
Committee's recommendations were driven by the desire to ensure that all
parties were fully open and transparent about the origins of their income.
Indeed, the Committee effectively prescribed a completely new regulatory
regime for parties which would impose the desired transparency. This would
entail, among other things:

- the establishment of an independent and authoritative election commission with 'wide executive and investigative powers';
- new rules for the auditing and accounting of parties;
- full public disclosure of donations (in cash or in kind) of £5000 or more
  nationally, and £1000 or more locally;
- a ban on foreign donations;
- a ban on 'blind trusts' (whereby donations can be channelled to parties
  while politicians supposedly remain ignorant of the identities of contributors);
- a ban on anonymous donations of £50 or more;
- a new system of scrutiny by a special Honours Scrutiny Committee
  where there might be a connection between the receipt of an honour and
  the giving of a political donation;
- controls on non-party organizations and individuals spending more than
  £25,000 nationally on political activity during an election campaign;
- shareholder consent for the making of company donations.

Each of these recommendations was embraced by the Government in its
response to the Report (Cm.4413 1999), though it is worth re-emphasizing that
the decision to reject Neill's recommendation on tax-relief for small donations
seems ill-judged; such a scheme was designed to reduce the parties' growing
dependence on large contributions from corporations, unions or wealthy
individuals – precisely the kinds of donation associated with allegations of
improper influence, as we have already seen in respect of the Ecclestone and
Sainsbury cases. In the absence of ceilings on the amount that can be donated,
significant new state grants to extra-parliamentary party organizations or a
scheme of tax-relief for small donors, it is virtually certain that the major parties will continue to earn large (and possibly growing) proportions of their

income in the form of large donations. Sadly, this could mitigate at least some – perhaps much – of the effect of the new regulatory regime. Nevertheless, this new framework, though hardly a panacea, must generally be judged sensible and long overdue – and it should leave fair-minded citizens in little doubt that the parties are doing something meaningful to put their houses in order.

The systemic functionality of political parties in Britain

If impropriety is one obvious source of public disaffection with political parties, then the perception that they are failing to perform well is another. There are a number of classic political functions that can be examined in order to gauge the performance of parties in modern Britain and such an evaluation allows us directly to assess how well they serve the political system. Specifically, this chapter considers the following functions: governance and political recruitment; representation; political communication; and political participation.

Governance and political recruitment

Two important aspects of the governing function of political parties need addressing: the *personnel* and *policy* of government. Broadly speaking, parties cannot be regarded as central to the provision of governance unless they provide the key personnel and policies of government. Discussion of these issues tends to become complex, and leads to further questions concerning matters such as the distinctiveness and effectiveness of party policies. These concerns are extremely important, however, and are almost certainly central to an understanding of dissatisfaction with the role of parties in government; recall, for instance, the evidence of Table 9.1 (items e–h) which suggested a degree of voter cynicism about the impact of parties in government. If voters doubt whether it really makes much difference which party is in power, either because they all share similar policies or because no party has the power to resolve certain policy dilemmas, then it may be reasonable to conclude that parties are failing in respect of one of their most important political functions. So, what is the evidence?

Turning first to the question of government personnel, it can be argued that party penetration of the British state in this sense is generally high and has become higher since 1960. Technically, we are dealing with the related function of *political recruitment* here – that is, the process by which individuals become members of representative and governing elites. In this context it is essential to recall that Cabinet ministers are, by longstanding convention, obliged to be parliamentarians – and the latter are almost entirely party politicians. In 1997, the election of the former BBC journalist Martin Bell as an Independent MP for the Cheshire constituency of Tatton (on an anti-corruption ticket), constituted a rare counter-example to the domination of the

House of Commons by party politicians.[3] Even the occasional selection of non-parliamentarians (and, indeed, of non-party members) for junior governmental posts is something entirely in the hands of the leading party politicians;[4] taken together with evidence that voters are overwhelmingly concerned with party rather than candidate considerations (Webb 1995: 305), this seems to confirm unequivocally that national governmental recruitment is primarily a party-oriented rather than a candidate-centred process.

Furthermore, as we saw in Chapter 1, this has even become largely true of local government. While it was not uncommon for independent non-partisan councillors to play a significant role in local politics until the major reorganization of local government in 1973–74, this has now become comparatively rare except at the lowest level of sub-national government (in the rural parishes, for instance). To this extent, therefore, there is actually a case for arguing that party penetration of the polity has increased since 1960. The constitutional reforms by which the new Labour government of 1997 introduced devolution and city-wide government in London are unlikely to alter the essential picture, since candidacies for these new offices will almost certainly be dominated by party nominees. Moreover, it should not be overlooked that there is a whole layer of non-elective public office which is part of the means by which Britain's public institutions are governed and resources allocated – that of the 'quangocracy'. Quango (an acronym for quasi-autonomous non-governmental organization) appointments may now number as many as 65,000 (though much depends on one's definition: Weir and Hall 1994; Viney and Osborne 1995) and cover an enormous range of activities and public provision, including school governorships, Training and Enterprise Councils (TECs), local health authorities and hospital trusts, prison visitorships, museum trustees and a variety of funding councils. Many of these positions are in the gift of the political parties, and it should be said that the increasingly naked exploitation of this vast reservoir of patronage by the Conservative governments between 1979 and 1997 became a subject of some controversy in the 1990s. Often the quangocracy's domain seemed to be enhanced at the expense of elective local authorities, and increasingly the Tories regarded it as vital to the exercise of power that sympathizers – especially from the world of business – outnumbered their rivals' appointees on all these bodies:

> What was extraordinary was the lengths to which ministers went to ensure that the membership of these bodies was loyal to them, and distant from any link with local democracy. Not until the Nolan Committee report in May 1995 on standards in public life did they begin to concede that they might have gone too far in this respect, being forced to accept an independent monitor of quango appointments which for 20 years had been crudely partisan. (Jenkins 1995: 264–5)

The second broad aspect of party government concerns *policy* rather than personnel: as Richard Katz puts it, under party government public policy should emanate from party sources which can clearly be identified and held to account by the citizenry (1986: 43). There are a number of potential challenges to this, however, the first of which is breakdown of party cohesion. That is, uncohesive, fluid and unpredictable patterns of alignment in parliamentary parties can undermine the capacity of the executive to effect its legislative programme, and make it difficult for electors to hold accountable specific parties or coalitions of parties which might be regarded as the authors of policy. In the UK, though, this condition is still largely satisfied by the prevalence of single-party government. It is true that cross-party negotiations and collaboration are not entirely absent and, as we have seen, are likely to become more evident, especially in the government of Scotland and Northern Ireland. But there is no evidence as yet that such coalitions will be uncohesive. Moreover, party discipline at Westminster is still strong enough for governments to enact most (and often all) of their preferred legislative programmes, notwithstanding the evidence we noted in Chapter 6 of a growth in backbench dissent since 1970. With the exception of certain authorities in local government, there is little difficulty in concluding that public policy can still generally be clearly identified as the policy of a given party or (occasionally) coalition of parties in Britain.

The second challenge to the idea that government policy is primarily party policy lies in the claim that government is becoming increasingly 'prime ministerial'; the most notable example of this is Michael Foley's argument that a de facto 'presidentialization' of British politics has occurred as the prime minister has become far more than merely a 'first among equals' (Foley 1993). This presents us with the possibility that an essentially collegial form of party government is stealthily being usurped by a new form of candidate-centred executive leadership. However, it must be said that while British prime ministers can often appear firmly in control of the ship of government, they still depend critically on the confidence of their Cabinet colleagues and backbench supporters in the Commons – as the reluctant departure from government of Margaret Thatcher in 1990 illustrates. This means that governmental policy remains party policy rather than prime ministerial policy; though leaders clearly play a central role in developing policy, they are constrained in various ways by the political impact of frontbench colleagues, backbenchers and even extra-parliamentary 'sub-leaders' (as we saw in Chapters 6 and 7).

A third challenge to party policy in government is posed by civil service power. In Britain, both central and local bureaucrats are career civil servants who are legally obliged to refrain from active engagement in party political activity. Clearly, therefore, the official bureaucracy remains formally impervious to parties. However, though formally subservient to their political masters, it is certain that senior bureaucrats often play an influential role in influencing and implementing policy. Bureaucrats working closely with Cabinet ministers hold many advantages, in that they often have greater general knowledge of government and specific knowledge of certain policy fields, they control information flows to ministers and also influence their agendas. That said, there is equally little doubt that politicians retain the final word; moreover, experienced ministers and governments with a clear pro-grammatic purpose and electoral mandate can undoubtedly impose themselves on the civil servants, as the Thatcherite administrations of the 1980s demonstrated (Budge 1996a: 44–5). In addition, ministers have sought to enhance their autonomy by appointing teams of political advisors answer-able to them rather than the civil service. Sometimes such appointments have been associated with the development of formal bodies such as Edward Heath's Central Policy Review Staff (colloquially the 'think-tank') in the 1970s, though more often ministers have usually preferred to appoint indi-vidual advisors, some of whom have had high and occasionally controversial public profiles.[5] Thus, while it represents a significant constraint, the fact of civil service power should not be seen as fundamentally undermining the party government model in Britain.

So, national governmental policy in Britain is still predominantly party rather than prime ministerial or bureaucratic policy. However, we can delve deeper into the matter of party autonomy in government by addressing a question famously posed by Richard Rose (1980): do parties make a difference to public policy? This bears once again upon the issue of accountability, it should be noted, for if parties are fundamentally unable to shape public policy, who does (if anyone) and who should be held to account (if anyone)? In fact, it is well recognized that a variety of macro-social developments can seriously constrain the scope for autonomous action by party governments, including technological changes (which can, for instance, increase the scope and cost of public health provision), demographic trends (including increased longevity and changing birth-rates), social changes (such as the growth of single-parent families) and economic cycles (with their attendant implica-tions for welfare budgets). Indeed, the whole question of global economic constraints on national governmental autonomy has become one of the defin-ing political themes of the contemporary era – and a highly vexed issue for politicians and intellectuals alike (see, for example, Hirst and Thompson 1996). The power of these implacable and impersonal forces can seem daunt-ing and they make it unsurprising that commentators should question the ability of parties to make any real difference. In fact, the broad question of whether or not they do breaks down into a number of more specific issues: addressing each of these in turn better enables us to get to grips with the over-all problem. First, do parties actually offer the electorate reasonably distinct policy alternatives, or are they so convergent as to render the idea of 'choice' meaningless? Second, irrespective of what they might promise to electors, do they actually generate real differences in terms of policy outputs once they get the opportunity to wield power? And finally, even if parties say and do dis-tinctive things, do any of them succeed in achieving 'effective' solutions to policy problems? Overall, these three questions go to the heart of the prob-lems of party legitimacy implicit in the evidence of Table 9.1.

The question of distinctiveness is potentially a very important one in the context of British party competition which, as we saw in Chapter 4, is pre-dominantly centripetal. That is, given the normal distribution of voter preferences on the critically important socialism–capitalism dimension of party competition, it clearly behoves rational vote-maximizing parties to locate themselves as close to the median voter as possible. Yet, notwith-standing the degree of major party policy convergence implicit in this classic Downsian conception, Figure 4.1 revealed that Labour and the Conservatives always manage to retain a degree of ideological distinctiveness, and never 'leapfrog' over each other in terms of overall manifesto emphases. This is con-firmed by Klingemann and his colleagues, who argue that Labour and the Conservatives have remained 'sharply distinguished' throughout the period after 1945 (1994: 59).

So parties may safely be regarded as offering a meaningful degree of choice in terms of the promises they make to electors, but do they really make any difference to policy outputs in practice? Since Rose's initiatives in the early 1980s a number of scholars have researched the impact of British party gov-ernments on public policy, and the general conclusion is that parties can and do make a difference. Brian Hogwood (1992) discovered that while overall levels of public expenditure (relative to population size and GDP) tended to climb regardless of which party was incumbent between 1945 and 1990, cer-tain policy fields (especially housing and defence) were clearly susceptible to party effects. This broad argument is confirmed in the far more theoretically ambitious and methodologically sophisticated approach of Klingemann et al., who suggest that while party governments struggle to control spending in areas characterized by entitlement rights (such as the automatic rights to ben-efit once a person is defined as unemployed or disabled), they can and do implement meaningful policy changes in other areas. Overall, they claim that their evidence 'offers a clear picture of the operation of the party mandate in Britain' (1994: 70). Indeed, given the preponderance of single-party govern-ments in the post-war era, Britain is precisely the sort of country in which one would expect to find a definite link between manifesto promises and gov-ernment action. Indeed, this point has been systematically confirmed in cross-national comparative research conducted by Manfred Schmidt, who discovered that 'large partisan effects typify majoritarian democracies' (1996: 155). Britain is perhaps not quite the classical exemplar of majoritarian democracy it once was – given, for instance, the advent of devolution and the independence of the Bank of England after 1997; nevertheless, it is far from being a genuine consensus democracy, and the continuing predominance of single-party national governments helps ensure a definite partisan impact on public policy. As noted in Chapter 1, moreover, similar research by Sharpe and Newton has confirmed that parties also make a discernible difference to policy outputs in local government (1984: ch. 9).

To the largely quantitative evidence supplied by researchers like Hogwood and Klingemann, two further points are worth adding. First, most observers would probably concur in the view that parties can also effect quite distinc-tive qualitative shifts in public policy once in power. One need only think of the Conservative governments' legislative initiatives which restricted the powers of trade unions in the 1980s, or the various reforms affecting the agencies delivering social policy during the same period; similarly, Labour's agenda of constitutional reform post-1997 is less quantitative than qualitative in its implications for the British state, yet it is nonetheless profound for all that. Second, it should be borne in mind that the longer parties are in power, the greater their policy impact is likely to be. As has often been pointed out, public policy tends to have a momentum of its own, and it can take considerable time and effort to change its direction. This fact may well explain an asymmetry in the party effects discovered by Klingemann and his colleagues, in that the Conservatives have tended to have a greater impact on policy outputs when in office than Labour. When one bears in mind that, between 1945 and 1997, the Conservatives enjoyed 35 years in office compared to Labour's 17, including unbroken spells of 18 years and 13 years, compared to Labour's maximum incumbency of 6 years, it is readily apparent that the former have experienced significantly greater opportunities for exerting long-term influence over the development of national policy. In essence, therefore, the overall conclusion must be that the majority of electors in the country who feel that it does make a difference which party is in power (refer again to Table 9.1, item e) are broadly justified in their view.

But even if the major British parties offer distinctive alternatives to voters and can make significant differences to policy outputs, are they able to achieve 'effective' solutions to the policy problems which confront the country? Since the end of the long post-war boom (that is, since the mid-1970s), one suspects that parties have particularly suffered from the increasingly widespread perception that they are ineffectual in this sense; the apparent failures of government to resolve persistent national policy problems are bound to undermine the popular status of parties – especially when these failures are associated with both sides of the partisan spectrum. While we might outline a number of such issues (see Table 9.1, items f–h), it is probably sufficient to mention the key area of economic performance. For several generations now the question of Britain's relative decline as an economic power (Gamble 1985; Sked 1987; Coates 1994; English and Kenny 1999) has dogged the country's political elites. In the light of this, it is interesting to recall that in Chapter 2 we encountered evidence that voters who perceive a long-term weakening of the British economy are significantly more likely to express hostility or indifference to the major parties and (not surprisingly) are significantly less likely to believe that election outcomes matter (Webb 1996: 376–7). However, while these data may illustrate the dangers of ineffectiveness, they do not directly demonstrate whether it is in fact appropriate to judge British party governments 'ineffective' or not.

Defining governing or policy 'effectiveness' is not at all straightforward. We might simply regard it as the capacity to devise and implement policies which provide solutions to problems in the public domain. However, 'effectiveness' in this sense is highly likely to be conditioned by subjective political preferences. Consider, for instance, the 'problem' of industrial unrest: one's view of how 'effective' the Conservative governments of the 1980s were in resolving this problem is bound to depend critically on one's ideological standpoint. While a neo-liberal or a Thatcherite Conservative would doubt-less be convinced of the effectiveness of the Thatcher governments' strategy in emasculating trade union power and reducing the number of working-days lost to industrial action, a socialist could surely not help but abjure such an approach and would certainly argue that it entailed the suppression of workers' rights. Since this could hardly be regarded as a desirable objective from a leftist perspective, there would be little chance of agreement between left and right that this constituted an 'effective' policy solution. Indeed, ideo-logical standpoint will even condition a voter's opinion of exactly what 'problems' should define a government's agenda. In essence, then, values tend to influence views about both the ends and means of governmental policy, and confound attempts to make detached analytical judgements about whether political parties provide effective governance or not.

There are two potential ways around this problem. The first is to focus on governing performance in respect of *valence* issues, where there are policy goals on which all the main parties and most voters can be assumed to agree (low unemployment, stable prices, crime control, and so on [Butler and Stokes 1974]). On reflection, however, this does not necessarily progress matters a great deal, since there is rarely much consensus of opinion about governing effectiveness on even these issues (as the debate over British 'decline' clearly illustrates [English and Kenny 1999]). It is interesting to note, however, that a number of comparative studies agree that majoritarian democracies such as the UK do not appear to perform any better than consensus democracies in terms of macro-economic management, notwithstanding the common argu-ment that single-party governments are 'strong' governments (Rose 1992; Castles 1994; Lijphart 1999: ch. 15).

A second way out of this intellectual maze is to adopt a more manageable conception of effectiveness, whereby it is simply defined as the capacity of parties to implement their preferred policies. Indeed, from this perspective, it is encouraging to note that British parties generally have a good record of redeeming their manifesto pledges (Rallings 1987) – something we should perhaps expect to find in a country dominated by single-party governments. Though undeniably 'effective' in this limited sense, however, we should not be too easily seduced by the impression that British party governments can straightforwardly identify problems and implement their preferred solutions. This is primarily because one must take account of the messy reality of 'incre-mentalism' in public policy. That is, we might imagine an ideal-type of a process according to which a party's strategists prioritize something they consider to be a problem, then devise a policy solution and implement it. In one sense, this might be regarded as the epitome of 'effective' governance, but in reality research has revealed many areas in which public policy is not made according to such 'heroic' or 'rationalist' dictates (Simon 1945); more commonly, a process of bargaining between politicians and interested social groups takes place which leads to incremental 'mutual partisan adjustment' in policy (Lindblom 1959; 1965; 1977; Braybrooke and Lindblom 1963). Though parties may be thought of as important actors (or perhaps brokers) in this process, it suggests a reality in which their autonomy is once again limited. Research provides a good deal of empirical support for this incrementalist perspective (Ham and Hill 1993: 87; Jordan and Richardson 1982), but it is conceivable that such an approach to policy-making is less than inspiring for many citizens; one can easily imagine how a diffuse, if vague, sense that parties are simply making marginal adjustments to public policy by 'muddling through' in this manner leads to the feeling that 'it doesn't really matter which party is in power, in the end things go on much the same' (Curtice and Jowell 1997: 93).

Does this imply that incrementalism amounts to ineffective party government? A number of points merit consideration before such a conclusion can be reached. First, not *all* policy-making is unspectacularly incremental in the UK. As we have seen, single-party governments with comfortable parliamentary majorities can enact ambitious legislative programmes, especially if they win two or more consecutive elections; such conditions have allowed certain administrations to be quite 'heroic' in their approach to governing (the second and third Thatcher terms being prime examples). Second, incremental shifts in policy are not necessarily insignificant anyway, especially if their impact accumulates in a succession of small steps over time (Ham and Hill 1993: 93). Again, the Conservative legislation on industrial relations provides a good example: having, perhaps, learnt from the disastrous experience of the Heath government's Industrial Relations Act 1972, the Thatcher governments enacted far-reaching reform through a series of laws introduced throughout the 1980s. Each successive piece of legislation had a relatively limited scope in itself, but the cumulative impact on the legal framework of industrial relations in the country was dramatic (Webb 1992a: 69). Third, it should in any case be borne in mind that incrementalism can be defended as a prescription for effective policy-making in democratic societies. Certainly, its chief proponent Charles Lindblom saw 'muddling through' as a way of avoiding serious policy mistakes, since it obliges policy-makers to secure the consent of interested parties; by contrast, the 'rational' model of policy-making, which is generally regarded as the polar antithesis of incrementalism, may encourage a 'futile attempt at superhuman comprehensiveness' (Lindblom 1959: 88). The dangers of this approach are well illustrated by the Thatcher government's disastrous poll tax fiasco. If anything merited the 'rational' or 'heroic' decision-making label it was this policy, in so far as it clearly eschewed accommodation with vested interests; the government simply identified a preferred solution to a perceived problem, and pushed it through regardless of opposition inside and outside parliament. The outcome of such an approach, however, can only be judged to be destabilizing and 'ineffective' by any standards. The widespread campaign of public protest and civil disobedience which confronted the new tax plainly ran contrary to the hopes and expectations of the government of the day; indeed, it is surely not inappropriate to describe the whole affair as a 'policy failure' (Butler et al. 1995). In this sense, then, it is perfectly possible for party government to be 'ineffective' even when its capacity to identify and introduce preferred policies is apparently high. On reflection, therefore, a mild if diffuse sense of popular frustration with the limits of party government may be a low price to pay for a predominantly incremental approach to policy-making. In fact, we may note that the prevalence of incrementalism in British government lends a surprisingly 'consensual' tenor to a generally majoritarian political context; this may well be critically important for retaining a deeper legitimacy in the system as a whole, in that it helps ensure some influence over the direction of public policy even for those who oppose particular governments.

Overall, it seems fair to conclude that parties continue to provide the most obvious way in which the body politic can generate a range of democratically accountable and distinct policy alternatives. In reality, the capacity of parties to act as autonomous policy-makers in government is undoubtedly limited by a variety of factors, and these challenges to party government may even help weaken the popular standing of parties in some ways. All the same, parties remain undeniably central to the provision of meaningful and accountable governance in Britain.

Representation

It is impossible to consider the role of parties as mechanisms of democratic representation in Britain without addressing the debate about electoral reform. The single-member plurality (SMP) system used in Westminster elections has been widely criticized for many years now, and in December 1997 the Blair government established the Independent Commission on the Voting System (chaired by Lord Jenkins) to investigate and make recommendations on electoral reform for Westminster elections. The Commission duly reported in October 1998. At the time of writing, the government is expected to call a referendum on the question of replacing the present electoral system, though the timing of this move is uncertain and it is by no means clear whether the government will endorse the alternative to SMP recommended by the Commission. Thus, while it currently remains possible to make the case that the legitimacy of the political system has been undermined by the growing failure of the party system to provide an overwhelmingly legitimate pattern of representation, it is not certain that the status quo will endure.

As Jenkins noted, SMP is 'not an inherent part of the British parliamentary tradition' (1998: para. 21). Until 1885 most constituencies had two members, and some urban and university seats had three or four members each. Indeed, a number of multi-member seats persisted until 1950, and it was the norm in these constituencies for elections to be conducted under the Single Transferable Vote (STV). The representative defects of the SMP system have been widely rehearsed in the past, and a number of the major ones were effectively summarized in the Jenkins Report. First, it is 'peculiarly bad at allowing third party support to express itself' (in terms of parliamentary representation). A party may receive a wide degree of support throughout the country, but if it is seldom concentrated in particular parliamentary constituencies, then it is unlikely to win many seats. To put it slightly differently, a party may succeed in winning many votes across the UK as a whole, but if this only enables its candidates to come second or third in most of the seats which it contests, then it will go substantially unrepresented in parliament. This barely registered as a problem in the 1950s when the Liberals won less than 5% of the national vote; by 1974, however, they were claiming 19.3% of the vote, yet still receiving only 2.2% of the seats in the Commons, and in 1983 the Liberal-SDP Alliance jointly garnered 25.4% of the vote, yet scraped together a paltry 3.5% of parliamentary seats. All of this reflected the fact that the centre parties frequently did well enough to come second or third in constituency contests, but only occasionally well enough to win. Interestingly, in 1997, Conservative Party support dropped so far that it was punished by the electoral system which it had defended staunchly for so long. It has been estimated that once a party's overall level of electoral support drops below one-third of the popular vote, then SMP will start to discriminate heavily against it (Dunleavy and Margetts 1997: 227); this is, of course, precisely the fate which befell the Tories, as they won just 30.7% of the vote in the UK (and 25% of Commons seats).

So long as a party has pockets of geographically concentrated support, however, it may still be surprisingly well rewarded, which explains why a far smaller party like Plaid Cymru could win 0.6% of the seats on just 0.5% of the vote cast in 1997. This also sheds light on a second major criticism of the system, which is that it can produce enormous geographical divergence in patterns of parliamentary support. In Chapter 2 we noted evidence of the 'north-south divide' in electoral support and representation which gradually developed between 1955 and 1987; thus, in the two general elections of the 1980s, Labour only won three seats south and east of an imaginary line running between the Wash and the River Severn estuary, excluding Greater London. By the same token, in 1997 the Conservatives lost all representation in Scotland, Wales and metropolitan England. Once again, these are features of a system which does not reward candidates who come second, even if their parties are relatively well-supported across a region as a whole.

Overall, these first two problems with SMP can be measured in terms of 'deviation from proportionality' (DV). This is calculated in a simple manner, by subtracting the percentage of votes received by a party from the percentage of seats it wins, totalling these scores for all parties in the system, and then dividing this sum by two. This gives an index with a potential range running from 0–100; the higher the score, the more disproportional an election outcome. Thus, in 1997 Labour won 44.4% of the vote outside Northern Ireland, but fully 65.4% of the seats, giving an individual party DV score of 21%. The total of all party DV scores was 42.1%, which resulted in an overall deviation from proportionality in terms of party representation in the House of Commons of 21% (op. cit.: 226). Moreover, deviation from proportional party representation within certain regions of the country has often been far in excess of this national mean; at its most extreme, for instance, in 1992 the

Conservatives took 97% of parliamentary seats in the south-east, despite winning only 55% of the votes there, giving a regional DV score of 43% (Dunleavy et al. 1993: 186–7).

The third defect which Jenkins identified with SMP was that it exaggerates (aggregate) movements of public opinion so much that it is liable to produce landslide victories for one side or another from time to time, an outcome which is not conducive to the 'effective working of the House of Commons' (placing as it does too much unfettered power in the hands of the executive), and which the public tends to regard with suspicion. Labour has won majorities of over 100 in 1945, 1966 and 1997 (this last occasion on the strength of just 44.4% of the vote), and the Conservatives in 1959, 1983 and 1987. Indeed, the exaggerative effects can generate quite perverse results overall, the most obvious of which occurred in 1951 (when Labour actually polled 250,000 votes more than the Tories nationwide, and piled up its best ever percentage of the popular vote [48.8%], yet lost the election), and February 1974 (when Labour emerged as the biggest single party at Westminster, despite being out-polled by the Conservatives). A further drawback of SMP is that it substantially narrows the electoral terrain on which the real battle for power is fought; since the bulk of Westminster constituencies are safe seats which only one party's candidate has a realistic prospect of winning, the election outcome is effectively determined by party competition in a maximum of 150 seats (out of 659). 'Outside the chosen arena, voters were deprived of (or spared from) the visits of party leaders, saw few canvassers, and were generally treated (by both sides) as irrevocably damned or sufficiently saved as to qualify for being taken for granted' (Jenkins 1998: para. 33). This produces a situation in which many votes are 'wasted' in so far as they cannot influence the result either way; winning parties pile up far more votes in safe seats than are required to win control of them, which means that individual electors (whether supporters or opponents) have little reason to regard their particular votes as important to the outcome.[6] Given the prevalence of safe seats, moreover, local party 'selectorates' are the people who really determine the choice of most MPs at Westminster; by contrast, certain other electoral systems (such as STV, AMS, and 'open' list PR) enable voters to express both a party (and, by implication, a governmental) preference and an individual candidate choice. Finally, Jenkins implies that SMP tends to be less good at providing for what we might refer to as 'social representation' – which is to say, a parliament which broadly approximates to a microcosm of British society in its demographic profile. Again, systems such as STV and AMS, by allowing multiple representation within a given constituency, permit voters to target some of their choices on candidates with particular social characteristics – women or ethnic minorities, for example. Given that women, ethnic minorities and the working class are known to be 'under-represented' in parliament (Norris and Lovenduski 1995), one of these other systems might be preferable on grounds of social representativeness.

If these are the shortcomings which the Jenkins Commission ascribes to the SMP system, what alternative does it recommend? The Commission's terms of reference stated that any such recommendations should 'observe the requirement for broad proportionality, the need for stable government, an extension of voter choice and the maintenance of a link between MPs and geographical constituencies' (Jenkins 1998: 1). Fulfilling all of these requirements simultaneously inevitably proved a considerable challenge, in that most existing systems operating in the democratic world tend to privilege one or more of these objectives, but few, if any, are known to satisfy all of them. Jenkins sought to meet the challenge, however, by proposing a novel piece of institutional engineering referred to variously as 'AV top-up', 'AV plus' or 'limited AMS'. The main features of this are as follows. First, it is a hybrid or mixed system under which the overwhelming majority of Westminster parliamentarians (between 80% and 85%) would continue to be elected on an individual constituency basis. The system used for the election of these members, however, would be the Alternative Vote (AV) rather than SMP; this is preferable, in the view of Jenkins and most other Commission members,[7] on the grounds that it would ensure that every constituency member would have the express support of an absolute majority of his or her local constituents – something which does not necessarily happen under SMP elections. In 1997, for instance, 345 (52.4%) of successful candidates won with absolute majorities. Such a requirement enhances both the consensual nature of the election and the representative legitimacy of the chosen MP. The remaining 15% to 20% of MPs would be allocated according to an open list system based on comparatively small 'top-up areas' (that is, existing counties or metropolitan districts). The express purpose of these additional members is to provide a corrective mechanism which would remove the most blatant deviations from proportional representation in the Commons.[8] At the same time, the Commission designed this system in such a way as to achieve 'broad proportionality without imposing a coalition habit on the country' (op. cit.: ch. 9, para. 7). Thus, where strong surges in public opinion favour one party or another, the Commission argued that 'no purpose of justice or efficacy' would be served by contriving a coalitional situation (para. 121), and it would certainly be undesirable to leave any pivotal party (such as the Liberal Democrats) permanently holding the balance of power; on the other hand, the Report noted the dangers to 'effective and responsive government' of situations (which have become more common since 1970) whereby big single-party majorities have been won on the basis of substantially lower levels of support than hitherto (para. 122). It contended, for instance, that any system which might have brought about coalitions during the 1974–79 or 1992–97 parliaments would have been preferable to SMP. AV top-up is just such a system, in the view of the Commission.

While those long wedded to purer notions of proportional representation than Jenkins proposed were, predictably, disappointed (see, for instance, Ellis 1998), the report was greeted with a wide degree of interest in political circles. Moreover, there is almost certainly a significant block of popular support for electoral reform, although quite how big this is unclear, since attitudes vary according to the precise wording of survey questions asked on the subject: at a minimum, however, it can safely be said that a third of voters would like a change in the electoral system (Curtice and Jowell 1997: 102), while some estimates have placed the figure as high as 55% (Dunleavy and Margetts 1997: 240). Research conducted on the Jenkins proposals in 1998 showed 43% of respondents preferring AV plus to the status quo (Dunleavy and Margetts 1999: 31). While it is not clear that popular dissatisfaction with SMP has become more widespread since 1979, the long Conservative incumbency between 1979 and 1997 presented critics with ample opportunity to high-light the dangers of the system. The lack of power-sharing, growing centralization of control within a unitary state, exploitation of the quangoc-racy and the accumulated spoils of office which accrued to the governing party over such an extended period rendered it, in the eyes of some, a domi-nant party (King 1993) – yet this dominance was sustained on the support of little more than one-third of registered electors. Whether such power can be fully legitimate in what purports to be a pluralist democracy is questionable. In any case, it can be argued that the time has come for government to recog-nize that the increasingly plural nature of British society and the more diffuse pattern of party support can no longer be adequately expressed by two-party majoritarianism and the winner-takes-all principle which accompanies it. Any electoral system will have its detractors but seen in this light the pre-scriptions of the Jenkins Commission deserve to be regarded as, at the very least, a step in the right direction, and perhaps as an ingenious method for achieving a sustainable blend of legitimate representation and stable, account-able party government.

At the time of writing, however, the prospects of the Jenkins recommen-dations ever being enacted remain very uncertain. Politically, they represent a compromise between Labour and the Liberal Democrats (Dunleavy and Margetts 1999: 14–17), which might be expected to maximize the parliamen-tary support for such measures under present circumstances. However, it is clear that there remains significant opposition to any kind of electoral reform within the PLP; it is unlikely that the promised referendum on the issue will take place prior to the next general election, and it is even less sure that the government will actively endorse AV plus in any eventual referendum cam-paign. Without such support, the likelihood of there being an electoral majority in favour of reform hangs in the balance. It is probable, therefore, that the outcome of the next general election, and Labour's calculations about the importance of its relationship with the Liberal Democrats, will determine the path of electoral reform in the foreseeable future.

The question of electoral reform, though undeniably central to any dis-cussion of parties and political representation in Britain, by no means exhausts the topic. In particular, it is important to take some account of the related functions of the articulation and aggregation of interests, which jointly and severally constitute key elements of representative activity. The *articula-tion of interests* refers to the role played by parties and other institutions (typically single-interest groups or social movements) in publicly expressing and pursuing the political demands of particular social groups. For instance,

in the context of Britain's two-class, two-party model, Labour classically articulated working-class interests while the Tories articulated the interests of the
middle class. The *aggregation of interests* refers to a related but broader process
by which parties bundle together the demands of a variety of social groups;
a modern left-wing party, for instance, might seek to express the interests of
the working class, women, immigrants and ethnic minorities, environmen-
talists, and so on. The aggregation of social group interests in this fashion is
not quite so straightforward as the articulation of a narrower set of interests,
since it requires the prioritization of demands. Where all social group
demands which a party seeks to aggregate are compatible, this will be relatively unproblematic, but this is by no means always the case. It is quite
possible, for example, that the pursuit of certain environmental policies
designed to restrict pollution and the over-exploitation of natural resources
could conflict with other policies aimed at maximizing industrial output and
job opportunities; under such circumstances, a left-wing party will be obliged
to make the difficult decision about which set of group interests it should prioritize – those of the environmental lobby or those of the working classes who
could be expected to benefit if output were maximized and unemployment
minimized.

Processes of social and political change have almost certainly confronted
the parties with new challenges as articulators and aggregators of group
interests. In particular, the growing heterogeneity of British society has
brought new social group demands and issues onto the political agenda to
which the parties have sometimes struggled to respond adequately (see
Chapter 1). Thus, as new issue cleavages such as environmentalism, sexual
minority, ethnic minority and women's rights have become prominent, those
concerned have often felt that single-issue groups and social movements
have articulated their particular demands more quickly and effectively than
parties (Byrne 1997). This argument is akin to the view sometimes pro-
pounded in comparative research that, when parties 'fail' (or perhaps just
falter) in this way, alternative organizations emerge to link state to society
(Lawson and Merkl 1988). To repeat an argument expressed earlier in this
book, the emergence of social heterogeneity and new cleavages has generated
more or less simultaneous effects, including partisan dealignment, membership decline and the rise of single-issue group activity (refer back to Figure
8.1).

If social heterogeneity poses a direct challenge to the capacity of political
parties to articulate interests, however, it also complicates their task of interest aggregation, though it does not render it obsolete. For notwithstanding the
challenge of growing societal complexity, it is hard to see an alternative vehicle to the political party for the aggregation of political demands in a country
like the UK. Though in principle demands can certainly be aggregated into
coherent legislative programmes by other actors (individual politicians in
candidate-centred presidential systems like the USA's, bureaucrats in non-
democratic systems) really it is only parties which can do so legitimately in
parliamentary democracies, and there is little doubt that the citizenry look

overwhelmingly to the parties to fulfil this function in Britain. Single-issue groups or social movements may be challenging parties as articulators of particular group demands, but by definition they are not in the business of bundling together a multiplicity of interests into ordered and coherent programmes of legislative action; interest aggregation, then, remains a core party function. Even so, this task has become more complex given the growing number of cross-cutting cleavages; in effect, the major parties have been challenged to build increasingly broad coalitions of support at a time when such a task has become inherently more difficult. Moreover, not only have major parties struggled to aggregate interests as effectively as hitherto, but their attempts to do so may even have undermined their ability to articulate traditional group demands; for Labour at least, the adoption of a more broadly aggregative inter-class appeal (the catch-all strategy) has probably weakened its role as a working-class tribune. In short, in attempting to develop its aggregative capacity, Labour may well have weakened its ability to articulate (some) demands.

Overall, however, while it is undoubtedly true that social and political changes have complicated parties' traditional tasks of articulating and aggregating social group demands, a sense of perspective should be retained about how far-reaching such effects have been. It would be a gross exaggeration to suggest that British political parties are generally failing to match the agendas or respond to the demands of the electorate. In fact, contemporary British parties are more likely to be criticized for pandering to the vagaries of public opinion, given the development of political marketing techniques (a classic accusation made by New Labour's detractors); looked at in a different light, this is just another way of saying that parties are increasingly responsive to citizens. Not that parties always provide programmes which are wholly acceptable to the electorate, and of course we have already unearthed evidence that citizens are often unconvinced that parties know or care about voter opinions. In view of this, it seems obvious that group activity and political protest must be regarded as vital supplementary channels of preference-articulation, and indeed, these channels of expression occasionally reveal enormous pressure for change in public policy. This was apparent, for instance, in the poll tax affair; as we have already noted, this generated a startling campaign of protest and civil disobedience which suggested that the government had not only misread popular preferences on the issue, but had also fatally overestimated the public's capacity for passively indulging even a powerfully placed administration. Ultimately, this episode almost certainly contributed to Margaret Thatcher's replacement by John Major and the rescinding of an unpopular law. It could be said that this demonstrated the remaining capacity of the party system to respond to the public agenda, although plainly it did not do so without the 'assistance' of demands which were articulated in channels quite external to the party system. On the whole, then, it seems clear that, while parties remain central to the complex task of aggregating interests, the function of articulating group demands is one they are increasingly compelled to share with single-issue groups and new social movements; indeed, their representative capacity can be rendered more effective when they work in conjunction with these other actors.

Political communication

Since the 1960s, British parties have undoubtedly been challenged by other actors as political communicators and educators. It is clear that reliance on non-partisan forms of media for political information and comment has increased dramatically in the country since 1960 (Dunleavy and Husbands 1985: 111). For instance, some 65.9% of British Election Survey respondents indicated that they saw a national TV news at least once a day during the 1997 election campaign, and all but 5% claimed to see some TV news during the course of a week; over two-thirds claimed to pay at least 'some attention' to the political content of this news. By contrast, 43% of respondents claimed to read a daily newspaper, and 58% to see a paper at least once a week; in any case, the press are probably increasingly autonomous of the parties, notwithstanding the well-known partisan biases of most papers (Norris et al. 1999: 82–4). The parties themselves could only directly contact around a quarter of electors via canvassing. As we saw in Chapter 5, all of this implies that the capacity of the political parties to inform, educate and set the agenda of political debate has most probably been reduced, and it certainly means that the most authoritative source of political information for most citizens is apt to be critical of any and all of the political parties. Indeed, the standard manner in which the public broadcasting networks interpret their brief to provide 'balanced' (which is to say, non-partisan) coverage of politics is by adopting an acutely adversarial stance in dealing with party spokesmen and women. Ultimately, one might plausibly speculate that this serves to weaken the popular legitimacy of parties, though it is hard to think of a way in which this can be conclusively demonstrated. When broadcasting's more notoriously aggressive interrogators grill politicians what unfolds is often a tense verbal jousting contest in which the viewer's/listener's understanding of policy questions is obscured by the ultra-defensive attitudes of the politician and the frequent and intolerant interjections of the interviewer. It is hard for party politicians to avoid giving the impression that they have something to hide during these ritualistic attempts at public humiliation. Since this applies to politicians of all sides, but especially to those associated with whichever party happens to be in office, the upshot is likely to be negative for the party system as a whole. It may be, therefore, that indications of public cynicism about parties (such as items a–d of Table 9.1) reflect, in part, the particular way in which parties are obliged to share the terrain of political communication with the mass media in Britain.

That said, party politicians have no right to expect supine deference from the media in a competitive and pluralist democracy, and they are by no means entirely passive victims. As we have seen in this book, since the first 'television election campaign' of 1959, parties have taken enormous pains to transform themselves into highly sophisticated political communicators capable of exploiting all the technological and professional resources at their disposal in their quest to inform and persuade voters. It certainly seems reasonable to conclude that, in conjunction with the mass media, parties in contemporary Britain still manage to play a considerable role in defining the political agenda, framing responsibility for public policy, and providing an informational basis for citizens' cognitive understanding of politics. Nevertheless, as in the case of the representational function, parties are no more than co-protagonists in performing these roles.

Political participation

Do British political parties foster political participation to a satisfactory extent? We have encountered a variety of evidence relating to parties and participation in this book, most notably that revealing the decline of party membership and activism in Chapters 7 and 8. Indeed, on the whole, it seems that citizens are far more inclined to take part in political activity via interest groups, direct protest (mainly restricted to the signing of petitions, it should be said) or contact with public officials – elected and unelected (Parry et al. 1992). Yet an overall assessment of the importance of political parties for political participation in Britain demands that a number of other factors should be borne in mind.

First, it should not be forgotten that the clear majority of voters still make the effort to vote for one party candidate or another, at least at national elections, and there is no decisive evidence of falling turnout. Not that one should be overly sanguine about electoral participation; while it is true that there is on the whole only trendless fluctuation since 1945, turnout for the 1997 general election was the lowest since the War, and it is well known to be significantly lower for most 'second-order' (that is, local and European) elections (Reif and Schmitt 1980; Heath et al. 1999). Second, developments over the past two decades or more suggest that, at least for those who remain sympathetic to parties, the opportunities to participate are significantly greater. This is evident in a number of ways: for one thing, the growth of the quangocracy offers myriad opportunities for participation in the governance of public sector institutions, and, as we have seen, many of these positions remain in the gift of the parties. Even more notably, the various reforms by which the main parties have sought to democratize their internal procedures have afforded ordinary members new rights of participation and influence in candidate-selection, leadership-selection and (albeit to a lesser extent) policy-making.

Most significantly, however, it must be understood that any answer to the question of whether parties foster a satisfactory level of participation will depend fundamentally on one's normative preferences concerning democracy itself. Thus, it is precisely from the perspective of the participationist vision of democracy that political parties most often tend to be regarded as 'failing'; those preferring more elitist and representative models of democracy, on the other hand, are unlikely to see great cause for concern in the

present situation. Indeed, disciplined and cohesive (rather than highly participatory) political parties are central to the competitive elitism exemplified
by writers like Max Weber and Joseph Schumpeter. They started from the
observation that the average elector is poorly informed about public affairs
and inclined to think about them in emotive or, to recall Schumpeter's
account, 'primitive' terms (1952: 262). Therefore, the democratic elitist would
argue, the primary function of public participation should be to select and
hold accountable powerful, informed and able political elites. The system
should permit a strong executive, competitive parties which dominate parliament, and an independent, expert and well-trained bureaucracy. The
competition for power between rival political elites, and the limited but
important role of citizens in legitimizing power through their electoral participation, should be sufficient to ensure that power is not exercised in a
tyrannical fashion (Held 1996: ch. 5).

For the participationist critic of this conception of democracy, however,
processes matter as much as the outcomes of politics, and any system which
involves popular participation on the limited scale of the contemporary
British model of party-dominated politics fails on at least three key criteria.
The first of these is the criterion of personal development. That is, participa-
tionists have long argued that direct involvement by citizens in processes of
political decision making is critical to their sense of civic responsibility and
moral development. The second criterion by which the participationist eval-
uates any system is its legitimizing mechanisms, and here too the elitist model
is said to fall short, for 'people are more prone to accept decisions they help
to make, even if they do not like the decisions reached' (Katz 1997: 67). Hence,
perhaps, Geoff Mulgan's lament about party structures which are 'centralized, pyramidal, national with strictly defined rules of authority and
sovereignty'. Finally, and crucially, participation in the democratic process is
generally held to be vital to ensuring that governments are sensitized to
public opinion and are therefore responsive to 'the will of the people'. In particular, the participationist critic could argue that British parties are not
always responsive enough to the popular will because the electorate has too
few opportunities to transmit clear messages about its aggregate distribution
of preferences on *individual* policy issues. While general elections are obviously of enormous basic importance to achieving government which
embodies the popular will, on their own they are far too crude and infrequent
to satisfy the participationist vision of how a democracy should operate. By
bundling together very broad programmes of legislative proposals (that is, by
aggregating interests), general election manifestos fail to elicit clearly the
preferences of the electorate on specific issues. Coupled with the majoritarian
'winner-takes-all' context of British politics, this can produce policy disasters
such as the poll tax fiasco; thus, a single-party government with a degree of
unfettered power that is highly unusual among Western democracies, can
push ahead with patently unpopular (and therefore fundamentally illegiti-
mate) policies on specific issues. This line of argument, it should be said,
cannot be ignored in view of the evidence we noted earlier concerning voter

doubts over whether parties really know or care about public opinion (Figures 9.1 and 9.2).

It could be suggested that one way around this problem would be through a greater willingness to utilize mechanisms of direct democracy, such as referenda (especially those which are popularly initiated). Such an argument contends that these participatory devices can complement the normal processes of representative democracy by serving to clarify popular preferences in respect of specific issues. It should be noted that this is *not* an argument for 'participatory democracy', where that term is understood to imply a form of highly egalitarian and consensual decision making in which the modus operandi is discussion in small, homogeneous groups without recourse to voting (Catt 1999: ch. 3). Such a model, which can operate in local politics (as de Tocqueville noted) or small-scale organizations, is not feasible for national politics where representative democracy is virtually inevitable in some form or other.[9] However, citizen participation remains important even to representative democracy, for the reasons outlined above (that is, personal development, legitimacy, and responsiveness); hence, it is important to consider whether participatory mechanisms such as referenda or popular initiatives might enhance the quality of representative democracy, and the implications such reforms might hold for political parties.

It might be added that there is evidence to suggest many voters feel that representative democracy as constituted at present is inadequate. An ICM opinion poll conducted in March 1994, for example, revealed that 60% of respondents considered that 'voting every four to five years' did not 'give them enough power'. More to the point, citizens have consistently favoured greater opportunities for direct democracy; thus, while a Gallup poll reported 69% of respondents supporting the use of referenda in 1968, fully 77% of respondents to a MORI poll conducted in 1991 (soon after the culmination of poll tax protest, it should be noted) agreed with the proposition that 'it would be a good idea if the British people could force government to hold a referendum on a particular issue by raising a petition with signatures from, say, a million electors' (Adonis and Mulgan 1994: 8). Similar findings hold in respect of countries where the use of direct democracy is widespread, such as the USA (Bowler and Donovan 1998a: 251). In view of this, it is interesting that the major parties appear to have become more willing to utilize referenda of late. Thus, on attaining national office in 1997, the Labour government quickly initiated referenda on Scottish, Welsh and Northern Irish devolution proposals, and the reintroduction of London-wide governance; in addition, British citizens were promised (by both major parties) a referendum on European Monetary Union and (by Labour and the Liberal Democrats) on the question of electoral reform. Apart from these national or regional exercises in popular consultation (note that none of these referenda outcomes legally bind the government), referenda are also used quite widely by local authorities.

Would the introduction of a greater component of direct democracy really help enhance the popular legitimacy and relevance of political parties? There are a number of possible counter-arguments, two of which merit particular attention here. First, many critics of direct democracy have suggested that it tends to produce undesirable policy outcomes: if this is true, there would be little point in pursuing it since, even if it did enhance the responsiveness of parties, it could damage their governing performance and would therefore be most unlikely to popularize them. Second, it can also be argued that the existence of direct democracy in places like Italy and the USA has not prevented the development of similar indications of public disaffection with parties and politicians as we find in the UK, so what would be the point of introducing it? Let us consider these points in turn.

First, why do critics contend that direct democracy produces undesirable outcomes? To simplify greatly, it is widely argued that it can generate policies which are short-sighted, serve narrowly defined interests or damage vulnerable minorities. For instance, critics doubt that many ordinary citizens can maintain the high levels of interest, information and reasoning which direct democracy requires of them, and this leads to the risk that decisions may be taken which are relatively ill-considered and perhaps even inconsistent with each other. In particular, the realities of budgetary constraints may be ignored by voters who want effective intervention by the state, but shrink from meeting the true costs involved (Budge 1996b: 37); and powerful, well-financed, but essentially narrow interests might be able to run campaigns which would sway public opinion (Magleby 1984; 1994; Magleby and Patterson 1998).

In effect, these arguments turn on two kinds of alleged problem with direct democracy. The first is that many voters are inherently incapable of coping with the complex cognitive demands which it places upon them: once again, we are drawn back to Schumpeter's 'primitive' citizen. That said, recent empirical research suggests that such a pessimistic view of voter ability is greatly exaggerated (Bowler and Donovan 1998b); relatedly, voters are not especially prone to passing anti-minority measures (Donovan and Bowler 1998b), nor do they appear particularly susceptible to the influence of special interests (Banducci 1998). The second fundamental flaw with direct democracy, however, is that it bypasses the normal channels of party politics and, therefore undermines the critically important aggregative function which parties perform. If direct democracy marginalizes parties, there is a risk that there would be no 'realistic rank-ordering of expensive policies' (Budge 1996b: 37). Indeed, the general consequences of marginalizing parties greatly alarm some commentators; Arthur Lipow and Patrick Seyd (1996), for instance, deride the anti-party 'techno-populism' of the 'new plebiscitarianism', and see in it the potential for manipulation of the masses by elites and demagogues – the very antithesis of democracy. However, it has also been argued that while direct democracy *can* bypass political parties, it is not necessarily *bound* to do so. Ian Budge, for instance, has outlined a model of democracy in which direct legislation would remain absolutely contingent on precisely the sorts of linkage which parties have traditionally supplied in representative democracies. For him, 'any feasible form of direct democracy would also be run by parties'. This is so largely because of the complexity of policy detail which confronts citizens; in the face of this, ordinary voters – no less than legislators in contemporary parliaments – would require parties to organize and lead debates. Thus: 'it is simply unrealistic to think that democracy could function without groupings resembling political parties . . . Mediating institutions, above all parties, facilitate rather than impede policy decisions and must be recognized as doing that under democracy in whatever form it occurs' (1996b: 175).

Is this argument plausible? Critics might point out that in places such as the USA, direct democracy (in conjunction with the substitution of primary elections for candidate selection by party caucuses) *has* succeeded in undermining parties to some extent.[10] Indeed, this is hardly surprising since direct democracy in America grew out of a series of reforms inspired originally by the Populist movement of the 1890s, the express purpose of which was to weaken and undermine the influence of political parties (Cronin 1989: 43ff.). But America is not necessarily a helpful comparative referent given that parties there have always been more loosely organized and disciplined than their British counterparts; it may be argued that direct democracy is far less likely to marginalize parties in parliamentary systems such as the UK's, where they already play a central and entrenched role. Although this is hardly an overwhelmingly powerful argument, it implies that Budge's proposals cannot be dismissed on the grounds that American evidence shows them to be implausible.

It is not inconceivable, therefore, that representative democracy could be supplemented by an extension of direct democracy without fundamentally undermining parties, and this could enhance the responsiveness of party governments by obliging them to consult voters more regularly on the impact of individual policies. Note too that the role they would play in organizing, leading and responding to policy debate implies that parties could be central to the revival of participatory linkage without their necessarily even recruiting more members. To summarize this argument, then: (a) political parties in contemporary Britain can currently be regarded as fostering an acceptable degree of political participation only from the narrow perspective of competitive elitism; (b) it is nevertheless possible to conceive of ways in which the existing structures and processes of representative democracy could be supplemented by a greater degree of direct democracy without fundamentally marginalizing parties; and (c) empirical evidence suggests that such a model is by no means certain to produce an increase in plainly inconsistent or bad laws, the influence of powerful interests or anti-minority legislation. This is not to suggest that direct democracy is some kind of panacea for all of the British political system's shortcomings, but it does imply a way in which parties could place themselves at the hub of an enhanced mechanism of participatory linkage and, potentially, revive their popular standing; at the very least, it would be far harder to accuse them of neither knowing nor caring what ordinary voters think about the issues of the day.

But what of the counter-argument that such reform is pointless since political parties are often unpopular and distrusted anyway in those political systems which already have a substantial component of direct democracy?

This is not an easy question to deal with since the countries concerned are in many ways fundamentally dissimilar to Britain, rendering comparison problematic. Italy is an obvious case in point: it has utilized 'abrogative referenda' (that is, popularly initiated referenda, the purpose of which is to seek the repeal of existing laws) since the 1970s, yet all the evidence suggests that parties and politicians there are singularly unpopular with the citizenry at large. Italy, however, is a Western country quite unlike most others, with a very particular set of problems relating to a dominant party system which allowed no alternation in power for nearly half a century, and which fostered immobilist government and an extraordinarily complex and profoundly corrupt network of relationships between state and society. Occasional recourse to the mechanisms of direct democracy can hardly be expected to counter all these evils single-handedly. Overall, the Italian case admits too many sources of extraneous variance for us to draw any safe comparative inferences.

A better test might seem to be provided by consideration of the USA, where few, if any, states of the Union replicate the acute exceptionalism of the Italian case. Budge suggests that 'it is very difficult to detect any systematic pattern of differences' (1996b: 122) in the standing and authority of parties between those American states which have recourse to direct legislation and those which do not. If this is so, then one might wonder if there is any point in extending direct democracy to a country like Britain. However, we have already seen that direct democracy in the USA is usually only weakly mediated by political parties, which means that it also offers a rather poor object of potential comparison. Indeed, the relative lack of party involvement in referenda and initiatives in America explains precisely why we should not expect the presence or non-presence of direct democracy to make any difference to the popular standing of parties there; their legitimacy could hardly be affected where they play no overt role in organizing direct legislation. Consequently, since it does not offer a model to which Britain is likely to approximate, the USA is once again a poor comparative referent.

Of potentially greater interest, however, is the case of contemporary Germany, where the major parties have in recent years sought to introduce greater direct democracy at state (*land*) level in a federal setting. Susan Scarrow argues that,

> Whatever the reality of the situation, in the early 1990s politicians in all parties subscribed to the diagnosis that Germany faced an upsurge of popular disenchantment which might threaten the health of the political system. They also accepted a conclusion which was widely proclaimed in contemporary analyses of anti-party sentiment, that the perceived 'problems with parties' might be overcome by giving citizens new ways to participate in political life. (1997: 465)

Though perhaps still too early to make a definitive judgement, her view is that these recent experiments in direct democracy have 'not immediately cured popular discontent with the political establishment' (op. cit.: 467).

Given, however, that this is a European parliamentary democracy based on a strong 'party state' which has recently introduced mechanisms of direct democracy in order to address problems of party legitimacy, Germany offers a more relevant point of comparison for those interested in British reform. Even so, there are significant limitations on the relevant institutional innovations in Germany, most notably in that politicians there have steadfastly refused to introduce direct democracy at the national level. Nevertheless, it is a case where developments should be monitored by proponents of direct democracy in Britain.

All in all, it must be said that there is as yet no really conclusive evidence from abroad as to the likely consequences of direct democracy for party legitimacy in Britain. It is virtually certain that it would not eradicate all disaffection with political elites and institutions, not least because a greater propensity to criticize is probably inherent in the irreversible processes of cognitive mobilization which have affected all Western electorates (Fuchs and Klingemann 1995: 432). Nevertheless, it could at least help parties avoid the (possibly unjustified) perception that they neither know nor care what voters think; more significantly, however, it could significantly affect the capacity of British parties to foster political participation and the attendant virtues of personal development and political responsiveness.[11] More generally, it seems fair to conclude that parties remain important, if flawed, channels of political participation for ordinary citizens in contemporary Britain. Even for advocates of greater direct democracy there can be little point in writing them off, for they remain a vital ingredient in the institutional recipe of participation; moreover, they could have the potential to help foster a revitalized participatory linkage if political elites are willing to engage in a little imaginative institutional engineering.

Conclusion

The evidence reviewed in the course of this chapter, and indeed the book as a whole, suggests a variety of challenges to political parties in modern Britain. Party managers and leaders cannot afford to be complacent about some of the indicators of popular distrust and cynicism which regularly emerge from opinion research, and it is not hard to identify certain shortcomings in parties' systemic performance – for instance, in their roles as mechanisms of representational and participatory linkage, or in the persistent policy problems which confront party governments. Equally, however, it is starkly apparent that they remain at the heart of the political system in a number of vital ways: thus, while increasingly compelled to share the functions of political communication and interest-articulation with other political actors, they are absolutely central to the aggregation of demands and the provision of accountable governance. To some extent, it is inevitable that parties will fail to perform all such tasks equally well, since there are certain trade-offs between them: for instance, there is clear potential for tension between articulating particular social group demands and aggregating multiple interests. Parties, therefore, should be given credit for pursuing a delicate balancing act between the various responsibilities which are thrust upon them in a parliamentary democracy such as Britain.

Overall, it should also be clear that the evidence we have reviewed makes it impossible to sustain the simplistic argument that political parties in Britain are in decline. After all, they remain functionally relevant (indeed, vital) to the political system in a number of ways; they have more than maintained their organizational strength and sophistication; and the overwhelming majority of voters still see politics through the lens of party competition. So why this apparent resilience? Mainly, perhaps, because parties are adaptable mechanisms. Nowhere is this more apparent than in the way they have forged new approaches to political communication and in the emergence of political marketing. Similarly, even though the rise of single-issue groups poses a certain challenge to parties as articulators of group interests, it also offers new opportunities for political mobilization. For instance, Labour not only maintains its formal organizational links with the affiliated trade unions, but it has developed less formal links with a host of groups concerned with the environment, nuclear energy and armaments, housing, social welfare, women's and ethnic issues. This suggests that party penetration of society is not always substantially weakened by the rise of single-issue groups, though it may be more mediated. Moreover, it is typical of parties to respond to membership decline or electoral defeat by organizational and political reforms designed, among other things, to offer new incentives to individual members and to enhance party responsiveness to the popular will. In short, even though political parties in the UK may have to contend with a variety of challenges, they are skilled at adapting and surviving; more than this, they remain of central importance to the structures and processes of democracy in the country.

Nevertheless, it is equally plain that there is considerable scope for reform which might further benefit parties and the political system more generally. In particular, the need for institutional innovation is pressing in the context of party finance (so as to enhance levels of popular trust in parties), and the electoral system (in order to improve parties' representative performance); greater recourse to direct democracy may also be desirable in order to enhance the capacity of parties to foster participatory and representative linkages. To some extent or other, change is either imminent or under consideration in each of these areas at the time of writing, which provides an upbeat note for the conclusion of our journey through the landscape of British party politics. The outcomes of any such reform are highly uncertain, however. Thus, while it is clearly appropriate to conclude that political parties remain central to democratic life in Britain today, it is equally apparent that they will be compelled to continue adapting to the evolving political system.

Notes

1 Indeed, recent research suggests that support for democracy generally remains high in established democracies, even though the tendency for citizens to be critical of the major institutions of representative government (including parties) has grown (Norris 1999: 26).

2 This was not easy, since the Sainsbury supermarket chain was known to have invested heavily in controversial genetically modified (GM) food products; given his position as Science Minister, Sainsbury could easily be perceived to be in a position to influence the outcome of government research into GM foods.

3 Even then, his success depended on the decisions by the Labour and Liberal Democratic parties to withdraw their own candidates in the constituency and support him.

4 Tony Blair demonstrated a certain proclivity for this practice on assuming office in 1997, in appointing one or two prominent businessmen with little or no background in party politics to junior ministerial posts: examples include Lord Simon, Lord Sainsbury and Lord MacDonald. In order to maintain constitutional tradition, however, these men took their places on the Labour benches in the House of Lords.

5 This is true, for instance, of Charlie Whelan, Chancellor Gordon Brown's closest aide until forced to resign over allegations that he leaked to the media embarrassing private financial details about the former Trade and Industry Minister Peter Mandelson (Watt 1998: 2).

6 Note that when the number of votes cast for losing candidates is added to the number of 'supernumerary' or 'surplus majority' votes (that is, the total above the winning threshold cast for the winning candidate), the overall sum of 'wasted' votes can be quite staggering. Dunleavy and Margetts calculate, for instance, that in the south Wales region in 1997, some 45% of votes were supernumerary, while a further 37% were cast for losing candidates. This produces an overall total of 82% of the popular vote which was 'wasted'(1997: 230)!

7 Note that Commission member Lord Alexander of Weedon issued a 'note of reservation' to the main report in which he defended the use of SMP for the election of constituency members.

8 The corrective mechanism proposed by Jenkins would operate as follows. The number of second ('additional') votes cast for each party would be counted and divided by the number of constituency MPs plus 1 gained by each party in each area. This produces a 'second votes' quota for each party, and the party with the highest such quota would then be allocated the first top-up member. Assume, for instance, that two parties competing in a given area win an identical number of second votes (say, 50,000), but while one of them (party A) has already won 4 constituency MPs in that same area, the other (party B) has only won 3 constituency members. The second vote quotas for the two parties would be 10,000 for A (50,000/[4+1]) and 12,500 for B (50,000/[3+1]). Thus, party B, which has clearly been discriminated against by the working of the electoral system in terms of the contest for constituency members in the area, is compensated by the award of the first 'top-up' member. Any further top-up members would then be allocated according to the same method, but adjusting for the fact that one party has already gained an additional member (Jenkins 1998: ch. 9, para. 6). In reality, if Jenkins's recommendations were to be adopted, there would probably only be a single top-up member to be allocated to most areas (that is, for each county or metropolitan district).

9   That direct democracy of the type discussed in this section constitutes no more than a participatory supplement to representative democracy is illustrated by the fact that even in Switzerland (which accounts for nearly half the modern world's referenda), direct legislation only comprises approximately 10% of all laws that are passed (Budge 1996b: 96).

10 Critics of direct democracy in America argue that this is a major problem. For instance, Magleby contends that the bypassing of parties leaves voters without clear cues for decision making and can permit well-resourced private interests undue influence in referendum campaigns (1984; 1994).

11 Readers interested in specific models for the extension of direct democracy in a country such as Britain might usefully refer to McLean 1989: 132; Adonis and Mulgan 1994; Budge 1996b, ch. 7; or even Held 1996: ch. 9. Advice on the organization and regulation of referenda is also abundant (see, for instance, Cronin 1989: ch. 9; Neill 1998: ch. 12; Seyd 1998).

APPENDIX: CLUSTER ANALYSIS

The goal of the cluster analysis performed in Chapter 6 is to identify homogeneous groups (or clusters) of MPs in terms of their core ideological values. This is achieved by using SPSS's[1] Cluster program, which can measure how close cases are to each other in terms of (squared) Euclidian distance. This may sound like an obscure formulation to readers who are not quantitatively minded, but a simple example demonstrates that it is conceptually quite straightforward. Assume that we are interested to know how far two individuals are from one another in terms of their core beliefs, and that we wish to calculate this in terms of squared Euclidian distance. These individuals are located as follows on our attitudinal scales:

Case	Socialism–Capitalism	Liberty–Authority
Individual 1	1.5	2.0
Individual 2	4.5	4.0
Euclidian distance	3.0^2	2.0^2

Recall that both scales run from 1–5, with 1 representing the most socialist or the most libertarian possible location, while 5 represents the most capitalist or authoritarian location. In the example, it is clear that we have two rather different cases; individual 1 is obviously nearer to the socialist and libertarian poles of the two scales, while individual 2 is closer to the capitalist and authoritarian extremes. How do we measure their overall distance in Euclidian terms? On the socialism scale the two individuals are fully 3 units apart, while on the libertarianism scale they are 2 units distant from one another. According to the formula, each of these distances must be squared, then totalled to give the overall Euclidian distance in our two-dimensional attitudinal space (thus, $3^2 + 2^2 = 13$).

This way of measuring distances provides the basis on which a cluster analysis of MPs in the BCS and BRS samples can be executed. In *hierarchical clustering*, there are as many clusters as there are cases at the outset of the analysis. At the first stage of analysis, the two cases which are nearest to each other in terms of Euclidian distance are merged into a single cluster. At the next stage, the next nearest case is then added to this cluster, or two other cases which are nearer to each other are joined together to form a new cluster. This proceeds until all cases have been merged into a single cluster, though it is almost certain that this final 'unified' formation will actually be very heterogeneous, and therefore substantively uninteresting. Once a cluster has been formed it cannot be split apart at a later stage of analysis; it can only be merged with other cases or clusters (Romesburg 1984; Norusis 1992: chs 3, 4). It is the task of the researcher to interpret cluster analysis results in the light of substantive knowledge and theory, so as to uncover a model in which each cluster consists of MPs who share relatively similar core political beliefs, while each cluster is relatively distinct from others within the party.

It is important to understand that cluster analysis does not necessarily produce any single statistically 'correct' solution to our problem. Rather, it provides indications of a range of statistically acceptable solutions, and allows the researcher to select among them in the light of substantive and theoretical knowledge. As Romesburg says, the researcher is ultimately obliged to make a 'subjective' decision about the trade-off between the desire for detail (many classes) and simplicity (few classes):

> The guiding rules for subjective decisions are the norms that professional fields sanction. The norms map out the range of what is and is not acceptable, rather than constraining the decision to one possibility. (1984: 241)

In Chapter 6, a number of statistical and 'subjective' criteria are applied. The first statistical criterion to offer us guidance is the *distance coefficient*.[2] This coefficient is based on the value of the distance between the most dissimilar points of the clusters being combined at each stage of the clustering process. Thus, as a general rule, small coefficients indicate that homogeneous clusters are being merged, while large coefficients suggest that clusters containing quite dissimilar cases are being forced together. It makes sense, therefore, to examine the schedule of distance coefficients (sometimes referred to as an *agglomeration schedule*) at each stage of the cluster analysis in order to observe where sudden, relatively large increases in value occur. In Table 6.1, for instance, this happens as the clustering process takes the data from a six-cluster model to a five-cluster model, and constitutes a prima facie indication that it would be prudent not to accept any solution containing five clusters or less (Norusis 1992: 102–3).

To rely on the distance coefficient alone would constitute a very crude approach, however. The next criterion on which we focus, therefore, is the *mean score on each of the two attitudinal scales* of each of the clusters generated by a particular model. This is of obvious importance since it is the basic measure by which we are able to locate the clusters in two-dimensional space. Cluster means inform us on average precisely how left-wing, right-wing, libertarian or authoritarian each of the clusters is, and thus identify the nature of each in a substantive sense. This information can be valuable in choosing between alternative models. Implicit in this part of the discussion is the 'subjective' criterion that a solution should be *substantively interpretable*. More precisely, there should be nothing in an accepted model which is counter-intuitive.

Beyond this, further statistical criteria are employed, each of which derives from analysis of variance. Specifically, the *F-ratios* generated by analysis of variance confirm whether the differences between cluster means are statistically significant; in Chapter 6 no model is accepted unless cluster means are significantly different on both the socialism and liberty scales. In addition, we can look to the eta^2 coefficient which measures the strength of these cluster differences (or more exactly, the ratio of variation explained by cluster group differences to that which is unexplained by them); as a general rule of thumb, a cluster model is not considered acceptable for our purposes unless eta^2 indicates that it explains at least 50% of the variation in each of the attitudinal scales. Finally, the standard deviation around the mean location on each scale is a useful indicator of cluster cohesion.

The final criterion which is applied is a cornerstone of modern political science, the principle of *parsimony*. That is, as a general rule, it makes sense to opt for the simplest meaningful model which conforms to the statistical criteria and captures the main nuances of intra-party attitudinal differences. Where, for instance, two alternatives seem acceptable on all other criteria, and both are substantively interpretable, then it is preferable to opt for the model containing fewer clusters.

These criteria explain the form in which the results of cluster analyses are reported in Chapter 6. That is, the distance coefficients generated by the final few stages of initial exploratory clustering are reported, so that the stage or stages at which the clustering process might cease are illustrated. Thereafter, details of the preferred cluster model are reported; these include cluster means and standard deviations for each of the attitudinal scales, along with significance levels derived from F-ratios, and eta^2 for each scale. All cluster models reported have been generated by SPSS's 'Cluster' program, which measures distances between cases in terms of squared Euclidian distance, and employs the 'average linkage between groups' method (as recommended by Leece and Berrington 1977: 530).

Notes

1   For the uninitiated, SPSS is the Statistical Package for the Social Sciences.
2   Note that distance coefficients can be calculated in a number of different ways, and are sometimes referred to as resemblance, similarity or dissimilarity coefficients. In Chapter 6, the distance between two cases is the sum of the squared differences in values for each variable, given by the formula:

$$\text{Distance } (X,Y) = \Sigma (X_1 - Y_1)^2$$

REFERENCES

Aarts, K (1995) 'Intermediate organizations and interest representation' in HD Klingemann and D Fuchs *Citizens and the State* (Oxford: Oxford University Press).

Adonis, A (1996) 'A guide to Britain's four Tory parties' The *Observer* 6 October.

Adonis, A and G Mulgan (1994) 'Back to Greece: the scope for direct democracy' *Demos Quarterly* 3, pp. 2–9.

Aldrich, JH (1995) *Why Parties? The Origin and Transformation of Political Parties in America* (Chicago: University of Chicago Press).

Alford, R (1963) *Party and Society: Anglo-American Democracies* (Chicago: Rand McNally).

Alt, JE, B Sarlvik and I Crewe (1976) 'Partisanship and policy choice: issue preferences in the British electorate' *British Journal of Political Science* 6, pp. 273–90.

Amery, LS (1947) *Thoughts on the Constitution* (Oxford: Oxford University Press).

Anderson, P (1961) 'Sweden: Mr Crosland's dreamland' *New Left Review*, pp. 7 and 9.

Anderson, P (1965) 'Problems of Socialist Strategy' in P Anderson and R Blackburn *Towards Socialism* (London: Collins).

Aughey, A (1994) 'The political parties in Northern Ireland' in L Robins, H Blackmore and R Pyper (eds) *Britain's Changing Party System* (London: Leicester University Press), pp. 166–82

Axelrod, R (1970) *Conflict of Interest* (Chicago, IL: Markham).

Baker, D, A Gamble and S Ludlam (1993a) 'Conservative splits and European integration' *Political Quarterly* 64/2, pp. 420–35.

Baker, D, A Gamble and S Ludlam (1993b) 'Whips or scorpions? The Maastricht vote and the Conservative Party' *Parliamentary Affairs* 42/2, pp. 151–66.

Baker, D, I Fountain, A Gamble and S Ludlam (1994) 'Conservative parliamentarians and European integration'. Paper presented to the *Annual Conference of Elections, Parties and Public Opinion Specialist Group of PSA*, Cardiff, September.

Baker, D, I Fountain, A Gamble and S Ludlam (1995) 'Sovereignty – the San Andreas fault of Conservative ideology'. Paper presented to *Annual Conference of Political Studies Association*, York, April.

Baker, D, A Gamble, S Ludlam and D Seawright (1999) 'Backbenchers with attitude: a seismic study of the Conservative Party and dissent on Europe' in S Bowler, DM Farrell and RS Katz (eds) *Party Discipline and Parliamentary Government* (Columbus: Ohio State University Press), pp. 72–93.

Banducci, S (1998) 'Direct legislation: when is it used and when does it pass?' in S Bowler, T Donovan and C Tolbert (eds) *Citizens as Legislators: Direct Democracy in the United States* (Columbus, OH: Ohio State University Press).

Barker, R (1978) *Political Ideas in Modern Britain* (London: Methuen).

Barnes, J (1994) 'Ideology and factions' in A Seldon and S Ball (eds) *The Conservative Century: The Conservative Party Since 1900* (Oxford: Oxford University Press), pp. 315–46.

Barnes, J and R Cockett (1994) 'Making party policy' in A Seldon and S Ball (eds) *The Conservative Century: The Conservative Party Since 1900* (Oxford: Oxford University Press), pp. 347–82.

Barnes, SH (1974) 'Italy: Religion and Class in Electoral Behaviour' in R Rose (ed.) *Electoral Behaviour: A Comparative Handbook* (London: Collier-Macmillan), pp. 171–226.

Barnes, SH and Kaase, M (1979) *Political Action: Mass Participation in Five Western Democracies* (Beverly Hills: Sage).

Bartle, J, I Crewe and A King (1997) 'Was it Blair wot won it?: leadership effects in the 1997 British general election'. Paper presented to conference *Assessing The 1997 Election*, University of Essex, September.

Bartolini, S and P Mair (1990) *Identity, Competition and Electoral Availability: The Stabilisation of European Electorates 1885–1985* (Cambridge: Cambridge University Press).

Bell, D (1959) *The End of Ideology* (New York: Free Press).

Belloni, FP and DC Beller (1978) *Faction Politics: Political Parties and Factionalism in Comparative Perspective* (Santa Barbara, CA: ABC-Clio).

Bennie, L, J Curtice and W Rudig (1996) 'Party members' in D MacIver (ed.) *The Liberal Democrats* (Hemel Hempstead: Prentice Hall), pp. 135–54.

Berlin, I (1969) 'Two concepts of liberty' in I Berlin *Four Essays on Liberty* (Oxford: Oxford University Press), pp. 118–72

Berrington, HB (1973) *Backbench Opinion in the House of Commons, 1945–55* (Oxford: Pergamon Press).

Berrington, H and R Hague (1997) ' The Liberal Democrat campaign' in P Norris and NT Gavin (eds) *Britain Votes 1997* (Oxford: Oxford University Press), pp. 47–60.

Beveridge, WH (1942) *Social Insurance and Allied Services: A Report* (London: HMSO).

Birch, AH (1984) 'Overload, ungovernability and delegitimation: the theories and the British case' *British Journal of Political Science* 14, pp. 135–60.

Blondel, J (1968) 'Party systems and patterns of government in western democracies' *Canadian Journal of Political Science* 1, pp. 180–203.

Bonham-Carter, J (1997) 'The Liberal Democrats' media strategy'. Paper presented to conference *Assessing the 1997 Election*, University of Essex, September.

Bowler, S and T Donovan (1998a) 'Two cheers for direct democracy or who's afraid of the initiative process?' *Representation* 35, pp. 247–54.

Bowler, S and T Donovan (1998b) *Demanding Choices: Opinion, Voting and Direct Democracy* (Ann Arbor, MI: University of Michigan Press).

Bowler, S, DM Farrell and RS Katz (1999) 'Party cohesion, party discipline and parliaments' in S Bowler, DM Farrell and RS Katz (eds) *Party Discipline and Parliamentary Government* (Columbus: Ohio State University Press), pp. 3–22.

Brack, B (1996) 'Liberal Democrat policy' in D MacIver (ed.) *The Liberal Democrats* (London: Prentice-Hall), pp. 85–110.

Braggins, J, M McDonagh and A Barnard (1993) *The American Presidential Election 1992 – What Can Labour Learn?* (London: Labour Party).

Brand, J (1989) 'Faction as its own reward: Groups in the British parliament 1945–1986' *Parliamentary Affairs* 42/2, pp. 148–65.

Brand, J (1992) *British Parliamentary Parties: Policy and Power* (Oxford: Clarendon Press).

Braybrooke, D and CE Lindblom (1963) *A Strategy of Decision* (New York: Free Press).

British Broadcasting Corporation (1999) *Vote 99: Local Elections in England, Scotland and Wales* (London: BBC).

Brittan, S (1977) *The Economic Consequences of Democracy* (London: Temple Smith).

Brock, M (1983) 'The Liberal tradition' in V Bogdanor (ed.) *Liberal Party Politics* (Oxford: Clarendon Press), pp. 15–26.

Brown, A (1997) 'Scotland: paving the way for devolution?' in P Norris and NT Gavin (eds) *Britain Votes 1997* (Oxford: Oxford University Press), pp. 150–63.

Budge, I (1994) 'A new spatial theory of party competition: uncertainty, ideology and policy equilibria viewed comparatively and temporally' *British Journal of Political Science* 24, pp. 443–67.

Budge, I (1996a) 'Great Britain and Ireland: Variations on dominant party government' in JM Colomer (ed.) *Political Institutions in Europe* (London: Routledge), pp. 18–61.

Budge, I (1996b) *The New Challenge of Direct Democracy* (Cambridge: Polity Press)

Budge, I (1999) 'Party policy and ideology: reversing the 1950s?' in G Evans and P Norris (eds) *Critical Elections: British Parties and Voters in Long-Term Perspective* (London: Sage), pp. 1–21.

Budge, I and D Farlie (1983) *Explaining and Predicting Elections: Issue Effects and Party Strategies in 23 Democracies* (London: George Allen & Unwin).

Budge, I, I. Crewe and D. Farlie (1976) *Party Identification and Beyond* (New York: Wiley).

Bulmer-Thomas, I (1953) *The Party System in Great Britain* (London: Phoenix House).

Burke, E (1906) 'Thoughts on the Cause of the Present Discontents' in H Frowde (ed.) *The Works of the Right Honourable Edmund Burke* (London: Oxford University Press), pp. 1–88; first published 1770.

Burke, E (1968) *Reflections on the Revolution in France* (London: Penguin); first published 1790.

Butler, D and D Kavanagh (1988) *The British General Election of 1987* (London: Macmillan).

Butler, D and D Kavanagh (1997) *The British General Election of 1997* (Basingstoke: Macmillan).

Butler, D and R Rose (1960) *The British General Election of 1959* (London: Macmillan).

Butler, D and D Stokes (1974) *Political Change in Britain* (Harmondsworth: Penguin) 1st edition 1969.

Butler, D, A Adonis and T Travers (1995) *Policy Failure in British Government: The Politics of the Poll Tax* (Oxford: Oxford University Press).

Byrd, P (1986) 'The Labour Party in Britain' in WE Paterson and A Thomas *The Future of Social Democracy* (Oxford: Clarendon Press), pp. 59–107

Byrne, P (1997) *Social Movements in Britain* (London: Routledge).

Cambridge Political Economy Group (1974) *Britain's Economic Crisis* (Nottingham: Spokesman).

Campbell, A, P Converse, WE Miller and D Stokes (1960) *The American Voter* (New York City: John Wiley).

Castles, FG (1994) 'The policy consequences of proportional representation: a sceptical commentary' *Political Science* 46, pp. 161–71.

Catt, H (1999) *Democracy in Practice* (London: Routledge).

Central Statistical Office (1963) *Annual Abstract of Statistics 100* (London: HMSO).

Central Statistical Office (1976) *Annual Abstract of Statistics 113* (London: HMSO).

Central Statistical Office (1989) *Annual Abstract of Statistics 125* (London: HMSO).

Chandler, JA (1996) *Local Government Today* (Manchester: Manchester University Press).

Clarke, P (1983) 'Liberals and social democrats in historical perspective' in V Bogdanor (ed.) *Liberal Party Politics* (Oxford: Clarendon Press), pp. 27–42.

Cm.3883 (1998) *Northern Ireland Peace Agreement* (London: The Stationery Office).

Cm.4413 (1999) *The Funding of Political Parties in the UK: The Government's Proposals for Legislation in Response to the Fifth Report of the Committee on Standards in Public Life* (London: The Stationery Office).

Coates, D (1994) *The Question of UK Decline: the Economy, State and Society* (Hemel Hempstead: Harvester Wheatsheaf).

Coates, K and T Topham (1986) *Trade Unions and Politics* (Oxford: Basil Blackwell).

Cockett, R (1994) 'The party, publicity and the media' in A Seldon and S Ball (eds) *The Conservative Century: The Conservative Party Since 1900* (Oxford: Oxford University Press), pp. 547–77.

Conservative Party (1997) *Blueprint for Change: A Consultation Paper for Reform of the Conservative Party* (London: Conservative Party).

Conservative Party (1998) *Fresh Future* (London: Conservative Party).

Converse, P (1964) 'The nature of belief systems in mass publics' in D Apter (ed.) *Ideology and Discontent* (New York: Free Press).

Cowley, P and P Norton with M Stuart and M Bailey (1996) 'Blair's Bastards: Discontent within the PLP' *Centre for Legislative Studies Research Paper 1/96* (Hull: University of Hull).

Cox, GW (1987) *The Efficient Secret: The Cabinet and the Development of Political Parties in Victorian England* (Cambridge: Cambridge University Press).

Cox, GW and MD McCubbins (1993) *Legislative Leviathan: Party Government in the House* (Berkeley, CA: University of California Press).

Crewe, I (1985) 'Great Britain' in I Crewe and D Denver (eds) *Electoral Change in Western Democracies: Patterns and Sources of Electoral Volatility* (Beckenham: Croom Helm), pp 100–50.

Crewe, I (1986) 'On the death and resurrection of class voting: some comments on *How Britain Votes*' *Political Studies* 34, pp. 620–38.

Crewe, I (1988) 'Why Mrs Thatcher was returned with a landslide' *Social Studies Review* 3, pp. 2–9.

Crewe, I (1993) 'Parties and electors' in I Budge and D. McKay (1994) *The Developing British Political System: The 1990s* (London: Longman), pp. 83–111.

Crewe, I and D Searing (1988) 'Ideological change in the British Conservative Party' *American Political Science Review* 82, pp. 361–85.

Crewe, I, N Fox and A Day (1995) *The British Electorate: A Compendium of Data from the British Election Surveys 1963–1992* (Cambridge: Cambridge University Press).

Cronin, TE (1989) *Direct Democracy: The Politics of Initiative, Referendum and Recall* (Cambridge, MA: Harvard University Press).

Crosland, CAR (1956) *The Future of Socialism* (London: Jonathan Cape).

Crosland, CAR (1975) *Social Democracy in Europe* (London: Fabian Society).

CSE-LCC (1980) *The Alternative Economic Strategy* (London: Conference of Socialist Economists-Labour Coordinating Committee).

Curtice, J (1988) 'Great Britain: Social liberalism reborn?' in E Kirchner (ed.) *Liberal Parties in Western Europe* (Cambridge: Cambridge University Press).

Curtice, J and R Jowell (1997) 'Trust in the political system' in R Jowell, J Curtice et al. (eds) *British Social Attitudes: 14th Report* (Aldershot: Ashgate), pp. 89–109.

Curtice, J and A. Park (1999) 'Region: New Labour, new geography?' in G Evans and P Norris (eds) *Critical Elections: British Parties and Voters in Long-term Perspective* (London: Sage), pp. 124–47.

Curtice, J and H Semetko (1994) 'Does it matter what the papers say?' in A Heath, R Jowell and J Curtice (eds) *Labour's Last Chance? The 1992 Election and Beyond* (Aldershot: Dartmouth), pp. 43–64.

Curtice, J and M Steed (1982) 'Electoral choice and the production of government: the changing operation of the UK electoral system since 1955' *British Journal of Political Science* 12, pp. 249–98.

Curtice, J and M Steed (1993) 'Appendix 2: the results analysed' in D Butler and D Kavanagh (eds) *The British General Election of 1992* (Basingstoke: Macmillan), pp. 322–62.

Dahl, R (1971) *Polyarchy* (New Haven, CT: Yale University Press).

Dalton, R (1996) *Citizen Politics: Public Opinion and Political Parties in Advanced Western Democracies* (Chatham, NJ: Chatham House); 2nd edition.

Dalton, R (forthcoming) 'Partisan dealignment' in R Dalton and M Wattenberg (eds) *Parties Without Partisans: Political Change in Advanced Industrial Democracies* (Oxford: Oxford University Press).

Denham, A and M Garnett (1999) 'Influence without responsibility? Think tanks in Britain' *Parliamentary Affairs* 52, pp. 46–57.

Denver, D (1989) *Elections and Voting Behaviour in Britain* (Hemel Hempstead: Harvester Wheatsheaf); 2nd edition 1994.

Denver, D (1998)'The government that could do no right' in A King, D Denver, I McLean, P Norris, P Norton, D Sanders and P Seyd *New Labour Triumphs: Britain at the Polls* (Chatham, NJ: Chatham House), pp. 15–48.

Denver, D and G Hands (1992a) 'Constituency campaigning' *Parliamentary Affairs* 45, pp. 528–44.

Denver, D and G Hands (1992b) *Issues and Controversies in British Electoral Behaviour* (Hemel Hempstead: Harvester Wheatsheaf).

Denver, D and G Hands (1997) *Modern Constituency Campaigning: The 1992 General Election* (London: Frank Cass).

Donovan, T and S Bowler (1998) 'Direct democracy and minority rights' *American Journal of Political Science* 43, pp. 1020–5.

Dorfman, G (1979) *Government versus the Trade Unions in Britain since 1968* (London: Macmillan).

Downs, A (1957) *An Economic Theory of Democracy* (New York: Harper Row).

Drucker, H (1979) *Doctrine and Ethos in the Labour Party* (London: George Allen and Unwin).

Drucker, H (1982) 'The influence of the trade unions on the ethos of the Labour Party' in B Pimlott and C Cook (eds) *Trade Unions in British Politics* (London: Longman), pp. 258–71.

Dunleavy, P (1979) 'The urban basis of political alignment: social class, domestic property ownership and state intervention in consumption processes' *British Journal of Political Science* 9, pp. 409–33.

Dunleavy, P (1980) 'The political implications of sectoral cleavages and the growth of state employment' *Political Studies* 28, pp. 364–83, 527–49.

Dunleavy, P (1987) 'Class dealignment revisited: why odds ratios give odd results' *West European Politics* 10, pp. 400–19.

Dunleavy, P and C Husbands (1985) *British Democracy at the Crossroads: Voting and Party Competition in the 1980s* (London: George Allen & Unwin).

Dunleavy, P and H Margetts (1997) 'The electoral system' in P Norris and NT Gavin (eds) *Britain Votes 1997* (Oxford: Oxford University Press), pp. 225–41.

Dunleavy, P and H Margetts (1999) 'Mixed electoral systems in Britain and the Jenkins Commission on electoral reform' *British Journal of Politics and International Relations* 1, pp. 12–38.

Dunleavy, P and H Ward (1981) 'Exogenous voter preferences and parties with state power: some internal problems of economic models of party competition' *British Journal of Political Science* 11, pp. 351-80.

Dunleavy, P, H. Margetts and S Weir (1993) 'The 1992 election and the legitimacy of British democracy' in D Denver, P Norris, D Broughton and C Rallings (eds) *British Elections and Parties Yearbook 1993* (Hemel Hempstead), pp. 177–92.

Dunleavy, P, H Margetts, B O'Duffy and S Weir (1997) 'Remodelling the 1997 General Election: how Britain would have voted under alternative electoral systems'. Paper presented to conference on *Assessing the 1997 Election*, University of Essex, September.

Duverger, M (1954) *Political Parties: Their Organisation and Activity in the Modern State* (London: Methuen).

Ellis, T (1998) 'The Jenkins Commission: editorial comment' *Representation* 35, pp. 87–9.

English, R and M Kenny (1999) 'British decline or the politics of declinism?' *British Journal of Politics and International Relations* 1, pp. 252–66.

Epstein, LD (1967) *Political Parties in Western Democracies* (London: Pall Mall Press).

Epstein, LD (1986) *Political Parties in the American Mold* (New York: Madison).

Esping-Andersen, G (1985) *Politics Against Markets: The Social Democratic Path to Power* (Princeton, NJ: Princeton University Press).

Eurig, A (1999) 'Welsh Assembly elections: history in the making' in C Rallings and M Thrasher (eds) *New Britain, New Elections: The Media Guide to the New Political Map of Britain* (London: Vacher Dod), pp. 89–90.

Evans, G (1998) 'How Britain views the EU' in R Jowell, J Curtice, A Park, L Brook, K Thomson and C Bryson *British and European Social Attitudes: The 15th Report* (Aldershot: Ashgate), pp. 173–90.

Evans, G (1999) 'Europe: a new cleavage?' in G Evans and P Norris (eds) *Critical Elections: British Parties and Voters in Long-Term Perspective* (London: Sage Publications), pp. 207–22.

Evans, G and M Duffy (1997) 'Beyond the sectarian divide: the social bases and political consequences of Nationalist and Unionist party competition in Northern Ireland' *British Journal of Political Science*, 1, pp. 47–81.

Evans, G and P Norris (eds) (1999) *Critical Elections: British Parties and Voters in Long-Term Perspective* (London: Sage Publications).

Evans, G, A Heath and C Payne (1999) 'Class: Labour as a catch-all party?' in G Evans and P Norris (eds) *Critical Elections: British Parties and Voters in Long-Term Perspective* (London: Sage Publications), pp. 87–101.

Ewing, K (1987) *The Funding of Political Parties in Britain* (Cambridge: Cambridge University Press).

Farrell, DM and PD Webb (forthcoming) 'Political parties as campaign organizations' in R. Dalton and M. Wattenberg (eds) *Parties Without Partisans: Political Change in Advanced Industrial Democracies* (Oxford: Oxford University Press).

Farrell, DM, I McAllister and D Studlar (1998) 'Sex, money and politics: sleaze and the Conservative Party in the 1997 election' in D Denver, J Fisher, P Cowley and C Pattie (eds) *British Elections and Parties Review 1998* (London: Frank Cass), pp. 80–94.

Farrell, S, D Kennedy, M Henderson and J Landale (1997) 'The Millbank tendency' *The Times*, 21 April.

Field, W (1997) *Regional Dynamics: The Basis of Electoral Support in Britain* (London: Frank Cass).

Finer, SE (1975) *Adversary Politics and Electoral Reform* (London: Anthony Wigram).

Finer, SE (1980) *The Changing British Party System, 1945–1979* (Washington: American Enterprise Institute).

Finer, SE (1987) 'Left and Right' in V Bogdanor (ed.) *The Blackwell Encyclopaedia of Political Institutions* (Oxford: Blackwell), pp. 324–5.

Finer, SE, HB Berrington and DJ Bartholomew (1961) *Backbench Opinion in the House of Commons, 1955–59* (Oxford: Pergamon Press).

Fisher, J (1996a) *British Political Parties* (Hemel Hempstead: Prentice Hall).

Fisher, J (1996b) 'Party finance' in P Norton (ed.) *The Conservative Party* (Hemel Hempstead: Prentice Hall), pp. 157–69.

Flanagan, SC and R Dalton (1985) 'Parties under stress: realignment and dealignment in advanced industrial societies' *West European Politics* 7, pp 7–23.

Foley, M (1993) *The Rise of the British Presidency* (Manchester: Manchester University Press).

Franklin, B (1994) *Packaging Politics* (London: Edward Arnold).

Franklin, M (1985) *The Decline of Class Voting in Britain, 1964–83* (Oxford: Clarendon Press).

Franklin, M (1992) 'Britain' in MN Franklin, TT Mackie and H Valen (eds) *Electoral Change: Responses to Evolving Social and Attitudinal Structures in Western Countries* (Cambridge: Cambridge University Press), pp. 101–22.

Freeden, M (1999) 'The ideology of New Labour' *Political Quarterly* 70, pp. 42–51.

Fuchs, D and H-D Klingemann (1995) 'Citizens and the state: a relationship transformed' in HD Klingemann and D Fuchs *Citizens and the State* (Oxford: Oxford University Press), pp. 419–43.

Gamble, A (1985) *Britain in Decline* (London: Macmillan).

Gamble, A (1988) *The Free Economy and the Strong State* (Basingstoke: Macmillan).

Game, C and Leach, S (1995) 'Monopolistic and hung councils: outcomes of the 1995 local elections' *Representation* 33, pp. 66–72.

Garner, R and R Kelly (1998) *British Political Parties Today* (Manchester: Manchester University Press); 2nd edition.

Garrett, G (1994) 'Popular capitalism: the electoral legacy of Thatcherism' in A Heath, R Jowell, J Curtice and B Taylor *Labour's Last Chance? The 1992 Election and Beyond* (Aldershot: Dartmouth), pp. 107–24.

Garry, J (1995) 'The British Conservative Party: Divisions over European policy' *West European Politics* 18, pp. 170–89.

Gavin, NT and D Sanders (1995) 'The impact of televisual economic news on public perceptions of the economy and government, 1993–1994'. Paper presented to specialist *PSA conference on Parties, Elections and Public Opinion*, London: Guildhall University, September.

George, S and M Sowemimo (1996) 'Conservative foreign policy towards the European Union' in S Ludlam and MJ Smith *Contemporary British Conservatism* (Basingstoke: Macmillan).

Giddens, A (1994) 'What's left for Labour?' *New Statesman and Society* (30 September).

Giddens, A (1998) *The Third Way: The Renewal of Social Democracy* (Cambridge: Polity Press).

Goldthorpe, J and C.Payne (1986) 'Trends in inter-generational class mobility in England and Wales, 1972–1983' *Sociology* 20, pp. 1–24.

Goldthorpe, JH, D Lockwood, F Bechofer and J Platt (1968) *The Affluent Worker: Political Attitudes and Behaviour* (Cambridge: Cambridge University Press).

Goodhart, CAE and RJ Bhansali (1970) 'Political economy' *Political Studies* 18, pp. 43–106.

Goodman, LA (1972) 'A modified multiple regression approach to the analysis of dichotomous variables' *American Sociological Review* 37, pp. 28–46.

Graetz, B and I McAllister (1987) 'Party leaders and election outcomes in Britain, 1974–1983' *Comparative Political Studies* 19, pp. 484–507.

Graham, BD (1993) *Representation and Party Politics* (Oxford: Blackwell).

Gray, J (1994) *The Undoing of Conservatism* (London: Social Market Foundation).

Green, TH (1888) 'Liberal legislation and freedom of contract' in RL Nettleship (ed.) *The Works of Thomas Hill Green, Volume 3* (London: Longmans, Green & Co.).

Guardian, The (1999) 'Lilley the pink' *Leading article*, 24 April, p. 19.

Gunter, B, J Sancho-Aldridge and P Winstone (1994) *Television and the Public's View* (London: John Libbey).

Gyford, J, S Leach, and C Game (1989) *The Changing Politics of Local Government* (London: Unwin Hyman).

Hall, PA (1998) 'Social capital in Britain'. Paper presented to *Annual Meeting of the American Political Science Association*, Boston, September.

Ham, C and M Hill (1993) *The Policy Process in the Capitalist State* (Hemel Hempstead: Harvester Wheatsheaf).

Hansard Society (1982) *Paying for Politics* (London: Hansard Society).

Harrison, M (1982) *Trade Unions and the Labour Party since 1945* (London: Allen & Unwin).

Haseler, S (1969) *The Gaitskellites* (London: Macmillan).

Hatfield, M (1978) *The House The Left Built: Inside Labour Policy Making, 1970–1975* (London: Victor Gollancz).

Hay, C and M Watson (1998) 'Rendering the contingent necessary: New Labour's neo-liberal conversion and the discourse of globalization'. Paper presented to the *Annual Meeting of the American Political Science Association*, 3–6 September, Boston, MA.

Heath, A and R Jowell (1994) 'Labour's policy review' in A. Heath, R Jowell and J Curtice (eds) *Labour's Last Chance? The 1992 Election and Beyond* (Aldershot: Dartmouth), pp. 191–212.

Heath, A and S-K McDonald (1988) 'The demise of party identification theory?' *Electoral Studies* 7, pp. 95–107.

Heath, A, G Evans and J Martin (1993) 'The measurement of core beliefs and values: The development of balanced socialist/laissez faire and libertarian/authoritarian scales' *British Journal of Political Science* 24, pp. 115–58.

Heath, A with G Garrett (1991) 'The extension of popular capitalism' in A Heath, J Curtice, R Jowell, G Evans, J Field and S Witherspoon (eds) *Understanding Political Change: The British Voter 1964–1987* (Oxford: Pergamon Press), pp. 120–35.

Heath, A, R Jowell and J Curtice (1985) *How Britain Votes* (Oxford: Pergamon).

Heath, A, R Jowell and J Curtice (1987) 'Trendless fluctuation: A reply to Crewe' *Political Studies* 35, pp. 256–77.

Heath, A, I McLean, B Taylor and J Curtice (1999) 'Between first and second-order: a comparison of voting behaviour in European and local elections in Britain' *European Journal of Political Research* 35, pp. 389–414.

Heath, A, R Jowell, J Curtice, G Evans, J Field and S Witherspoon (1991) *Understanding Political Change* (Oxford: Pergamon).

Held, D (1996) *Models of Democracy* (Oxford: Polity Press); 2nd edition.

Hencke, D and L Ward (1998) 'Tories purge staff over 50' The *Guardian*, 20 July, p. 1.

Heywood, A (1994) 'Britain's dominant party system' in L Robins, H Blackmore and R Pyper (eds) *Britain's Changing Party System* (London: Leicester University Press), pp. 10–25.

Hibbs, J (1999) 'Resignation call over Sainsbury's £2m gift to Labour' The *Daily Telegraph*, 9 September.

Hill, R (1998) *Social Democracy and Economic Strategy: The Labour Party in Opposition 1979–1992*. Doctoral thesis, Brunel University, Middlesex.

Himmelweit, HT, P Humphreys and M Jaeger (1981) *How Voters Decide* (Milton Keynes: Open University Press); 2nd edition 1985.

Hine, D (1982) 'Factionalism in West European parties: A framework for analysis' *West European Politics* 5, pp. 36–53.

Hirst, P and G Thompson (1996) *Globalisation in Question* (Cambridge: Polity Press).

Hix, S (1998) 'Elections, parties and institutional design: a comparative perspective on European Union democracy' *West European Politics* 21, pp. 19–52.

Hix, S and C Lord (1997) *Political Parties in the European Union* (Basingstoke: Macmillan).

Hobhouse, LT (1964) *Liberalism* (Oxford: Oxford University Press), first published 1911.

Hobsbawm, E (1981) 'The forward march of Labour halted?' in M Jacques and F Mulhearn (eds) *The Forward March of Labour Halted?* (London: New Left Books).

Hobson, JA (1909) *The Crisis of Liberalism: New Issues of Democracy* (London: PS King and Son).

Hogwood, B (1992) *Trends in British Public Policy* (Buckingham: Open University Press).

Holland, S (1975) *The Socialist Challenge* (London: Quartet).

Holme, R and A Holmes (1998) 'Sausages or policeman? The role of the Liberal Democrats in the 1997 general election campaign' in I Crewe, J Bartle and B Gosschalk (eds) *Political Communications: Why Labour Won the General Election of 1997* (London: Frank Cass).

Holroyd-Doveton, J (1996) *Young Conservatives: A History of the Young Conservative Movement* (Durham: Pentland Press).

Houghton, Lord (1976) *Report of the Committee on Financial Aid to Political Parties.* (London: HMSO).

House of Commons Select Committee on Home Affairs (1994) *Report on the Funding of Political Parties, HC301* (London: HMSO).

Hughes, C and Wintour, P (1990) *Labour Rebuilt: The New Model Party* (London: Fourth Estate).

Ingle, S (1996) 'Party organisation' in D MacIver (ed.) *The Liberal Democrats* (Hemel Hempstead: Prentice Hall), pp. 113–33.

Inglehart, R (1971) 'The silent revolution in Europe: political change in post-industrial societies' *American Political Science Review* 66, pp. 991–1017.

Inglehart, R (1977) *The Silent Revolution* (Princeton, NJ: Princeton University Press).

Inglehart, R (1990) *Culture Shift in Advanced Industrial Society* (Princeton, NJ: Princeton University Press).

Inglehart, R (1997) *Modernization and Postmodernization: Cultural, Economic and Political Change in 43 Societies* (Princeton, NJ: Princeton University Press).

Iyengar, S and D Kinder (1987) *News That Matters: Television and American Opinion* (Chicago, IL: University of Chicago Press).

Jacques, M (1993) *The Amazing Case of the Shrinking Politicians*, Broadcast on BBC2, 25 October.

Jenkins, Lord (1998) *Report of the Independent Commission on the Voting System* (London: The Stationery Office).

Jenkins, R (1979) *Bevanism: Labour's High Tide* (Nottingham: Spokesman).

Jenkins, S (1995) *Accountable to None: The Tory Privatization of Britain* (London: Penguin).

Johnston, RJ and CJ Pattie, (1989) 'The changing electoral geography of Great Britain' in J Mohan (ed.) *The Political Geography of Contemporary Britain* (Basingstoke: Macmillan).

Johnston, RJ, C Pattie and J Allsopp (1988) *A Nation Dividing? The Electoral Map of Great Britain 1979–1987* (Harlow: Longman), pp. 51–68.

Johnston, RJ, C Pattie and E Fieldhouse (1994) 'The geography of voting and representation: regions and the declining importance of the cube law' in A Heath, R Jowell and R Curtice (eds) *Labour's Last Chance? The 1992 Election and Beyond* (Aldershot: Dartmouth), pp. 255–74.

Jones, T (1996) 'Liberal Democrat thought' in D MacIver (ed.) *The Liberal Democrats* (Hemel Hempstead: Prentice Hall), pp. 63–84.

Jordan, G and J Richardson (1982) 'The British policy style or the logic of negotiation?' in J Richardson (ed.) *Policy Styles in Western Europe* (London: George Allen & Unwin), pp. 80–110.

Katz, RS (1986) 'Party government: a rationalistic conception' in FG Castles and R Wildenmann (eds) *Visions and Realities of Party Government* (Berlin: de Gruyter), pp. 31–71.

Katz, RS (1990) 'Parties as linkage: a vestigial function?' *European Journal of Political Research* 18, pp. 143–62.

Katz, RS (1997) *Democracy and Elections* (New York: Oxford University Press).

Katz, RS and P Mair (1995) 'Changing models of party organization and party democracy: the emergence of the cartel party' *Party Politics* 1, pp. 5–28.

Kavanagh, D (1995) *Election Campaigning: The New Marketing of Politics* (Oxford: Basil Blackwell).

Kavanagh, D (1997) 'The Labour campaign' in P Norris and NT Gavin (eds) *Britain Votes 1997* (Oxford: Oxford University Press), pp. 24–33.

Keating, M (1997) 'The political economy of regionalism' in M Keating and J Loughlin *The Political Economy of Regionalism* (London: Frank Cass).

Kellner, P (1997) 'Virgin MPs set a radical agenda' The *Observer* 11 May.

Kelly, RN (1989) *Conservative Party Conferences: The Hidden System* (Manchester: Manchester University Press).

Key, VO (1955) 'A theory of critical elections' *Journal of Politics* 17, pp. 3–18.

Keynes, JM (1936) *The General Theory of Employment, Interest and Money* (London: Macmillan).

King, A (1976a) 'Modes of executive-legislative relations: Great Britain, France and West Germany' *Legislative Studies Quarterly* 1, pp. 11–36.

King, A (1976b) *Why is Britain becoming harder to govern?* (London: BBC Publications).

King, A (1993) 'The implications of one-party government' in A King, I Crewe, D Denver, K Newton, P Norton, D Sanders and P Seyd *Britain at the Polls 1992* (Chatham, NJ: Chatham House), pp. 223–48.

King, A (1998) 'Why Labour won – at last' in A. King, D Denver, I McLean, P Norris, P Norton, D Sanders and P Seyd *New Labour Triumphs: Britain at the Polls* (Chatham, NJ: Chatham House), pp. 177–207.

Kingdom, J (1991) *Local Government and Politics in Britain* (Hemel Hempstead: Philip Alan).

Kingdom, J (1999) *Government and Politics in Britain: An Introduction* (Cambridge: Polity Press); 2nd edition.

Kirchheimer, O (1966) 'The transformation of western European party systems' in J LaPalombara and M Weiner (eds) *Political Parties and Political Development* (Princeton, NJ: Princeton University Press), pp. 177–200.

Kitschelt, H (1993) 'Class structure and social democratic party strategy' *British Journal of Political Science* 23, pp. 299–337.

Klingemann, H-D, R Hofferbert and I Budge (1994) *Parties, Policies and Democracy* (Boulder, CO: Westview Press).

Kobach, KW (1994) 'Switzerland' in D Butler and A Ranney *Referendums Around the World* (Basingstoke: Macmillan), pp. 98-152.

Kogan, M and D Kogan (1982) *The Battle For The Labour Party* (London: Fontana).

Koole, R (1994) 'The vulnerability of the modern cadre party in the Netherlands' in RS Katz and P Mair (eds) *How Parties Organize: Change and Adaptation in Party Organizations in Western Democracies* (London: Sage), pp. 278–303.

Koole, R (1996) 'Cadre, catch-all or cartel? A comment on the notion of the cartel party' *Party Politics* 2, 507–23.

Kuhnle, S (1997) 'Reshaping the welfare state' in I Budge, K Newton, R McKinley, E Kirchner, D Urwin, K Armingeon, F Müller-Rommel, M Walter, M Shugart, M Nentwich, S Kuhnle, H Keman, H-D Klingemann, B Wessels and P Frank *The Politics of the New Europe: Atlantic to Urals* (Harlow: Addison Wesley Longman), pp. 241–358.

Laakso, M and P Taagepera (1979) 'Effective number of parties: a measure with application to Western Europe' *Comparative Political Studies* 12, pp. 3–27.

Labour Party (1918) 'Labour and the new social order: a report on reconstruction, revised in accordance with the resolutions of the Labour Party conference, June 1918' (London: Labour Party).

Labour Party (1983) *New Hope for Britain* (London: Labour Party).

Labour Party (1989) *Meet the Challenge, Make the Change: The Final Report of Labour's Policy Review for the 1990s* (London: Labour Party).

Labour Party (1992) *It's Time to Get Britain Working Again* (London: Labour Party).

Labour Party (1997a) *Labour into Power: A Framework for Partnership* (London: Labour Party).

Labour Party (1997b) *Partnership in Power* (London: Labour Party).

Labour Party (1998) *Selecting Labour's European Candidates for 1999* (London: Labour Party).

Labour Party (1999) *Benefits of Labour Party Membership* (London: Labour Party).

Lane, JE and SO Ersson (1999) *Politics and Society in Western Europe* (London: Sage); 4th edition.

Laver, M (1997) *Private Desires, Political Action: An Invitation to the Politics of Rational Choice* (London: Sage).

Laver, M (1998) 'Party policy in Britain 1997: results from an expert survey' *Political Studies* 46, pp. 336–47.

Laver, M and WB Hunt (1992) *Policy and Party Competition* (London: Routledge).

Laver, M and N Schofield (1998) *Multiparty Government: the Politics of Coalition in Europe* (Ann Arbor: University of Michigan Press).

Laver, M and K Shepsle (1999) 'How political parties emerged from the primeval slime: party cohesion, party discipline and the formation of governments' in S.

Bowler, DM Farrell and RS Katz (eds) *Party Discipline and Parliamentary Government* (Columbus, OH: Ohio State University Press), pp. 23–52.

Laver, M, C Rallings and M Thrasher (1987) 'Coalition theory and local government coalition payoffs in Britain' *British Journal of Political Science* pp. 501–8.

Lawson, K and P Merkl (1988) *When Parties Fail: Emerging Alternative Organizations* (New Jersey: Princeton University Press).

Leach, R (1991) *British Political Ideologies* (Hemel Hempstead: Philip Allan).

Leece, J and H. Berrington (1977) 'Measurement of backbench attitudes by Guttman scaling of Early Day Motions: a pilot study, Labour – 1968–69' *British Journal of Political Science* 7, pp. 529–49.

Liberal Party (1928) *Britain's Industrial Future: Being the Report of the Liberal Industrial Inquiry* (London: Benn).

Lievesley, D and D Waterton (1985) 'Measuring individual attitude change' in R Jowell and S Witherspoon *British Social Attitudes the 1985 Report* (Aldershot: Gower), pp. 177–94.

Lijphart, A (1984) *Democracies: Patterns of Majoritarian and Consensus Government in Twenty-One Countries* (New Haven and London: Yale University Press).

Lijphart, A (1999) *Patterns of Democracy: Government Forms and Performance in Thirty-Six Countries* (New Haven and London: Yale University Press).

Lindblom, CE (1959) 'The science of "muddling through"' *Public Administration Review* 19.

Lindblom, CE (1965) *The Intelligence of Democracy* (New York: The Free Press).

Lindblom, CE (1977) *Politics and Markets* (New York: Basic Books).

Linder, W (1994) *Swiss Democracy* (New York: St. Martin's Press).

Linton, M (1992) 'Unblocking the block vote' *Fabian Review* 104/4.

Linton, M (1994a) *Money and Votes* (London: Institute for Public Policy Research).

Linton, M (1994b) 'The mad hatter's Tory party' The *Guardian* 14 April, p. 22.

Lipow, A and P Seyd (1996) 'The politics of anti-partyism' *Parliamentary Affairs*, 49, pp. 273–84.

Lipset, SM and S Rokkan (1967) 'Cleavage structures, party systems and voter alignments: an introduction' in SM Lipset and S Rokkan (eds) *Party Systems and Voter Alignments: Cross National Perspectives* (New York: Free Press), pp. 1–64.

Lowell, AL (1908) *The Government of England, Volume 1* (London: Macmillan).

Ludlam, S (1996) 'The spectre haunting Conservatism: Europe and backbench rebellion' in S Ludlam and MJ Smith (eds) *Contemporary British Conservatism* (Basingstoke: Macmillan), pp. 98–120.

Lynch, P (1998) 'Devolution in the UK and new territorial politics'. Paper presented to *Annual Meeting of the American Political Science Association*, Boston, September.

MacAskill, E (1998) 'Party membership: Stuff that envelope, say the activists' The *Guardian*, 23 June, p. 17

Magleby, DB (1984) *Direct Legislation: Voting on Ballot Propositions in the United States* (Baltimore: Johns Hopkins University Press).

Magleby, DB (1994) 'Direct legislation in the United States' in D Butler and A Ranney *Referendums Around the World* (Basingstoke: Macmillan), pp. 218–54.

Magleby, DB and KD Patterson (1998) 'Consultants and direct democracy' *Political Science and Politics* 31, pp. 160–9.

Maguire, M (1983) 'Is there still persistence? Electoral change in Western Europe, 1948–1979' in H Daalder and P Mair (eds) *Western European Party Systems: Continuity and Change* (London: Sage) pp. 67–94.

Mair, P (1984) 'Party politics in contemporary Europe: a challenge to party?' *West European Politics* 6, pp. 128–34.

Mair, P (1990) 'Introduction' in P Mair (ed.) *The West European Party System* (Oxford: Oxford University Press), pp. 1–22.

Mair, P (1994) 'Party organizations: from civil society to state' in RS Katz and P Mair (eds) *How Parties Organize: Change and Adaptation in Party Organizations in Western Democracies* (London: Sage Publications), pp. 1–22.

Mair, P (1995) 'Political parties, popular legitimacy and public privilege' *West European Politics* 18, pp. 40–57.

Mair, P (1997) *Party System Change: Approaches and Interpretations* (Oxford: Clarendon Press).

Maor, M (1997) *Political Parties and Party Systems: Comparative Approaches and the British Experience* (London: Routledge).

Marr, A (1998) 'Blair's big secret: he's a Liberal' The *Observer*, 26 July, p. 21.

Marquand, D (1988) *The Unprincipled Society: New Demands and Old Politics* (London: Fontana).

Marshall, G, H Newby, D Rose and C Vogler (1988) *Social Class in Modern Britain* (London: Hutchinson).

Maslow, A (1954) *Motivations and Personality* (New York City: Harper & Row).

May, JD (1973) 'Opinion structure of political parties: the special law of curvilinear disparity' *Political Studies* 21, pp. 135–51.

McAllister, I and R Rose (1984) *The Nationwide Competition for Votes* (London: Frances Pinter).

McCombs, M and D Shaw (1972) 'The agenda-setting function of the mass media' *Public Opinion Quarterly* 36, pp. 176–87.

McIver, J (1995) 'The first elections to the new Scottish unitary councils – April 1995' *Representation* 33, pp. 73–9.

McKee, V (1991) 'Fragmentation on the Labour right, 1975-77' *Politics*.

McKee, V (1996) 'Factions and groups' in D MacIver (ed.) *The Liberal Democrats* (Hemel Hempstead: Prentice-Hall), pp. 155–70.

McKenzie, RT (1955) *Political Parties* (London: Heinemann).

McLean, I (1989) *Democracy and New Technology* (Cambridge: Polity).

McLean, I, A Heath and B Taylor (1995) 'Were the 1994 Euro- and local elections in Britain really second-order?' Paper presented to *Annual Conference on Elections, Public Opinion and Parties*, London Guildhall University, September.

McSmith, A (1999) 'Major vents fury as Hague slams Tory record in office' The *Observer*, 14 March, p. 2.

Mellors, C (1989) 'Non-majority British local authorities in a majority setting' in C Mellors and B Pijnenburg (eds) *Political Parties and Coalitions in European Local Government* (London: Routledge), pp. 68–112.

Menard, S (1995) *Applied Logistic Regression Analysis* (London: Sage Publications).

Mezey, ML (1979) *Comparative Legislatures* (Durham, NC: Duke University Press).

Miliband, R (1972) *Parliamentary Socialism: A Study in the Politics of Labour* (London: Merlin).

Miller, W, H Clarke, M Harrop, L le Duc and P Whiteley (1990) *How Voters Change: The 1987 British Election Campaign in Perspective* (Cambridge: Cambridge University Press).

Miller, WE and Shanks, JM (1996) *The New American Voter* (Cambridge, MA: Harvard University Press).

Miller, WL (1978) 'Social class and party choice in England: a new analysis' *British Journal of Political Science* 8, pp. 257–84.

Miller, WL (1983) 'The denationalisation of British politics: The reemergence of the periphery' *West European Politics* 6, pp. 103–29.

Miller, WL and Mackie, T (1973) 'The electoral cycle and the assymetry of government and opposition popularity' *Political Studies* 21, pp. 263–79.

Miller, WL, S Tagg and K Britto (1986) 'Partisanship and party preference in government and opposition: the mid-term perspective' *Electoral Studies* 5, pp. 31–46.

Minkin, L (1980) *The Labour Party Conference: A Study in the Politics of Intra-Party Democracy* (Manchester: Manchester University Press); first published by Allen Lane in 1978.

Moran, M (1985) *Politics and Society in Britain* (Basingstoke: Macmillan).

Mughan, A (1995) 'Party leaders and presidentialism in the 1992 election: a postwar perspective' in D Denver, P Norris, C Rallings and D Broughton (eds) *British Elections and Parties Yearbook 1993* (Hemel Hempstead: Harvester Wheatsheaf), pp. 193–204.

Mulgan, G (1994a) 'Party-free politics' *New Statesman and Society* 15 April.

Mulgan, G (1994b) *Politics in an Anti-Political Age* (Cambridge: Polity Press).

National Union of Conservative and Unionist Associations (1988) *Rules and standing orders of the National Union of Conservative and Unionist Associations* (London: National Union).

Neill, Lord (1998) *Report of the Committee on Standards in Public Life on the Funding of Political Parties in the UK, vol. 1, Cm 4057–1* (London: The Stationery Office).

Newton, K (1991) 'Do people believe everything they read in the papers?' in I Crewe et al. (eds) *British Elections and Parties Yearbook 1991* (Hemel Hempstead: Harvester Wheatsheaf).

Newton, K (1993) 'Caring and competence: the long, long campaign' in A King, I Crewe, D Denver, K Newton, P Norton, D Sanders and P Seyd *Britain at the Polls 1992* (Chatham, NJ: Chatham House), pp. 129–70.

Norris, P (1990) *British By-elections: The Volatile Electorate* (Oxford: Clarendon Press).

Norris, P (1994) 'Labour party factionalism and extremism' in A Heath, R Jowell and J Curtice (eds) *Labour's Last Chance? The 1992 Election and Beyond* (Aldershot: Dartmouth), pp. 173–190.

Norris, P (1995) 'May's law of curvilinear disparity revisited: leaders, officers, members and voters in British political parties' *Party Politics* 1, pp. 29–47.

Norris, P (1996) *Electoral Change Since 1945* (Oxford: Basil Blackwell).

Norris, P (1997) 'Anatomy of a Labour landslide' in P Norris and NT Gavin (eds) *Britain Votes 1997* (Oxford: Oxford University Press), pp. 1–24.

Norris, P (1998) 'The battle for the campaign agenda' in A King, D Denver, I McLean, P Norris, P Norton, D Sanders and P Seyd *New Labour Triumphs: Britain at the Polls* (Chatham, NJ: Chatham House), pp. 113–44.

Norris, P (1999) 'Introduction: the growth of critical citizens?' in P. Norris (ed.) *Critical Citizens: Global Support for Democratic Governance* (Oxford: Oxford University Press), pp. 1–27.

Norris, P and J Lovenduski (1995) *Political Recruitment: Gender, Race and Class in the British Parliament* (Cambridge: Cambridge University Press).

Norris, P, J Curtice, D Sanders, M Scammell and H Semetko (1999) *On Message: Communicating The Campaign* (London: Sage Publications).

Norton, P (1975) *Dissension in the House of Commons: Intra-Party Dissent in the House of Commons Division Lobbies 1945–74* (London: Macmillan).

Norton, P (1978) *Conservative Dissidents: Dissent Within the Parliamentary Conservative Party 1970–74* (London: Temple-Smith).

Norton, P (1980) *Dissension in the House of Commons 1974–79* (Oxford: Oxford University Press).

Norton, P (1990) 'The lady's not for turning, but what about the rest? Margaret Thatcher and the Conservative Party 1979-89' *Parliamentary Affairs* 43, pp. 41–58.

Norton, P (1994a) 'The parties in parliament' in L Robins, H Blackmore and R Pyper *Britain's Changing Party System* (London: Leicester University Press), pp. 57–74.

Norton, P (1994b) 'The parliamentary party and party committees' in A Seldon and S Ball *The Conservative Century: The Conservative Party Since 1900* (Oxford: Oxford University Press), pp. 97–144.

Norton, P (1996) 'Philosophy: the principles of Conservatism' in P. Norton (ed.) *The Conservative Party* (Hemel Hempstead: Prentice Hall), pp. 68–82.

Norton, P (1998) 'The Conservative Party: "in office but not in power"' in A King, D Denver, I McLean, P Norris, P Norton, D Sanders and P Seyd *New Labour Triumphs: Britain at the Polls* (Chatham, NJ: Chatham House), pp. 75–112.

Norton, P and A Aughey (1981) *Conservatives and Conservatism* (London: Temple Smith).

Norton, P and P Cowley (1996) 'Are Conservative MPs revolting? Dissension by Government MPs in the British House of Commons 1976–96' *Centre for Legislative Studies Research Paper 2/96* (Hull: University of Hull).

Norusis, MJ (1992) *SPSS/PC+ Professional Statistics Version 5.0* (Chicago, IL: SPSS Inc).

Norusis, MJ (1994) *SPSS Advanced Statistics Version 6.1* (Chicago, IL: SPSS Inc).

Office for National Statistics (1999) *Annual Abstract of Statistics 135* (London: The Stationery Office).

O'Leary, B and G Evans (1997) 'Northern Ireland: La fin de siecle, the twilight of the second protestant ascendancy and Sinn Fein's second coming' in P Norris and NT Gavin (eds) *Britain Votes 1997* (Oxford: Oxford University Press), pp. 164–72.

Olson, M (1965) *The Logic of Collection Action* (New York: Schocken Books).

O'Shaughnessy, N (1990) *The Phenomenon of Political Marketing* (London: Macmillan).

Ostrogorski, M (1902) *Democracy and the Organisation of Political Parties, Volume 1* (London: Macmillan).

Owen, D (1981) *Face the Future* (London: Jonathan Cape).

Panebianco, A (1988) *Political Parties: Organisation and Power* (Cambridge: Cambridge University Press).

Panitch, L (1976) *Social Democracy and Industrial Militancy* (Cambridge: Cambridge University Press).

Parry, G and G Moyser (1990) 'A map of political participation in Britain' *Government and Opposition* 25, pp. 147–69.

Parry, G, G Moyser, and N Day (1992) *Political Participation and Democracy in Britain* (Cambridge: Cambridge University Press).

Paterson, WE and A Thomas (1977) *Social Democratic Parties in Western Europe* (London: Croom Helm).

Pattie, C, R Johnston and E Fieldhouse (1993) 'Plus ca change? The changing electoral geography of Great Britain, 1979–92' in D Denver, P Norris, D Broughton and C Rallings (eds) *British Elections and Parties Yearbook 1993* (Hemel Hempstead: Harvester Wheatsheaf), pp. 85–99.

Pattie, CJ, RJ Johnston and JG Allsopp (1988) *A Nation Dividing?: Electoral Map of Great Britain 1979-87* (London: Longman), pp. 41–66.

Pattie, CJ, RJ Johnston and EA Fieldhouse (1995) 'Winning the local vote: the effectiveness of constituency campaign spending in Great Britain, 1983–1992' *American Political Science Review* 89, pp. 969–86.

Pattie, CJ, P Whiteley, R Johnston and P Seyd (1994) 'Measuring local campaign effects: Labour Party constituency campaigning at the 1987 general election' *Political Studies* 42, pp. 469–79.

Pedersen, M (1979) 'The dynamics of European party systems: changing patterns of electoral volatility' *European Journal of Political Research* 7, pp. 1–26.

Pedersen, M (1983) 'Changing patterns of electoral volatility in European party systems 1948-1977: explorations in explanation' in H Daalder and P. Mair (eds) *Western European Party Systems: Continuity and Change* (London: Sage), pp. 29–66.

Pinto-Duschinsky, M (1980) *British Political Finance, 1932-1980* (Washington: American Enterprise Institute).

Poguntke, T (1994) 'Parties in a legalistic culture: the case of Germany' in RS Katz and P Mair (eds) *How Parties Organize: Change and Adaptation in Party Organizations in Western Democracies* (London: Sage), pp. 185–215.

Poguntke, T (1996) 'Anti-party sentiment – conceptual thoughts and empirical evidence: explorations in a minefield' *European Journal of Political Research* 29, pp. 319–44.

Poguntke, T and S Scarrow (1996) 'Anti-Party Sentiment'. Special issue of *European Journal of Political Research* 29/3.

Pulzer, P (1967) *Political Representation and Elections in Britain* (London: George Allen & Unwin).

Punnett, RM (1992) *Selecting The Party Leader: Britain in Comparative Perspective* (Hemel Hempstead: Harvester Wheatsheaf).

Radice, G (1992) *Southern Discomfort* (London: Fabian Society pamphlet 555).

Raelin, JA (1991) *The Clash of Cultures: Managers Managing Professionals* (Cambridge, MA: Harvard Business School Press).

Rallings, C (1987) 'The influence of election programmes: Britain and Canada, 1945-79' in I Budge, D Robertson and D Hearl *Ideology, Strategy and Party Change* (Cambridge: Cambridge University Press), pp. 1–14.

Rallings, C and M Thrasher (1997a) *Local Elections in Britain* (London: Routledge).

Rallings, C and M Thrasher (1997b) 'The local elections' in P Norris and NT Gavin (eds) *Britain Votes 1997* (Oxford: Oxford University Press), pp. 173–84.

Rallings, C and M Thrasher (1999) *New Britain, New Elections: The Media Guide to the New Political Map of Britain* (London: Vacher Dod).

Reif, K, and H Schmitt (1980) 'Nine second-order national elections' *European Journal of Political Research* 8, pp. 3–45, 146–62.

Riker, W (1962) *The Theory of Political Coalitions* (New Haven, CT: Yale University Press).

Robbins, K (1994) *The Eclipse of a Great Power* (London: Longman).

Robertson, D (1984) *Class and the British Electorate* (Oxford: Basil Blackwell).

Romesburg, HC (1984) *Cluster Analysis for Researchers* (Belmont, CA: Lifetime Learning Publications).

Romzek, BS and JA Utter (1997) 'Congressional legislative staff: political professionals or clerks? *American Journal of Political Science* 41, pp. 1251–79.

Rose, R (1964) 'Parties, factions and tendencies in Britain' *Political Studies* 12, pp. 33–46.

Rose, R (1980) *Do Parties Make a Difference?* (Chatham, NJ: Chatham House); 2nd edition, London, Macmillan, 1984.

Rose, R (1992) *What are the Economic Consequences of PR?* (London: Electoral Reform Society).

Rose, R and I McAllister (1986) *Voters Begin to Choose: From Closed-Class to Open Elections in Britain* (London: Sage).

Rose, R and D. Urwin (1970) 'Persistence and change in Western party systems since 1945' *Political Studies* 18, pp. 287–319.

Rosenbaum, M (1997) *From Soapbox to Soundbite: Party Political Campaigning in Britain Since 1945* (Basingstoke: Macmillan).

Saggar, S (1998) *Race and British Electoral Politics* (London: UCL Press).

Saggar , S and A Heath (1999) 'Race: Towards a multicultural electorate?' in G Evans and P Norris (eds) *Critical Elections: British Parties and Voters in Long-Term Perspective* (London: Sage), pp. 102–23.

Sanders, D (1991) 'Government popularity and the next general election' *Political Quarterly* 64, pp. 235–61.

Sanders, D (1993) 'Why the Conservatives won – again' in A King, I Crewe, D Denver, K Newton, P Norton, D Sanders and P Seyd *Britain at the Polls 1992* (Chatham, NJ: Chatham House), pp. 171–213.

Sanders, D (1996) 'Economic performance, management competence and the outcome of the next general election' *Political Studies* 64, pp. 203–31.

Sanders, D (1997) 'Conservative incompetence, Labour responsibility and the feel-good factor: why the economy failed to save the Conservatives in 1997'. Paper presented to the conference on *Assessing the 1997 general election: voters, parties, polls and the media*, University of Essex, September.

Sanders, D (1999) 'The impact of left-right ideology' in G Evans and P Norris (eds) *Critical Elections: British Parties and Voters in Long-Term Perspective* (London: Sage), pp. 181–206.

Sanders, D and M Brynin (1999) 'The dynamics of party preference change in Britain, 1991–1996' *Political Studies* 47, pp. 219–39.

Sanders, D and P Norris (1997) 'Does negative news matter? The effect of television news on party images in the 1997 British general election'. Paper presented to the conference *Assessing the 1997 general election: voters, parties, polls and the media*, University of Essex, September.

Sanders, D, D Marsh and H Ward (1992) 'Macroeconomics, the Falkands War and the popularity of the Thatcher government: a contrary view' in H Norpoth, J-D Lafay and M Lewis-Beck (eds) *Economics and Politics: The Calculus of Support* (Ann Arbor: Michigan University Press), pp. 161–84.

Sanders, D, D Marsh and H Ward (1993) 'The electoral impact of press coverage of the British economy 1979–1987' *British Journal of Political Science* 23, pp. 175–210.

Sarlvik, B and I Crewe (1983) *Decade of Dealignment: The Conservative Victory of 1979 and Electoral Trends in the 1970s* (Cambridge: Cambridge University Press).

Sartori, G (1976) *Parties and Party Systems: A Framework for Analysis* (Cambridge: Cambridge University Press).

Scammell, M (1995) *Designer Politics: How Elections Are Won* (Basingstoke: Macmillan)

Scammell, M (1999) 'Political marketing: lessons for political science' *Political Studies* 47, pp. 718–39.

Scarbrough, E (1984) *Political Ideology and the Electorate* (Oxford: Clarendon).

Scarbrough, E (1986) 'The British electorate twenty years on: Reviewing electoral change and election surveys' *Essex Papers in Politics and Government* (Colchester: Essex University).

Scarrow, SE (1994) 'The paradox of enrolment: Assessing the costs and benefits of party memberships' *European Journal of Political Research* 25, pp. 41–60.

Scarrow, SE (1996) *Parties and Their Members* (Oxford: Oxford University Press).

Scarrow, SE (1997) 'Party competition and institutional change: the expansion of direct democracy in Germany' *Party Politics* 3, pp. 451-72.

Scarrow, SE (forthcoming) 'Parties without members? Party organization in a changing electoral environment' in R Dalton and M Wattenberg (eds) *Parties Without*

Partisans: Political Change in Advanced Industrial Democracies (Oxford: Oxford University Press).

Schmidt, M (1996) 'When parties matter: a review of the possibilities and limits of partisan influence on public policy' *European Journal of Political Research* 30, pp. 155–183.

Schumpeter, JA (1952) *Capitalism, Socialism and Democracy* (London: George Allen & Unwin); 5th edition (1st edition 1942).

Scottish Labour Party (1998) *Labour's Future, Scotland's Future: Procedural Guidelines for the Scottish Parliament Selections* (Glasgow: Scottish Labour Party).

Scruton, R (1980) *The Meaning of Conservatism* (London: Macmillan).

Seenan, G and E McAskill (1999) 'Angry Lib Dems finally agree coalition deal' The *Guardian*, 14 May.

Seyd, B (1998) 'Regulating the referendum' *Representation* 35, pp. 191–9.

Seyd, P (1987) *The Rise and Fall of the Labour Left* (New York City: St. Martin's Press).

Seyd, P (1998) 'Tony Blair and New Labour' in A. King, D Denver, I McLean, P Norris, P Norton, D Sanders and P Seyd *New Labour Triumphs: Britain at the Polls* (Chatham, NJ: Chatham House), pp. 49–73.

Seyd, P (1999) 'New parties/new politics: a case study of the British Labour party' *Party Politics* 5, pp. 383–405.

Seyd, P and P Whiteley (1992) *Labour's Grassroots: The Politics of Party Membership* (Oxford: Clarendon Press).

Seyd, P, P Whiteley, and J Richardson (1993) 'Who are the true blues? The Conservative Party members'. *Paper to the Annual Conference of the Political Studies Association*, April.

Seymour-Ure, C (1997) 'Newspapers: editorial opinion in the national press' in P Norris and NT Gavin *Britain Votes 1997* (Oxford: Oxford University Press), pp. 78–100.

Sharpe, LJ and K Newton (1984) *Does Politics Matter? The Determinants of Public Policy* (Oxford: Clarendon Press).

Shaw, E (1994) *The Labour Party Since 1979: Crisis and Transformation* (London: Routledge).

Simon, HA (1945) *Administrative Behaviour* (Glencoe, IL: Free Press).

Sked, A (1987) *Britain's Decline* (Oxford: Basil Blackwell).

Smith, G (1979) 'Western European party systems: on the trail of a typology' *West European Politics* 2, pp. 128–43.

Smith, G (1989) 'Core persistence: change and the "people's party"' in P Mair and G Smith (eds) *Understanding Party System Change in Western Europe* (London: Frank Cass), pp. 157–68. (Originally a special issue of *West European Politics* 12.)

Smith, M (1992) 'A return to revisionism? The Labour Party's policy review' in M. Smith and J Spear (eds) *The Changing Labour Party* (London: Routledge), pp. 13–28.

Sowemimo, M (1996) 'The Conservative Party and European Integration 1988–95' *Party Politics* 2, pp. 77–97.

Steed, M and Curtice, J (1982) 'Electoral choice and the production of government: the changing operation of the UK electoral system 1955–79' *British Journal of Political Science* 12, pp. 249–98.

Stewart, J and G Stoker (1989) *The Future of Local Government* (Basingstoke: Macmillan).

Stewart, MC and Clarke, HD (1992) 'The (un)importance of party leaders: leader images and party choice in the 1987 British election' *Journal of Politics* 54, pp. 447–70.

Taggart, P (1996) 'Rebels, sceptics and factions: Euroscepticism in the British Conservative Party and the Swedish Social Democratic Party' *Contemporary Political Studies 1996*, pp. 589–97.

Taylor, A (1987) *The Trade Unions and the Labour Party* (London: Croom Helm).

Taylor, M and J Cruddas (1999) *New Labour, New Links* (London: Unions 21).

Thatcher, M (1988) 'Britain and Europe', text of *speech to the College d'Europe, Bruges*, 20 September.

Thorpe, A (1997) *A History of the British Labour Party* (Basingstoke: Macmillan).

Tomlinson, J (1999) 'Nothing new under the sun? Understanding New Labour' *Brunel Discussion Paper in Government, 99/2* (Uxbridge: Brunel University).

Topf, R (1994) 'Party manifestos' in Anthony Heath, R Jowell and J Curtice with B Taylor (eds) *Labour's Last Chance? The 1992 Election and Beyond* (Aldershot: Dartmouth), pp. 149–72.

Viney, J and J Osborne (1995) *Modernising Public Appointments* (London: Demos).

von Beyme, K (1985) *Political Parties in Western Democracies* (Aldershot: Gower).

Wald, KD (1983) *Crosses on the Ballot: Patterns of British Voter Alignment Since 1885* (Princeton, NJ: Princeton University Press).

Walker, A (1986) 'The future of the British welfare state: privatization or socialization?' in A Evers et al. (eds) *The Changing Face of Welfare* (Aldershot: Gower).

Ware, A (1987) *Citizens, Parties and the State* (Oxford: Polity Press).

Ware, A (1996) *Political Parties and Party Systems* (Oxford: Oxford University Press).

Watt, N (1998) 'The fall of Mandelson: knives out for Chancellor's ebullient confidant' The *Guardian*, 28 December.

Webb, PD (1992a) *Trade Unions and the British Electorate* (Aldershot: Dartmouth).

Webb, PD (1992b) 'Election campaigning, organisational transformation and the professionalisation of the British Labour Party' *European Journal of Political Research* 21, pp. 267–88.

Webb, PD (1992c) 'The United Kingdom' in RS Katz and P Mair *Party Organizations: A Data Handbook* (London: Sage), pp. 837–70.

Webb, PD (1994) 'Party organizational change in Britain: the iron law of centralization?' in RS Katz and P Mair (eds) *How Parties Organize: Change and Adaptation in Party Organizations in Western Democracies* (London: Sage Publications), pp. 109–33.

Webb, PD (1995) 'Reforming the party-union link: an assessment' in D Broughton, D Farrell, D Denver and C Rallings *British Parties and Elections Yearbook 1994* (London: Frank Cass) pp. 1–14.

Webb, PD (1996) 'Apartisanship and anti-party sentiment in the UK: correlates and constraints' *European Journal of Political Research* 29, pp. 365–82.

Webb, PD (1997) 'Attitudinal clustering within British parliamentary elites: Patterns of intra-party and cross-party alignment' *West European Politics* 20, pp. 89–110.

Webb, PD and DM Farrell (1999) 'Party members and ideological change' in G Evans and P Norris (eds) *Critical Elections: British Parties and Voters in Long-term Perspective* (London: Sage), pp. 44–63.

Webster, P (1993) 'Citizen Smith ends Labour backing for state control' *The Times*, 8 February.

Webster, P (1995) 'Tory MP defects to Liberal Democrats' *The Times*, 30 December.

Weir, S and W Hall (1994) *Ego Trip* (London: Demos).

Wellhofer, ES (1979) 'Strategies for Party Organisation and Voter Mobilisation: Britain, Norway and Argentina' *Comparative Political Studies*, 12.

White, M (1998) 'On the edge, ex-Tory admirer of Blair' The *Guardian*, 20 April, p. 18.

White, M (1999) 'Howard refuses to back Lilley public service stand' The *Guardian*, 26 April, p. 10.

Whiteley, P and P Seyd (1992) 'The Labour vote and local activism: The local constituency campaigns' *Parliamentary Affairs* 45, pp. 582–95.

Whiteley, P and P Seyd (1998) 'New Labour – new grass-roots party?'. Paper presented to the *Annual meeting of the Political Studies Association*, Keele, April.

Whiteley, P, P Seyd and J Richardson (1994) *True Blues: The Politics of Conservative Party Membership* (Oxford: Clarendon Press).

Wilensky, HL (1959) *Intellectuals in Labor Unions* (New York: The Free Press).

Willetts, D (1992) *Modern Conservatism* (London: Penguin).

Wintour, P (1991) 'Labour in cash crisis over subscriptions' The *Guardian*, 26 November.

Wintour, P and A McSmith (1997) 'Last post sounds for first past the post system' The *Observer* 2 March, p. 1.

Wring, D (1996a) 'From Mass Propaganda to Political Marketing' in C Rallings, D Farrell, D Denver and D Broughton (eds), *British Elections and Parties Yearbook 1995* (London: Frank Cass), pp. 105–24.

Wring, D (1996b) 'Political Marketing and Party Development in Britain' *European Journal of Marketing* 30, pp. 100–11.

Young, H (1999) 'Lilley knocks up the first plank in Tory life raft' The *Guardian*, 22 April, p, 20.

INDEX